Reading Freud's Reading

Literature and Psychoanalysis
General Editor: Jeffrey Berman

Reading Freud's Reading

Edited by Sander L. Gilman, Jutta Birmele,
Jay Geller, and Valerie D. Greenberg

NEW YORK UNIVERSITY PRESS
NEW YORK AND LONDON

NEW YORK UNIVERSITY
New York and London

Copyright © 1994 by New York University

Library of Congress Cataloging-in-Publication Data
Reading Freud's reading / edited by Sander L. Gilman . . . [et. al.].
p.   cm. — (Literature and psychoanalysis ; 5)
Includes bibliographical references and index.
ISBN 0-8147-3051-5 (alk. paper)
1. Freud, Sigmund, 1856-1939—Books and reading.
2. Psychoanalysis and literature—History.   I. Gilman, Sander L.
II. Series.
BF109.F74R43   1994
150.19'52'092—dc20   93-11102
                            CIP

New York University Press books are printed on acid-free paper,
and their binding materials are chosen for strength and durability.

Manufactured in the United States of America

10 9 8 7 6 5 4 3 2 1

Contents

Foreword

As New York University Press inaugurates a new series of books on literature and psychoanalysis, it seems appropriate to pause and reflect briefly upon the history of psychoanalytic literary criticism. For a century now it has struggled to define its relationship to its two contentious progenitors and to come of age. After glancing at its origins, we may be in a better position to speculate on its future.

Psychoanalytic literary criticism was conceived at the precise moment in which Freud, reflecting upon his self-analysis, made a connection to two plays and thus gave us a radically new approach to reading literature. Writing to his friend Wilhelm Fliess in 1897, Freud breathlessly advanced the idea that "love of the mother and jealousy of the father" are universal phenomena of early childhood (*Origins*, 223–24). He referred immediately to the gripping power of *Oedipus Rex* and *Hamlet* for confirmation of, and perhaps inspiration for, his compelling perception of family drama, naming his theory the "Oedipus complex" after Sophocles' legendary fictional hero.

Freud acknowledged repeatedly his indebtedness to literature, mythology, and philosophy. There is no doubt that he was a great humanist, steeped in world literature, able to read several languages and range across disciplinary boundaries. He regarded creative writers as allies, investigating the same psychic terrain and intuiting similar human truths. "[P]sycho-analytic observation must concede priority of imaginative writers," he declared in 1901 in *The Psychopathology of Everyday Life* (SE 6:213), a concession he was generally happy to make. The only exceptions were writers like Schopenhauer, Nietzsche, and Schnitzler, whom he avoided reading because of the anxiety of influence. He quoted effortlessly from Sophocles, Shakespeare, Goethe, and Dostoevsky, and was himself a master prose stylist, the recipient of the coveted Goethe Prize in 1930. When he was considered for the Nobel Prize, it was not for medicine but for literature. Upon being greeted as the discoverer of the unconscious, he disclaimed the title and instead paid generous tribute to the poets and philosophers who preceded him.

And yet Freud's forays into literary criticism have not been uniformly welcomed by creative writers, largely because of his allegiance to science rather than art. Despite his admiration for art, he viewed the artist as an introvert, not far removed from neurosis. The artist, he wrote in a well-known passage in the *Introductory Lectures on Psycho-Analysis* (1916–17), "is oppressed by excessively powerful instinctual needs. He desires to win honour, power, wealth, fame and the love of women; but he lacks the means for achieving these satisfactions" (SE 16:376). Consequently, Freud argued, artists retreat from reality into the world of fantasy, where they attempt to make their dreams come true. While conceding that true artists manage to shape their daydreams in such a way as to find a path back to reality, thus fulfilling their wishes, Freud nevertheless theorized art as a substitute gratification. Little wonder, then, that few artists have been pleased with Freud's pronouncements.

Nor have many artists been sympathetic to Freud's preoccupation with sexuality and aggression; his deterministic vision of human life; his combative, polemical temperament; his self-fulfilling belief that psychoanalysis brings out the worst in people; and his imperialistic claim that psychoanalysis, which he regarded as his personal creation, would explore and conquer vast new territories. He chose as the epigraph for *The Interpretation of Dreams* (1900) a quotation from *The Aeneid*: "Flectere si nequeo superos, Acheronta movebo" ("If I cannot bend the Higher Powers, I will move the Infernal Regions"). Although he denied that there was anything Promethean about his work, he regarded himself as one of the disturbers of the world's sleep. The man who asserted that "psychoanalysis is in a position to speak the decisive word in all questions that touch upon the imaginative life of man" (SE 19:208) could hardly expect to win many converts among creative writers, who were no less familiar with the imaginative life of humankind and who resented his intrusion into their domain.

Freud viewed psychoanalysts as scientists, committed to the reality principle and to heroic self-renunciation. He perceived artists, by contrast—and women—as neurotic and highly narcissistic, devoted to the pleasure principle, intuiting mysterious truths which they could not rationally understand. "Kindly nature has given the artist the ability to express his most secret mental impulses, which are hidden even from himself," he stated in *Leonardo da Vinci and a Memory of His Childhood* in 1910 (SE 11:107). The artist, in Freud's judgment, creates beauty, but the psychoanalyst analyzes its meaning and "penetrates" it, with all the phallic implications thereof. As much as he admired artists, Freud did not want to give them credit for knowing what they are doing. Moreover, although he always referred to artists as male, he assumed that art itself was essentially female; and he was drawn to the "seductive" nature of art even as he resisted its embrace, lest he lose his masculine analytical power. He wanted to be called a scientist, not an artist.

From the beginning of his career, then, the marriage Freud envisioned between the artist and the analyst was distinctly unequal and patriarchal. For their part, most creative writers have remained wary of psychoanalysis. Franz Kafka, James Joyce, and D. H. Lawrence were fascinated by psychoanalytic theory and appropriated it, in varying degrees, in their stories, but they all remained skeptical of Freud's therapeutic claims and declined to be analyzed.

Most artists do not want to be "cured," fearing that their creativity will be imperiled, and they certainly do not want psychoanalysts to probe their work; they agree with Wordsworth that to dissect is to murder. Vladimir Nabokov's sardonic reference to Freud as the "Viennese witch doctor" and his contemptuous dismissal of psychoanalysis as black magic are extreme examples of creative writers' mistrust of psychoanalytic interpretations of literature. "[A]ll my books should be stamped Freudians Keep Out," Nabokov writes in *Bend Sinister* (xii). Humbert Humbert speaks for his creator when he observes in *Lolita* that the difference between the rapist and therapist is but a matter of spacing (147).

Freud never lost faith that psychoanalysis could cast light upon a wide variety of academic subjects. In the short essay "On the Teaching of Psycho-Analysis in Universities" (1919), he maintained that his new science has a role not only in medical schools but also in the "solutions of problems" in art, philosophy, religion, literature, mythology, and history. "The fertilizing effects of psycho-analytic thought on these other disciplines," Freud wrote enthusiastically, "would certainly, contribute greatly towards forging a closer link, in the sense of a *universitas liter-arum*, between medical science and the branches of learning which lie within the sphere of philosophy and the arts" (SE 17:173). Regrettably, he did not envision in the same essay a cross-fertilization, a desire, that is, for other disciplines to pollinate psychoanalysis.

Elsewhere, though, Freud was willing to acknowledge a more recip-rocal relationship between the analyst and the creative writer. He opened his first published essay on literary criticism, "Delusions and Dreams in Jensen's *Gradiva*" (1907), with the egalitarian statement that "creative writers are valued allies and their evidence is to be highly prized, for they are apt to know a whole host of things between heaven and earth of which our philosophy has not yet let us dream" (SE 9:8), an allusion to his beloved Hamlet's affirmation of the mystery of all things. Conceding that literary artists have been, from time immemorial, precursors to sci-entists, Freud concluded that the "creative writer cannot evade the psy-chiatrist nor the psychiatrist the creative writer, and the poetic treatment of a psychiatric theme can turn out to be correct without any sacrifice of its beauty" (SE 9:44).

It is in the spirit of this equal partnership between literature and psy-choanalysis that New York University Press launches the present series. We intend to publish books that are genuinely interdisciplinary, theo-retically sophisticated, and clinically informed. The literary critic's in-sights into psychoanalysis are no less valuable than the psychoanalyst's insights into literature. Gone are the days when psychoanalytic critics assumed that Freud had a master key to unlock the secrets of literature. Instead of reading literature to confirm psychoanalytic theory, many critics are now reading Freud to discover how his understanding of lit-erature shaped the evolution of his theory. In short, the master-slave relationship traditionally implicit in the marriage between the literary critic and the psychoanalyst has given way to a healthier dialogic rela-tionship, in which each learns from and contributes to the other's discipline.

Indeed, the prevailing ideas of the late twentieth century are strikingly different from those of the late nineteenth century, when literature and psychoanalysis were first allied. In contrast to Freud, who assumed he was discovering absolute truth, we now believe that knowledge, partic-ularly in the humanities and social sciences, is relative and dependent upon cultural contexts. Freud's classical drive theory, with its mechanistic implications of cathectic energy, has given way to newer relational models, such as object relations, self psychology, and interpersonal psychoanalysis, affirming the importance of human interaction. Many early psychoanalytic ideas, such as the death instinct and the phylogenetic transmission of memories, have fallen by the wayside, and Freud's theorizing on female psychology has been recognized as a reflection of his cultural bias.

Significant developments have also taken place in psychoanalytic literary theory. An extraordinary variety and synthesis of competing approaches have emerged, including post-Freudian, Jungian, Lacanian, Horneyan, feminist, deconstructive, psycholinguistic, and reader response. Interest in psychoanalytic literary criticism is at an all-time high, not just in the handful of journals devoted to psychological criticism, but in dozens of mainstream journals that have traditionally avoided psychological approaches to literature. Scholars are working on identity theory, narcissism, gender theory, mourning and loss, and creativity. Additionally, they are investigating new areas, such as composition theory and pedagogy, and exploring the roles of resistance, transference, and countertransference in the classroom.

"In the end we depend/On the creatures we made," Freud observed at the close of his life (*Letters*, 425), quoting from Goethe's *Faust;* and in the end psychoanalytic literary criticism depends on the scholars who continue to shape it. All serious scholarship is an act of love and devotion, and for many of the authors in this series, including myself, psychoanalytic literary criticism has become a consuming passion, in some cases a lifelong one. Like other passions, there is an element of idealization here. For despite our criticisms of Freud, we stand in awe of his achievements; and even as we recognize the limitations of any single approach to literature, we find that psychoanalysis has profoundly illuminated the human condition and inspired countless artists. In the words of the fictional "Freud" in D. M. Thomas's extraordinary novel *The White Hotel* (1981), "Long may poetry and psychoanalysis continue to highlight, from their different perspectives, the human face in all its nobility and sorrow" (143n.).

JEFFREY BERMAN
Professor of English
State University of New York at Albany

Works Cited

Freud, Sigmund. *The Letters of Sigmund Freud.* Ed. Ernst Freud. Trans. Tania and James Stern. New York: Basic Books, 1975.

———. *The Origins of Psychoanalysis.* Ed. Marie Bonaparte, Anna Freud, and Ernst Kris. Trans. Eric Mosbacher and James Strachey. New York: Basic Books, 1954; rpt. 1977.

———. *The Standard Edition of the Complete Psychological Works of Sigmund Freud.* Ed. James Strachey. 24 vols. London: Hogarth Press, 1953–74.

Nabokov, Vladimir. Introduction, *Bend Sinister.* New York: McGraw-Hill, 1974.

———. *Lolita.* London: Weidenfeld and Nicolson, 1959.

Thomas, D. M. *The White Hotel.* New York: Viking, 1981.

Preface

Freud's reading is "the heart of the matter" of this book and it is this "heart" which informed the project out of which this book grew. "Kern der Sache," the heart of the matter, is the line which Sigmund Freud scribbled in the margin of a number of his books when he found what seemed to him the essence of a text and its author. The heart of the matter in this volume is Freud's books, his reading, his library. Decades ago I had the pleasure of reading in Nietzsche's library, then buried in the recesses of the research library of the Goethe-Schiller Archive in Weimar. Along with Nietzsche's papers, it had been the centerpiece of the shrine which Nietzsche's sister, Elizabeth Förster-Nietzsche, had constructed and which became a centerpiece of Nazi political culture. The Nietzsche-Archive was disbanded and its holdings, including Nietzsche's library, were amalgamated into the holdings of the Goethe-Schiller Archive run by the National Research and Museum Organization of the German Democratic Republic.

As I learned in the mid-1970s, it is more than romanticization to read the books read by great thinkers. Reading their books gives you an insight to what they read and what they did not read; what they included in their reading of a text, and what they excluded. I was certain that I knew what reading of Emerson had shaped Nietzsche—it was the early *Essays* to which every scholar interested in the antecedents or parallels of Nietzsche's thought had referred since the beginning of this century. This certainty was shattered when I read in his library and found a dog-eared single issue of the *Atlantic Monthly* with a late, idealized essay on Brook Farm which Nietzsche, unsure about his English, had translated into German by one of his traveling companions ("Nietzsches Emerson Lektüre: Eine unbekannte Quelle," *Nietzsche-Studien* 9 [1980]: 406–31).

Here was the failed socialist dream of which Nietzsche was so contemptuous and here was his unknown, hidden Emerson.

Likewise with Freud—I found myself sitting at the Freuds' dining room table in the newly opened Freud Museum reading Freud's sources for his study of Leonardo ("Leonardo Sees Him-Self: Reading Leonardo's First Representation of Human Sexuality," *Social Research* 54 [1987]: 149–71). Freud's essay had been the subject of a devastating (and quite correct) attack by the famed art historian Meyer Schapiro, who pointed out that Freud's entire theory rests on a mistranslation—the "vulture" which Freud claimed to see in Leonardo's painting of the Holy Family with St. Anne was a ghost—it was a mistranslation of the Italian word for another bird, the kite ("Two Slips of Leonardo and a Slip of Freud," *Psychoanalysis* 4 [1955–56]: 3–8 and "Leonardo and Freud: An Art-Historical Study," *Journal of the History of Ideas* 27 [1956]: 147–78). Here Schapiro was quite right. But it was not Freud's mistranslation—rather it was to be found throughout the German-language source books Freud used to prepare his reading. But most importantly, it was to be found in the master narrative against which he wrote—the Russian mystic Dmitri Merezkovsky's fin-de-siècle novel based on Leonardo's life. Freud thus stood in an important contemporary tradition of the creative misreading, of which his was only the most visible. This framed my reinterpretation of Freud's text as part of a turn-of-the-century fictive reading of Leonardo's life as art.

But it is not only the philological drive—the search for sources or analogues—which is satisfied by reading in the libraries of creative individuals; perhaps more important one is able to frame the intellectual context of the author. While it is possible to reconstruct such a context from knowledge about a period or an individual's reading patterns, it is even more striking to see what the author read, to hold specific editions in one's hand, to read those texts which would seem most peripheral to any specific work and yet which provided its intellectual and emotional frame. How extraordinary to pick up those books purchased by the young Nietzsche or Freud when they were students! One can read those texts against which they came to define themselves. One can read their most mundane books, their travel guides or, in the case of Nietzsche, their diet books, and begin to unravel how the world which bounded them as well as their very bodies were constructed in the texts which mirrored and shaped their world.

I was so struck by my experience that I wanted others to share it. In the summer of 1992 I had the pleasure to direct a National Endowment for the Humanities Summer Seminar for College Teachers on the topic of Freud's reading. Held at the Freud Museum in London, it consisted of twelve colleagues from throughout the United States ranging from Alaska to Maine. We met in the museum and all read in Freud's library from a series of different perspectives. Some of the fruits of these readings can be found here. In addition to the members of the seminar, the editors, all of whom participated in the group, requested that a few colleagues, some of whom were involved during the period of the seminar, contribute to this project. They all agreed to do so and we are very pleased with their contributions.

Writing about Freud's reading and his library is not always the same thing. Freud's letters reveal passing references to an extraordinary range of authors and the wide range of cited literature in his scholarly work is proof that his library is but a fragment of his reading. Even determining what books Freud owned is not simple. While there are a small number of books from Sigmund Freud's personal library at the Rare Book Room of the College of Physicians and Surgeons, Columbia University, and the Library of Congress, the bulk of Freud's library remains at the Freud Museum in Hampstead. The question of what volumes actually belonged to Freud remains a complicated one. Nolan D. C. Lewis and Carney Landis ("Freud's Library," *Psychoanalytic Review* 44 [1957]: 327–28 and the catalogue, 28 pp.) provided a reprint of the bookseller's catalogue for the volumes purchased in 1938 for the Psychiatric Institute (and which are now at Columbia). David Bakan ("The Authenticity of the Freud Memorial Collection," *Journal of the History of the Behavioral Sciences* 11 [1975]: 365–67) drew the attribution of some of these titles into question, showing that a number of them had simply been added by the bookseller to those books purchased by him from Freud. K. R. Eissler ("Bericht über die sich in den Vereinigten Staaten befindenen Bücher aus Sigmund Freuds Bibliothek," *Jahrbuch der Psychoanalyse* 9 [1977]: 10–50) provided further information about the origin of some of the volumes now at the Columbia Medical College and reproduced the bookseller's catalogue. Eissler also listed those titles now at the Library of Congress. Further comments on Freud's books in New York are to be found in the work of Ernest Harms ("A Fragment of Freud's Library," *Psychoanalytic Quarterly* 40 [1971]: 491–95) and, concerning the small number of books in the Freud Museum in Vienna, the essay by Hans Lobner ("Some Additional Remarks on Freud's Library," *Sigmund Freud House Bulletin* 1 [1975]: 18–29). The library which Freud retained and which is now housed at the Freud Museum, 20 Maresfield Gardens, London was first catalogued by Harry Trosman and Roger Dennis Simmons ("The Freud Library," *Journal of the American Psychoanalytic Association* 21 [1973]: 646–87). A more complete catalogue is now available at the Freud Museum, compiled by Keith Davies. Unlike the citations from Freud's works, it is clear that Freud did not read all of the books in his possession (some of them are uncut dedication copies).

The studies in this volume reflect both Freud's reading in general and, in many cases, Freud's specific reading of specific volumes. Both approaches can be found in earlier introductions to Freud's reading such as Peter Brückner, *Sigmund Freuds Privatlektüre* (Cologne: Verlag Rolf Horst, 1975); Robert R. Holt, "Freud's Adolescent Reading: Some Possible Effects on his Work," in Paul Stepansky, ed., *Freud: Appraisals and Reappraisals*, 3 vols. (Hillsdale, N.J.: Analytic Press, 1988), 3: 167–92; and Edward Timms, "Freud's Library and His Private Reading," in Edward Timms and Naomi Segal, eds., *Freud in Exile: Psychoanalysis and its Vicissitudes* (New Haven: Yale University Press, 1988), pp. 65–79.

All of the quotations from Freud's works in this study, unless otherwise noted, are to Sigmund Freud, *Standard Edition of the Complete Psychological Works of Sigmund Freud*, ed. and trans., J. Strachey, A. Freud, A. Strachey, and A. Tyson. 24 vols. (London: Hogarth, 1955–74). (Referred to in the notes as SE.) Unless translations are cited in the notes, all of the other translations in this study are by the authors of the essays.

I am especially grateful for the work which the director of the Freud Museum, Erica Davies, and her staff, Alex Bento, Paul Cobley, Keith Davies, Michael Molnar, Susan O'Cleary, and Ivan Ward, put into helping all of us in our time at the Museum. We also want to thank the National Endowment for the Humanities Summer Seminar for College Teachers program for their support and Jeffrey Berman for expressing his interest in including this volume in his distinguished series on literature and psychoanalysis.

SANDER L. GILMAN, *Ithaca, New York*

Contributors

JUTTA BIRMELE studied German Literature at San Francisco State University and Case Western Reserve after having received a Law degree from the Free University of Berlin. She received her Ph.D. in European Studies (History) at Claremont and teaches courses on Modern Germany in the Departments of German and History at California State University, Long Beach.

HAROLD P. BLUM is Clinical Professor of Psychiatry, New York University, College of Medicine; Training and Supervising Analyst, The Psychoanalytic Institute, New York University; Executive Director, The Sigmund Freud Archives; and Past Editor-in-Chief, *Journal of the American Psychoanalytic Association*.

JAY GELLER is a Lecturer of Religion at Princeton University. His publications include *The Nose Job: Freud and the Feminized Jew* (forthcoming) and articles on Freud, Hegel, Hitler, Nordau, Schreber, and representations of the male Jewish body.

SANDER L. GILMAN is the Goldwin Smith Professor of Humane Studies at Cornell University and Professor of the History of Psychiatry at the Cornell Medical College. A member of the Cornell faculty since 1969, he is a cultural and literary historian and the author or editor of over thirty books, the most recent—*The Jew's Body* (Routledge) and *Inscribing the Other* (Nebraska)—having appeared in the fall of 1991. He is the author of the basic study of the visual stereotyping of the mentally ill—*Seeing the Insane*—published by John Wiley in 1982 as well as the standard study of *Jewish Self-Hatred,* the title of his Johns Hopkins University Press monograph of 1986.

VALERIE D. GREENBERG, Associate Professor of German at Tulane University, is author of *Transgressive Readings: The Texts of Franz Kafka and Max Planck* (University of Michigan Press, 1991) and *Literature and Sensibilities in the Weimar Era.* With the support of a fellowship from the Guggenheim Foundation, she is writing a book on Freud's readings in language theory.

NED LUKACHER, Associate Professor of English, University of Illinois-Chicago, is the author of *Primal Scenes: Literature, Philosophy, Psychoanalysis* (Ithaca: Cornell University Press, 1986) and is the translator of several works of French theory, most recently Jacques Derrida's *Cinders* (University of Nebraska Press, 1991). His recently completed new book is tentatively entitled "Allegories of Conscience: Shakespeare, Freud, Heidegger."

PHILLIP MCCAFFREY is Professor of English and Writing at Loyola College (Baltimore). He teaches Medieval and Renaissance literature, creative writing, and Freudian stylistics. He has published articles on English mystery plays, *Le Roman de la Rose,* Chaucer, Malory, and Milton and a book on *Freud and Dora* (Rutgers, 1984).

ROBIN N. MITCHELL-BOYASK currently teaches Classics at Temple University and writes about Greek and Latin literature and comparative topics. He received a B.A. in Classics from the University of Chicago and a Ph.D. in Comparative Literature from Brown University.

MICHAEL MOLNAR has worked at the Freud Museum, London, since its opening in 1986. As well as listing the archive and handling research inquiries, he has translated and edited Freud's *Kürzeste Chronik* which was published as *The Diary of Sigmund Freud 1929–1939* (New York: Scribner's; London: Hogarth; Paris: Albin Michel, 1992).

URSULA REIDEL-SCHREWE is Assistant Professor of German at Colby College, Waterville, Maine. Her publications include *Die Raumstruktur des narrativen Textes. Thomas Mann, der Zauberberg* (Würzburg: Königshausen, 1992) and articles on narrative structures in the early twentieth-century novel. She is currently working on literary representations of androgyny.

RITCHIE ROBERTSON was educated at the universities of Edinburgh, Vienna, and Oxford. Since 1989 he has been University Lecturer in German at Oxford University and Fellow of St. John's College, Oxford. He has published *Kafka: Judaism, Politics, and Literature* (Oxford University Press, 1985: German translation published by Metzler, 1988) and *Heine* in the series "Jewish Thinkers" (London: Peter Halban; New York: Grove Press, 1988). Together with Edward Timms, he edits the yearbook *Austrian Studies* (published by Edinburgh University Press).

PETER L. RUDNYTSKY is Associate Professor of English and Director of the Institute for Psychological Study of the Arts at the University of Florida. He is the author of *Freud and Oedipus* (1987) and *The Psychoanalytic Vocation: Rank, Winnicott, and the Legacy of Freud* (1991) and most recently the editor with Ellen Handler Spitz of *Transitional Objects and Potential Spaces: Literary Uses of D. W. Winnicott* (1993), also published by New York University Press.

1. Freud's Début in the Sciences

Ursula Reidel-Schrewe

Montaigne doesn't know yet of what he is capable and like all débutants, he imitates. He follows the fashionable; and he follows it even in that which is concerned with ideas.[1]

This short paragraph about Montaigne was carefully and completely underlined in an edition of selected writings by Montaigne which I came across in Freud's personal library in Hampstead, London. It was a small red leather volume that looked like it had been used frequently. Each Montaigne text was preceded by a brief commentary on the development of Montaigne's style. Some parts were marked with short vertical pencil lines in the margin of the page until the page with the quoted lines. They were boldly underlined instead of being marked in the margin. After this page the marking stopped altogether, as if the reader had lost interest in the book after he had been struck by this remark about Montaigne as a beginning writer.

The underlined passage says that three features are characteristic of Montaigne, as of beginners in general: unawareness of one's own capability, imitation, and conforming with the *Zeitgeist*. Why should it be of interest that Freud underlined these words about Montaigne? First of all, can we be sure that it was Freud who made the pencil marks in this book?

During our NEH research seminar in London we examined dozens of volumes in Freud's library. After a while, a certain pattern in Freud's reading could be observed. If there were markings at all from Freud's hand, they usually consisted of short vertical lines in the margin, sometimes one-word commentaries or an exclamation mark carried out with unsharpened lead or red or green or blue pencil. They reflected one reader's impulsive reaction rather than a systematic practice. As in the Montaigne volume, the marking often was not continued through to the end of a volume. We also found that the markings occurred for the most part in secondary rather than in primary texts. Thus, the marking in the *commentary* sections of the Montaigne volume was representative of Freud's reading interests. I did not find any words or exclamation marks in this volume, but it did have the characteristic heavy lead pencil marks in the margin, and in addition, the unusual underlining of every entire line in that one paragraph which drew my attention.

Freud was at least 58 years old when he came across this Montaigne volume published in 1914. At the time, Freud had already published his essays on Leonardo da Vinci, Michelangelo, and Jensen's *Gradiva* dealing with the creative powers of the genius.[2] Throughout his life Freud took great interest in the psychic sources of creativity and he often expressed his ambivalent feelings about his artistic and/or scientific talents.[3] Numerous comments about his own writing testify to his awareness of language, style, and audience. Thus, underlining the paragraph on the undeveloped talent of Montaigne illustrates Freud's interest in the mechanisms of the creative mind. We can read it as yet another comment on writing. Did Freud mark these lines because this description of an unconscious capability reminded him of his own beginnings? In my reading this underlining is a marking of identification providing an appropriate epigraph for my analysis of Freud's 1877 publication in the Proceedings of the Imperial Academy of Sciences in Vienna, an article on eels: "Observations on the configuration and finer structure of the lobed organs in eels described as testes."[4]

By today's perspective on science, the title of this paper sounds ludicrous, even more so in German, and the topic seems odd and outdated. In the ongoing reassessment of Freud's work and the culture of his time, however, the eel article is a significant document in the history of science as well as a source for Freud's development as a writer and scientist. My analysis will focus on the conceptual and linguistic features of the eel article and point out the ambiguity of its outcome. In juxtaposition to his first scientific writing, I will take a closer look at the letters from Trieste in which Freud describes his research on the eels to his friend Eduard Silberstein; my comparison of Freud's personal and the official account of his stay in Trieste and my discussion of their discrepancies in content and language aim at a more accurate understanding of Freud's beginnings foreshadowing the literary and scientific eminence of his later works.

Biographers have treated the "eel article" and its preceding research in Trieste as an episode in the context of Freud's student years rather than as a significant component of Freud's work.[5] This is not surprising since we still do not have immediate access to the part of Freud's writings preceding his psychoanalytic work. Apart from four articles on the brain that Freud wrote for an encyclopedia, all of his early scientific articles have yet to be translated into English.[6] The Standard Edition contains the "Abstracts of the Scientific Writings of Dr. Sigm. Freud. 1877–1897" compiled by Freud himself while pursuing a professorship at the University of Vienna in 1897, but, as James Strachey reminds the reader, "Freud's 'complete psychological works' are very far from coinciding with Freud's 'complete works.' "[7]

Freud was a student of medicine at the University of Vienna, not yet 21 years old, when his zoology professor Carl Claus, director of the Institute for Zoological Comparative Anatomy, sent him to Trieste to conduct research on the sexual organ of eels. Claus had founded the Marine Zoological Station in Trieste in 1875, and Freud was one of his first students to do research there. Carl Claus was a fervent Darwinist; as Lucille Ritvo relates, "the very year in which Freud enrolled at the University of Vienna, Carl Claus was brought from Göttingen to modernize the zoology department, which at that time meant bringing it into line with the new paradigm being established in biology by Darwin's work" (Ritvo 1990:113). Siegfried Bernfeld gives a vivid account of the enthusiasm for Darwin's theory of evolution in the last decades of the 19th century at the University of Vienna. Darwin had created an entirely new worldview by pursuing the path of natural science and elaborating his theories about the origin of life. Methods of scientific research were changing from the statistical and descriptive to the experimental and microscopic observation of the dynamic energies in organisms. As a student of two Darwinist teachers, Carl Claus the zoologist, and Ernst Brücke the physiologist, Freud found himself at the source of these new ideas as he conducted his laboratory work on primitive species.[8]

Within the context of this "New Biology," the sexual organ of the eel was a typical Darwinist topic since at that time it was not certain if the eel was a hermaphroditic species or if the male and female eel were separate fish. Proving that the eel was bisexual would have been very much in line with Darwin's idea of the "descent of man" from hermaphroditic or androgynous origins. Carl Claus had studied hermaphroditism in animals[9] and must have felt challenged by Simon Syrski's claim that he had discovered a lobed-shaped organ in the eel "which could be nothing else than the testicles. . . . Therefore the eels are of separate gender."[10]

Syrski had conducted his research on the eels in the capacity of director at the Museum for Natural History in Trieste, a position he held from 1866 to 1875. Syrski was an accomplished zoologist who had studied in Warsaw and later became professor of zoology at the University of Lemberg (Lwow). His article, "Über die Reproductions-Organe der Aale," was published in the *Proceedings of the Academy of Sciences* in 1874.[11] The results of Syrski's research discharged the idea that the eel belonged to the hermaphroditic species, as two Italian zoologists had previously argued (Syrski 1874:323). Syrski found that the lobe-shaped organ was different from the ovaries in eels as they were known thus far. Even though the lobed organ and the ovaries looked similar in an early stage of their development, Syrski believed that these organs developed separately in the female and male eels, respectively. Yet, one thing was missing in Syrski's discoveries: the proof that these lobed-shaped testicles would produce sperm. Therefore, the probability that the eel belonged indeed to the hermaphroditic species remained plausible and further study was necessary to confirm one theory or the other.

It was not an easy task for the young Freud: to take up this controversial issue and to fulfill the expectations of his mentor Professor Claus by providing evidence that would refute Syrski's findings. The results of this research were going to be published in the Academy's Proceedings, the same publication in which Syrski's article had appeared three years before. The Academy was the forum where the conflicting directions in scientific research were continuously discussed. The study of the eels placed the student Freud right in the middle of that debate. His findings would either undermine the Darwinist theories of his professor or the validity of the research done by Syrski. It is precisely his ambivalence between two paradigms that makes Freud's final report on this subject inconclusive.

Bernfeld was the first to point out that the results of Freud's research were "inconclusive," but he did it based on the assumption that Freud had failed to substantiate the validity of Syrski's observations. A similar presupposition, namely that Freud had aimed to produce evidence of testicles in the eel, can be noticed in Jones's remark "that the future discoverer of the castration complex was disappointed at not being able to find the testes of the eel" (Jones 42; see also Bernfeld 1949:166). Just as Jones and Bernfeld, we tend to project our present knowledge of the separate gender of eels to be the objective of Freud's research at the time. We read Freud's paper expecting that it will support and expand Syrski's observations and we are disappointed to find that Freud fails to make use of this opportunity.

Freud repeats and verifies Syrski's anatomical description of the "Lappenorgan," but he does not validate the difference between the male and the female reproductive organ in eels; instead, he casts doubt on Syrski's findings by stating that "for the reader of Syrski's information the supposition suggests itself readily that the lobed-shaped organ would be nothing else than a modified ovary."[12]

While Syrski tries to establish the evidence for the different anatomical features of the ovaries and the testicles, Freud emphasizes that these organs are similar in appearance, providing that the eel is not full-grown and has not exceeded the length of approximately eight inches (Freud 1877b:423).

Only after histological examination does Freud admit that the cells of the lobed organ show a variety of characteristics distinct from the cells of the ovaries. Freud gives a careful account of their varying size, structure, position, and ability to proliferate. He suggests that the shape of some cells, their conglomeration, and proliferation indicate the possibility of forming spermatozoa. Thus, Freud comes very close to the discovery of the eel's sperm, the missing link in Syrski's discovery of the male organ. But Freud does not abandon the paradigm of hermaphroditism; before discussing the possibility of spermatozoa he repeats that "the opinion cannot be rejected that the lobed organ is a modification of the ovary, which derives from an earlier developmental phase of the latter, because there was no proof that the first disposition of both organs was already different."

He then continues by considering the contrary: "But this is not very probable, since as far as the development of the lobed organ has been traced, it proved to be different from the immature ovary."[13]

Repeatedly, Freud disregards his findings and those of Syrski by emphasizing that the proliferating characteristics of cells could be found in any organ that is not yet full-grown. He stresses again that the lobed organ that Syrski had found was an immature organ: "Even if one would admit that the lobed organ is the testicle, nobody really has seen a mature lobed organ and a mature male eel."[14]

Throughout his paper, Freud avoids conclusions for fear of excluding either the bisexual nature of the eel or the division of male and female. This way, Freud echoes his Darwinist professor, who set out to challenge Syrski's claim, and yet, he does not entirely dismiss Syrski's discovery. Being caught in the scrutinizing authoritative gaze of two opposed scientific factions, Freud chose indeterminacy in order to circumvent the constraint in which he found himself in relation to his teacher Claus. In this regard, the eel article is a reflection of biographical circumstance as well as a resource which documents the scientific debate about the Darwinist ideas on the evolution of reproductive functions. Freud's inconclusive study certainly contributed to the continuation of this debate and to the delay in the acceptance of Syrski's findings.[15]

When we discussed the eel article at the Freud Seminar in London, one sarcastic remark was that "the essence of it is sex! What else is new?" Indeed, the topic of the eel article invited ironic rather than serious comments. Bernfeld refers to these beginnings as a singular incident since Freud "let almost twenty years go by before he gave sexuality another scientific thought." Bernfeld wonders whether the topic might have been "repulsive" for Freud: "The eighteen-seventies were prudish and hypocritical and the moral standards of Freud's family were strictly Victorian; Freud shared them with conviction" (Bernfeld 1949:168). Bernfeld assumes that Freud himself was dissatisfied with his paper and suggests that working under Claus must have been a frustrating experience for the young student.[16]

Gay reminds us of another "coincidence" concerning Freud who would become the discoverer of the Oedipus complex; Freud had to translate 33 verses of Sophocles' *Oedipus Rex* in the final examination at the Gymnasium. Gay hesitates to interpret this biographical data: "Both [the translation and the eel article], after all, were assignments" (Gay 32). Rather than viewing them as accidental assignments, I would like to consider the impact of these early exercises on the potential capabilities of the young student and their significance for the progression of Freud's ideas.

Following Frank Sulloway's lead, we become aware of the continuity in the debate about Darwin's theory of evolution and Freud's continuous involvement in this debate after he had finished working for Claus and became more engaged in the Physiological Institute of Ernst Brücke. Sulloway points out that Freud's early studies prepared him well for the exchange of ideas with Wilhelm Fliess that started in 1887 and in which the biological bisexual nature of man became a major issue (Sulloway 160).[17] Thus, we may conclude that the eel article was not an awkward, isolated incident in Freud's life, but an essential part of the biological preparation which informed Freud's later insights into the psycho-biological mechanisms of human nature.

The debated functions of sexual organs in eels led Freud to produce a text prefiguring the rhetoric of uncertainty and reflection that we find in many of his later writings.[18] In this regard, the eel article is a gold mine for stylistic studies. First, let us look at the article as a piece of scientific writing. Could this kind of language have been written by any other scientist of that time? Did Freud follow the rules and adopt the style of the dry "Wissenschaftsdeutsch" and thus "imitate," as it was said of Montaigne? Syrski's article could have served Freud as a guideline for writing his first scientific report to the Academy. As we shall see, Freud followed the customary pattern to some extent in his outline but not in his style.

Freud introduces his subject matter by delineating the scope of his research: the time frame, what kind of eels, their number and size. He then states the objective of his research and takes Syrski's results as the departure point for his investigation. An extensive description of the anatomical characteristics of the lobed organ and the ovaries in eels follows, recapitulating for the most part Syrski's findings. Freud concludes this part of his paper by stating that the *anatomical* evidence does not confirm a clear distinction between the male and the female organ. A *histological* examination would be necessary:

Even though the smallest ovaries which one can find in animals of less than 8' in length are still two to three times wider than the smallest not lobed-shaped forms of the Syrski-organ in animals of the same size, one has to admit that the appearance of the undeveloped "Lappenorgan" comes so close to that of an immature ovary, that with this identity of all topographical circumstances in both organs, only the histological examination can determine, if the lobed organ is an organ *sui generis* or a modification of the ovary which develops from a very early state of the latter.[19]

Freud then presents the results of his histological research. He lists noticeable differences between the arrangement and composition of the cells in ovaries and the "Lappenorgan." In contrast to Syrski's final conclusion summarizing his findings in five points and restating the claim that eels are of separate gender, Freud's ending reiterates the inconclusive results on the grounds that Syrski's, as well as his own research, did not produce the evidence of a male organ in a sexually mature condition.

Syrski's conclusion is followed by a description of the external characteristics of two types of eels including their color and the measurements of their eyes and stomach. Syrski's intention to make "a preliminary contribution to the systemic record of the Adriatic eels" gives us a glimpse of a major scientific objective at that time (Syrski 324). Measuring external differences and compiling a systematic record of species was the common biological method during most of the 19th century.

It is of interest that Freud's article ends in a similar but more extensive detour than Syrski's. Here, Freud takes a firm stand against the notion that measurements and external characteristics like color or large eyes in certain varieties of eels could be an indicator for their sex, fertility, or sterility. Familiar with microscopic histological analysis, Freud points clearly to the direction that future scientific investigation would take.

Apart from the fact that Freud concludes his report with a digression, as did Syrski, it is noteworthy that Freud ends on a note that leads away from the actual topic and deals with methodological problems. Such digression and change of perspective typify Freud's work; he meticulously recapitulated, reconsidered, or rewrote introductions, footnotes or endings as a result of a new understanding or a modifying methodological insight. One remarks examples of this practice in the *Interpretation of Dreams* (1900), the *Three Essays on the Theory of Sexuality* (1905), and, in a most perplexing way, in *Moses and Monotheism* (1939).

Besides the appended methodological discussion, the eel article, as we have seen, is appropriately structured. Still, it is a confusing experience to read through this paper; the organizing principles are not explicit to the reader. We are wondering what Bernfeld meant when he praised Freud's style in the following manner: "Although it is written in a precise and animated style, always self-assured—at times even cocky—its content is neither exciting nor brilliant" (Bernfeld 1949:166). A closer look at Freud's language in the eel article reveals that precision and self-assurance characterize only those parts of the article where Freud gives a detailed description of his anatomical and histological findings. These parts are written in the indicative and show an impressive linguistic accuracy, as in this example: "The cells themselves [of the lobed organ] are smaller than the ovarian cells and also otherwise easy to distinguish; they are rounded when they lie individually in the loops of the network, but cubic when more of them lie together in a space of the tissue and have flattened each other."[20]

Here, and even more pronounced in his other reports to the Vienna Academy (1877a, 1878, 1882), Freud already demonstrates his skill in articulating observations of extremely complicated systems in a clear and inventive language. He is describing fibres arranged like Pinsel (brush), Büschel (bunch), Bündel (bundle), Rosetten (rosettes), Schlingen (loops), Netze (nets), or Sterne (stars). Once he says, "as if a knitted pouch is pulled over a toy ball" ("wie wenn ein gestrickter Beutel über einen Spielball gezogen ist" (Freud 1882:25). From his psychoanalytical texts we are familiar with similar, strikingly simple but perfect comparisons. As Ritvo comments, "even as a biologist, Freud deviated from the academic style of the day and reported his scientific work from the beginning in a straight-forward German, simple enough even for Darwin" (1990:11). Ritvo, as well as Bernfeld, is certainly right concerning the "objective" rendering of facts in Freud's biological writings. The language in the eel article, however, doesn't match this positive evaluation in those parts that deal with the interpretation of the evidence.

In the eel article we find a recurrent hesitation to come to the "Kern der Sache." Freud cannot bring himself to argue that he had indeed found the male eel organ. These interpretative passages are written in the subjunctive and are characterized by redundant phrases like: "it seems" (es scheint), "cannot be totally dismissed" (ist ja nicht völlig auszuschließen), "doesn't speak directly for it, neither against it", (spricht nicht direct dafür, spricht aber auch nicht dagegen), "seem at least not to contradict" (scheinen wenigstens nicht zu widersprechen), "seemed to be not at all indisputable" (durchaus nicht unanfechtbar zu sein schien), "almost entirely to confirm" (fast durchgehends zu bestätigen), "it seemed to be appropriate" (es schien angezeigt), "in some likelihood" (mit einiger Wahrscheinlichkeit), "this at least can only be said" (es läßt sich dies höchstens sagen), and "appears to be not very convincing" (wenig zwingend erscheinen). Some of these phrases appeared already in my discussion in full quotations, illustrating the ambiguity of the conveyed message.

One asks whether this type of language is the rhetoric of a conscientious, articulate scientist or the uncomfortable, biased voice of a person who avoids conclusiveness in view of possible rejection? Awareness of his audience leads Freud to employ a mode of expression that forecloses his opponents without diminishing their or his own stature. We are familiar with this rhetorical tendency from later texts, such as the *Studies in Hysteria*, the *Case Histories*, or the *Interpretation of Dreams*. Rather than making authoritative statements Freud chooses to make the processes of his thoughts accessible and to incorporate probable objections; thus, he displaces and postpones an outcome and distances himself from his subject matter.

It can be said that the topical inconclusiveness of the eel article, swaying between hermaphroditism and the division of sexes, is strikingly reflected in its discourse. This discursive feature clearly distinguishes the article from the three other publications (1877a, 1878, 1882) in the Proceedings of the Academy of Sciences. These publications dealt with nerve fibres and nerve cells of the crayfish and the petromyzon, a primitive species of eel-like fish, and were the results of Freud's work in Ernst Brücke's laboratory. Their subject matter was certainly less charged than the topic of the eel's sex, which was a concern of Claus's. In these papers on the nervous system, Freud engages in an extensive, well-informed and thorough discussion of previous studies done by other scientists. His findings are presented as unbiased contributions to the field of neuro-biological research; the same cannot be said of the eel article.

The peculiarity of Freud's début becomes even more apparent when we look at Freud's letters to his friend Eduard Silberstein in April 1876.[21] It is a fortunate circumstance that we have a "personal" report on the stay in Trieste side by side with the "official" report to the Academy. The letter of April 5, 1876 in particular, shows how deeply Freud immersed himself in his scientific work at the Zoological Station in Trieste. He gives a detailed description of its location and the setup of his working area, accompanied by a sketch that illustrates the position of the microscope, the vials and bowls, and the tools needed for dissecting; even four pencils and a sheet of paper are mentioned and appear in the drawing ("in der Mitte vier Bleistifte neben einem Blatt Papier"). The entire narrative of the letter is interspersed with little sketches: a tiny donkey, a face, the layout of the worktable, a variety of fish species and several eels. To our surprise, we also find sketches of the reproductive organ: similar-looking testes and ovaries as well as spermatozoa and ovary cells. As in a scientific text, Freud even numbers his illustrations from "Fig. 1" to "Fig. 17" and comments ironically "my drawings are not without value as caricatures" (meine Zeichnungen sind als Karikaturen nicht ohne Wert). [22] It may be added here that the scientific illustrations attached to Freud's articles of 1877a, 1877b, 1878, and 1882 were drawn by Freud himself. In their precision and soft colors these depictions of biological structures reveal some talent and are not without a special beauty.

Freud writes on April 5, 1876 that once a day his daily work is interrupted; the fishermen have arrived and he hurries down to the courtyard to inspect the catch of the day, which is then distributed for dissection among Freud and his colleagues:

That way I receive daily sharks, rays, eels and other beasts, which I anatomically examine in general then in regard to *one particular point. This point* is the following. You know the eel. *For a long time* only the female of this beast was known, *even Aristotle did not know* from where these take the male and therefore had the eels arise from the mud. *Throughout the Middle Ages and modern times* a kind of a chase for the male eels was carried on. [23]

In his witty account of the quest for the male eel, Freud clearly demonstrates his awareness of the "one particular point." In fact, besides providing a sketch of the sperm, he already hypothesizes the outcome of his research: "Under microscope the testes show spermatozoa, the ovaries eggs even with naked eye." [24]

The reader is led to believe that Freud indeed did see what he describes, were it not that he concludes his biology "lesson" by breaking the illusion and presenting the fact that he had only dissected eels of the "gentler sex." [25] Freud's unabashed dealing with the "one particular point" proves that the topic of the eel's sex was certainly not repulsive to him, as Bernfeld suggests in his discussion of Freud's attitude toward his first zoological effort (Bernfeld 1949:166). On the contrary, Freud clearly found pleasure in his work and even greater pleasure in writing about it to his friend Silberstein. The letter conveys the presumptive certainty of making the discovery of spermatozoa which Syrski had failed to come up with. Why was Freud not as straightforward and explicit when it came to addressing this "one particular point" in his report to the Academy? Did he suppress evidence in order to keep the issue open and, as I have suggested earlier, to side with Claus on the issue of hermaphroditism? Held against the letter to Silberstein, we are puzzled by Freud's report to the Academy in its avoidance of clarifying the point that would end the discussion about the eel's sex.

Let us turn to the other lines emphasized in the quotation above. The phrases "even Aristotle did not know" and "throughout the Middle Ages and modern times" indicate that Freud, under the cover of irony, embraces the idea of the historical dimension of his project. This notion reappears in the official report as "the question, pending for centuries" ("die seit Jahrhunderten schwebende Frage"; Freud 1877b:420) and reminds the reader of Syrski's earlier formulation in his eel article of 1874: "Since it might be of interest to learn how I arrived at the solution of the task that so many researchers have been struggling with in vain from Aristotle to our days, sometimes for several months and years, I want to recall this first, before I will deal with the subject matter itself."[26]

Freud's adaptation of Syrski's historical perspective in his letter to Silberstein and in his official report can be read as a way of counteracting the boldness of Syrski's claim to have discovered the testicles of the eel. Freud reacts with an almost cynical reproach to Syrski's discovery: "Recently, a zoologist from Trieste has found, as he says, the testes, that means the male eel, but has not given a precise description of those, because he seems not to know what a microscope is."[27]

Freud can allow this sneer against Syrski in a private humorous letter to his friend, whereas he would encounter difficulty in articulating the intricacies of the issue in his official report. There he would employ all the *ifs* and *whens* with the result that Syrski's discovery appeared dubious.

Freud's letters from Trieste reveal still another literary, feature that I would like to address. Kurt Eissler has taken a closer look at the literary talent of the young Freud. He assumes that a gifted youth like Freud "could easily have become a renowned professor of German literature."[28] Eissler suggests that Freud's decision to study medicine was influenced by Freud's defense against feelings of sexual arousal and passion after renouncing his infatuation with Gisela Fluß, the sister of his boyhood friend Emil Fluβ. In his letter of August 1873 to Silberstein, Freud explained that no other person had taken her place; that place could stay empty, or rather had filled itself with something else, as with air (*Jugendbriefe* 52). Two months after writing this, Freud would be enrolled as a student of medicine at the University of Vienna. The "empty place" was filled with something else: philosophy, biology, anatomy, and chemistry. A rigorous daily schedule, starting early in the morning, protected the young man from the pitfalls of emotional turmoil.

Does that mean that Freud also abandoned his talent and the pleasure of writing as Eissler records and illustrates with Prospero saying, "I'll break my staff, Bury it certain fathoms in the earth, And deeper than did ever plummet sound I'll drown my book?"[29] Letters to Emil Fluβ and Eduard Silberstein seem to demonstrate Freud's continued enjoyment and awareness of his performance as a writer.

Freud's changing mood and attitude toward writing, depending on the involvement in his scientific research, becomes apparent when we look at the Trieste letters sequentially. After his arrival in Trieste, Freud sent a brief undated note to Silberstein saying that "writing would be the most stupid thing that he could do" and that he would tell him everything orally later on.[30] The beginning of his next letter on April 5 suggests that letter writing is an obligation that has to be met at certain times: "Today is a day of letter writing, all parties have to be satisfied today."[31] Nevertheless, Freud is carried away by his own story, and this letter, filled with his "scientific" illustrations, will become one of the most creative and imaginative letters Freud has ever written. Finally, the last letter from Trieste to Silberstein, dated April 23, 1876, states explicitly the enjoyment of writing. It begins like this: "I thoroughly enjoyed your writing, since it gives me the opportunity to answer and since sometimes it is most desirable to be able to write letters. Don't be amazed about this "sudden" change in my attitude: that I previously tried to get rid of the burden of responding and now long for it. My mood has totally changed according to the reigning law of nature in me."[32]

As the zoological study of the eels ends, Freud indulges in writing. Phrases such as "just like novel writers would depict it" ("ganz wie die Romanschreiber schildern"), or "I am coming in *medias res*" ("komme ich in medias res"), show how consciously he worked on the narrative (*Jugendbriefe* 175).

From a literary viewpoint, this letter of April 23 deserves a closer look.

Here, Freud tells Silberstein about an excursion he made on a Sunday with one of his colleagues from the Station. They went by steamboat to a small village in one of the adjacent bays near Trieste: "I have to tell you more about this excursion, some things have touched me in a special way."[33] "Being touched" sets the tone for the subsequent story leading the reader to a most lively depiction of village and country life in the taverns of Muggia, the town for which "respect" is demanded.

The scene is filled with drunkards, joking innkeepers, women and children, and even animals. An ailing woman with a guitar is entering the tavern accompanied by her young son who is playing the accordion. These impoverished figures lead Freud to the compassionate comment "that we became inclined to believe in real misery which is indeed not that rare in the world."[34] Before leaving the boat on their return trip, Freud kisses the "loveliest child" in the arms of a beautiful woman. As a farewell, he reaches out and touches the world by which he had been touched so deeply (*Jugendbriefe* 179). There is a Goethean quality to this narrative. It reminds us of Werther's revelling about the beauties of country life and his recollection of the startling encounter with the deranged young man and his mother to whom Werther reaches out by handing them some money before he leaves.

The "Muggia" letter of April 23 was written a few days before Freud left Trieste and returned to Vienna. Its tone and immediacy are almost poetic compared with the letter with the "caricatures" which Freud wrote three weeks earlier on April 5, 1876, when he was still fully occupied with his research on the eels. Here, the prevalent mode of expression is irony reflecting a detachment from his inner feelings and the outside world. Writing this letter meant gaining a new perspective on the work and the daily routine; Freud's creative talent is set free and the research project on the eels becomes an amusing story:

When I take a walk in the evening at 6:30, my hands stained from the white and red blood of the sea animals and in front of my eyes the glimmering debris of cells, which still disturb me in my dreams, and in my mind nothing but the big problems connected with the names of testicles and ovaries—universally significant names—so when I take my walk at night after work, I only see very little of the physiology of the Triestians.[35]

Obviously, the lonely young man Freud is joking about his horniness. Ironic exaggeration and "scientific" language—"physiology of the Triestians"—are the means by which Freud distances himself from his surroundings and his new experiences. Moreover, this passage illustrates Freud's intense self-observation and his talent for depicting a situation in terms of its psychological effects on a person. He speaks of himself as of a blood-stained offender of animals who is victimized by his own actions. He incorporates in his narrative various states of consciousness such as "preoccupation of the mind," "traumatic experience," and "isolation"; a case history in a nutshell is sketched in a few lines.

Further on in the letter Freud talks about the variety of people in Trieste, much in the same way he summed up the variety of fish in the Zoological Station: "I understand by 'people' all living creatures, who as inhabitants and workers populate Triest."[36] He switches from horses, bulls, and donkeys to men, from cats to women, and finally describes the children. In another passage the human world turns into a submarine habitat; animals take on human features: "Fish and other beasts are simply not going out in bad weather. The sharks and rays are sitting in their little rooms on the bottom of the sea..."[37]

The word "beasts" ("Bestien") appears several times. Freud uses it like a code when he refers to the women in Trieste. In context, it is less derogatory than it sounds. Rather than a qualification, it is an ironic label for a certain species of creatures in the vast biological universe. Freud, impregnated by the Darwinist idea of evolution, understood himself to be a "Naturforscher." As he explains in his letter to Emil Fluβ, of May 1, 1873: "I will take insight in the millennium-old chronicles of nature, perhaps even listen to their eternal process and share my benefits with everybody who wants to learn."[38]

Freud's idea of the study of nature is highly idealized, if not romantic. In the same vein, I would read the nickname "Ichthyosaura" for Gisela Fluβ as imaginative and witty, rather than demeaning as Eissler suggests (471). This nickname complements well the metaphor of the "hydrographical system" for the "Flüsse" (rivers), meaning the three Fluβ brothers—Emil, Richard, Alfred—and their sister Gisela (Letter to Emil Fluβ, August 23, 1875; Grubrich-Simitis 1987:116).

Freud continuously borrows language from his zoological studies and uses it in an imaginative and ironic way as a means to deal with professional pressure and emotional confusion. He speaks of "anatomical features" when he describes people and he even confesses that "since it is not allowed to dissect humans, I actually have nothing to do with them."[39] Notwithstanding its ironic tone and intention, this remark conveys the chilling idea that people only count as objects of analysis. This sentence has been quoted as a sign of Freud's defenses against emotional involvement presaging his recourse to psychoanalysis to "dissect" the complicated makeup of the human condition (Eissler 471; Gay 32; McGrath 134). In any case, this remark seems to indicate that Freud was coming to terms with his vocation as a scientist and that "dissecting humans" was part of Freud's comprehensive understanding of life where humans and animals are interrelated in the realm of nature.

The juxtaposition of Freud's article on the eels and his letters from Trieste discussed here reveals a dialectic in Freud's self-understanding during this early period of his life. His talents were channeled in two different directions. Letter writing became a means to stimulate his own imagination, with personal friends providing a congenial audience. In the eel article, on the other hand, we confront a document that reflects the frustration of a young scientist trying to cope with the expectations of a scrutinizing audience, which included his immediate superior Carl Claus, the "challenger" Simon Syrski, and the authority of an institution such as the Academy of Sciences. Freud would continue to immerse himself in the professional sphere, becoming at times a captive in the struggle for recognition of his scientific achievements. At this point, the young Freud did not yet know that he was capable of creating a work in which his literary and scientific talent would be closely intertwined, setting in motion a new understanding of the human psyche.

Notes

1. René Radonant: *Montaigne. Oeuvre Choisi* (Paris: Hatier, 1914), p. 29: "Montaigne ne sait pas encore de quoi il est capable et comme tous les débutants, il imite. Il suit la mode; et il suit même pour ce qui est des idées."

2. S. Freud (1907a) "Delusions and Dreams in Jensen's 'Gradiva' " (SE 9:3). id. (1910c) "Leonardo da Vinci and a Memory of his Childhood" (SE 11:59). id. (1914) "The Moses of Michelangelo" (SE 13).

3. Two books have dealt exclusively with Freud as a writer. Walter Schönau evaluates Freud's language and style on the basis of the claim that his work is that of a scientist—rather than literary artist—representing a milestone in the intellectual history of our age. Walter Schönau, *Sigmund Freuds Prosa* (Stuttgart: Metzler, 1968). Patrick Mahoney, in his book *Freud as a Writer* (expanded edition, New Haven: Yale UP, 1987) takes a different viewpoint

by perceiving Freudian expression as a phenomenon in itself, from which an evolution in the understanding of human behavior resulted.

4. Sigmund Freud, stud.med. "Beobachtungen über Gestaltung und feineren Bau der als Hoden beschriebenen Lappenorgane des Aals." (Mit 1 Tafel). Vorgelegt in der Sitzung am 15. März 1877. Arbeiten aus dem zoologisch-vergleichend-anatomischen Institute der Universität Wien. *Sitzungsberichte der Mathematisch-Naturwissenschaftlichen Classe der Kaiserlichen Akademie der Wissenschaften.* Abteilung I. Wien. 75/1–4 (1877b) 419–431. This publication will be referred to as *Proceedings of the Academy of Sciences.*

In the "Abstracts of the Scientific Writings of Dr. Sigm. Freud" (SE 3:227), Freud listed this paper as his first. As protocols show, Freud actually submitted a report on his research in Trieste on June 8, 1876. As a recipient of a study grant from the Austrian Ministry of Education, which Professor Claus had initiated for Freud's eel project in Trieste, he was required to submit a report to the administration; see Jos. Gicklhorn, "Wissenschafts-geschichtliche Notizen zu den Studien von S. Syrski (1874) und S. Freud (1877) über männliche Flußaale," *Sitzungsberichte der Österreichischen Akademie der Wissenschaften.* Mathematisch-Naturwiss. Klasse. Abteilung I. Wien. 164/1–2 (1955) 1–24.

In September of that same year (1876) the grant was renewed and Freud returned to Trieste for a second round of research on the eels. Subsequently, the final report was published in the *Proceedings of the Academy* in March 1877. In the meantime, Freud finished his next research project, this time for Ernst Brücke; it was published two months earlier than the eel article in the *Proceedings* of January 1877.

Until graduation, and in the year following his graduation as medical doctor in 1881, Freud published three other papers in the *Proceedings of the Academy of Sciences* and one in the *Zentralblatt der medizinischen Wissenschaft* (SE 3:227, 328). See note 8 for their titles.

5. The most detailed account of Freud's years as a student of medicine and young scientist is given by Siegfried Bernfeld, "Freud's Scientific Beginnings," *American Imago* 6 (1949):163–196. A German translation of this article is included in Siegfried Bernfeld and Suzanne Cassirer-Bernfeld, *Bausteine der Freud-Biographik,* intr., ed., transl. by Ilse Grubrich-Simitis (Frankfurt: Suhrkamp TB, 1988). Bernfeld's research data and their interpretation have been an important resource for Freud scholars. His work resurfaces almost verbatim in the fourth chapter of Ernest Jones's *Sigmund Freud: Life and Work,* 3 Vols. (London: Hogarth, 1953; 1980). Grubrich-Simitis, in her introduction to Bernfeld's *Freud-Biographik,* comments that Jones's debt to Bernfeld was worth more than a few footnotes and that in this case the right of authorship had been infringed upon.

William J. McGrath, in *Freud's Discovery of Psychoanalysis* (Ithaca: Cornell UP, 1986), p. 133, draws on the vivid letters Freud wrote to Eduard Silberstein in April 1876 while in Trieste. See also Peter Gay, *Freud: A Life for Our Time* (New York: Norton, 1988), p. 31. Lucille Ritvo's study deals predominently with the life and work of Carl Claus. Claus's influence on Freud and the "eel article" are discussed in the larger context of the Darwinist school at the University of Vienna. See "Carl Claus as Freud's Professor of the New Darwinian Biology," *International Journal of Psycho-Analysis* 53 (1972): 277–283. See also Ritvo's more recent book *Darwin's Influence on Freud. A Tale of Two Sciences* (New Haven: Yale UP, 1990).

6. Mark Solm and Michael Saling: *A Moment in Transition* (London: Karnac, 1990).

7. SE 3: 226.

8. Bernfeld (1949). The studies under Ernst Brücke resulted in four publications on the histology of the nervous system in an elementary specimen of fish: S. Freud, "Über den Ursprung der hinteren Nervenwurzeln im Rückenmarke von Ammocoetes (Petromyzon Planeri)," *Sitzungsberichte der Kaiserlichen Akademie der Wissenschaften Wien.* (Mathematisch-Naturwissenschaftliche Classe) III. Abteilung 75(1877a)15–27. S. Freud, "Über Spinalganglien und Rückenmark des Petromyzon," *Sitzungsberichte der Kaiserlichen Akademie der Wissenschaften Wien.* (Mathematisch-Naturwissenschaftliche Classe) III. Abteilung. 78(1878)81–167. S. Freud, "Eine Notiz über eine Methode zur anatomischen Präparation des Nervensystems," *Zentralblatt der medizinischen Wissenschaft* 17/26(1879)468–469. S. Freud, "Über den Bau der Nervenfasern und Nervenzellen beim Flußkrebs," *Sitzungsberichte der Kaiserlichen Akademie der Wissenschaften Wien.* (Mathematisch-Naturwissenschaftliche Classe) III. Abteilung. 85(1882)9–47.
    These studies in biological science led eventually to Freud's neurological research on the human brain after he obtained his medical degree in 1881. Most Freud scholarship emphasizes this neurological component rather than the early zoological studies in the "cathartic prehistory" of psychoanalysis (S. Freud (1935) *An Autobiographical Study* SE 20:71). Freud recalls the six years he worked for Ernst Brücke at the Institute of Physiology as the most professionally and personally rewarding experience of his early life. That Freud did not pay similar tribute to his teacher and mentor Carl Claus indicates, according to Bernfeld and other later scholars, that the student-teacher relationship between Freud and Claus was not as positive and productive as the one with Brücke.

9. Frank J. Sulloway, *Freud, Biologist of the Mind* (New York: Basic Books, 1979), p. 159 and Bernfeld (1949:166).

10. "Diese Organe können daher nichts anderes als Hoden sein.... Die Aale sind demnach getrennten Geschlechts" ("Über die Reproductions-Organe der Aale" von Dr. Syrski [mit 2 Tafeln], *Sitzungsberichte der Kaiserlichen Akademie der Wissenschaften. Mathematisch-Naturwissenschaftliche Classe.* Abteilung I. Wien: 69/4 (1874) 315–327. Quotes on pp. 322 and 323).

11. More extensive biographical information about Simon Syrski was collected by Jos. Gicklhorn (1955): Syrski (1829–1882) was born in Galicia. At the

time Galicia was part of the Austrio-Hungarian Hapsburg Empire; in 1918 it became part of Poland. Gicklhorn raises the question of why Syrski's accomplishments in the field of science were not fully recognized. Syrski published several articles on the eel and related topics in German, English, Italian, and Polish. According to Gicklhorn, a skeptical attitude toward Syrski's discovery of the eel's male organ prevailed in subsequent studies; until four decades later the Syrski-organ was not an accepted fact. We might add to this, that Freud's eel article was probably the first to contribute to the delay of Syrski's recognition.

Contrary to Syrski's low esteem in the sciences are the high honors he received from the Austrian government. He was awarded the Franz Joseph Medal for Civil Services after his return from an expedition to East Asia under the auspices of the Ministry of Agriculture. On the occasion of the World Exhibit in Vienna in 1873, he established an aquarium, the well-known Vienna "Vivarium" (destroyed in World War II). In recognition of his accomplishments, Syrski was raised to nobility, which at the time meant both adding a "von" to your name and being exempt from taxes (Gicklhorn 7–9).

12. Freud 1877b:420: "Besonders nahe lag für den Leser der Syrski'schen Mitteilung die Vermutung, daß das Lappenorgan doch nichts anderes als ein modifizierter Eierstock sei." All English translations of quotations in this paper are my own. For verification purposes, I include the German, since the quotations come from texts that have not been translated.

13. Freud 1877b:427–428: "Die Meinung, daß das Lappenorgan eine Modifikation des Ovariums ist, welche von einem frühen Entwicklungszustand des letzteren ausgeht, ist zwar nicht völlig auszuschließen, denn es ist ja nicht gelungen nachzuweisen, daß die erste Anlage beider Organe schon eine verschiedene sei. Sie ist aber gar nicht wahrscheinlich, denn soweit das Lappenorgan in seiner Entwicklung zurückverfolgt worden, hat es sich als different vom unreifen Ovarium erwiesen."

14. Freud 1877b:429: "Denn selbst wenn man zugibt, daß das Lappenorgan der Hoden ist, so hat doch niemand ein reifes Lappenorgan und ein reifes Aalmännchen gesehen."

15. See note 11.

16. Bernfeld's perception of Freud's "hostile attitude toward his first scientific study" (1949:167) derives from a psycho-analytic interpretation of his observation that the abstract of the eel article is the only piece in which Freud mentions the name of Claus (Bernfeld 1949:168; Freud, S. (1897) "Abstracts of the Scientific Writings of Dr. Sigm. Freud, 1877–1897," (SE 3:227). The basis for this interpretation appears to be less solid, if one takes into account the "Curriculum Vitae" (1885/1960) where Freud with even emphasis pays tribute to both of his teachers, to Carl Claus, including the stay at the Zoological Station in Trieste, and to Ernst Brücke. The "Curriculum Vitae" was written twelve years before the "Abstracts" (1897) and thirty years before

the first version of the "Selbstdarstellung" (1925). That Claus was not mentioned in the latter, gave rise to the perception that studying under Claus
was not a very rewarding experience for Freud. The long interim between
the "Curriculum" and the "Selbstdarstellung" could also be an explanation
why Freud saw the importance of the rather short Claus period in a different
light from the years at Brücke's institute. See also note 8. The "Curriculum
Vitae" is included in the volume, edited by Ilse Grubrich-Simitis, *Sigmund
Freud: "Selbstdarstellung." Schriften zur Geschichte der Psychoanalyse*
(Frankfurt: Fischer, 1987), p. 125.

17. *The Complete Letters of Sigmund Freud to Wilhelm Fliess: 1887–1904*, ed.
and transl. by Jeffrey Moussaieff Masson (Cambridge: Belknap, 1985).

18. According to Schönau, Freud distinguished between two techniques of writing: the genetic method and the dogmatic method. The genetic method includes the reader in the process of developing a new theoretical concept by
discussing its propositions and conclusions and taking into account probable
comments and objections. The "Introductory Lectures on Psycho-Analysis"
(SE 15–16), stand out in this quality of gradually building upon and expanding
the knowledge of the reader. The dogmatic method, of which "An Outline
of Psycho-Analysis" (1938) is the most characteristic example, approaches
the reader with theoretical results, assuming the reader's familiarity and consent with the underlying reasoning, and evoking the impression of a final
stand. For a more extensive discussion of Freud's didactic methods and rhetorical strategies, see Schönau 35–37.

19. Freud 1877b:423: "Obwohl also die kleinsten Ovarien, die man bei Tieren
von 200mm findet, immer noch zwei bis drei Mal breiter sind als die kleinsten
ungelappten Formen des Syrski'schen Organs bei gleich großen Tieren, so
muß man doch zugestehen, daß das Aussehen des unentwickelten Lappen-
organs sich dem eines ganz unreifen Ovariums so sehr nähert, daß bei der
Identität aller topographischen Verhältnisse beider Organe nur mehr die his-
tologische Untersuchung entscheiden kann, ob das Lappenorgan ein Organ
sui generis oder eine Modifikation des Eierstocks ist, die sich aus einem frühen
Zustand des letzteren entwickelt."

20. Freud 1877b:425: "Die Zellen selbst sind kleiner als die Eizellen und auch
sonst leicht von diesen zu unterscheiden, sie sind rundlich, wenn sie einzeln
in den Maschen des Gerüstes liegen, dagegen kubisch wenn sie zu mehreren
in einer Gewebslücke beisammen liegen und sich gegenseitig abgeplattet
haben."

21. Walter Boehlich, ed., *Sigmund Freud: Jugendbriefe an Eduard Silberstein:
1871–1881* (Frankfurt: Fischer, 1989).

22. This line in parentheses reads in the printed text: "meine Zeichnungen sind
also Karikaturen nicht ohne Wert." The "also" doesn't make sense and might
be a typographical error. A closer look at the facsimile of Freud's handwritten
letter, which is included in the edition of the Freud-Silberstein letters, con-
firms that it should be read as "als Karikaturen" (*Jugendbriefe* 161/171).

23. *Jugendbriefe* 63, emphasis added: "So bekomme ich Haie, Rochen, Aale und andere Bestien täglich, die ich allgemein anatomisch und dann in Bezug auf einen besonderen Punkt untersuche. Dieser Punkt ist folgender. Du kennst den Aal. Lange Zeit hindurch war von dieser Bestie nur das Weibchen bekannt, schon Aristoteles wußte nicht, woher diese die Männchen nehmen, und ließ deshalb die Aale aus dem Schlamm entstehen. Durchs ganze Mittelalter und die Neuzeit hindurch wurde eine förmliche Hetzjagd auf die Aalmännchen angestellt."

24. *Jugendbriefe* 164: "Unter Mikroskop zeigen die Hoden Samentierchen, die Eierstöcke schon mit freiem Auge Eier."

25. *Jugendbriefe* 164: "Ich plage nun mich und die Aale, seine Aalmännchen wiederzufinden, aber vergebens, alle Aale, die ich aufschneide, sind vom zarteren Geschlecht."

26. Syrski 315 emphasis added: "Indem es aber nicht ohne Interesse sein dürfte zu erfahren, wie ich zur Lösung der Aufgabe gelangt bin, mit der so viele Forscher, *seit Aristoteles bis auf den heutigen Tag, darunter mehrere Monate und Jahre lang,* sich umsonst abgemühet haben, so will ich dieses, bevor ich auf den Gegenstand selbst eingehe, früher anführen."

27. *Jugendbriefe* 164: "Vor kurzem hat ein Triester Zoolog, wie er sagt, die Hoden, somit die Männchen des Aals aufgefunden, aber weil er, wie es scheint, nicht weiß, was ein Mikroskop ist, keine genaue Beschreibung davon gegeben."

28. Kurt R. Eissler, "Creativity and Adolescence. The Effect of Trauma in Freud's Adolescence," *The Psychoanalytic Study of the Child,* Vol. 33, ed. Ruth S. Eissler (New Haven: Yale UP, 1978).

29. Eissler's quote (475) refers to a poem which Freud wrote on the occasion of Gisela Fluß' wedding. After this poetic effort Freud had announced: "A new time may commence without secretly active forces, a time that does not need poesy and fantasy" (quoted after Eissler, 475).

30. *Jugendbriefe* 158: "Glauben mir Euer Gnaden, daß Schreiben das allerdümmste wäre, was ich tun könnte. Ich werde Ihnen alles mündlich erzählen."

31. *Jugendbriefe* 158: "Es ist heute ein Tag des Briefschreibens, alle Parteien müssen heute befriedigt werden, ... "

32. *Jugendbriefe* 174: "Dein Schreiben hat mir umsomehr Freude gemacht, als es mir Gelegenheit gibt, es zu beantworten, und es mitunter höchst erwünscht ist, Briefe schreiben zu können. Wundre Dich nicht über diese "plötzliche" Veränderung meiner Haltung: daß ich ferner die Last des Beantwortens von mir abzuwälzen suchte und sie jetzt herbei sehne. Meine Stimmung ist einem bei mir giltigen Naturgesetz gemäß ganz umgeschlagen."

33. *Jugendbriefe* 175: "Von dem Ausflug muß ich Dir mehr erzählen, denn es hat mich manches besonders berührt."

34. *Jugendbriefe* 178: "... sie sah so elend aus, ... daß wir geneigt wurden, an wirkliches Elend, das ja in der Welt nicht so selten ist, zu glauben."

35. *Jugendbriefe* 158: "Wenn ich abends 1/2 7 Uhr, die Hände befleckt vom
    weißen und roten Blut der Seetiere und vor den Augen flimmernde Zell-
    trümmer, die mich noch in den Träumen stören, und in Gedanken nichts als
    die großen Probleme, die sich an die Namen Hoden und Ovarien—welt-
    bedeutende Namen knüpfen, wenn ich also am Abend nach der Arbeit spa-
    zierengehe, sehe ich nur recht wenig von der Physiologie der Triestiner."
36. *Jugendbriefe* 160: "Ich verstehe unter 'Leuten' alle lebenden Wesen, die als
    Bewohner und Arbeiter Triest bevölkern."
37. *Jugendbriefe* 175: "Denn die Fische und anderen Bestien gehen bei schlechtem
    Wetter einfach nicht aus. Die Haie und die Rochen sitzen in ihren Kämmerlein
    auf dem Meeresgrund . . . "
38. Grubrich-Simitis 1987:116: "Ich werde Einsicht nehmen in die jahrtausen-
    dealten Akten der Natur, vielleicht selbst ihren ewigen Prozeß belauschen
    und meinen Gewinn mit jedermann teilen, der lernen will." In this letter of
    May 1, 1873 to Emil Fluß, Freud announced his choice of study in very
    general terms: "I decided to become a natural scientist . . . " ("Ich habe fest-
    gestellt, Naturforscher zu werden . . . " Grubrich-Simitis 1987:106) In En-
    glish "natural scientist" (*Naturwissenschaftler*) connotes a field of study,
    whereas the German term "Naturforscher" carries the meaning of an adven-
    turous search into the secrets of nature. As such it was meant by Freud,
    when he speaks of "millennium-old chronicles" and the "eternal process."
39. *Jugendbriefe* 160: "Da es nicht gestattet ist, die Menschen zu sezieren, habe
    ich eigentlich gar nichts mit ihnen zu tun."

2. Freud's Reading of Classical Literature and Classical Philology

Robin N. Mitchell-Boyask

Further, we must be guided by the insight for a thorough reading of the authors, that we alone find what is important for us.—A passage marked by Freud in his copy of Burckhardt's *Griechische Kulturgeschichte*[1]

From his student days until his death in London Freud took great interest in classical antiquity and the scholarly study of it, and he frequently drew inspiration from Greece and Rome to name and to enrich many of his most important ideas; Oedipus, Narcissus and his famous comparison of psychoanalysis to archaeology spring to mind.[2] Freud's deep and abiding interest in antiquity can be seen in his library's extensive holdings of books, both primary and secondary, about all aspects of Greece and Rome, and I believe Freud's books about classical myth and literature can tell us at least as much about him as his famous collection of classical statuary.[3] I shall not here tease out at length allusions in Freud's writings to specific classical texts, but I shall examine primarily Freud's interest in scholarship on classical literature in order to show the context for his understanding of poets like Sophocles who were to play such a great role in his thought. Further, I believe the simple goal of imparting information about the breadth and thoroughness of Freud's reading in classical culture is worthwhile in itself. Since my interest in presenting a broad picture (as well as limitations in my knowledge) will lead me at times not to dwell on some areas which need detailed exposition, I ask for my reader's patience.

The scope of Freud's acquisitions, the fact that he retained them when he moved to London, and the sheer volume of his annotations in his books, do not show a man casually interested in the study of Greco-Roman culture. Far surpassing what might be expected of an educated man of his time, Freud's library in the humanities was an integral part of his work, as was expressed by the location of his analyst couch in his study surrounded by books. Challenging the view advocated by Ernest Jones and Peter Brückner that Freud read primarily for relaxation or escape, Edward Timms has argued that we cannot separate Freud's literary interests from his scientific work since "Freud's essential gift lay in his ability to synthesize ideas derived from both literary and scientific sources. Certainly his scientific discoveries cannot be fully understood without reference to their cultural matrix."[4]

Containing such items as German translations of Greek texts which he bought as a student, books about Oedipus which may have significantly influenced *The Interpretation of Dreams* and ten years of copies of a Classics journal to which he subscribed, Freud's library offers a fascinating glimpse into his involvement in the study of classical antiquity from boyhood to old age, the possible effects this had on his work, especially for *The Interpretation of Dreams,* as well as an overview of the concomitant professionalization of psychoanalysis and classical philology during Freud's life, and the significance the latter discipline may have held for the aged Freud.

Literature: Sophocles and Others

I begin with an anecdote. Freud, corresponding with the exiled Arnold Zweig in 1934 (3 April), believed he had erred in his Greek when reporting the story from Xenophon in which 10,000 soldiers, having marched through Persia, finally reach the sea and call out *"thalassa, thalassa"* ("the sea! the sea!").[5] Freud inscribed the exclamation in correct Greek, but the next day he wrote Zweig again to report that he had written the Greek word with a second lambda. Commented Freud, "I have always been proud of how much Greek I have remembered (choruses from Sophocles, passages from Homer)." Freud's Greek, despite his fears, had been correct, but Zweig, perhaps still smarting from Freud's strenuous objections to his plans to write a historical novel about Nietzsche, failed to communicate this to his idol.

As a student in a nineteenth-century *Gymnasium*, Freud experienced the normal rigors of a curriculum heavily weighted with Greek and Roman literature, but the particular contents of Freud's studies were to influence his life and work for decades. Public ceremonies to mark the end of the school year in 1871 featured a fifteen-year-old Freud in Act IV, Scene iii of Shakespeare's *Julius Caesar,* a classical subject which would feature in his analysis of the *Non Vixit* dream in *The Interpretation of Dreams* (SE 5:422–24), and the exhibition continued with other students reciting passages from Sophocles' *Electra* and the Laocoon episode from Book 2 of Virgil's *Aeneid,* a passage featuring the intrusion of the very dark, infernal powers which are evoked in the Virgilian epigraph of *The Interpretation of Dreams.*[6] We should note the constellation of Shakespeare, Virgil and Sophocles which returns with such mature force in *The Interpretation of Dreams.* Freud's *Matura* (graduation exam), as is well known, featured the beginning of the Nisus and Euryalus episode in the *Aeneid* (Book 9.176–223) and lines 14–57 (the Priest's address to Oedipus) of Sophocles' *Oedipus the King.* During this period Freud wrote letters to friends like Emil Fluß documenting how engrossed he was with Sophocles and Virgil.[7] Jean Starbonski speculates on the role of Nisus and Euryalus in Freud's imagination that "[o]ne might see, as an extension of the text, the tracing of Freud's friendship and heroic rivalry with Fleischl, with Fliess, and so on . . . "[8] Hence, the die was cast for the role of Classics both in Freud's work and in his life.

Despite Freud's professed pride in maintaining his knowledge of Greek almost seventy years after his school days, no books in Greek or Latin remain in his library. However, in scholarly works, particularly those by Constans and Laistner, Freud does frequently mark and comment on passages in ancient Greek. It is entirely possible that, between Freud's death in 1939 and the opening of the Freud Museum in 1986, some misguided admirer decided to walk off with Freud's Greek Sophocles and his Latin Virgil, but we cannot assume so. His copies of Laistner and Constans were marked roughly 35 years before the letter to Zweig, and any modern student of Greek knows that it is not remembered at all well without regular use. On the other hand, passages one has memorized as a student do tend to leave a lasting impression. Perhaps Freud does retain passages *"im Gedächtnis"* (in memory), perhaps he exaggerates to his awe-struck younger admirer, but in any case Freud finds it important to stress the continued priority of classical literature in his life.

Of primary texts only translations remain. Among these, the oldest, and potentially the most significant, are German translations of Sophocles and Aristophanes, both by J. C. Donner.[9] Both volumes appear to be of the same vintage and are bound similarly, and since the Aristophanes has hundreds of small, seemingly meaningless pencil marks, the kind one makes as an eager, rapaciously reading adolescent, my guess would be that Freud acquired these volumes as a student during his *Gymnasium* or university days, although I doubt Aristophanes was typical fare in straight-laced Vienna. Because passages from Donner's translation appear throughout Freud's discussion of *Oedipus the King* in *The Interpretation of Dreams*, the volume in the library is indubitably the very one Freud consulted during the years he was composing his work.

Remarkably, only one passage, but a most critical one for Freud's understanding of Oedipus, in the entire volume is marked, Jocasta's assurances to Oedipus that all men dream of bedding their mothers (981– 83 in Greek, 955–57 in Donner); the lack of other marks suggests this was not the text Freud used to help him prepare for his *Matura*—in other words, Freud did read the Greek, but that text has been lost. The shift to the German, however, adds an element which might have been significant, as Donner, while generally a quite fine translator, steps back from literal translation. To demonstrate, I list here (1) Donner's German; (2) a literal English translation of Donner; and (3) a literal translation of the Greek.

(1) Denn viele Menschen sahen auch in Träumen schon
Sich zugesellt der Mutter: Doch wer alles dies
Für nichtig achtet, trägt die Last des Lebens leicht.

(2) For many men have already seen also in dreams
Themselves mated with mother: But who holds all this as
nothing, bears the burden of life lightly.

(3) For many mortals already also in dreams
Have slept with (their) mother. But to whom these things
Are nothing, he bears life most easily.

Two aspects of this translation stand out. First, the German preserves the Greek's plural "men" who dream about a singular "mother," thus increasing the effect of the universality of the paradigm. Second, Donner adds a level of mediating representation to the repressed wish for incest: instead of merely dreaming about sleeping with mother, Donner's text has men *seeing themselves in dreams* doing such. Freud here reads not just about dreams, but about their function in human consciousness; Donner's minor shift away from literal translation may have been enough to start Freud thinking. Since Freud will make much of the narratability of dreams and the effects of condensation and displacement on their representation, this extra layer of distance in Donner's translation of the literary text most important to Freud could have influenced his thought subsequently in *The Interpretation of Dreams*.

Apart from this, little primary literature remains. There is an old (1881) unmarked German translation of Artemidorus' *Symbolism of Dreams,* a German edition of the Presocratics, a translation of the *Iliad* by Albrecht Schaffe which was dedicated to Freud on his 75th birthday, a very old (1744) edition of Hippocrates, a German edition of Plato's *Symposium,* and an English translation of Euripides' *Ion,* presented to Freud by its translator, H. D.[10] Freud acquired these books at every stage of his life, and continued to inspire translators of classical literature, again demonstrating the symbiosis between Freud and classical culture.

Theodor Gomperz

Books also remain documenting Freud's personal link with Classics through his friendship with the great Viennese classicist Theodor Gomperz, who influenced Freud's early thought on dreams; specifically, Freud's annotated copy of Gomperz's three-volume *Griechische Denker (Greek Thinkers),* and an unmarked, but apparently read, translation by Gomperz of Aristotle's *Poetics.*[11] Freud had a fairly extensive relationship, both personal and professional, with the Gomperz family. A secular, anglophilic, intellectual Jew like Freud, although more successful at achieving a chair at the University of Vienna, Gomperz hired Freud to translate John Stuart Mill.[12] Freud later treated his wife, Elise, and his son, Heinrich.[13] Elise Gomperz even attempted to advance Freud's academic career through personal intervention.[14] Gomperz distinctly affected Freud's life and work. Freud later, in a letter to Elise Gomperz dated 12 November 1913, counted Gomperz among the greater influences on him in his youth: "I heard from him the first remarks about the role played by dreams in the psychic life of primitive men—something that has preoccupied me so intensively ever since."[15] If Gomperz in fact began Freud's thought about dreams, then we cannot underestimate his significance. Freud here was probably referring to the lectures Gomperz gave which were published in 1866 as *Traumdeutung und Zauberei*, and which Freud listed in the bibliography to the first edition of his own book on the subject.[16]

While Gomperz's work on dream interpretation did not accompany Freud to London, *Griechische Denker* did, although the books do not contain many annotations. However, this paucity should not lead us to surmise Freud did not read the books very closely, since in the third volume Freud corrects misspellings and typographical errors; the very last entry in the book is a reference to the work of the British Aristotelean Bywater, whose misspelled name Freud amends.[17] Freud's few markings show him to be interested in Gomperz's focus on the progression from mysticism to science; on page 58 of volume one, Freud jotted "*Forscher vs. Mystiker*" ("Researcher vs. Mystic") in the margin. In the third volume (172) Freud indicates interest in Aristotle's *Metaphysics*, underlining Gomperz's discussion of Aristotle's definition of God. These markings, in addition to the next book we shall discuss, show Freud to have been distinctly aware of the Greek whose thought, grounded in philosophy and biology and covering all facets of human life, is so productively comparable to the Viennese psychoanalyst's.[18]

The translation of Aristotle's *Poetics*, the other work by Gomperz in the library, involves many disparate figures in Freud's life, from Martha Freud's uncle to Josef Breuer. This text is remarkable because it also contains an essay by Alfred Freiherrn von Berger, *Wahrheit und Irrtum in der Katharsis-Theorie des Aristoteles* (*Truth and Error in Aristotle's Catharsis Theory*), which directly ties Aristotle's theory of catharsis to Freud's work with Breuer, via Jacob Bernays, the uncle of Freud's wife and Professor of Classical Philology at the University of Bonn in the middle of the nineteenth century. Like Gomperz, Bernays concentrated on Greek philosophy and was the first, as von Berger noted (72), to see Aristotle's literary terminology in the context of his medical language. Bernays, Rudnytsky observes,[19] was also one of the few philologists to defend Nietzsche's *Birth of Tragedy*, which Nietzsche wrote when still a classical philologist at the University of Basel. Von Berger's essay, surprisingly synthesizing in its scope, securely grounds Freud's thought in the scholarly currents of nineteenth-century philology, psychology and medicine by explicitly connecting Jacob Bernays's work to the early work on hysteria by Freud and Breuer (81): "The cathartic treatment of hysteria, which the physicians Dr. Josef Breuer and Dr. Sigmund Freud have described, is very appropriate for making the cathartic theory of tragedy understandable."[20] At this early stage in Freud's career, he is still known only as "Arzt" (physician), and, published in 1897, I believe this is the first scholarly work in the humanities to see the significance of Freud's work for areas other than psychology. The presence of Aristotle's *Poetics,* the first and most influential tract to canonize *Oedipus the King,* also supports Rudnytsky's argument that Freud consciously worked not with some vague impression of the Oedipus myth, but with Sophocles' Oedipus.[21] Gomperz, and especially this latter book, is paradigmatic of the complex and densely interwoven relationship of Freud's thought with so many facets of the cultural and intellectual life of his time.

The Interpretation of Dreams and Fin de Siècle Scholarship

We now turn to Freud's reading of three roughly contemporary scholarly works on Greek literature and myth which may have influenced *The Interpretation of Dreams:* Jacob Burckhardt, *Griechische Kulturgeschichte (The History of Greek Civilization);* Leopold Constans, *La Légende d'Oedipe: Étudiée dans l'antiquité, au moyen âge et dans les temps modernes en particulier dans le Roman de Thèbes, texte français du Xiie siècle;* and Ludwig Laistner, *Das Rätsel der Sphinx: Grundzüge einer Mythengeschichte (The Riddle of the Sphinx: Characteristics of a History of Myths).*[22] These three works fall outside the strict bounds of classical scholarship, but they are all representative of the study of ancient Greek myth and culture in the late nineteenth century. I shall examine here the possible significance of these three books, as well as of Burckhardt himself, for Freud's work.

As one of the great scholars of classical and Renaissance culture, two areas immensely important to Freud, and as a colleague of Friedrich Nietzsche, Burckhardt's thought held great interest for Freud, who possessed six of his books. We should note briefly here that Nietzsche was not only a philosopher who recognized the power of the irrational, but he was also the first to recognize it in Greek culture. Nietzsche's dark vision of Greece, we shall see, influenced Burckhardt, and through Burckhardt, Freud. One imagines that the posthumous publication, during the gestation period of *The Interpretation of Dreams,* of a book on Greek culture by Burckhardt would have been an exciting prospect for Freud. Although Freud does not annotate his copy of Burckhardt as heavily as his volumes of Laistner and Constans, Burckhardt matters because of his remarks on the function of Greece for modern culture, his willingness to see the darker sides of Greek myth and society, as well as his link to Nietzsche (which is supported in turn by the presence of Rohde's *Psyche* in Freud's library).[23] While Freud in his publications never cites Burckhardt's work on Greece, his letters to Fliess during the time of *The Interpretation of Dreams* clearly evince its significance for him. On 30 January 1899, Freud writes to his colleague, "For relaxation I am reading Burckhardt's *History of Greek Civilization,* which is providing me with unexpected parallels. My predilection for the prehistoric in all its human forms has remained the same."[24] In the same letter Freud reports to Fliess of breakthroughs in his thought concerning such factors as conflict and fantasy, and given Burckhardt's interest in such matters in Greek culture (perhaps as a result of Nietzsche's influence), Freud could indeed have found "unexpected parallels" between his thought and the Swiss historian's. Freud adds three weeks later as a postscript of 19 February 1899 to his letter, "I am deep in Burckhardt's *History of Greek Civilization.*" Burckhardt frequently stressed the productive dialectical relationship between antiquity and its modern interpreters, thoughts which must have struck a chord with Freud, who frequently marked such passages in red pencil. The passage which opened this essay is one such instance.

Freud seems in particular to have taken an interest in Burckhardt's thoughts on Greek myth and religion.[25] Burckhardt wrote (32) that Greek religion originated not with priests, but with the people, in the *Volksbewußtsein,* "their national consciousness." Burckhardt further indicated in a footnote which Freud marked that gods of Greek myth were generated not by events in nature but the emotions excited by human struggle and man's inner life (*aus seinem innern Leben*). As we shall see, Laistner also saw the genesis of myths in man's unexpressed emotional life. Burckhardt continued with an almost Viconian stress on the role of the *Volk* and the *Volksphantasie* (33) in the formation of myth and archaic literature.

Burckhardt saw the myth of the three-step progression of the divine dynasty from Uranus to Zeus as purely the product of human imagination (*Phantasie*). The Greeks only ever believed in the Zeus-ruled Olympians, he argued (41), and the dynasties of Cronos and Uranus were projected backwards "as prehistory." Freud marked Burckhardt's contention that "The dynasties of Uranus and Cronos are not really gods which in older times were really worshipped, but are hypotheses of a theologically and politically affected imagination, to which the sight of changes in rulers was nothing unusual, and Zeus shows completely the form of an earthly usurpator."[26]

Writing in Nietzsche's shadow, Burckhardt continued to undermine the Victorian vision of a Greece filled with sweetness and light by observing in the Hesiodic myth of the divine power struggle "that pessimism, which penetrates the whole Greek myth" (42), a pessimism which the myth's sexual violence underscores: "Misery and evil in human existence begins with the great sin in the divine world, the castration of Uranus by Cronos."[27]

From the castration come all of the "things which cause anxiety for mankind (*jene Ängstiger des Menschengeschlechtes*)," the first of which is *Schicksalstod* (fated death). Freud marks this passage with a double line (a mark rarely used) in the margin with a lead pencil, not red as elsewhere in the volume,[28] and thus Freud probably returned to this passage after his initial study of the book, having seen something of significance for his own work: a myth concerning a struggle between a father and a son, which leads to a castration, which in turn introduces *Angst* to the world, and the primary example of which is *Schicksalstod*. This matters because, during the year Freud said he read this book, he identified *Oedipus the King* as a tragedy of *Schicksal* and hence any contemporaneous extended discussion of destiny in Greek literature left some mark on Freud's thought. Freud later in the same volume (125) marks another passage on *Schicksal*. At several points (e.g., 76, 349), Burckhardt compares the figures in Greek myths and the events of the myths themselves to dreams and notes the difficulty of differentiating between truth and dream in Greek stories. Freud, who marked these passages, may have seen in them support for his contention that the Greek myth achieved the most unrepressed expression of the Oedipus complex, which Sophocles' Jocasta believed is expressed by dreams. Freud continually underlined Burckhardt's returns to Greek pessimism and fantasy. Clearly, this is a key source for Freud.

• • •

Leopold Constans's careful study of all aspects of the Oedipus myth and its centrality to European culture must have influenced Freud, who underlined passages on almost every page, and who probably found in this book thoughts which corroborated and supplemented many of his own.[29] Constans encompassed a wide range of mythic traditions which survived antiquity, and he provided Freud with linguistically sophisticated parallels from Sanskrit, comments by scholiasts, fragments from lost Greek tragedies and much evidence for the continuing vitality of the Oedipus myth in medieval and modern culture. Throughout, Freud paid close attention to a wealth of detail, especially passages in Greek; obviously this was a book he read with utmost care. We must keep in mind that the Oedipus Freud recounts in *The Interpretation of Dreams* is the Oedipus he drew, albeit selectively, from Sophocles; even in that version Freud excludes certain elements, such as the mutilation of Oedipus's feet. A short survey of what Freud found interesting in Constans will show that Freud made a highly conscious choice to keep to the Sophoclean Oedipus.

It seems likely that Freud was in fact reading Constans's book during his work on *The Interpretation of Dreams,* although there is no direct evidence of this. In a letter to Fliess dated 24 March 1898 Freud reports to his friend about his progress on his *magnum opus:* "Comments on *Oedipus the King,* the talisman folk tale, and possibly *Hamlet,* will find their place. I first must read up on the Oedipus legend—do not know yet where."[30] Masson, in a footnote to this letter, announces the existence of Constans in Freud's library, but then completely distorts the nature of Freud's reading. His remark, "Freud marked those passages in the work having to do with incest," gives the impression that Freud *only* marked those passages, whereas, as will become very apparent shortly, Freud annotated almost every page in the book. In fact, the section on incest is marked less than many other pages.[31]

Constans provided Freud with information and analysis concerning such topics as Oedipus's name, Jocasta's age and Laius's sexuality. Oedipus's name puns doubly on verbs for knowing and swelling, and Freud would have known the latter implication from *Oedipus the King* when the messenger, explaining to Oedipus that he was not Polybus's son, reminds him of the connection between his name and his lamed feet. It is curious that Freud—despite occasionally calling his daughter Anna "Antigone" and despite the medallion he received in 1906 with images of himself on one side and Oedipus on the other[32]—never really discussed his personal identification with Oedipus as a bold intellectual explorer solving the riddles of human existence. In fact Freud read early in Constans about Oedipus as a figure of Enlightenment; the first passage he underlined states unequivocally (5), "Oedipus is a hero of the same character as Zeus, Apollo, Heracles, Bellerophon, etc., that is to say, a personification of light" (or "enlightenment"—"*une personnification de la lumière*"). Constans continued on the next page (also marked by Freud) by initially explaining Oedipus's name as derived from the Greek verb *oida*, "I know." After covering the range of versions of the Oedipus myth, Constans detailed these etymologies on pages 24–25, which are very heavily marked. Freud especially paid attention to the original Greek sources, which are given completely, including the extensive quotes from Apollodorus detailing the prophecies given to Laius, and the riddle of the Sphinx.

Freud's detailed attention to passages on pages 25 and 26 concerning the crimes, both violent and sexual, committed by Laius raises the question of Freud's neglect of this structural aspect of the myth. Constans, after explaining the mutilation of Oedipus's feet, digressed into a discussion of Laius's behavior and its possible role in his son's fate. Laius had earlier violated the hospitality of Pelops by raping his son, Chrysippus, and Pelops in turn cursed Laius, thus resulting in Oedipus's fate. Constans called this "*le premier l'exemple d'un amour contre nature.*" Freud gave this passage a double vertical line in the margin, a mark he rarely used (recall it also appeared next to the discussion of Uranus's castration in Burckhardt). A few pages later (30), Freud marked Constans's mention of the possibility that the Sphinx was sent by Juno to punish the crime of Laius. These marks suggest this image of violent, illicit sexuality was a powerful one for Freud and could have been productively explored by the psychoanalyst, yet he never mentions it. Why? I have two possible answers. First, the idea of the sins of the father being visited on the son would have violated Freud's focus on the fantasy life of the son. Second, Sophocles deliberately excluded earlier traditions about Laius such as this one since they too would have distracted from the powerful drama about a man discovering and coming to grips with a destiny which was both determined by the gods and freely chosen. Given Freud's frequent discussions of homosexuality, however, it does seem odd that he neglects that of Oedipus's father.[33]

The variety of markings in Constans's book suggest Freud carefully read and repeatedly returned to this work about the Oedipus myth and was aware of all of the myth's permutations. The Oedipus he chose was the result of long and careful deliberation. Freud's exclusion of Laius's homsexuality and its consequences marks Freud's insistence on the experiences of the specifically Sophoclean hero and their implications for all individual men.

Supplementing the factual information concerning the Oedipus myth but also providing Freud with theories about the relationship between dream and myth and with evidence about the universality of the Oedipus myth was Laistner's massive and comprehensive work, *The Riddle of the Sphinx.* While, as in the case of Burckhardt's books about Greece and Constans's study, Freud never cites Laistner in his published work, only listing his work in the bibliography to *The Interpretation of Dreams,* we know from a letter to Wilhelm Fliess on 4 July 1901 that he was aware of Laistner:

Dr. von der Leyen from Munich has called my attention to a book by L. Laistner, *The Riddle of the Sphinx,* which very forcefully maintains that myths go back to dreams. So far I have read its delightful preface, but my laziness has kept me from reading on. I see that he knows nothing of what is *behind* dreams; on the other hand, he appropriately seems to focus on the *anxiety* dream.[34]

Freud had reported in 1898 to Fliess a need to read more about Oedipus, but without naming any books. Perhaps *The Riddle of the Sphinx* was one source. I do not think that Freud was completely straight with Fliess in the 1901 letter, for it was written when their relationship had already collapsed into hostility. The previous summer the two had met near Innsbruck for what turned out to be their last "congress," but fell into vehement arguments and never saw each other again. Marie Bonaparte observed that the friendship declined in 1900 because Fliess envied the superiority Freud manifested with the publication of *The Interpretation of Dreams.*[35] The letter just quoted lacks the almost embarrassingly effusive affirmations of respect and affection typical of their earlier correspondence, and its opening seems awkward and tentative. Freud needed or wanted to protect himself. Hence, I regard with caution, if not skepticism, Freud's assertion that he was too busy and lazy actually to have read Laistner, especially since Freud's extensive annotations in both volumes suggest the opposite. I suspect that Freud was trying to deflect attention away from what he read while working on *The Interpretation of Dreams*. Since his relationship with Fliess was growing increasingly hostile, Freud may have been afraid of an accusation of plagiarism and was trying to cover his tracks. This reference to Laistner may also indicate an anxiety of influence on the part of Freud. Freud only admits reading and being influenced by Burckhardt in a letter written while Fliess's friendship was still warm and does not cite Burckhardt at all in *The Interpretation of Dreams*, and thus we cannot use the letters or Freud's published writings as reliable guides to decide when he read these books. In fact, it is difficult to be absolutely certain about the dates of Freud's reading, so we have to rely on informed guesses and deduction. While Freud displayed an on-going interest in Oedipus, he does not mark later books about Oedipus, such as his copy of Carl Roberts's more philologically oriented study, and the intensity and extensiveness of the markings in these volumes seem more likely to indicate they were made when he was actively working on the Oedipus myth than later, and the markings in Laistner strongly resemble those made in Burckhardt, which we know he was reading before 1900. The balance of the evidence suggests to me that Freud studied Laistner before the publication of his own book.

If in fact Freud was reading *The Riddle of the Sphinx* during the work on *The Interpretation of Dreams*, then it would have proved a powerful catalyst. Every passage I mention in the following discussion Freud marked. Laistner saw the myth of Oedipus and the Sphinx as a model to examine myth in general. As Freud himself observed, Laistner put the source of myths in dreams, verifying the old German saying, "*Alb ist Alp*" ("elf is nightmare", x), although Laistner carefully distinguished between a normal dream and the myth-generating nightmare. Laistner argued that "legends which report (*berichten*) from nightmare afflictions . . . these reports agree with dream experiences (*Traumerlebnissen*)" (x).

Since we can understand myths, then, presumably, we can understand nightmares; they make sense, possessing a logic of their own. The mythological world is not a "fantasy picture" ("*ein Phantasie Gebilde*") but is one of most sensible reality: "If we consider how intimately poetry and religion hang together with myth, so the surprising fact emerges, that the first embryo of this most important manifestation of the life of mankind moves not in the activity of the awake spirit, but in sleep . . . " (xiii).[36]

Simply put, *"Mythus ist ... der Bericht vom Alptraum"*—"myth is the report from the nightmare"—a phrasing which suggests the Freudian idea that dreams are the report from the unconscious. Dreams generate the related phenemona of myth, poetry and religion, and "the most exceptional object of mythological poetry according to its actual being is nothing other than the racial difference (*Geschlechtsgegensatz*) between the worlds of men and gods" (xix).

Laistner proceeded to discuss his theoretical ideas using the myth of Oedipus and the Sphinx as his main example and model, and Freud paid close attention. Freud's annotations are remarkable in their range and in their ability to draw connections. Since the space and scope of my study are limited, I shall concentrate on what may have influenced Freud or at least seemed agreeable to him. In the table of contents Freud only checked the title of the chapter specifically on the mythical pattern of Oedipus's life, *"Das Schicksalskind,"* and Freud underlined it again at the actual beginning of the chapter, and this resonates in Freud's designation of *Oedipus the King* as "a tragedy of destiny (*Schicksalstragödie*)" (S E 4: 262). This is not to suggest Freud took his language from Laistner (or from Burckhardt for that matter), but that he found corroboration in others for his own intimations. Freud marked passages on etymology, mythic parallels, sources and a host of other subjects, interjecting comments about Heracles, Samson and Shakespeare's Pericles. This is not a mind concerned solely with the manifestation in Oedipus of the desire for incest; presented with a text about the relationship between dreams, myth and literature, he responded in kind.

Since dreams generate myths, mythical stories exert a strong force over their audience. The Sphinx myth, resulting from a specific type of nightmare (43), that of being questioned and then killed for one's ignorance, can thus be found in the structure of dozens of myths about questioning female monsters throughout the world, a pattern Laistner explored at length. Since everyone has nightmares about being compelled to answer about what one does not know, the Sphinx myth has a particular power. Moreover, mythological poetry (48) "brings into prominence difficulty breathing (*Atemnot*), anguish and anxiety at having a nightmare (*am Alpdrücken*)." "The sphingial questioning-pain (*die sphingische Frage-pein*) ... is only the poetic representation of the oppressive nightmare condition." The idea that a story's power arises from its relation to dreams agrees well with Freud's remarks about the continuing vitality of *Oedipus the King*.

Since Laistner struggled somewhat in providing precise statements of his theories, he seems, at first glance, to lack an explanation of why dreams become thus expressed in myth, an explanation such as Freud's theories of censorship, condensation and displacement. However, in his second volume, Laistner came remarkably close (in 1889): "The night-maremyth, as we have seen, is the typical result of the nightmare. If the natural supposition of such a dreamstory, the sleep of man, is silent, so stories come into being, whose mythical character is not clear at first sight" (169).[37]   Mythical stories come from the inability of dreams to be reported by the conscious mind. Strangely, so close to a Freudian thesis of the censorship of sleeping thoughts, Laistner steps back and does not develop this insight.

Freud must have found both the conclusions and the methodology conducive to his own work, and his reading of Laistner was far more extensive than he admitted to Fliess. While I cannot prove the date of his reading, I have drawn the conclusion, based on the number and type of Freud's annotations and the similarity of the marks and the colors of pencils used to read Laistner with those in Burckhardt, that it did occur during his work on *The Interpretation of Dreams*. Freud's thoughts about *Oedipus the King* and about the relationship among dreams, myth and literature did not arise in a vacuum, and I believe that these three works give us a good idea of some of the contemporary scholarly ground work. Finally in this section, I believe that the last two books support (or at least explain) some of Freud's discursive practices. Although later criticized for seeking and finding the Oedipus complex everywhere, Freud was merely following the practice of fin de siècle scholars of mythology and folklore like Laistner and Constans, who sought corroborations for their theories in a variety of texts from different eras and cultures. Freud was not alone in thinking the Oedipus myth said something universal about the human condition.

Classical Philology and the Psychoanalyst

In the late years of the nineteenth century and in the early decades of the twentieth, while Sigmund Freud occupied himself with defining and demarcating the techniques and objects of psychoanalysis as a science, Ulrich von Wilamowitz-Möllendorf was similarly circumscribing the terrain of classical philology under the banner of *Altertumswissenschaft*. The famous attack by Wilamowitz against Nietzsche's *The Birth of Tragedy* proved to be the warning shot in the fight for the soul of classical studies.[38] Sharing Freud's devotion to the author of *Faust*, Wilamowitz allowed Goethe into the history of his discipline, but, aside from a fondness for Ibsen which infected his view of Euripides, he never developed much taste for contemporary cultural figures. Although Wilamowitz's influence led to a codification of hostility among philologists to the intrusion of "outsiders" importing their "foreign" methodologies to the scientific study of antiquity, an attitude which hardened with time, Freud continued to explore what seemed to him to be the best known and thought about Greco-Roman culture.

In this final section I examine the aged Freud's interest, often strangely personal, in classical philology through an examination of his ten-year subscription from 1929 to 1938 to *Die Antike: Zeitschrift für Kunst und Kultur des Klassichen Altertums (Antiquity: Journal for the Art and Culture of Classical Antiquity)*. Because of the importance of this subject for Freud and because this was the only non-medical journal which he brought with him to London, *Die Antike* offers a fascinating glimpse into Freud's interests in the last decade of his life. Freud was keenly aware in 1929 of his stature and of his advanced years, as the commencement in that year of his *Kürzeste Chronik* demonstrates.[39] Since Freud only cut the pages of the articles which he actually read, we are provided with a unique glimpse into his reading.

The role of *Die Antike* in Freud's life and his self-conception during the final years of his life can be seen in many of the photographs by Edmund Engelmann, who extensively photographed Freud's apartment at Berggasse 19 several weeks before the Freuds departed Vienna.[40] In many of the photographs of Freud's apartment, the current issue of *Die Antike* is prominently displayed on a small table next to his desk. This would indicate that Freud was actively reading this publication and he wanted people to know it. The journal's presence, along with the statuary around it, suggests Freud's determination to continue his work, to preserve the order and tradition of culture as far he could, at least within the confines of his own home, despite what was happening outside.

Freud's interests here were at times startling, both in the areas new to Freud and in those continuous with the Freud of *The Interpretation of Dreams*. Each issue of this quarterly journal clearly displayed its contents, without needing its pages cut, on the inside cover. The editor of *Die Antike*, Werner Jaeger, dedicated the first issue of Freud's subscription (vol. V, no. 1, 1929) to Wilamowitz on his 80th birthday, complete with a large picture of the master. I shall return to Wilamowitz later. Freud read most of this issue but all of the next; presumably his interested had been piqued. However, Freud only cut half of the third issue and left the fourth intact, an edition which featured an essay "Im Memoriam Hugo von Hofmannsthal"—Freud could not stand the Viennese poet and presumably had read as much about his passing as he could tolerate. Volume VI (1930) was relatively uneventful, but in the first issue of Volume VII Freud only cut the pages of an essay by Stadleman on Jacob Burckhardt's *Griechische Kulturgeschichte*, that book so beloved by Freud 30 years earlier, which argued that since Burckhardt did not like Greece (!!) he could not possibly treat it well, and, anyway, Burckhardt was too much influenced by Rohde—a code word for Nietzsche. As Freud saw here, the tension between Nietzsche and Wilamowitz had not abated. In the second issue of the same year, Freud read an article by Borchardt on Virgil. In 1932 Freud studied Klingner on Tacitus in issue three, and the next edition gave Freud the chance to return to his adolescent predilection for Aristophanes with a long essay by Paul Friedländer, an essay whose continuation in issue two of the next year Freud also read. In Volume XI (1935), Karl Reinhardt, the classicist who most successfully integrated the legacies of Wilamowitz and Nietzsche, entered the picture. Freud's copy of the first issue retains a loose insert advertising Reinhardt's magisterial interpretative work, *Sophokles*, but, more tellingly, Freud read in issue two Reinhardt's brilliant, comprehensive essay on Nietzsche, *Nietzsches Klage der Ariadne*, which shows, once again, the vanity of Freud's protestations of ignorance concerning Nietzsche.[41]

In addition to indicating Freud's interests in the years before the Second World War, *Die Antike* could also shed light on Freud's own state of mind because of its links with the founder of modern classical philology, Ulrich von Wilamowitz-Möllendorf, whose final book, *Der Glaube der Hellenen* (1932), also remains in Freud's library. The journal was founded in 1925 by a group of Wilamowitz's students, led by the proponent of the "Third Humanism," Werner Jaeger, which was dissatisfied with the dry historicism of their teacher and wanted to unite it with the more Dionysian ideas of his infamous *bête noire*, Friedrich Nietzsche.[42] I suspect Freud may have felt some kind of identification with Wilamowitz. This sounds somewhat crazy, I realize, and there is absolutely no external evidence for my suggestion, but please allow me to speculate. Wilamowitz is the last Classics scholar one would expect to find in Freud's library, and we must remember that, since Freud had carefully sorted through his library, every volume at Maresfield Gardens is, as a Prague linguist would say, "marked." Wilamowitz's presence has meaning. There are a few interesting parallels between the lives of Wilamowitz and Freud. They were both German-speaking scholars who, during the same era, took two peculiarly German interests, the mind and Greece, and built them into the wide-ranging, substantial, codified intellectual disciplines of classical philology and psychoanalysis, two fields whose scientificity has not always been uncontested. At the beginning of his career Wilamowitz was considered a radical precisely because of his insistence on turning classical philology into a science. Freud surely also knew of Wilamowitz's attacks on Nietzsche, a predecessor about whom Freud was famously ambivalent. As mentioned earlier, Freud's subscription to *Die Antike* begins with an issue dedicated to Wilamowitz on his 80th birthday, thus making him Freud's elder by only seven years. This dedication and this age probably were not lost on a man who was always keenly aware of his age and who spent an enormous amount of time and energy enaging in love-hate relationships with his own disciples. In 1932 Freud cut the first three pages of Jaeger's memorial essay on Wilamowitz, something he had not done in 1929 for a similar piece on Hofmannsthal. Sometime between then and his departure for England, he purchased Wilamowitz's last book, the posthumously published *Der Glaube der Hellenen*, although he never cut its pages and read it, perhaps because of his business, perhaps because of his illness.[43] Nonetheless, since he deemed it important enough to carry to London with him, he must have intended to read it. I cannot stress this enough: the 80-year-old, cancer-ridden Sigmund Freud was planning to devote time and energy to the work of the master of classical philology of the first half of the twentieth century.

As the fourth decade of the twentieth century wore on, its unhappy events increasingly forced their way even into Freud's readings about classical antiquity. What is perhaps most remarkable about Freud's subscription to *Die Antike*, and indeed about his general interest in classical antiquity, is its homology with Freud's intellectual life and with its place in history. Freud could occasionally see his name in the pages of *Die Antike*—for example, an essay (pages cut) by Binswanger at the beginning of Volume XI (1935) where Binswanger mentioned him prominently— and he could have easily found his name by looking in the index at the end of each year; curiously he sometimes did not cut the pages where he is mentioned. Freud could also see his future in its pages. In the second issue of 1937, a year in which he cut the pages of all of the first three quarterly issues, Werner Jaeger, whose wife was Jewish, suddenly dis- appeared from the editorship of *Die Antike* (to resurface soon in American universities) and was replaced by a triumvirate of scholars who were more comfortable with being Nazi stooges. Given Freud's awareness, shown by his letters and by the *Kürzeste Chronik*, of the growing Nazi threat, we can only imagine Freud's worries when reading the distinctly Nazi rhetoric and language of the editorial statement affirming then, to stand the title of Butler's famous book on its head, the tyranny of Germany over Greece; the new editors wanted their readers to know about the important historical changes occurring, their relationship to the study of classical antiquity, and the reincarnation of the Greek spirit in *"unser Volk."* Always an unstable mix, Jaeger's Third Humanism, co-opted by the Third Reich, had blown up in his face.[44] Exactly one year later Freud, like Jaeger, left the Nazi-controlled world, and thus his subscription to *Die Antike* ended. And one year after that, Freud, like Wilamowitz, was dead.

A final parallel between the two giants concerns as much their legacies, intended and unintended, in their disciplines as any pattern in their lives, once classical philology and psychoanalysis became incorporated as sci- entific procedures, separated by history and by professionalization from the culture which spawned them. Wilamowitz's goal was a philological science objectively studying the works of classical antiquity, free of in- terference from contemporary or personal concerns and devoid of any aesthetic or cultural interest. Even a text's *Nachleben* became an object of philology, the province of specialists. Especially once the cultural tradition of Europe was weakened in the aftermath of the Second World War, the result has been, arguably, an impoverished discipline, cut off from the culture which nourished it. Writing about the departure of psychoanalysts from Europe during the war, Frederic Wyatt has observed a similar impoverishment of psychoanalysis, as the culture which also nourished Freud's thought was lost: "In a deeper sense, quoting from the classics is an appeal for, or a confirmation of, the continuity of an unbroken tradition. . . . What was lost was the unfolding of images and ideas from Sophocles through Shakespeare and Goethe and Freud—a continuity which for psychoanalysis had provided the support of a high cultural tradition to guide and confirm it."[45]

Notes

1. "Weiter muß uns zum Ganzdurchlesen der Authoren die Einsicht bestimmen, daß das, was für uns wichtig ist, nur wir finden." Jakob Burckhardt, *Griechische Kulturgeschichte*, 4 vols. (Berlin: W. Spemann, 1898–1902), 9.

2. On the importance of Sophocles for Freud, see Peter L. Rudnytsky, *Freud and Oedipus* (New York: Columbia University Press, 1987). On Virgil's role in Freud's thought, see Jean Starbonski, *"Acheronta Movebo," Critical Inquiry* 13 (1987), 394–407.

3. My study does not address Freud's interest in archaeology and ancient art, as these subjects have been well treated elsewhere and have been subject to public viewing in a touring exhibition. See *Sigmund Freud and Art: His Personal Collection of Antiquities*, Intro. by Peter Gay, eds. Lynn Gamwell and Richard Wells (SUNY, Binghamton and Freud Museum, London, 1989).

4. Edward Timms, "Freud's Library and His Private Reading," in *Freud in Exile: Psychoanalysis and Its Vicissitudes*, eds. Edward Timms and Naomi Segal (New Haven: Yale University Press, 1988), 67.

5. *The Letters of Sigmund Freud and Arnold Zweig*, ed. Ernst L. Freud; trs. Elaine and William Robson-Scott (New York: Harcourt Brace Jovanovich, 1970).

6. For the *Jahresbericht* for the Leopoldstädter Communal-Real- und Obergymnasium in which Freud was enrolled, see *Sigmund Freud: His Life in Pictures and Words*, eds. Ernst Freud, Lucie Freud and Ilse Grubich-Simitis; tr. Christine Trollope (New York: Harcourt Brace Jovanovich, 1978), 74–75. My understanding of the detailed events in Freud's life has relied on Peter Gay, *Freud: A Life for Our Time* (New York: W. W. Norton, 1988). On the importance of *Julius Caesar* in Freud's imagination, see William McGrath, *Freud's Discovery of Psychoanalysis: The Politics of Hysteria* (Ithaca: Cornell University Press, 1986), 83–83 and 285–87.

7. See the letters of 17 March and 16 June 1873 in *Letters of Sigmund Freud, 1873–1939*, ed. Ernst Freud; trs. Tania and James Stern (New York: Basic Books, 1971).

8. See Starbonski (note 2 above), 396.

9. *Sophokles, Deutsch in den Versmaßen der Urschrift*, vol. 1, J. C. Donner, tr. (Leipzig and Heidelberg: E. Winter'sche, 1868); *Die Lustspiele des Ar-*

istophanes, Deutsch in den Versmaßen der Urschrift, Donner, tr. (Leipzig and Heidelberg: E. Winter'sche, 1861). The Sophocles volume contains the two Oedipus plays, *Antigone* and *Philoctetes*. The Aristophanes contains *The Clouds, Knights, The Frogs, Birds, Peace* and *Wealth*.

10. Artemidorus of Daldis, *Symbolik der Träume*, tr. with commentary by Friederich S. Kraus (Vienna: Hartleben, 1881); *Die Vorsokratiker*, tr. Wilhelm Kapelle (Leipzig: Alfred Kröner, 1935); *Ilias*, tr. Albrecht Schaffe (Berlin: Hartleben, 1929); Plato, *Gastmahl*, trs. F. Kobler and E. Müller (Vienna: Saturn, 1932); Euripides, *Ion* (London: Chatto, 1937). On Artemidorus and Freud, see S. R. F. Price, "The Future of Dreams: From Freud to Artemidorus," in *Before Sexuality: The Construction of Erotic Experience in the Ancient World*, eds. D. Halperin, J. Winkler and F. Zeitlin (Princeton: Princeton University Press, 1990), 365–88.

11. Theodor Gomperz, *Griechische Denker: Eine Geschichte der Antiken Philosophien*, 3 vols. (Leipzig: Veit, 1896); *Aristoteles' Poetik*, tr. and intro. Theodor Gomperz (Leipzig: Veit, 1897). The former was one of then "good" books which Freud listed in reply to a request for such a list from his publisher Hugo Heller in 1907; see Gay (note 6 above), 166.

12. The cultural interconnections and resonances here are complex and rich, for it was Freud's insistence on exploring intellectual life outside his medical studies which led him to Gomperz; in 1879 Brentano recommended his occasional student Sigmund Freud to Gomperz, who was editing the German edition of Mill; see Gay (note 6 above), 36. Because of Mill's influence, Gomperz, the greatest scholar of ancient philosophy of Freud's time, disliked the Presocratics. Freud, perhaps after reading Gomperz's great history of Greek thought, bought a German edition of the Presocratics which he brought with him to London. Gomperz involved Freud in the last volume of the Mill translations, undertaken by Freud in 1879, which contained essays on women's liberation, Plato and socialism.

13. Gomperz was one of a number of polymaths, mostly Jewish, like Freud and Popper-Lynkeus, whom fin de siècle Vienna nurtured. On Gomperz's stature, which was considerable, in Vienna, see *Theodor Gomperz: Ein Gelehrter im Bürgertum der Franz-Josefs-Zeit*, ed. Robert Kahn (Vienna: Österreichische Akademie der Wissenschaften, 1974).

14. See Gay (note 6 above), 122.

15. *Letters of Sigmund Freud*, number 165 (note 7 above).

16. Gomperz published this essay again in *Essays und Erinnerungen* (Stuttgart: Deutsche Verlags-anstalt, 1905).

17. There are four other sets of corrections, the only marks in the volume, in Freud's hand on pages 119, 123, 129 and 172. Until I found these marks I had believed Freud did not read these books carefully, but I then decided not to take any absence of marks as a sign of Freud skimming the pages. I discovered several similar instances in Freud's Burckhardt, where dozens of pages would pass without comment until Freud found a mistake. I wonder

whether Freud took pleasure in finding the errors of others or he was simply annoyed at the carelessness.

18. Freud is frequently compared to Plato because of their shared interest in eros and its repression, but Aristotle's attempt, beginning from biology, to explain and to categorize rationally all facets of human experience, from the effect of tragedy to the nature of the mind, seems much more like Freud's project.

19. *Freud and Oedipus* (note 2 above), 217. Rudnytsky is a useful source on Nietzsche's anticipation of Freud and Freud's ambivalence towards him.

20. Die kathartische Behandlung der Hysterie, welche die Ärzte Dr. JOSEF BREUER und Dr. SIGMUND FREUD beschrieben haben, ist sehr geeignet, die kathartische Wirkung der Tragödie verständlich zu machen.

   Unless otherwise indicated, all subsequent translations of German and French are mine.

21. Rudnytsky succinctly observes (note 2 above, 338), "Aristotle joins with Freud in adopting an *Oedipus-centered* perspective, and hence in elevating Sophocles' tragedy to its unique place in the life of the Western mind."

22. Jacob Burckhardt, *Griechische Kulturgeschichte*, 4 vols. (Berlin: W. Spemann, 1898–1902); Leopold Constans, *La Légende d'Oedipe: Étudiée dans l'antiquité, au moyen âge et dans les temps modernes en particulier dans le Roman de Thèbes, texte français du Xiie siècle* (Paris: Maissonneuve, 1881); and Ludwig Laistner, *Das Rätsel der Sphinx: Grundzüge einer Mythengeschichte*, 2 vols. (Berlin: Wilhelm Herz, 1889). Only the first three volumes of Burckhardt are still in Freud's library, but, since Freud barely touched the third volume (see below) I suspect he never acquired the fourth.

23. Erwin Rohde, *Psyche: Seelenkult und Unsterblichkeit der Griechen*, 3rd ed. (Tübingen and Leipzig: J. C. B. Mohr, 1903). Rohde, one of the few classicists not to break completely with Nietzsche, is still read today.

24. *The Complete Letters of Sigmund Freud to Wilhelm Fliess 1887–1904*, tr. and ed. Jeffrey M. Masson (Cambridge, Mass.: Harvard University Press, 1985).

25. The overwhelming majority of Freud's marks are in the first of the three volumes. The marks disappear in the first volume when Burckhardt discusses Greek politics, mirroring Freud's withdrawal from Austrian politics. Freud displays little interest in the third volume, which deals with Greek art, and barely seems to have touched Burckhardt's sections on Greek tragedy. As I indicated earlier, because of the corrections Freud made to an otherwise virgin copy of Gomperz's *Griechische Denker*, I hesitate to assert that Freud did not read any of his books closely, but, judging from the uncharacteristic stiffness of the pages, I do not think Freud spent much time with the third volume.

26. Die Dynastien des Uranos und Kronos sind nicht etwa Götter, welch in ältern Zeiten wirklich verehrt werden wären, sondern Voraussetzungen einer theologisch und auch schon politisch berührten Phantasie, welcher der Anblick von Herrscherwechseln nichts Ungewohntes war, und Zeus verrät (vergl. 390) völlig die Art eines irdischen Usurpators.

27. Das Unglück und das Böse im Menschenleben beginnt mit dem großen Frevel in der Götterwelt, der Entmannung des Uranos durch Kronos.

Remarkably, Freud's own main reference to Cronos in *The Interpretation of Dreams* errs by making Cronos the subject of castration by Zeus. He admits in a footnote that only in a few versions of the myth is this so, but he fails to cite any sources. I have never seen such a version of the myth.

28. Freud does use a lead pencil much later in the book. In any case, he returned to this passage.

29. In *Freud in Exile* (note 4 above, 79, n. 12), Edward Timms observes that Freud's annotations in Constans show "the systematic way in which he studied literary interpretations of the Oedipus myth." Freud also later acquired and read the twentieth-century philological counterpart to Constans, Carl Roberts's *Oidipus: Geschichte eines Poetischen Stoffes im Griechischen Altertum* (Berlin: Weidmannische Buchhandlung, 1915).

30. I have altered, I hope not pedantically, Masson's translation, changing the title of Sophocles' play from the latinate *Oedipus Rex*, since Freud himself chose the German title, and, substituting "folk tale" for "fairy tale," since the latter has child-like overtones I doubt Freud intended.

31. I dwell on this glaring distortion because I find it inexcusable that someone in Masson's position was so sloppy. Masson seems to want us to believe Freud was obsessed with incest, but the briefest glance at Constans refutes this insinuation.

32. See Rudnytsky (note 2 above), 4–6.

33. On the possible implications of Laius's homosexuality for Freud's theories, see Marianne Krüll, *Freud und Sein Vater* (Munich: C. H. Beck, 1979), 82.

34. I add the emphasis on "behind" ("hinter") and "anxiety," from the German edition, which is generally more faithful to the facsimiles. *Sigmund Freud: Briefe an Wilhelm Fliess*, ed. Jeffrey M. Masson, rev. of German edition by Michael Schröter (Frankfurt am Main: S. Fischer, 1989).

35. See Gay (note 6 above, 101–2) on the quarrel. Bonaparte's unpublished notebook is quoted by Masson (note 24 above, 3). Masson does not mention the presence of Laistner's book in Freud's library, lending credence to my suspicion that his distorted stress on incest when mentioning Constans was a deliberate obfuscation. Or Masson simply unquestioningly bought Freud's obfuscations.

36. Erwägen wir, wie innig Dichtung und Religion mit dem Mythus zusammenhängen, so tritt die überraschende Tatsache hervor, daß der erste Keim zu diesen hochwichtigen Lebensäußerungen der Menschheit nicht in einem Tun des wachen Geistes sich regte, sondern im Schlafe . . .

37. Der Alpmythus, haben wir gesehen, ist die typische Wiedergabe des Alptraumes. Wird die natürliche Voraussetzung einer solchen Traumgeschichte, der Schlaf des Menschen, verschwiegen, so entstehen Erzählungen, deren mythischen Charakter nicht auf den ersten Blick einleuchten . . .

38. For a brief survey of Wilamowitz's role in the history of classical philology,

see the introduction by Hugh Lloyd-Jones to the English translation of
Wilamowitz's *History of Classical Scholarship*, tr. Alan Harris (London:
Duckworth, 1982). On the competing claims of culture, interpretation, sci-
ence and history in classical philology, see Karl Rheinhardt, "Die klassische
Philologie und das Klassiche," in *Vermächtnis der Antike* (Göttingen: Van-
denhoeck & Ruprecht), 334–60.

39. Freud began "The Briefest Chronicle" on 31 October of that year with the
observation that he had once again been passed over for the Nobel Prize. I
thank my colleague in the seminar Jay Geller for drawing my attention to
this. See *The Diary of Sigmund Freud, 1929–1939*, ed. Michael Molnar (New
York: Scribner's, 1992).

40. *Berggasse 19, Sigmund Freud's Home and Offices, Vienna 1938: The Photographs of Edmund Engelmann* (New York: Basic Books, 1976). The current
edition of *Die Antike* can be prominently seen in plates 27, 28, 29, 31, 35
and 36, on the small table which was to Freud's right as he sat at his desk.
The cover of the journal in the English edition is difficult to read due to the
poor quality of the prints. The librarian of the Freud Museum, Keith Davies,
who called the photographs to my attention, has shown me that the French
edition of this book has much clearer photographs.

41. Fortunately, this essay has been reprinted in *Vermächtnis der Antike* (see
note 38 above).

42. See William Calder III, "The Credo of a New Generation: Paul Friedländer
to Ulrich von Wilamowitz-Möllendorf," *Antike und Abendland* 26 (1990),
90–102.

In addition to his interest in Wilamowitz, Freud read the masterpiece of
Theodor Mommsen, the great German ancient historian, *Römische Geschichte*
(Vienna: Phaidon, 1932), as well as *Das Weltreich der Caesaren* (Vienna:
Phaidon, 1933).

43. *Der Glaube der Hellenen*, 2nd. vol. (Berlin: Weidmannsche Buchhandlung,
1932). The few pages cut allow one to see the table of contents and index,
as well as the posthumous memorial epigraph by Wilamowitz's publisher,
who wrote of the pain and sadness such a publication incurred.

44. In 1945 *Die Antike* became *Antike und Abendland*, a journal still published
today, and its editorial offices were moved from Berlin to Hamburg, a city
with more positive associations. Presumably the title was changed to "de-
Nazify" and re-situate the legacy of antiquity not in Germany, but in the
West as a whole.

45. Frederic Wyatt, "The Severance of Psychoanalysis from its Matrix," in *Freud
in Exile* (note 4 above), 13–54.

3. Sigmund Freud and the Sexologists: A Second Reading

Sander L. Gilman

Certainly one of the most valuable contributions of Frank Sulloway's study of Freud and the biological thought of the nineteenth century was to position Freud within the debates about the meaning and nature of sexuality.[1] Freud was indebted to the sexologists—those professional students of human sexuality, most of them physicians, most of them involved in the definition, identification, and treatment of the pathological aspects of human sexuality, as defined by late nineteenth-century legal codes. Whether it was the radical reinterpreters of sexual pathology, such as Havelock Ellis or Magnus Hirschfeld, or the more conservative commentators on the topic, such as Albert Moll, Freud positioned himself carefully in regard to them. And yet Freud was also careful to position himself in terms of the other great charge, one which Sulloway did not address, of the discussions of the special associations of the racial definition of the Jew and the Jew's (especially the Jewish male's) deviant sexuality.

In the fin de siècle medical literature there is a clear association of the Jew with sexual crimes, with criminal perversions. This is an ancient topos which harks back to Tacitus's description of the Jews as the "projectissima ad libidinem gens"—the most sensual of peoples. By the close of the nineteenth century it had become part of the new forensic literature in Germany which described the nature of the Jew as it was stated in one of the standard forensic studies of the time: "Further it must be noted that the sexuality of the Semitic race is in general powerful, yes, often greatly exaggerated."[2] Or, as John S. Billings, the leading American

47

student of Jewish illness and the head of the Surgeon General's Library in Washington, noted, that when Jewish males are integrated into Western culture they "are probably more addicted to . . . sexual excesses than their ancestors were."[3] The physiognomy of the "sexual" male is "dark" (Biérent), or has a "dark complexion" (Bouchereau), or has "brown skin" and "long noses" (Mantegazza).[4] Jewish physicians of the period understood the implications of this charge. The Viennese Jewish physician Hanns Sachs, who was involved in the earliest development of psychoanalysis, commented in his memoirs on this version of the "timeworn prejudice that the Jewish . . . mind was abnormally preoccupied with matters of a sexual nature."[5] Some Jewish scientists of the fin de siècle, such as the Munich neurologist Leopold Löwenfeld, were forced to confront this charge and were unable to dismiss it. He argued, in a study of sexual constitution published in 1911, that the role of racial predisposition in structuring the sexual drives can be confused by the mediating role which climate, nutrition, or culture can play.[6] But he, and his Jewish contemporaries such as Iwan Bloch, have no doubt that racial identity does play some role in structuring sexual constitution. Freud's Jewish lodge brother and one of the original members of the Viennese Psychoanalytic Society, Eduard Hitschmann, believed that "neuroses, psychoses, suicides, etc. play a more important role among the Jews, . . . they have many more sexual experiences than others and—a fact that must be particularly emphasized—take them much more seriously."[7] The Jews' mental states, specifically the psychopathologies associated with the Jews, are closely linked to their intense sexuality.

In terms of the medical world of the fin de siècle, the criminality of the Jew was also a major factor in understanding the Jew's sexuality. The discussion about the nature of Jew and the Jew's relationship to the world of anti-social activity became a central theme in the medical literature of the late nineteenth century. The statistical evidence of forensic psychiatry argued for a greater rate of criminality, in some specific spheres, among the Jews. Such activity was read as not only being sociopathic but also psychopathic, it was a sign of the degeneracy of the Jews because of their endogamous marriages and the resultant inbreeding.[8] The etiology for the Jew's hysteria, for example, like the hysteria of the woman, was to be sought in "sexual excess."[9] Specifically in the inbreeding within this endogenous group: "Being very neurotic, consanguineous marriages among Jews cannot but be detrimental to the progeny."[10] This view was even advocated by Rudolf Virchow, whose liberal views on the ability of Jewish acculturation were paralleled by his sense of the dangers of Jewish consanguinity.[11] Virchow pointed out the much greater occurrence of inherited diseases among the Jews. Such dangerous marriages were labeled as a criminal activity, even when such "inbreeding" was not consanguineous. In historical terms, writers such as Houston Stewart Chamberlain could comment on the origin of the Jews and its "refreshingly artless expression in the genealogies of the Bible, according to which some of these races owe their origin to incest, while others are descended from harlots."[12] This was answered, at least in the data gathered by Jewish social scientists and their medical allies, in the claim that either the totality of the image presented was incorrect and correct statistical data could be amassed or that a higher incidence could be found but only for certain crimes (usually economic ones) or among specific subsets (such as Eastern Jews).[13] These were linked in the view that the "destructive impact of certain professions (such as that of the stock market speculator) on the nerves predisposed individuals to commit sexual crimes."[14] What is most striking is the counterargument, the Jewish "immunity" for sexual crimes, such as incest, was stressed by other groups.[15] Such immunity was often read as a form of latent criminality, a hidden disposition which was simply not triggered because of the sexual barriers erected by Jewish religious practices. This literature must be set against the ubiquitous charge of Jewish criminal sexuality which haunted European culture of the fin de siècle.

The face of the Jew and that of the criminal as sexual criminal had merged in the course of the fin de siècle in the figure of "Jack the Ripper" as an Eastern European Jew.[16] The charge was made in 1894 in the anti-Semitic newspapers in Germany, that Jack was an Eastern European Jew functioning as part of the "International Jewish conspiracy."[17] This image of the Jewish Jack the Ripper rested on a long association of the image of the Eastern Jew in the West with the image of the mutilated, diseased, different appearance of the genitalia. It is especially in the image of the Eastern Jew as criminal (as described in Western literature) that this view seems to be fixed. The overall medical view is that Jews in the East demonstrate a higher incidence of criminal insanity than do Western Jews. While Eastern Jews argue that they actually evidence a lower rate of criminality,[18] the overall assumption among Western forensic scientists, both Jews and non-Jews, is that the Eastern Jew is dangerous. Rafael

Becker, reporting from a Jewish mental hospital near Warsaw, notes that 13% of the mental patients examined for their legal competency were Jews.[19] In Vienna the legal attempt to identify those who were not German "by race or language" during the early 1930s led to an on-going representation of the Eastern Jews in Austria as the source of all criminality, including sexual crimes.[20] The theme of the criminality of the Eastern Jew continued into the Nazi period. Joachim Duckart documented the history of a "criminal community" of Eastern Jews back into the eighteenth century.[21] Though it has been argued that Jews, especially Eastern Jews, presented an overwhelming majority of those individuals involved in sexual commerce in Europe and South America from the 1880s through the beginning of the 1930s, the image of the Jew as sexual criminal in the medical and forensic debates of the fin de siècle rests on the special, sexualized nature of the Jew.[22] It is the debate about race which taints all other views of the social reality of the period.

Within the major psychoanalytic work dealing with criminality, a study written by the Berlin psychoanalyst Franz Alexander and the jurist Hugo Staub in 1929, there is absolutely no mention of the Jewish predisposition for any type of crime.[23] Indeed, race has completely vanished as a category of analysis. Only "idiots, paretics, schizophrenics, and epileptics" are considered under the label of those criminals showing a "biological etiology" for crime. All other crimes are either committed by neurotics, whose unresolved Oedipal complex provides the psychological basis for their acts, or "normal" criminals, whose acts are examples of the weakness of character deformed by a negative social context. Alexander and Staub actually evoke all of the rhetoric about the Jewish criminal—on all sides of the issue—but in completely removing the category of race from their analysis, they make criminality a universal rather than a racial activity. Sexuality becomes the hallmark of the neurotic criminal with his unresolved Oedipus complex; inheritance, the sign of the "born criminal" suffering from mental deficiency or impairment, and the social milieu mark the "normal" criminal. The authors do not create a nosology of crime. They do not place any group in a special relationship to any of these categories. In doing so they avoid all of the debates about the special status of the Jews in relationship to the world of sexuality and crime.

The Jew remains the representation of the male as outsider, the act of circumcision marking the Jewish male as sexually apart, as anatomically different. For fin de siècle medicine, madness was marked not only on the face but also on the genitalia. In the case of the signs of mental degeneration, "precisely the anomalies of the genitalia are of extreme importance and are rarely found alone."[24] The prostitute was the embodiment of the degenerate and diseased female genitalia in the nineteenth century.[25] From the standpoint of the normative perspective of the European middle class, it is natural that the Jew and the prostitute, Jack and his victims, must be in conflict and that the one "opens up" the Other, as they are both seen as "dangers" to the economy, both fiscal and sexual, of the state.[26] This notion of the association of the Jew and the prostitute is also present in the image of "spending" semen (in an illicit manner) which dominates the literature on masturbation in the eighteenth and early nineteenth centuries. For the Jew and the prostitute are seen as negating factors, outsiders whose sexual images represent all of the dangers felt to be inherent in human sexuality.

The debate about Jewish sexual crimes provides a further reading of the idea of the hidden nature of the Jew. Latent criminality becomes a component of the "common mental construction" of the Jews. In 1881 there appeared an anonymous, anti-Semitic pamphlet on *The Jews' Role in Crime* which began by asking its audience not to inquire "Où est la femme?" in searching for the origin of crime but "Where is the Jew?"[27] The Jew became the substitute for the woman as the source of criminality in society. The author cited the following statistics from the 1871 Prussian census. In 1871 Jews made up only 1.3% of the population. Thus there were 16,636,990 Protestants; 8,625,840 Catholics; and 339,700 Jews (or "1 Jew for every 74 Germans"). But they were accused of crimes against morality 20% more often than their Catholic or Protestant co-religionists (Catholic = 372; Protestant = 703; Jewish = 18). And this argument was made by the author across every arena of criminality. The argument is explicit that Jews are by their very nature criminals and all areas of criminality, including the area of sexual crimes, such as incest, rape, and sexual abuse of minors, find them overly represented.

This pamphlet called forth an immediate and intensive rebuttal on the part of Jewish social scientists. S. Löwenfeld attempted to answer it, labeling it a "statistical cry against the Jews."[28] Löwenfeld's argument was that while Jews may be accused of certain crimes more frequently than other groups, their conviction rate was actually lower than that of either the Catholic or the Protestant population, indeed they represented less than half of the numbers of convictions than their representation in the population. He stressed this in specific areas, such as the area of sexual crimes. In 1885 Ludwig Fuld, a lawyer in Mainz, published yet another tabulation of the "relationship between religion and criminality." Relying on the 1881 Prussian criminal census, his tabulation of sexual crimes noted that the sexual abuse of minors and statutory rape were the most often punished moral crimes among Jewish men, but also widely spread among non-Jews. Incest, on the other hand, was so rarely to be found that he sees its absence among Jewish men as a relic of the Biblical injunction which punishes this crime with death. He sees the lower rate of conviction of Jews for the crime of incest as an atavism which can be traced back to the ethnopsychology of the Jews. [29] At the same time the French Jewish community, in reviewing the crime statistics in France during 1885, argued that these statistics were "an honor to the Jews" as they revealed a much lower incidence in all areas including incest. [30]

The debate about Jewish criminality, with its subtext about the higher or lower rate of the incidence of sexual crimes among Jews, was serious enough that when the "Committee to Defend Against Anti-Semitic Attacks" began its publication series in 1896, its first statistical study was directed against the literature on Jewish criminality. [31] The statistics on sexual crimes reported in this study are revealing. Covering the period from 1882 to 1892, the statisticians found that, instead of the 44 cases of incest potentially projected for the Jewish population based on its representation in the population, only seven convictions are to be found; in the case of "unnatural inbreeding" ["Inzucht"], 20 cases as against the 50 predicted; and 21 cases of "crimes against morals" which was the number projected.

In 1905 Arthur Ruppin, the founder of Jewish social statistics in Germany, reported similar statistics for the period from 1899 to 1902. [32] Ruppin's rationale for the substantially lower rates of sexual crimes is the "greater education of the Jews." [33] Ruppin's work is reflected in his basic study of the sociology of the Jews published in 1904. [34] This view is seconded by Bruno Blau in a pamphlet in 1906 which, however, admits to a higher incidence of certain crimes (such as slander) because of the "temperament" of the Jews. [35] Here the contrast between evaluations based on nature or nurture can be judged. Ruppin saw the educational level of the Jews as a reflex of the older religious tradition now secularized. This is precisely the aspect of the Jewish mind which is most often evoked when the discussion is of the negative impact of the stresses of civilization on the Jew, given the Jew's predisposition for mental illness. Blau's comment on the temperament of the Jew looked at a characterological argument for criminal activity. Character was, however, formed by social stress, by the ghetto experience, according to many commentators. What was clearly an argument based on experience reveals itself to be analogous to one made on inheritance and vice versa. This can be most clearly seen in the comments of one of the leading criminologists of the early twentieth century in his 1910 handbook on sexual crimes: "The Jew is marked by his intellectual gifts, which in general serve as a preventative against the commission of crime. His ability to think logically and his cleverness provide an antidote to his passion and his sexual excitedness. In other crimes [than sexual ones], especially fraud and perjury these characters are a predisposing criminal factor."[36]

The view that race was a primary factor in criminality became the flashpoint of debate after the beginning of the twentieth century. In the second volume of the primary German periodical on criminology founded by the most eminent criminologist of his day, Gustav Aschaffenburg, there is a long essay on the topic of race and criminality by the physician Richard Weinberg from Dorpat/Tartu (Estonia).[37] Weinberg argued that criminality is inherently a reflex of race; that it is an inherited proclivity of a group. In looking at the Jews, Weinberg notes the "general tendency of the Jews for mental illness" and he sees this as a sign of their racial degeneration.[38] This degeneration has a clearly psychological aspect. It is the result of the mixing of races, a sign of the alteration of the character of the second generation of mixed racial types.[39] Madness and criminality result from racial mixing and both are forms of psychological degeneration as represented by physical signs. This is the view of the ideological orig- inator of modern biological anti-Semitism, Count Gobineau, who saw degeneracy of a people as the direct result of the decline of racial homogeneity.[40]

The madness of the Jews and their predisposition to disease were results of the inbreeding of the Jews, much as the noble families of Europe had decayed (and lost power) and the population of the Swiss villages had degenerated. This view is stated quite directly in the standard textbook of psychiatry of the fin de siecle, that of Emil Kraepelin.[41] Simon Scherbel, a Polish Jew and the son of a Rabbi, presented his dissertation to the medical faculty of the Berlin University in 1883 on the topic of consan- guineous marriages. He is confronted with an absolute contradiction.

How can the "laws of Moses, which are for the most part still valid for Protestants" advocate the marriage of their "daughters within the tribe."[42] For it is evident that these laws have "a negative result." Jews have higher incidences of deaf-mutism and mental illness.[43] Scherbel responds that the Jew has the necessary disposition for such illnesses, because of his economic or professional status or because of some factor yet unknown, which is triggered more frequently than his non-Jewish counterpart.[44] The laws which forbid consanguineous marriages are an attempt to avoid "incest and immorality" in families.[45] The entire debate on consanguineous marriage, from a religious as well as from a medical point of view in the 1920s, was summarized in the *Jewish Lexicon*.[46] The essay by Felix Theilhaber stressed that the result of such marriages is an increased rate of mental illness among the offspring.

In 1909, there are further statistics brought to argue a decrease in the conviction rate for Jews accused of sexually related crimes.[47] In Aschaffenburg's journal, the chief of the Dutch Bureau of Legal Statistics published an essay which asked quite directly: "It is racial criminality or is it a criminality which is a product of social circumstances?"[48] He presented the Dutch figures for the period from 1896 to 1906 and argued "that in spite of the various circumstances in which Jews live, they show the same pattern of criminality."[49] And this is especially true in the tendency to commit sexually related crimes. They may show fewer cases of incest and sexual criminality, but they are much more involved in the publication of pornography. For de Roos their criminality is the result of the "combination of the natural disposition and their social and economic circumstances."[50] Thus in 1911, Rudolf Wassermann was forced to confront the question of the "racial" cause of Jewish criminality directly. Spurred on by de Roos's essay, Wassermann stated his position most clearly: Jewish criminality mirrors the criminality of the society in which the Jews find themselves and is a purely social reflex rather than the result of inheritance.[51] And indeed this is the general view within the German-speaking Jewish scientific community.[52] Franz von Liszt attempted to further Wassermann's views, stressing that the criminality of any group, including that of the Jews, sprang from the specific social location.[53] What is different in von Liszt's approach is that he assumed that the choice of profession was a reflex of the "common mental construction" of the Jews.

It is striking that none of the studies suggested the evident control for such assumptions: the rate of criminality and the types of crimes committed by Jewish converts and their offspring. The assumption would be that conversion, given the contemporary discussion of its intent, would at least change the social localization of the convert and would permit the convert to engage in other professions, some of which were *de facto* barred to Jews. The rate of the commission of sexual crimes would also be reflected (positively or negatively) in the change of the structure of the family and of the social context of the Jew. The taboo about seeking to examine the convert can be attributed to the anxiety on all sides of the implications of boundary crossers.

It is important to clarify what these various "sexual" crimes were. Incest in the German legal and forensic discourse of the fin de siècle is "Blutschande," the violation of the blood.[54] The origin of this concept is that there is a real "pollution" of the blood by the sexual contact between relatives.[55] Its origin is the concept of the "sanguis contumelia" of Roman law.[56] Incest is understood as being "unnatural" because it comes from an "unnatural" desire and may lead to "unnatural," i.e., unhealthy offspring. Incest is a question of law, though there is a substantial debate among forensic scientists about its universal applicability or historical foundation. But it is also seen as a loss of control: "That the mentally ill tend to commit incest is easily explained, for the mentally ill there is complete loss of control as well as the law of the shortest way."[57] Incest is thus an activity which marks the atavistic nature of the mentally ill. In the course of the nineteenth century this concept moves from signifying incestuous behavior to meaning the violation of the purity of the race.[58] It is no longer the violation of the taboos created within the narrower definition of the social unity (such as the family), rather it becomes a definition of the boundaries of the wider unity, such as the race. Commit "Blutschande" and you violate the newly biologically defined taboos inherent in the purity of the racial stock. This act pathologizes the very concept of race by defining what will and does cause racial degeneration. For the very concept of "Blutschande" implies the degeneration of the race into illness and moral corruption.

It was of little wonder that the very debate about "incest" was fraught with racialist undertones. For Magnus Hirschfeld, the great German-Jewish sexologist, it was a moral not a legal question. The term which he and other researchers of the period preferred was "Unzucht" (indecency) rather than "Blutschande" (incest). "Inzest" (incest) was forbidden sexual contact between related individuals, but not necessarily related by consanguinity. This view was also stressed by Hermann Rohleder, who distinguished between incestuous relationships, which were forbidden by law, and "inbreeding" which he interpreted as any sexual contact within the wider blood-relationship.[59] Thus German and Austrian law at the fin de siècle punished sexual contact between in-laws.[60] The Christian preoccupation with the Jewish custom of the levirate marriage, the obligation of a man to marry the widow of his brother, comes into clear conflict with these European traditions.[61] Within the German understanding of the Jew's sexuality, this aspect of Jewish ritual practice had been a central focus. The "reader" appended to one of the very first grammars of Yiddish written in German which was to be used to train missionaries to the Jews in the seventeenth century consisted of two texts: one on leprosy and one on the levirate marriage.[62] The link between the diseased nature of the Jews and the Jews's marital practice was a long-established one. It is unimportant that by Talmudic times such marriages were seen as objectionable, indeed Abba Saul viewed them as equivalent to incest.[63] This obligation could be avoided through the institution of the ceremony of *chalitsah*.[64] Even though the levirate marriage was not a common ritual practice in nineteenth-century Europe, it remained a subject of endless fascination. In his history of marriage, one of Freud's major sources, Edvard Westermarck, evoked the practice among the Jews in his discussion of levirate marriage. He cited the obligation "of a man to marry the widow of his brother if he died childless, and the firstborn should succeed in the brother's name 'that his name should be not put out of Israel.'"[65] This type of marriage was one of the keys to the European debate about incest in the nineteenth century.[66] It is the incestuous implications of the levirate marriage which underlie the charge of brother-sister incest often lodged against the Jews. For a sexual relationship between a brother-in-law and his sister-in-law was considered to be the legal equivalent in German and Austrian law to brother-sister incest. C. G. Jung's charge that Freud had sexual relations with his sister-in-law, Minna Bernays, whom he called his "sister," is an evocation of this calumny.[67]

For German-Jewish scientists such as Hirschfeld "incest is the most frequent crime of solitary farms and narrow proletarian domiciles,"[68] not of the middle-class dwellings of Berlin or Viennese Jewry. It is in these venues, marked by endemic goiter and insanity, that the signs of the degenerate are permitted to be found. Another German-Jewish forensic psychiatrist, Max Marcuse, noted that "all human beings stem from in-breeding[, f]or the original sexual relationships were incestuous. . . . In people the marriage of consanguineous parents often evidence severe ill-nesses and deformities. The dangers of inbreeding can be illustrated by the degeneration and disappearance of many noble families, the racial pathology of the Jews, the endemic constitutional inferiority of people living in mountain villages, in which the inhabitants tend to mix only with themselves."[69] The acceptance of the view that inbreeding (and certainly incest) results in the decline of the group was a commonplace and was often applied to the Jew as an explanation, as we have seen, for a number of pathological conditions. The "cure" for the disease of Jew-ishness would be exogenous rather than endogenous marriages. The cure would be to marry outside of the group. In 1904 Heinrich Singer had argued against such positions. For him it is an error to imagine that Jews suffer from the physiological results of inbreeding. "Mixed marriages," he writes, "as the sole cure and the preventative of the collapse of the race are not necessary."[70] Such a cure can be accomplished by Jews moving into professions which are healthier and by the youth undertaking a "hygienic, body-building education."

The confusion surrounding the very concept of incest surfaced in the forensic literature of the fin de siècle. In 1907 Rudolf Wassermann pub-lished his basic introduction to the question of Jewish criminality.[71] Was-sermann accepted the question of the criminality of the Jews as one which is appropriate for statistical evaluation, even though there had been a debate in the criminological literature about the effectiveness and appro-priateness of using "religion" as a criterion for the tabulation of such statistics.[72] Wassermann, using the criminal census figures in Germany from 1899 to 1902, tabulated a slightly lower (about 10%) rate of sexual crimes on the part of Jews. But he also noted that during the year of 1895, there had been a 10% higher rate of these crimes among Jews.[73] In general Jews showed a higher rate of crimes against public morality than did Christians, but Christians showed a much higher incidence of incest.[74]

For Wassermann, and for many of the other commentators of the period, the Jews' lower rate of sexual crimes is closely tied to their rate of alcohol consumption. This motif, as we have seen in the discussion of the lower incidences of syphilis among Jews, presented a social practice linked to the inheritance of sobriety.[75] Hugo Hoppe, the author of the standard study of Jews and alcohol, sees the Jews as less likely to commit such crimes because of their lower alcohol consumption.[76] Jewish abstinence provided the key to the lower rate of incest. Incest was a crime, as Hirschfeld had noted, committed when one was completely out of rational control. The insane provided him a perfect model. And alcoholism or at least drunkenness provided precisely the same context. Alcoholism remains the major "social" context of sexual abuse, although it is seen as an inherited trait which passes other, more devastating inherited traits on to the children of alcoholics. Zola describes his *Nana* as the "story of a girl descended from four or five generations of drunkards, her blood tainted by an accumulated inheritance of poverty and drink, which in her case had taken the form of a nervous derangement of the sexual instinct."[77] If alcoholism leads to sexual degeneration and perversity, then the absence of such sociopathic acts on the part of the Jews must be the direct result of their abstinence.

The debates about Jews and alcohol reflect the overall debates about predisposition as opposed to socialization. Wassermann noted that the more visible the Jew is in society, the more he is placed in a position where alcohol consumption is needed.[78] Thus the latent criminality of the Jew can be triggered and he can commit sexual crimes. In 1909 Wassermann added to his argument about the social context of the Jew's criminality, seeing the changes of the patterns of Jewish criminality as a reflex of the changes in social status of the Jews.[79] He calculated that 59% of all sexual crimes were committed under the influence of alcohol. Alcohol consumption among Jews remains relatively low into the 1920s.[80] Incest figures for Jews during the period from 1899 to 1916, while higher than in the previous decade, also remain remarkably below those for all other groups.

The association between the illicit sexuality of the Jew and the discourse on criminal sexuality is linked, as has been observed, in the argument that there is a Jewish predisposition for specific forms of mental illness. The "perverse" sexuality of the Jew lies at the heart of this charge, for it is the inbreeding of the Jew which predisposes him to specific psychopathologies, precisely those such as "homosexuality, from which the Jew is understood to suffer. The "degenerate" Jew becomes closely associated with models of "degenerate" sexuality. Ludwig Woltmann, the noted eugenist and anthropologist, sees in the "physical collapse of the Jews the degeneration of their nervous systems."[81] The "degenerate," the greater category into which the nosologies of the nineteenth century placed the "pervert," was—according to Max Nordau, one of the very first supporters of Theodor Herzl's Zionism, quoting B. A. Morel—the "morbid deviation from an original type."[82] The difference between the original type, the middle-class, heterosexual, Protestant, white male, and the outsider was a morbid one—the outsider was diseased. Thus there is a general parallel drawn between the feminization of the Jew and the homosexual in the writings of assimilated Jews, Jews who did not seek to validate their difference from the majority during the late nineteenth century but did see themselves as potentially at risk by being perceived as such morbid deviations from the norm. Nowhere is this illustrated with greater force than in an essay written in 1897 by the future foreign minister of the Weimar Republic, Walter Rathenau. Rathenau, who begins his essay by "confessing" to his identity as a Jew, condemns the Jews as a foreign body in the cultural as well as the political world of Germany: "Whoever wishes to hear its language can go any Sunday through the Thiergartenstrasse midday at twelve or evenings glance into the foyer of a Berlin theater. Unique Vision! In the midst of a German life, a separate, strange race. . . . On the sands of the Mark Brandenburg, an Asiatic horde." As part of this category of difference, Rathenau sees the physical deformities of the Jewish male—his "soft weakness of form," his femininity (associated with his "orientalism")—as the biological result of his oppression. This was a restructuring of the charge that Jews were inherently feminine, rather than as a social reaction to their stigmatization.[83] Theologians such as David Friedrich Strauss, the great critic of Christianity, were even able to speak of the "especially female" nature of the Jews.[84] (Freud read this text as a young man and it made a considerable impression on him.)[85] The evils of Christianity lie in the mentality of their Jewish origin—a point which Nietzsche, and many of the "Christian" critics of Christianity during the late nineteenth century ascribed. And physicians such as Moses Julius Gutmann could translate this discussion of the "common mental construction" of the Jews into a reading of the anthropometric statistics of the woman as parallel those of the male Jew. Thus the Jew has an arm span less than equivalent to his height, as does the woman.[86] It is of little surprise therefore that the Jew is seen as overwhelmingly at risk for being (or becoming) a homosexual. Moses Julius Gutmann observes that "all of the comments about the supposed stronger sexual drive among Jews has no basis in fact; most frequently they are sexual neurasthenics. Above all the number of Jewish Homosexuals is extraordinarily high."[87] This view is echoed by Alexander Pilcz, Freud's colleague in the Department of Psychiatry at the University of Vienna, who noted that "there is a relatively high incidence of homosexuality among the Jews."[88] It is the very biological (or "ontological") difference of the Jew which is the source of his feminized nature. Among Jews, according to a lecture in 1920 by the Professor of Anthropology at the University of Vienna Robert Stigler, "the physical signs of the sexual characteristics are noticeably vague. Among them, the women are often found to have relatively narrow pelvis and relatively broad shoulders and the men to have broad hips and narrow shoulders. ... It is important to note the attempt on the part of the Jews to eliminate the role which secondary sexual characteristics instinctively play among normal people through their advocacy of the social and professional equality of man and woman."[89] Only Havelock Ellis denied this association noting that among his homosexual patients only "two are more or less Jewish." His (British) surprise is that "frequent presence of the German element" among his patients.[90] This charge of the general tendency of all Jews (male and female) toward homosexuality, as represented by their social and political acts as well as their biological reality, had to be modified by Jews such as Rathenau to provide a space where they were able to escape the stigma of feminization.

"Feminization" is here to be understood both in its general, cultural sense and in its very specifically medical sense. "Feminization" or the existence of the "feminized man" is a form of "external pseudo-hermaphrodism."[91] It is not true hermaphroditism, but rather the sharing of external, secondary sexual characteristics, such as the shape of the body or the tone of the voice. The concept begins in the middle of the nineteenth century with the introduction of the term: "infemminsce," to feminize, to describe the supposed results of the castration of the male.[92] By the 1870s, the term is used to describe the "feminisme" of the male through the effects of other disease, such as tuberculosis.[93] And Henry Meige, at the Salpêtrière, saw this feminization as a form of atavism, in which the male returns to the level of the "sexless" child.[94] "Feminization" was the direct result of actual castration or the physiological equivalent, such as intensely debilitating illness. And it reshaped the body. Freud, citing Taruffi, rejected any simple association of the form of the body of the hermaphrodite with the sexual preference of the homosexual.[95] He separated out the "common mental construction" of the homosexual from his/her physical form.

Freud's response to his own potential "deviancy" was complicated. In the 1890s he confronted the question of the relationship between inheritance and trauma as the two major sources for all mental illness. His struggle with the idea of predisposition and inheritance can be seen in his reading of Leopold Löwenfeld's work. Löwenfeld, one of Freud's most assiduous supporters, confronted the question of the racial predisposition of the Jews in his textbook of 1894. In his discussion of the etiology of neurasthenia and hysteria he examined the role which "race and climate" might play in the origin of these diseases:

Concerning the claimed predisposition of the Semitic race, one can only state the fact that among the Israelites today there is an unusually large number of neurasthenics and hysterics. Whether this is the result of a specific predisposition of the race seems very questionable. Historically, there is no trace of such as predisposition to be shown. The epidemics of mass hysteria observed in earlier centuries never affected members of the Semitic race. I believe it more likely that the great predisposition of the Israelites does not rest in racial qualities, but in their present quality of life. Among these would come into consideration—in East Europe, the physical poverty as well as the extraordinary moral pressure, the practice of early marriage, and the great number of children—in the West, the great number of Israelites who undertake intellectual activities.[96]

Freud read Löwenfeld's textbook very carefully. The opening pages are full of debates about the inheritability of hysteria and its relationship to trauma. Thus Löwenfeld claims that "inheritance plays a major role in the origins of neurasthenia and hysteria through the existence of an abnormal constitution of the nervous system." Freud retorts: "From where?" in the margin. Tucked away in a footnote, Löwenfeld quotes a source which claimed that to have seen a large number of cases of hysteria "without a trace of hereditary neurosis."[97] Freud chuckles: "Bravo! Certainly acquired." These comments reflected Freud's preoccupation with the universal question of whether all human beings could be divided into the healthy and the degenerate, the mentally sound and the hysteric. Löwenfeld's rejection of the predisposition for hysteria for *all* Jews meant it was possible to focus on the universal rather than the racialist question. And yet Löwenfeld's distinction between Eastern Jews with their mix of social and sexual causes for their mental states and Western Jews with their (highly sought) intellectual status shows that even there a dichotomy between the religious and the secular Jew is sought. Freud seems never to reach this section of the book; his eye remains fixed on the universal question and does not seem to enter into the debate about the Jews and madness. But in fact, he enters this debate in a complicated manner.

Freud's essay on "'Civilized' Sexual Morality and Modern Nervous Illness" (1908) is in many ways an unspoken dialogue on the association of race and insanity in contemporary science. In that paper Freud links the repressive nature of modern society with the deformation of human sexuality. He begins with a paraphrase of the work of the contemporary Prague philosopher and co-founder of *Gestalt* psychology Christian von Ehrenfels who held an essentially ethnopsychological position (for many of the same reasons as did Freud). Ehrenfels had solicited Freud's contribution to a new periodical, *Sexual Problems*, which first appeared in 1908.[98] The magazine was one of the successors of the older journal, *Mother Protection*, the official publication of a eugenics group to which Freud and Ehrenfels belonged. Upon founding the journal, Ehrenfels immediately wrote to Freud for a contribution and received the essay from him.

Ehrenfels stated, in the extract cited by Freud, that "the innate character of a people" could be compared with their "cultural attainments" in order to differentiate between "civilized" and "natural" sexual morality.[99] "Civilized" morality produces "intense and productive cultural activities," while "natural sexual morality maintains "health and efficiency." The disease of the cities, of urban life, is thus a product of the civilizing process. It is a necessary, though unfortunate, result of the suppression of human sexuality in culture. It is a problem of modern life, not of Jews in modern society.

Christian von Ehrenfels's monograph is a most interesting point of departure for Freud.[100] Published in a series of short monographs on "marginal questions" in neurology and psychology edited by Freud's friend Leopold Löwenfeld in Munich, Ehrenfels's text is explicitly indebted to Freud for much of its psychological framework. Highly influenced (like Freud) by a Darwinian model of sexual selection, Ehrenfels could not only contrast "natural" and "civilized" morality, but just as easily write of the competition between the "higher" and the "lower" races and about the "great problem of our time": resolving the demand of race in the light of the "liberal-humanistic fiction of the equality of all people."[101] For Ehrenfels, the purpose of "natural sexual morals" (which is for him a natural law) "is to conserve or improve the constitution of the tribe or people."[102] He saw the need for the "white, yellow, and black" races to remain "pure" and to avoid any sexual interbreeding. As with most of the racial scientists of his time, he justified colonial expansion with the rationale that the "sexual mission" of some races is best accomplished "if they place their generative powers in the service of others."[103] As the rhetoric of this statement seems to indicate throughout Ehrenfels's discussion of race, his prime example is the "Oriental." Indeed, Freud underlines the passage in his text where Ehrenfels warns of the risk of the "Yellow Peril" overwhelming Europe. Freud's own writing reflects this image in his formulation of 1915, in which he stated that the war which had been expected before 1914 was assumed to be between the "civilized" ("white") and "primitive" ("darker") races.[104] It is clear in this formulation that the Jews, seen as a people of culture, were to be considered to be "white" and, therefore, civilized.

The monograph however concludes with an index, prepared by the author and intended by him to enable his monograph to be used as a handbook for those seeking direct advise on topics of sexual morality. The final entry makes reference to the discussion on racial sexuality and concludes the volume with the following observation: "These same directives are applicable to the Jewish problem, in as much as these are the result of differences in their constitution and not—as is actually generally the case—the result of resolvable differences in their social milieu."[105] All of the discussions about race are, in fact, encoded references to the Jewish question. It is the claim for an innate, biologically rooted difference of the Jews which is the subtext of Ehrenfels's study of sexual ethics. For the Jews are understood as biologically different. Their strengths, like the strengths of each of the races, are preserved only when they remain within their own group. Intermixing leads to the corruption and the weakening of the race. Rather than intermixing with the Aryan the Jew, Ehrenfels implies, through their activity in Western culture, can place "their generative powers in the service of others."

Ehrenfels's demands for the purity of the race were not merely theoretical. Ehrenfels himself was an active spokesperson for eugenics and spoke on "breeding reform" in December 1908 before the Vienna Psychoanalytic Society. There again he warned about the dangers of monogamy as well as the threat of the "annihilation of the white race by the yellow race."[106] And yet the racial theorist who advocated the purity of the race and the distinction between "healthy" and "civilized morality" in the "higher" and "lower" races was himself Jewish by descent even though raised as a Christian. Ehrenfels publically acknowledged his own personal Jewish background and saw the rise of political anti-Semitism as a social anathema.[107] The real danger, Ehrenfels again stated in a talk given in 1911, is the "Yellow Peril," the "hoards of Mongols" poised to confront the "Caucasian" race: "Among 100 whites there stand two Jews. The German peasant has been awakened and armed with the holy weapons of his ancestors—not to struggle against 80 million Mongols but to confront two Jews! Is this not the height of folly!"[108]

Ehrenfels's response to the nature of the Jew can be best read in his review of Otto Weininger's *Sex and Character,* published in one of the most widely read eugenics journals of his day.[109] Weininger had published his revised dissertation, *Sex and Character,* in 1903, and killed himself shortly thereafter in the house in Vienna in which Beethoven had died.[110] Weininger's book both became an immediate best-seller and established him as a serious contributor to the discourse about the relationship between race and gender at the beginning of the century.[111] This is a work of intensive, undisguised self-hatred which had an unprecedented influence on the scientific discourse about Jews and women at the turn of the century. Thus the lesbian feminist Charlotte Perkins Gilman saw Weininger's work as a major contribution to the science of gender.[112] And Ludwig Wittgenstein, the homosexual, partially "Jewish" Catholic philosopher, accepted and incorporated aspects of Weininger's "philosophy" into his worldview.[113] Christian von Ehrenfels immediately identified the central problem in Weininger's work as the author's rejection of heterosexuality. But Ehrenfels is careful to separate Weininger's rejection of heterosexuality (and the parallel sexual ambiguity) from any discussion of Jewish identity. In regard to Weininger's overt anti-Semitism, Ehrenfels sees all of his traits as falling within Weininger's representation of the Jew. He is "superficial, impious, fivolous, impertinent, and publicity seeking." In other words, he sees Weininger as living out his own internalized negative self-image of the Jew in his own writing. For Ehrenfels, the central link to this classic of early twentieth-century sexology is Weininger's own reflection of the ambiguities of all identity formation—either as a male or as a Jew, but not as a gay Jew.

By 1911 Ehrenfels comes to deny any substantial physiological dif-

ference between Aryans and Jews. Indeed, he comes to see the Jews as
suffering from all of the diseases and dangers of modern society: "They
suffer more than we do from the present sexual and economic order."[114]
Primary among these are mental disease. Jews are, therefore, simply
exaggerated Aryans. Indeed, this seems a response to Oskar Rie's comment following his paper in Vienna that "would the Mongols, in taking
over our culture, not take over our potential for degeneration as
well..."[115] For a number of thinkers of the period assumed that the
Jews were the example of the worst cast of the impact of civilization
because of their weak nervous system. Franz Kafka mentions a response
which Ehrenfels made to a presentation by Felix Theilhaber on the "decline of Germany Jewry" to a public audience in Prague during January
of 1912.[116] Theilhaber had recapitulated the thesis of his controversial
book, that urbanization, the struggle for profit, as well as mixed marriages
and baptism were causing German Jewry to vanish. (The latter argument
was a social variant on the older biological argument that "mixed marriages between Jews and Aryans had a noticeably lower fecundity.")[117]
Ehrenfels's response, as Kafka noted, was a "comic scene" in which the
philosopher (whose Jewish antecedents were well known) "smiling spoke
in favor of mixed races." Freud and Ehrenfels both found themselves in
an unresolvable tension between accepting the discourse of science about
race and the need to position themselves in regard to this discourse. Freud
represses this discourse; Ehrenfels eventually valorizes it.

The image of the healthy family in " 'Civilized' Sexual Morality and
Modern Nervous Illness," Freud's model, is clearly not a Jewish one as
represented in nineteenth-century images of Jewish sexuality. It is of a
family, "living in simple, healthy, country conditions," which has become
ill when the members "had successfully established themselves in the
metropolis, and in a short space of time had brought their children to a
high level of culture."[118] It is, however, the Jews, who are the prime
examples for such social deformation in Freud's own primary sources.
Freud argued that these authorities were essentially correct but that they
"leave out of account precisely the most important of the etiological
factors involved. If we disregard the vaguer ways of being 'nervous' and
consider the specific forms of nervous illness, we shall find that the
injurious influence of civilization reduces itself in the main to the harmful
suppression of the sexual life of civilized peoples (or classes) (*Kulturvölker
[oder Schichten]*) through the 'civilized' sexual morality prevalent in

them."[119] Not race (Ehrenfels's point of departure)—but civilization or class determines pathology. But what do Freud's sources say: Otto Binswanger stated that "among the European races the Jews present the greatest number of cases of neurasthenia."[120] Wilhelm Erb, at a birthday celebration for the King of Baden, commented on the increased nervousness among the "Semites, who already are a neurotically predisposed race. Their untamed desire for profit and their nervousness, caused by centuries of imposed life style (*auferlegte Lebensweise*) as well as their inbreeding (*Inzucht*) and marriage within families (*Familienheiraten*) predisposes them to nervousness."[121] Richard Krafft-Ebing, in one of the standard medical handbooks of the day, simply quoted Erb, that "Jews are especially prone to nervousness."[122] None of this Freud commented upon. His desire is to move the argument about the madness of the Jews away from the question of race and to universalize it.

Human sexuality becomes the universal wellspring of psychoanalytic theory. There are many potential threads to Freud's discovery/construction of this fact. One of them which was quite evident is Freud's careful repression of the discourse on Jewish psychopathology and its relationship to sexual deviancy in the medical literature of his time. Freud "reads around" this problem, confronts all of its presuppositions—predisposition, inheritance, trauma—and concludes that what was present was the ubiquitous presence of human sexuality—in all of its manifestations—within the course of human development. Here too Freud masks the discussion of the meaning of the sexuality of the Jew. In 1926 Freud (in his essay on lay analysis) referred (in English) to female sexuality as the "dark continent" of the human psyche: "But we need not feel ashamed of this distinction; after all, the sexual life of adult women is a 'dark continent' for psychology. But we have learnt that girls feel deeply their lack of a sexual organ that is equal in value to the male one; they regard themselves on that account as inferior, and this 'envy for the penis' is the origin of a whole number of characteristic feminine reactions."[123] Elsewhere I have sketched the implications of this phrase in terms of the medicalization of the black female body during the nineteenth century.[124] But note Freud's vocabulary concerning the sense of inferiority attributed to the woman because of her " 'envy for the penis.' " The question of the woman's attribution of meaning to the female genitalia, specifically the clitoris, is raised by Freud in this context: "women possess as part of their genitals a small organ similar to the male one; and this small organ, the clitoris, actually plays the same part in childhood and during the years before sexual intercourse as the large organ in men."[125] The view that the clitoris is a "truncated penis" is generally rejected in contemporary psychoanalytic theory. To date the only explanation for this view has been found in the arguments about homologous structures of the genitalia.[126] But little attention has been given to what Freud could have understood within this generally accepted model.

The image of the clitoris as a "truncated penis," as a less than intact penis, reflects the popular fin de siècle Viennese view of the relationship between the body of the male Jew and the body of the woman. This clitoris was known in Viennese slang of the fin de siècle simply as the "Jew" (*Jud*).[127] The phrase "for a woman to masturbate" is to "play with the Jew." The "small organ" of the woman becomes the *pars par toto* for the Jew with his circumcised, shortened organ. This pejorative synthesis of both bodies because of their "defective" sexual organs reflects the fin de siècle Viennese definition of the essential male as the antithesis of the female and the Jewish male.

But the clitoris, the "Jew," becomes a sign of masculinity for Freud. In his *Three Essays on the Theory of Sexuality* Freud stressed the fact that the "assumption that all human beings have the same (male) form of the genital" is the primary fantasy of all children (male and female) about the structure of the body.[128] According to this view, all children believe that they have a penis and may lose it (male) or had a penis and lost it (female). The clitoris, the "truncated penis," becomes the sign of the missing (castrated) penis. In Freud's own theory the unitary fantasy of a "male" penis is transmuted into the image of the clitoris as a parallel to the penis (at least in terms of masturbatory activity). In the genital stage the little boy and the little girl masturbate using their "penis/clitoris." It is a unitary "male" penis which unites all the fantasies of the genitalia.

Everyone, male and female, seems to relate to this male organ. The woman must transcend her own fantasy of castration and her penis envy. She must not remain fixated at the level of masculine sexuality but must move to the higher level of vaginal (i.e., reproductive) sexuality. As late as his essay on female sexuality (1931), Freud stressed the need for female sexuality to develop from the early masturbatory emphasis on the masculine genital zone, the clitoris, to the adult sexuality of vaginal intercourse. The clitoris, the "Jew," is the sign of the masculine which must be abandoned if and when the female is to mature into an adult woman.[129] The "Jew" is the male hidden within the body of the female for Freud. The "Jewish" nature of "castrated" female sexuality is replaced by the universal "male" nature of the child's fantasy of the human body. It is this masculine aspect of the woman which must be transcended if she is to define herself antithetically to the male. But with which male is she to identify herself? For the body of the Jewish male is not identical with that of the Aryan. The Jew's penis is different and visibly so. It is the Aryan which is the "healthy," "normal" baseline which determines the pathological difference of the male Jew. In Freud's discussion of the nature of the female body the distinction between male Aryan and male Jew is repressed, to be inscribed on the body of the woman. All of this displacement is colored by the discourse on the Jewish male body (and mind) present within the medical (and sexological literature) of the time. Here is the second reading of Frank Sulloway's history of Freud and sexology—a subliminal one, but one which helped shape the rhetoric of Freud's own argument.

Notes

1. Frank Sulloway, *Freud, Biologist of the Mind: Beyond the Psychoanalytic Legend* (New York: Basic Books, 1979), pp. 277–319.
2. Erich Wulffen, *Der Sexualverbrecher* (Berlin: P. Langenscheidt, 1910), p. 302. This was considered to be one of the major innovative contributions to criminology of the day. See the review in the *Jahrbuch für sexuelle Zwischenstufen* NF 3 (1911): 376–78.
3. John S. Billings, "Vital Statistics of the Jews," *North American Review* 153 (1891): 70–84, here, 84.
4. All of these fin de siècle sources are cited by Havelock Ellis, *Studies in the Psychology of Sex*, 7 vols. (Philadelphia: F. A. Davis, 1900–1928), 5: 185–86. (In the Freud Library, London.)
5. Hanns Sachs, *Freud: Master and Friend* (Cambridge, MA: Harvard University Press, 1946), p. 19.
6. Leopold Löwenfeld, *Über die sexuelle Konstitution und andere Sexualprobleme* (Wiesbaden: J. F. Bergmann, 1911), pp. 75–76. (In the Freud Library, London.)
7. *Protokolle der Wiener Psychoanalytischen Vereinigung*, ed. Herman Nunberg and Ernst Federn, 4 vols. (Frankfurt a. M.: S. Fischer, 1976–81), 2: 41; translation from *Minutes of the Vienna Psychoanalytic Society*, trans. M.

Nunberg, 4 vols. (New York: International Universities Press, 1962–75), 2: 45.

8. The overall literature on this topic is available in M. L. Rodriques de Areia and A. M. Elias Abade, eds., *Consanguinidade: Bibliografia* (Coimra: Instituto de Antropologia, Universidade de Coimra, 1983).

9. Cecil F. Beadles, "The Insane Jew," *Journal of Mental Science* 46 (1900): 732.

10. Maurice Fishberg, *The Jews: A Study of Race and Environment* (New York: Walter Scott, 1911): 349.

11. Rudolph Virchow, "Über Erblichkeit I. Die Theorie Darwins," *Deutsche Jahrbücher für Politik und Literatur* 6 (1863): 339–58, here, 354.

12. Houston Stewart Chamberlain, *Foundations of the Nineteenth Century*, trans. John Lees, 2 vols. (London: John Lane/The Bodley Head, 1913), 1: 366. On Freud's reading of Chamberlain see Sigmund Freud, *Gesammelte Werke: Chronologisch Geordnet*, 19 vols. (Frankfurt a. M.: S. Fischer, 1952–87). (Referred to in the notes as GW.) Here Nachtragsband, 787.

13. On the question of Jews and crime, and the anxiety about violence, in the nineteenth century see Paul Brienes, *Tough Jews: Political Fantasies and the Moral Dilemma of American Jewry* (New York: Basic Books, 1990), pp. 106–12.

14. Wulffen, *Der Sexualverbrecher*, p. 302.

15. D. Ackner, "The Crime of Incest," *Medical and Legal Journal* 48 (1980): 79–91.

16. See the discussion in "The Jewish Murderer: Jack the Ripper, Race, and Gender," in Sander L. Gilman, *The Jew's Body* (New York: Routledge, 1991), pp. 104–27.

17. Peter Pulzer, *The Rise of Political Anti-Semitism in Germany and Austria* (London: Peter Halban, 1988), p. 6.

18. B. Goldberg, "Zur Kriminalität der Juden in Russland," *Zeitschrift für Demographie und Statistik der Juden* 8 (1912): 127–30.

19. Rafael Becker, "Die Hüfigkeit jüdischer Krimineller unter den geisteskranken Verbrecher in Polen," *Psychiatrische-Neurologische Wochenschrift* 33 (1931): 362–64.

20. Walter Pötsch, *Die jüdische Rasse im Lichte der Straffälligkeit: Zuchtstätten der Minderrassigkeit* (Ratibor: Hans W. Pötsch, 1933).

21. Joachim Duckart, *Die Juden von Betsche: Ein Beitrag zum 'Wirken' der Juden im deutschen Osten*. Veröfflichungen des Rassenpolitischen Amtes der NSDAP, Band 1 (Meseritz: P. Matthias, 1939).

22. See Edward Bristow, *Prostitution and Prejudice: The Jewish Fight against White Slavery, 1870–1939* (New York: Schocken, 1983) as well as his essay "History versus Memory: Jews and White Slavery," *Moment* 9 (1984): 44–49, which has an overview of the critical literature on this topic.

23. Franz Alexander and Hugo Staub, *Der Verbrecher und seine Richter: Eine psychoanalytischer Einblick in die Welt der Paragraphen* (Vienna: Interna-

tionaler Psychoanalytischer Verlag, 1929) (In the Freud Library, London); translated by Gregory Zilborg as *The Criminal, The Judge, and the Public: A Psychological Analysis* (New York: Macmillan, 1931). (In the Freud Library, London.)

24. Paul Näcke, "Über den Wert der sog. Degenerationszeichen," *Monatsschrift für Kriminalpsychologie und Strafrechtsreform* 1 (1904), pp. 99-11, here, pp. 110–11.

25. See Sander L. Gilman, *Sexuality: An Illustrated History* (New York: Wiley, 1989), pp. 231–62.

26. See the discussion by Alain Corbin, "Commercial Sexuality in Nineteenth-Century France: A System of Images and Regulations," *Representations* 14 (1986): 209–19.

27. *Der Juden Antheil am Verbrechen: Auf Grund der amtlichen Statistik über die Thätigkeit der Schwurgerichte, in vergleichender Darstellung mit den christlichen Confessionen* (Berlin: Otto Hentze, 1881).

28. S. Löwenfeld, *Die Wahrheit über der Juden Antheil am Verbrechen* (Berlin: Stuhr, 1881).

29. Ludwig Fuld, *Das jüdische Verbrecherthum: Eine Studie über den Zusammenhang zwischen Religion und Kriminalität* (Leipzig: Theodor Huth, 1885), pp. 24–25. He also notes the rate of convictions for incest in the census are for Catholics = 25 convictions; Protestants = 31 convictions; and Jews = 1 conviction.

30. *Archives Israélites: Recueil politique et religieux hebdomadaire* 46 (August 13, 1885): 260–61.

31. *Die Kriminalität der Juden in Deutschland* (Berlin: Siegfried Cronbach, 1896). This is followed up by *Die wirtschaftliche Lage, soziale Gliederung und die Kriminalstatistik der Juden* (Berlin: Verlag des Vereins zur Abwehr des Antisemitismus, 1912).

32. Arthur Ruppin, "Die Kriminalität der Christen und Juden in Deutschland 1899–1902," *Zeitschrift für Demographie und Statistik der Juden* 1 (1905): 6–9.

33. Ruppin, 9.

34. Arthur Ruppin, *Die Juden der Gegenwart* (Berlin: S. Calvary, 1904), chapter 15.

35. Bruno Blau, *Die Kriminalität der deutschen Juden* (Berlin: Louis Lamm, 1906).

36. Wulffen, *Der Sexualverbrecher*, p. 303.

37. Richard Weinberg, "Psychische Degeneration, Kriminalität und Rasse," *Monatsschrift für Kriminalpsychologie und Strafrechtsreform* 2 (1906): 720–30.

38. Weinberg, 727.

39. Weinberg, 729.

40. Arthur de Gobineau, *The Inequality of Human Races*, trans. Adrian Collins (New York: Howard Fertig, 1967), pp. 168–80.

41. Emil Kraepelin, *Psychiatrie: Ein Lehrbuch für Studierende und Ärzte*, 4 vols. (Leipzig: Johann Ambrosius Barth, 1909), 1: 189. (In the Freud Library, London.) See Kurt Kolle, *Kraepelin und Freud: Beitrag zur neueren Geschichte der Psychiatrie* (Stuttgart: Georg Thieme, 1957).

42. Simon Scherbel, *Über Ehen zwischen Blutsverwandten* (Berlin: Gustav Schade, 1883), p. 8.

43. Scherbel, pp. 12, 27 (deaf-mutism); pp. 40–42, (mental illness).

44. Scherbel, pp. 43–44.

45. Scherbel, p. 9.

46. Felix A. Theilhaber, "Blutverwandte, Ehen unter," *Jüdisches Lexikon*, ed. Georg Herlitz and Bruno Kirschner, 4 vols. in 5 (Berlin: Jüdischer Verlag, 1927–30): 1: 1088–92. (In the Freud Library, London.)

47. Bruno Blau, "Die Kriminalität der Juden in Deutschland während der Jahre 1903–1906," *Zeitschrift für Demographie und Statistik der Juden* 5 (1909): 49–53.

48. J. R. B. de Roos, "Über die Kriminalität der Juden," *Monatsschrift für Kriminalpsychologie und Rechtsreform* 6 (1909–10):193–205.

49. de Roos, 197.

50. de Roos, 205.

51. Rudolf Wassermann, "Ist die Kriminalität der Juden Rassenkriminalität?" *Zeitschrift für Demographie und Statistik der Juden* 7 (1911):36–39.

52. "Die Kriminalität der deutschen Juden," *Ost und West* 12 (1912):713–16.

53. Franz von Liszt, *Das Problem der Kriminalität der Juden* (Giessen: Alfred Töpelmann, 1907).

54. Magnus Hirschfeld, *Geschlecht und Verbrechen* (Leipzig: Verlag für Sexualwissenschaft, 1930).

55. Hirschfeld, p. 325.

56. Herbert Maisch, *Incest*, trans. Colin Bearne (London: André Deutsch, 1973), pp. 11–64. Compare Jack Goody, "A Comparative Approach to Incest and Adultery," *British Journal of Sociology* 7 (1956):286–305.

57. Hirschfeld, p. 326.

58. Christina von Braun, "Die 'Blutschande'—Wandlung eines Begriffs: Vom Inzesttabu zu den Rassengesetzen," *Die schamlose Schönheit des Vergangenen: Zum Verhältnis von Geschlecht und Geschichte* (Frankfurt a. M.: Verlag Neue Kritik, 1989), pp. 81–112.

59. Hermann Rohleder, *Monographien über die Zeugung beim Menschen*, 7 vols. (Leipzig: Thieme, 1911–21), 2. Teil: *Die Zeugung unter Blutsverwandten*, pp. 3–8.

60. Hirschfeld, p. 329.

61. Isser Yehuda Unterman, *Shevet mi-Yehudah: Berure Sugyot, Hidushe Torah ve-Hikre Halakhah be-a Rba ah Helka Shulhan Arukh* (Jerusalem: Mosad ha-Rab Kook, 1983).

62. Johann Christoph Wagenseil, *Belehrung der Jüdisch-Teutschen Red- und Schreibart* (Königsberg: Paul Friedrich Rhode, 1699). See my *Jewish Self-*

72   Sander L. Gilman

Hatred: Anti-Semitism and the Secret Language of the Jews (Baltimore: The Johns Hopkins University Press, 1986), p. 74.

63. *Yebamot,* 39b.

64. *Yebamot,* 109a.

65. Edvard Westermarck, *The History of Marriage,* 3 vols. (London: Macmillan, 1921), 3:216. (In the Freud Library, London, in the translation by L. Katscher and R. Grazer [Berlin: H. Barsdorf, 1902].) Of interest in this context is Westermarck's response to Freud, *Freuds Teori um Oedipuskomplexen* (Stockholm: Albert Bonnier, 1934). On the function of this tradition within the anthropological literature see Howard Eilberg-Schwartz, *The Savage in Judaism: An Anthropology of Israelite Religion and Ancient Judaism* (Bloomington: Indiana University Press, 1990), p. 36. On Westermarck see Timothy Stroup, ed., *Edward Westermarck: Essays on His Life and Works* (Helsinki: Societas Philosophica Fennica, 1982).

66. See the discussion of this theme in Hjalmar J. Nordin, "Die eheliche Ethik der Juden zur Zeit Jesu," trans. W. A. Kastner and Gustave Lewié in *Beiwerke zum Studium der Anthropophyteia* 4 (1911):99–104, a periodical which Freud both contributed to and used extensively (see SE 10: 215, n. 1; 11: 233–35; 12: 177–203; 21: 106–7). On the political implications of this theme see N. F. Anderson, "The 'Marriage with a Deceased Wife's Sister Bill' Controversy: Incest Anxiety and the Defense of Family Purity in Victorian England," *The Journal of British Studies* 21 (1982):67–86.

67. See the discussion in William J. McGrath, *Freud's Discovery of Psychoanalysis: The Politics of Hysteria* (Ithaca, NY: Cornell University Press, 1986), p. 280.

68. Hirschfeld, p. 326.

69. Max Marcuse, ed., *Handwörterbuch der Sexualwissenschaft* (Bonn: A. Marcus & E. Webers, 1926), p. 311. (In the Freud Library, London.)

70. Heinrich Singer, *Allgemeine und spezielle Krankheitslehre der Juden* (Leipzig: Benno Konegen, 1904), pp. 22–23.

71. Rudolf Wassermann, *Beruf, Konfession und Verbrechen: Eine Studie über die Kriminalität der Juden in Vergangenheit und Gegenwart* (Munich: Ernst Reinhardt, 1907).

72. Wassermann, *Beruf,* pp. 4–5.

73. Wassermann, *Beruf,* pp. 39–41.

74. Wassermann, *Beruf,* pp. 46–47.

75. See the discussion in my *The Jew's Body,* op. cit., pp. 96–102.

76. Hugo Hoppe, *Alkohol und Kriminalität in allen ihren Beziehungen* (Wiesbaden: J. F. Bergmann, 1906); "Die Kriminalität der Juden und der Alkohol," *Zeitschrift für Demographie und Statistik der Juden* 2 (1907):38–41.

77. Émile Zola, *Nana,* trans. George Holden (Harmonsworth: Penguin, 1972), p. 221.

78. Wassermann, *Beruf,* p. 55.

79. Rudolf Wassermann, "Die Kriminalität der Juden in Deutschland in den letzten 25 Jahren (1882–1906)," *Monatsschrift für Kriminalpsychologie und Rechtsreform* 6 (1909):609–19.

80. Felix A. Theilhaber, "Alkoholgenuss der jüdischen Jugend," *Zeitschrift für Demographie und Statistik der Juden* N.S. 3 (1926):128–34.

81. Ludwig Woltmann, "Rassenpsychologie und Kulturgeschichte," *Politisch-anthropologische Revue* 3 (1905):350–57–84, here, 355.

82. Cited from the English translation, Max Nordau, *Degeneration* (New York: Appelton, 1895), p. 16.

83. See his essay "Höre, Israel!" *Die Zukunft* (6 March 1897):454–62.

84. David Friedrich Strauss, *Der alte und der neue Glaube: Ein Bekenntnis* (Leipzig: G. Hirzel, 1872), p. 71.

85. H. Knöpfmacher, "Sigmund Freud in High School," *American Imago* 36 (1979):287–300 as well as Robert R. Holt, "Freud's Adolescent Reading: Some Possible Effects on His Work," in Paul Stepansky, ed., *Freud: Appraisals and Reappraisals*, 3 vols. (Hillsdale, NJ: Analytic Press, 1988), 3: 167–92, here, 185–88.

86. M. J. Gutmann, *Über den heutigen stand der Rassen-und Krankheitsfrage der Juden* (Berlin: Müller & Steinecke, 1920), p. 18.

87. Gutmann, pp. 25–26.

88. Cited by Hans F. K. Günther, *Rassenkunde des jüdischen Volkes* (Munich: J. F. Lehmann, 1931), p. 273. (First published in 1922).

89. Robert Stigler, "Die rassenphysiologische Bedeutung der sekundären Geschlechtscharaktere," *Sitzungsberichte der anthopologischen Gesellschaft in Wien* (1919–20), pp. 6–9, here p. 7. Published as a special number of the *Mitteilungen der anthropologischen Gesellschaft in Wien* 50 (1920).

90. Havelock Ellis, *Studies in the Psychology of Sex*, vol. 2: *Sexual Inversion* (Philadelphia: F. A. Davis, 1920), p. 264. (In the Freud Library, London.)

91. Freud's primary source on this topic was Cesare Taruffi, *Hermaphrodismus und Zeugungsunfähigkeit: Eine systematische Darstellung der Missbildungen der menschlichen Geschlechtsorgane*, trans. R. Teuscher (Berlin: H. Barsdorf, 1903), pp. 96–103.

92. Taruffi, p. 97.

93. Ferdinand-Valère Faneau de la Cour, *Du féminisme et de l'infantilisme chez les tuberculeux* (Paris: A. Parent, 1871).

94. Henri Meige, "L'infantilisme, féminisme et les hermaphrodites antiques," *L'Anthropologie* 15 (1895):257–64.

95. SE 7: 141–42.

96. Leopold Löwenfeld, *Pathologie und Therapie der Neurasthenie und Hysterie* (Wiesbaden: J. F. Bergmann, 1894), pp. 44–45. (In the Freud Library, London.)

97. Löwenfeld, p. 19 (inheritance); p. 20, note (on hysteria).

98. On the background to the essay see Wilhelm Hemcker, " 'Ihr Brief war mir so wertvoll...' Christian von Ehrenfels und Sigmund Freud—eine

verschollene Korrespondenz," in Jean Clair, Cathrin Pichler, Wolfgang Pircher, eds., *Wunderblock—eine Geschichte der modernen Seele* (Vienna: Löcker, 1989), pp. 561–70. See also Peter Brückner, *Sigmund Freuds Privatlektüre* (Cologne: Verlag Rolf Horst, 1975), p. 62.

99. Sigmund Freud, *Standard Edition of the Complete Psychological Works of Sigmund Freud*, ed. and trans., J. Strachey, A. Freud, A. Strachey, and A. Tyson, 24 vols. (London: Hogarth, 1955–74). (Referred to in the notes as SE.), here 9: 181.

100. Christian von Ehrenfels, *Sexualethik* (Wiesbaden: J. F. Bergmann, 1907). (In the Freud Library, London with extensive marginalia.) This is reprinted in Christian von Ehrenfels, *Philosophische Schriften*. ed. Reinhard Fabian, 4 vols. (Munich: Philosophia Verlag, 1982–90): 3: 265–356. All references are to this edition.

101. On his debt to Freud, *Sexualethik*, p. 296, n. 1; on the problem of our time, p. 362; on the question of the "higher" and "lower" races see his essay "Über den Einfluss des Darwinismus auf die moderne Soziologie," *Volkswirtschaftliche Wochenschrift* (Vienna) 42 (1904): 256–59 and *Die Wage* (Vienna) 7 (1904): 363–64, 382–85; *Philosophische Schriften*, 3: 251–64.

102. Ehrenfels, *Sexualethik*, p. 275.

103. Ehrenfels, *Sexualethik*, p. 276.

104. SE 14: 274.

105. Ehrenfels, *Sexualethik*, p. 356.

106. *Protokolle der Wiener Psychoanalytischen Vereinigung*, ed. Herman Nunberg and Ernst Federn, 4 vols. (Frankfurt a. M.: Fischer, 1976–81), 2: 84–91; translation from *Minutes of the Vienna Psychoanalytic Society*, trans. M. Nunberg, 4 vols. (New York: International Universities Press, 1962–75), 2: 93–100, here 93. He also discussed Fritz Wittels's monograph on sexuality, 2: 74–83; 2: 82–92.

107. On Ehrenfels's sense of his own Jewish ancestry see Max Brod, *Streitbares Leben* (Munich: Herbig, 1969), p. 211.

108. Christian von Ehrenfels, "Rassenproblem und Judenfrage," *Prager Tageblatt* 36 (December 1, 1911): 1–2. Reprinted in *Philosophische Schriften*, 4: 334–42, here, 337.

109. Christian von Ehrenfels, "Geschlecht und Charakter," *Politisch-anthropologische Revue* 3 (1905): 481–84, here, 483.

110. On Weininger see my *Jewish Self-Hatred*, op. cit., pp. 244–51; Jacques Le Rider and Norbert Leser, eds., *Otto Weininger: Werk und Wirkung* (Vienna: Österreichischer Bundesverlag, 1984); Peter Heller, "A Quarrel over Bisexuality," Gerald Chapple and Hans H. Schulte, ed., *The Turn of the Century: German Literature and Art, 1890–1915* (Bonn: Bouvier, 1978), pp. 87–116; Peter Gay, *Freud, A Life for Our Time* (New York: W. W. Norton, 1988), pp. 154–55; Katherine Arens, "Characterology: Hapsburg Empire to Third Reich," *Literature and Medicine* 9 (1989): 128–55 as well as her *Structures of Knowing: German Psychologies of the Nineteenth Cen-*

tury (Dordrecht, Boston: Kluwer Academic Publishers, 1989); H. Rodlauer, *Von 'Eros und Psyche' zu 'Geschlecht und Charakter': Unbekannte Weininger-Manuskripte im Archiv der Osterreichischen Akademie der Wissenschaften* (Vienna: Verlag der Österreichischen Akademie der Wissenschaften, 1987), pp. 110–39; Franco Nicolino, *Indagini su Freud e sulla Psicoanalisi* (Naples: Liguori editore, n.d.), pp. 103–10.

111. See, for example, the discussion in Carl Dallago, *Otto Weininger und sein Werk* (Innsbruck: Brenner-Verlag, 1912) and Emil Lucka, *Otto Weininger: Sein Werk und seine Persönlichkeit* (Berlin: Schuster & Loeffler, 1921), esp. pp. 37–80.

112. Charlotte Perkins Gilman, "Review of Dr. Weininger's *Sex and Character*," *The Critic* 12 (1906): 414.

113. Jacques Le Rider, "Wittgenstein et Weininger," *Wittgenstein et la critique du monde moderne* (Brussels: La Lettre Volée, 1990), pp. 43–65.

114. Ehrenfels, *Philosophische Schriften*, 4: 341.

115. *Protokolle der Wiener Psychoanalytischen Vereinigung*, ed. Herman Nunberg and Ernst Federn, op. cit., 2: 84–91; translation from *Minutes of the Vienna Psychoanalytic Society*, trans. M. Nunberg, op. cit., 2: 93–100, here, 99.

116. Franz Kafka, *Tagebücher*, ed. Hans-Gerd Koch, Michael Müller, and Malcolm Pasley (Frankfurt: S. Fischer, 1990), 370–71.

117. Heinrich Singer, *Allgemeine und spezielle Krankheitslehre der Juden* (Leipzig: Benno Konegen, 1904), p. 25.

118. SE 9: 182.

119. SE 9: 185: GW 7: 148.

120. Otto Binswanger, *Die Pathologie und Therapie der Neurasthenie* (Jena: Gustav Fischer, 1896), p. 46. SE 9: 184–85.

121. Wilhelm Erb, *Über die wachsende Nervosität unserer Zeit. Akademische Rede zum Geburtsfeste...Karl Friedrich am 22. November 1893* (Heidelberg: Universitäts-Buchdruckerei J. Höring, 1893), p. 22.

122. Richard Krafft-Ebing, *Nervosität und Neurasthenische Zustände* (Vienna: Alfred Hölder, 1895), p. 57. (This was also published as part of volume 12 of Hermann Nothnagel, ed., *Specielle Pathologie und Therapie*, 24 vols. [Vienna: Alfred Hölder, 1894–1908]), p. 54.

123. SE 20: 212.

124. Sander L. Gilman, *Difference and Pathology: Stereotypes of Sexuality, Race, and Madness* (Ithaca, NY: Cornell University Press, 1985), pp. 76–108.

125. SE 15: 155.

126. See, for example, F. D. F. Souchay, *De l'Homologie sexuelle chez l'homme* (Paris: Rignoux, 1855). This topic is central to the argument in Thomas Laqueur, *Making Sex: Body and Gender from the Greeks to Freud* (Cambridge, MA: Harvard University Press, 1990).

127. Karl Reiskel, "Idioticon viennense eroticum," *Anthropophyteia* 2 (1905): 1–13, here, 9. Freud makes reference to this volume in SE 10: 215, n. 1.

On Freud's relation to the editor of the journal see Johannes Reichmeyr, "Friedrich Salomon Krauss and Sigmund Freud—Begegnung unorthodoxer Gelehrter," *Luzifer Amor* 1 (1988): 133–55 and Mirjam Morad, "Friedrich Salomo Krauss. Vom Blick in die Seele zum Seelenzergliederer," in Jean Clair, Catharin Pichler, Wolfgang Pircher, eds., *Wunderblock: Eine Geschichte der modernen Seele* (Vienna: Löcker, 1989), pp. 501–6.

128. SE 7: 195.
129. SE 21: 232–33.

4. Reading the Look

Michael Molnar

An image that has been "talked away" is not seen again.[1]

As you enter Freud's library and study at 20 Maresfield Gardens you face a print of Moses with the tablets of the law. A plaster cast of "Gradiva" dominates the doorway; opposite her hangs a reproduction of Leonardo's cartoon *The Virgin and Child with St. Anne and St. John the Baptist*. These are exactly the works of art you might expect to be on display here. But there is one work of art whose absence from these walls is so complete that it never even arouses comment—the Orvieto frescoes of Luca Signorelli.

The Signorelli parapraxis was the first detailed examination of unconscious processes ever to be published and as such it may be considered as crucial an analysis as those of Michelangelo's *Moses* or Leonardo's *Virgin and Child*. But there is a good reason for Freud's apparent neglect of the Orvieto frescoes. Both the Leonardo and Michelangelo studies are in some way or other a form of art criticism, albeit of a totally new type: they talk *about* their object without ever losing sight of it and the image remains the primary material on which the discussion is founded. But in the Signorelli parapraxis images dissolve into words and fragments of words. The processes pivot on the lost name. The pictures which made that name of significance are only mentioned in passing. But these brief mentions are curious and inconsistent enough to arouse suspicion that they refer to charged topics.

Three different versions of the Signorelli episode exist: the initial ac-

"The Preaching and Acts of the Antichrist" from the Orvieto frescoes of Luca
Signorelli. By permission of the Freud Museum, London.

count is contained in a letter to Wilhelm Fliess in September 1898, the elaborated account was published the same year in the *Monatsschrift für Psychiatrie und Neurologie* and finally a modified version of this appeared as the opening chapter of *The Psychopathology of Everyday Life* (1901). The first and briefest account runs as follows:

I could not find the name of the renowned painter who did the *Last Judgment* in Orvieto, the greatest I have seen so far. Instead, Botticelli, Boltraffio occurred to me; but I was sure these were wrong. At last I found out the name, Signorelli, and immediately knew, on my own, the first name, Luca—as proof that it had been only a repression and not genuine forgetting. It is clear why *Botticelli* had moved into the foreground; only *Signor* was repressed; the Bo in both substitute names is explained by the memory responsible for the repression; it concerned something that happened in *Bo*snia and began with the words, *"Herr [Signor, Sir], what can be done about it?"* I lost the name of Signorelli during a short trip to *Her*zegovina, which I made from Ragusa with a lawyer from Berlin with whom I got to talking about pictures. In the conversation, which aroused memories that evidently caused the repression, we talked about death and sexuality. The word *Trafio* is no doubt an echo of Trafoi, which I saw on the first trip! How can I make this credible to anyone? (Freud-Fliess 22.9.1898)[2]

How indeed could that be made credible? The published version in the *Monatsschrift* involves 8 pages of closely argued evidence and includes the most persuasive item of all, the famous schematic diagram:

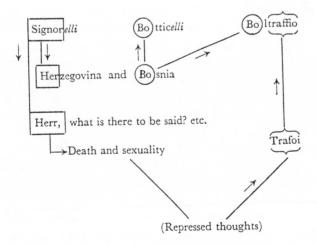

(Repressed thoughts)

Here the forgotten and remembered names have been fractured along fault lines that reveal a structure of linked morphemes and which "may serve as nothing more or less than a model for the pathological processes . . ."[3] The individual elements of this model are highly specific instances, only the "Repressed thoughts" could be held to constitute a general category: it is therefore the mode of connection, the bridged gaps, which provide the scientific paradigm.

The schema is in itself as idiosyncratic and intellectually intriguing as the images it displaces. The associations of sense and sound, the metaphorical and metonymical linkages, apparently form a set of dynamic relations. But there is also a topographic tinge to the plan because the repressed thoughts are at the bottom and the conscious material at the top. However, no fixed locus of consciousness can in fact be deduced. For although only the two substitute names were initially conscious, the remaining associations are eventually retrieved by analysis and become accessible as memories. Only the reticently bracketed "(Repressed thoughts)" remain unrevealed. How they relate to the charged theme of "Death and sexuality" is not made explicit, and though the two factors are connected by a bar, there is no arrow indicating influence. This raises the question—what form of influence or activity do those arrows represent?

At the time of forgetting, the true name (or the *Signor* part of it) was replaced by a sharp visual image of the painter and his work. This forms a synchronic correlate of the alternative names, *Botticelli* and *Boltraffio*, and acts as the conceptual correlate of "Death and sexuality." The arrows appear to demonstrate no more than phonemic substitutions or condensations. The events could all be simultaneous, they could all be happening in a sphere of "pure language." But although the diagram confines itself to verbal associations, the image of the painter should really stand in for the lost name, since it replaces the word in memory and fades when it is regained. It is as if clarity of vision and of verbal consciousness were incompatible.

The schema and the territory it charts are a sidestep on from the diagrams of hypothetical cortical tracks that illustrate the monograph *On Aphasia* (1891). They are one consequence of that book's conclusion, with its rejection of Wernicke and Lichtheim's "brain mythology"—that is, the belief that psychopathological events could be understood directly in terms of brain anatomy. Freud has instead followed Hughlings Jackson in postulating that the "relationship between the chain of physiological events in the nervous system and the mental processes is probably not one of cause and effect."[4] For the time being their interrelation eluded any available explanation.

Freud's "Psychological schema of the word concept" in *On Aphasia* is abstracted from direct physical correspondences. Instead of attempting localization of tracts or centers it presents a functional model of language and, most importantly, the "word concept is linked to the concept of the object via the sound image only."[5] This allowed Freud to divide speech disorders into two classes, namely: "(1) verbal aphasia, in which only the associations between the single elements of the word concept are disturbed; and (2) asymbolic aphasia, in which the association between word concept and object concept are disturbed."[6] The distinction evolved here is reflected in the Signorelli schema where the disturbances are, as here, along phonological or semantic lines of association.

In the *Monatsschrift* account of the episode Freud had stated that an "unmistakable feeling of irritation, similar to that which accompanies motor aphasia, now attends our further efforts to find the name..."[7] This gesture towards an earlier preoccupation is dropped in *The Psychopathology of Everyday Life,* in order not to confuse psychological and neurological issues, one assumes. But some of the conceptual territory of the Signorelli misremembering had already been sketched fairly thoroughly in that work, as can be seen in the passage on paraphrasia (the replacing of an appropriate word by an incorrect, but related word): "In paraphrasia words of a similar content, or linked by frequent association, are used in place of one another, e.g., "pen" instead of "pencil," "Potsdam" instead of "Berlin." Furthermore, words of a similar sound are mistakenly used for each other, such as "Butter" for "Mutter" or "Campher" for "Pamphlet"; and finally, if the patient makes mistakes in articulation (literal paraphrasia), single letters are replaced by others."[8]

There was no good reason for Freud to call attention to these previous states of development in the history of the parapraxis. But, returning to the specific circumstances of the Signorelli example, it is curious that the *Monatsschrift* account dismisses the connection between the Orvieto frescoes and the suppressed topics as only "very slight." The version in the *Psychopathology of Everyday Life* goes even further:—"At first sight it seems impossible to discover any relation between the topic in which the name *Signorelli* occurred and the repressed topic..."[9]. This is a rather surprising denial. The sensuality of Signorelli's nudes as well as the various tortures and executions depicted would seem, even at first sight, more than "very slightly" related to the sensitive issues. It can only be supposed that this virtual dismissal of the images at this point of the discussion is tactically advantageous, in order to focus attention on the acts of the signifiers alone.

As it turns out the repressed images do finally re-emerge, displaced into the following chapter and half-concealed as footnotes to the "aliquis" parapraxis. Here Freud concedes the relevance of the frescoes' theme and also alludes to the abnormal clarity of his visual memory at the time: ". . . so long as the painter's name remained inaccessible, the visual memory that I had of the series of frescoes and of the self-portrait which is introduced into the corner of one of the pictures was *ultra-clear*—at any rate much more intense than visual memory-traces normally appear to me."[10]

Another, minor, discrepancy between Freud's three accounts of the episode affects the actual name of the pictures. In the Fliess letter they are called the "Last Judgment"; in the *Monatsschrift* it is "the end of the world and the Last Judgment" and in the *Psychopathology* "the Four Last Things" [death, judgment, heaven and hell]. This is more or less correct as far as three of the large frescoes are concerned. One depicts the resurrection of the flesh, another the elect being received into heaven and a third the damned being cast into hell. But the fourth fresco, and in fact the only one to which there is a specific allusion in the text—for it is at its edge that the artist painted his self-portrait—portrays "The Preaching and Acts of the Antichrist." This is not strictly part of any Last Judgment, since the coming of the Antichrist only augurs the forthcoming end of the world. Also it is a theme which in itself is unusual enough in Renaissance art to attract any cultured person's attention, even leaving aside that undeniable magnificence of the work to which Freud refers.

This unusual theme has been variously interpreted. One version is that the Antichrist refers to the infamous Borgia pope Alexander VI.[11] However, the art historian A. Chastel convincingly suggests that the Antichrist may in fact represent the pope's great adversary, the puritanical preacher Savonarola,[12] who had dominated Florence until two years before Signorelli began the fresco in 1500. His republic ended 60 years of Medici rule: he took as his motto "Christ King in Florence." The mayhem in the picture could well have revived memories of the recent bloodshed and disorder there. Furthermore, the pile of precious objects in the fresco at the base of the Antichrist's pedestal gives weight to Chastel's interpretation. It appears to refer to the mound of "vanities" Savonarola twice collected from the citizens and burnt on the Piazza della Signoria—where his own hanged body was to be burnt soon afterwards. And it is, incidentally, Savonarola's shadow which falls across the late, religious works of the painter whose name replaces Signorelli's in Freud's diagram, Botticelli—just as the phonic shadow of the Piazza della *Signor*ia falls across the lost element of Signorelli's name.

Whether or not these allusions are actually implicated in Freud's parapraxis must remain undecidable. But there is a strategic respect in which the roles of Freud and Signorelli coincide and this hinges on the artist's self-portrait. In their frank revelation of hidden violence and sexuality, both the artist and the scientist feature as opponents of puritanical repression. Yet both of them, whether standing in the frame of the painting or as commentator of a dream, display a similar ambivalence or unease in relation to the carnal indulgence their work reveals.

In *The Resurrection of the Flesh* groups of sensuous nudes embrace, watched from the edge of the picture by a gaggle of grinning skeletons. These grotesque and anatomically impossible figures seem to have strayed into the picture from some medieval *danse macabre*. And in a sense they have, for there is a disparity in these frescoes between classical nudity and Christian iconography. The lithe bodies of the elect and the resurrected are sexual lures that can only be so blatantly displayed by being simultaneously denied by their religious context. The torments of the damned writhing in hell offer guilty justification to sado-masochist enjoyment. Facing this welter of uneasy sensuality the black figure of the artist himself fixes his severe gaze on the observer, who can hardly avoid the challenge it confronts him with—where does *he* (Dr. Freud) place himself in relation to these images?

In contrast to the other frescoes the bodies in *The Preaching and Acts of the Antichrist* are all clothed. Though violence and sexuality are also present here they are more enigmatic, both because of the curious theme and because of the presence of the artist as an intermediary consciousness reflecting a secondary impression of events through his quizzical glance. Moreover the artist is duplicated in the dark figure behind him. This is Fra Angelico, his dead precursor. Together with Benozzo Gozzoli he had begun the painting of the Chapel of San Brizio at Orvieto cathedral in 1447. During the work one of his helpers fell to his death from a scaffolding. Fra Angelico, finding himself unable to finish the work, resiliated his contract in 1449, having completed only *The Chorus of Prophets* and *Christ as Judge*. (The plunging figure of the artist, Giovanni d'Antonio, seems to be reproduced in Signorelli's frescoes, in the tumbling bodies of the damned and in the headlong fall of the Antichrist.)

Signorelli and Fra Angelico, in dark clothes that distinguish them clearly from all the other figures, stand to one side, half in and half out of the picture. Fra Angelico placidly watches the rampant violence and prostitution in front of him, his finger raised as if pointing out an unheard commentary on the scene. His body forms a single torso with Signorelli, who stands against the *trompe l'oeil* column that frames the scene. He, alone of all the characters, stares out at the observer.

The overlapping figures of Signorelli and Fra Angelico ("man" and "angel") are negatively reflected in a symmetrical couple in the center foreground—Antichrist and devil. These two also blend into a single torso and the devil is whispering in Antichrist's ear. Here is an emblem of deception (or paraphrasia?)—false words from a hidden source. (Savonarola had claimed—"It is not I who preach but God who speaks through me.") Around them figures argue or perform acts of torture or execution, all graphic correlates of the false preaching. Here neither words nor deeds can be trusted, they are all misleading, imposters of the truth. Only the figure of the artist stands in for truth. Its representation is his gaze, the questioning look directed at the observer.

Freud's admiration for the artist marks an identification that makes his parapraxis an act of self-forgetting (*Si*gnorelli and *Si*gmund share the same first syllable).[13] The replacement of the name by a hallucinatory vision of the artist links up with a further dimension of conflict. This is not, and could not, be indicated in the schema since it involves the conceptualization of mental events. The disturbance of the name/image relation and the troubling gaze of the artist might well revive the unsettling question of the place of consciousness in the psychical mechanism.

Freud's shift from neurology to psychoanalysis which occurred in the 1890s is already prefigured in *On Aphasia*, in the rejection of brain mythology and the attempt to establish a theoretical basis for word association. The half-way stage between the two disciplines is recorded in the heroic "Project for a Scientific Psychology" [1895–96] which foundered on the failure to account for consciousness in scientific terms. The stumbling block was that science was concerned with quantity whereas consciousness registers quality: "Consciousness gives us what are called *qualities*—sensations which are *different* in a great multiplicity of ways and whose *difference* is distinguished according to its relations with the external world. Within this difference there are series, similarities and so on, but there are in fact no quantities in it."[14] At the end of the section devoted to "The Problem of Quality" Freud was driven to an entirely negative conclusion: "This transmission of quality is not durable; it leaves no traces behind and cannot be reproduced."[15] In effect this was an admission that the crucial fact of consciousness evaded observation entirely. At this point there seemed no alternative but to abandon any attempt to define it as a process and turn instead to an examination of its representations. This was the sensible course, but the unequal struggle with this central concept had left its mark.

In the letter to Fliess of August 31, 1898 which immediately precedes the one relating the Signorelli case, Freud speaks lightly, almost dismissively, of his hysterical restlessness and complete disorientation. But this pessimism is partly bluff, for it serves as prelude to an optimistic note. There had been progress in his psychology and he had come to a far-reaching conclusion: "Consciousness is only a sense organ; all psychic content is only a representation; all psychic processes are unconscious" (Freud-Fliess 31.8.1898).[16] By marginalizing consciousness "... which was once so omnipotent and hid all else from view..."[17] Freud had at last bypassed the protean problem. But the triumphal and repeated "only" in his letter marks the scene of a long struggle and a strong wish to persuade himself that it was over. The devious tracks of the unconscious processes that are traced in the Signorelli schema are the first consequence of this theoretical advance. Representations and their relationships could now be examined independently of accession to consciousness. But at the time Freud was struggling with the name and image of the artist these consequences had not yet been consolidated and the gnawing problem of consciousness was still fresh in his mind.

In the *Psychopathology of Everyday Life* account a further significant detail was omitted that had been included in both previous versions, namely the spontaneous return of the artist's first name. In the *Monatsschrift* this phenomenon is linked with the fading of the portrait: "I was myself able to add the artist's *first* name, *Luca*. Soon my ultra-clear memory of the master's features, as depicted in his portrait, faded away."[18]

One can again assume that this detail was rejected in the final text as a distraction from the essential argument which concerns the distortions of the surname. But there is another reason why it should be a diversion, since it refers back to the problematic nature of the visual image and, indirectly, to its relation to consciousness. The ultra-clarity of the un-named portrait marks the absence of the word—and mocks the person struggling to remember it. This is a sort of revenge of the metaphor, for while the surname has been metonymically displaced the first name re-mains metaphorically present in the *lucid* vision of the portrait (*Luce* = "light"). Light is the overall context of the image and, like consciousness, it resists theory. Above the artist's head an angel casts the Antichrist down from heaven in a shower of violent rays that smite dead a troop of men, presumably his followers. The artist himself turns away from this cryptic scene in which the imposter is overcome by those merciless rays of angelic destruction. His sideways glance out of the picture is also charged with a potentially destructive force, for his look is at the same time *eine Lücke* "a gap"—or *eine Luke* "a hatch"—in the frame of the representation. As a mute commentary on the images he has created, the artist's glance is inexpressible, or is itself an image of consciousness con-fronting its objects.

Signorelli's frescoes stand at the threshold of modern culture. The medieval ideology they emerge from and the reborn classical art they incorporate are both visible, but breaking out of their frames into a new, baroque universe. Their symbolic content is of course highly relevant to the parapraxis they caused. Even though the admission was reluctant and relegated to a footnote, Freud could not eventually evade the implication that his neo-romantic themes of sexual repression and the transmutation and return of the repressed had been vividly prefigured in *The Resur-rection of the Flesh* and *The Damned Cast into Hell*. But at a structural and stylistic level too the frescoes are of equal relevance to the parapraxis.

On both sides of the doorway of the Chapel figures spill from an arc-shaped fresco above the entrance. On one side a fleeing crowd tumbles out, thunderstruck by fire from heaven; on the other armed men surround a Sybil and a Prophet who gestures towards the atrocities occurring in the scene above. Like Signorelli and Fra Angelico who stand next to them on the neighboring wall, these groups overlap the *trompe l'oeil* frame and thus bridge the gap between the observer and the pictorial space. This novel technique has never quite lost its capacity to surprise and to disturb; the viewer is drawn into the immanent drama of the scene depicted.

Previous commentators have taken up Freud's ambiguous hints about the connections between the frescoes themselves and his own parapraxis. They have not, however, related the parapraxis to the problem of consciousness, nor drawn parallels between the *form* of the frescoes and the nature of Freud's scientific preoccupations of that period. In constructing one such parallel, I have no intention of implying any direct cause-and-effect relationship between the incident in Freud's life and the conceptual problem it may have evoked or reflected. Such a simplistic connection between the life and the work would be the biographical equivalent of "brain mythology." My aim is to read the Signorelli frescoes as a sort of "pictorial metapsychology" and not just a source of charged images. The problems of perspective and viewpoint in renaissance art were quintessentially *scientific.* Conceptually they map out the terrain for future investigations of subjectivity, whether philosophical, physiological or psychological. In the structural complexity of Signorelli's frescoes, Freud might have sensed a foreshadowing of his own struggle to plot the determinants of mental activity. Freud repeatedly stated that artists and writers had prefigured the discoveries of psychoanalysis. His science was consequently predestined to become, among other things, an interpretation of art.

The frescoes inspire admiration as much for their structural innovations as their representational content—the figures in violent motion, the *trompe l'oeil,* the startling perspectives. All these effects are calculated to surprise the viewer, but Freud's *Monatsschrift* account mentions only one particular detail: "I saw before my eyes with especial sharpness the artist's self-portrait—with a serious face and folded hands—which he had put in a corner of one of the pictures, next to the portrait of his predecessor in the work..."[9] In the *Psychopathology,* the uncanny mediation of the artist and his dead predecessor in the broken frame has been shifted out of the picture entirely, reduced to an afterthought. And what of those folded hands, as if the image were refusing to disclose its significance? Yet it does seem as if it is the gaze of the artist which marks the site of Freud's memory disturbance. That glance might be seen, from another viewpoint, as a strange extrapolation of Byzantine iconography (which formed one of the bases of renaissance art). The gaze of a religious icon, however, annihilates its object, for the inverse perspective of the icon places the viewer at its vanishing point. The universe of the icon is infused with total consciousness, the full word which is the Creator and Pantocrator, and there is no space for independent human subjectivity. The Signorelli frescoes, at the opening of another tradition, reinterpret the iconic gaze. It is now *ironic*, it looks askance at the viewer from the edge of the image. Consciousness has shifted from a central deity to the periphery of creation—the unsettling eyes of the artist.

But in the Signorelli parapraxis the eyes are only part of the memory of a face. Beyond the eidetic image of that face the schema, like lines of perspective, creates its own virtual reality—fragmented words flickering in a series of metonymic exchanges. The forgetting and misremembering, all the significant action occurs outside the imagery. About that mechanism Freud states: "Of the whole course of events that have in ways like these produced the substitute names instead of the name *Signorelli* no information has been given to consciousness."[20]

At first reading this simple, and surely proud, statement also fails to yield all its implications, which point back as far as *On Aphasia* and forward to *The Unconscious*. The key phrase is that it is "the whole course of events" which has been concealed. This is important for future attempts to conceptualize the unconscious. The representations through which the unconscious processes advance must exist in a rudimentary form, they are not actually "seen" and there can be no true unconscious images for there is no unconscious observer. But, though they may be incomplete or temporarily forgotten, potential images can be brought to conscious attention. What is however truly and permanently hidden is the system of connections and it is this which is the definitive trait of the unconscious processes.

In *The Unconscious* (1915) what was implied in the Signorelli schema is finally made theoretically explicit in a psychic apparatus that pivots on the word presentation: " . . . the conscious presentation comprises the presentation of the thing plus the presentation of the word belonging to it, while the unconscious presentation is the presentation of the thing alone. The system *Ucs.* contains the thing-cathexes of the objects, the first and true object-cathexes; the system *Pcs.* comes about by this thing-presentation being hypercathected through being linked with the word-presentations corresponding to it."[21] Returning, then, to the 1890s, when the image had not yet been hypercathected, we can postulate an intermediate stage in the evolution of a metapsychology. It could be pictured in the form of Signorelli, standing in the frame between conscious and unconscious processes. In the context of Freud's misremembering, the ultra-clear portrait and the lost word are each split-off components of conscious representation. (When the word is found, the hallucinatory clarity fades, because it was a symptom of reduced consciousness.) The actual frescoes within their frames can stand for the thing-presentations. The figure of the artist acts as their potential cathexis, the channel through which they can be named. As the locus of the word-presentation his image belongs to the dual conscious (preconscious) system.

In condensing a corner of the Orvieto frescoes and a metapsychological schema, I do not aim to interfere directly either with biography or theory. In his writings Freud never returned to that work of art: speculation about its supposed effect on him fades inevitably into fiction. As for the theoretical status of a pictorial analogy, it may well end up restricting the scientific paradigm it supposedly depicts. My aim is rather to restore Signorelli's marvelous and hellish imagery at least to the margins of Freud's work, perhaps into the space between biography and theory where image and significance may cohabit without having to battle for mastery.

Signorelli's glance is wordless but full of inchoate meaning; that meaning cannot be directly connected to the painting, for his hands are crossed. The gesture which links sign and scene belongs not to him but to the dead Fra Angelico. The configuration tempts commentary. The visual image is timeless like the unconscious. If interpreted and drawn into full consciousness—and time—by words, it is doomed. Not to total extinction (an impossible fate) but to death, which is reification.

In a sense the archetypal parapraxis seemed to have "talked away" the magnificent Signorelli frescoes. But that secondary process can never be exhaustive. At this point, therefore, the epigraph with which I began this chapter should be completed: "... an image that has been talked away is not seen again. If nevertheless this does happen we can confidently assume that the second time the image will be accompanied by a new set of thoughts, or the idea will have new implications."[22] Though it has been Signorelli's name and not his work which has entered Freudian theory, the images remained in memory "... which we like to regard as an archive open to anyone who is curious ..."[23]. In the London Freud Museum a folio of prints and photos that had spent the last 50 years in drawers came to light. Most relate to Italy—landscapes, town scenes, reproductions of old masters—probably kept as mementoes of past holidays. And among them one finds a view of Orvieto cathedral and a set of reproductions of the Signorelli frescoes, including a close-up of the artist's portrait. Forty years after the visit to Orvieto, when Freud moved to London in 1938, these images were still with him.

Notes

The German translation of an earlier version of this chapter was published as "Luca Signorelli: Licht und Lücke" in *Wunderblock: Eine Geschichte der modernen Seele* (Editors: Jean Clair, Cathrin Pichler, Wolfgang Pircher) Wiener Festwochen Catalogue, Vienna 1989.

1. "Studies in Hysteria" SE 2:96.
2. J. M. Masson (Ed.) *The Complete Letters of Sigmund Freud to Wilhelm Fliess 1887–1904* (Cambridge, Mass.: Harvard University Press, 1985).
3. "The Psychical Mechanism of Forgetfulness" SE 3:295.
4. *On Aphasia* Imago (1953), p. 55.
5. Ibid., p. 77.
6. Ibid., p. 78.
7. "The Psychical Mechanism of Forgetfulness" SE 3:289.
8. *On Aphasia*, p. 22.
9. "The Psychopathology of Everyday Life" SE 6:5.
10. Ibid., p. 13.
11. R. and M. Karpe "The Significance of Freud's Trip to Orvieto," *The Israel Annuals of Psychiatry and Related Disciplines* 17:1 (1979):11.
12. A. Chastel "L'Apocalypse en 1500: la fresque de l'Antéchriste à la Chapelle St. Brice à Orvieto," *Humanisme et Renaissance* 14 (1952):124–140.
13. Didier Anzieu *Freud's Self-Analysis,* Trans. Peter Graham (London: Hogarth: 1986 [1975]), p. 362.
14. "Project for a Scientific Psychology" SE 1:308.
15. Ibid., p. 310.
16. Masson op. cit.
17. "The Interpretation of Dreams" SE 5:615.
18. "The Psychical Mechanism of Forgetfulness" SE 3:291.
19. "The Psychical Mechanism of Forgiveness" SE 3:291.
20. "The Psychopathology of Everyday Life" SE 7:5.
21. "The Unconscious" SE 14:201.
22. "Studies in Hysteria" SE 2:296.
23. "The Psychical Mechanism of Forgetfulness" SE 3:296.

5. Freud's Uncanny Woman

Phillip McCaffrey

All fear is the fear of death.—Wilhelm Fliess[1]

In an odd footnote in *Beyond the Pleasure Principle*, which he worked on before and after rewriting his essay on "The 'Uncanny'" in May of 1919, Freud argues that Plato's selection of stories for *The Symposium* is significant even when they were not of his own invention (SE 18:58 n.).[2] By the same logic, Freud's selection of examples in "The 'Uncanny'" should also be significant. The sheer *number* of those examples is worth noting; Samuel Weber calls them a "*Musterung.*"[3] Furthermore, although Freud adds list after list of them to his essay, they do not advance his argument which, instead, circles obsessively over the elusive "*besonderer Kern*" ("particular core") of the uncanny which Freud set out to seek but which he never clearly locates (SE 17:219; GW 12:229).[4] If the lists of examples do not fulfill their function of testing and validating Freud's successive reformulations of a definition of the uncanny,[5] then why are they so prominent in his text? It is a fair question, then, to ask why Freud chose some examples rather than others and, if we bear in mind his description of psychoanalysis as an inquiry "accustomed to divine secret and concealed things [*Geheimes und Verborgenes zu erraten*] from despised or unnoticed features, from the rubbish-heap, as it were, of our observations" (SE 13:222; GW 10:185), we might expect the most peripheral of his uncanny examples to be in some ways the most revealing.

The texts Freud refers to as examples in "The 'Uncanny,'" more than forty altogether, compose, in effect, a larger text, a secondary structure surrounding and informing the essay. The members of this secondary structure are linked to each other and to "The 'Uncanny' " by a network of recurring and crisscrossing associations. Since most of the texts are literary, these associations usually manifest themselves by means of literary structures—as plot developments, characters, scenes, symbols, and so on. In this article, I would like to examine one of the unifying elements in this secondary structure of texts, a single motif which centers on a character type which I have called the "Uncanny Woman." Because this motif is embodied in a series of (mostly) fictional characters, it is convenient to treat it as a kind of archetype, as Freud himself did in his "The Theme of the Three Caskets," discussed below. In addition, for reasons that should become progressively more apparent, this "archetype" is most likely to inhabit the "gaps" in the secondary collection of texts, those texts and sections of texts which are most obliquely connected to "The 'Uncanny'." Finally, in order to appreciate the complexity and texture of each of the examples to be examined, and the complexity of their relationships to one another and to "The 'Uncanny'," I will proceed in a roughly inductive fashion, basing comparisons and generalizations on my readings of the successive texts.

As an initial example we might consider Freud's reference to Oscar Wilde's "The Canterville Ghost," the last text he cites in "The 'Uncanny'."[6] He mentions it as a counter-example, a story which could have been uncanny but is not: "Even a 'real' ghost, as in Oscar Wilde's *Canterville Ghost,* loses all power of at least arousing *gruesome* feelings in us as soon as the author begins to amuse himself by being ironical about it and allows liberties to be taken with it" (SE 17:252, Strachey's italics). The point is the same that Freud had made about Mark Twain's *A Tramp Abroad* some fifteen pages earlier, that a humorous tone can reverse potentially uncanny effects (SE 17:237). Wilde's very British ghost is offered Tammany Rising Sun Lubricator for his noisy chains, is frightened by a jerry-built "double," and is repeatedly ambushed, tricked, and assaulted by formidable prepubescent twins. Since the family who has bought the Ghost's house is American, Wilde is able to combine social satire of both nationalities with a parody of gothic fictional conventions. Yet the story's humorous tone veils some satisfactorily gruesome material which might easily have been turned to uncanny effect. Lord Canterville murdered his wife, disappeared mysteriously, and during the next 300 years haunted an impressive number of the British aristocracy into suicide or insanity. His face is not humorous: he appears "in the wan moonlight, an old man of terrible aspect. His eyes were as red as burning coals" (Wilde, 64). But Freud is mainly right in his assessment of the story. It is a question of point of view: the reader sees most of the action through the ghost's eyes and, often enough, what the ghost sees is the vulgar Americans playing gothic tricks on him. What is puzzling, then, is why Freud ignores the one incident in the story which comes closest to creating uncanny effects, its climax. If the story illustrates the neutralizing effect of tone, surely this would be the passage to cite.

In fact, in the climax of "The Canterville Ghost" Wilde abandons his satirical tone in order to render effects which are very nearly uncanny. The narrative sequence begins when fifteen-year-old Virginia returns to the haunted house from a ride with her young suitor: she has torn her dress so badly that she decides to "go up by the back staircase so as not to be seen" (Wilde, 76). Passing a remote room, she discovers the Ghost who has become thoroughly disheartened at his treatment by the Americans and by his inability to frighten them. She sympathizes with his miseries, serious and comical, until finally he complains that he has not slept for 300 years and pleads with her to intercede with the Angel of Death for him. Because she has "the purity of a little child" she can open for him "the portals of Death's house." When she agrees to help him,

He rose from his seat with a faint cry of joy, and taking her hand bent over it with old-fashioned grace and kissed it. His fingers were as cold as ice, and his lips burned like fire, but Virginia did not falter, as he led her across the dusky room. On the faded green tapestry were broidered little huntsmen. They blew their tasselled horns and with their tiny hands waved to her to go back.... Horrible animals with lizard tails, and goggle eyes, blinked at her from the carven chimney-piece, and murmured "Beware! little Virginia, beware! we may never see you again," but the Ghost glided on more swiftly, and Virginia did not listen ... [she] saw the wall slowly fading away like a mist, and a great black cavern in front of her. A bitter cold wind swept round them, and she felt something pulling at her dress. "Quick, quick," cried the Ghost, "or it will be too late"... (Wilde, 79-80)

Thus Virginia disappears; during the rest of that day her family and suitor search for her with increasing anxiety until, at midnight, she reappears "out on the landing, looking very pale and white, with a little casket in her hand..." (Wilde, 82). Asked where she has been, Virginia replies quietly, "I have been with the Ghost. He is dead . . . and he gave me this box of beautiful jewels before he died" (Wilde, 83). Virginia's father offers to return the jewels to the Canterville family since Virginia is only "a child" and "these gems are of great monetary worth" but adds: "Perhaps I should mention that Virginia is very anxious that you should allow her to retain the box" (Wilde, 85). The current Lord Canterville demurs: "My dear sir, your charming little daughter rendered my unlucky ancestor, Sir Simon, a very important service" (Wilde, 85–6).[7] It seems that the reverse is true, as well. A little later, when Virginia has returned from her honeymoon and has laid fresh roses on the Ghost's grave, her new husband, Cecil, questions her:

" . . . you have never told me what happened to you when you were locked up with the ghost."

"I have never told any one, Cecil," said Virginia gravely.

"I know that, but you might tell me."

"Please don't ask me, Cecil, I cannot tell you. Poor Sir Simon! I owe him a great deal. Yes, don't laugh, Cecil, I really do. He made me see what Life is, and what Death signifies, and why Love is stronger than both." (Wilde, 87)

Virginia's casket of jewels may remind us of Dora's (SE 5:64); the transparent sexual symbolism attached to the "little girl" in the passages just quoted runs more or less throughout the story. It is only "little Virginia," for example, "who, for some unexplained reason, was always a good deal distressed at the sight of the blood-stain" which keeps reappearing on the library floor, supposedly the blood of the murdered wife. (The Ghost has stolen crayons from Virginia's crayon box to refurbish the stain [Wilde, 77]). Her disappearance with the Ghost and her return as a more worldly "little girl," complete with her casket of jewels, hints at a sexual initiation. At the same time, her mission has been to encounter the Angel of Death in order to negotiate the failing Ghost's final repose. Virginia thus manages to combine suggestions of innocence and sexuality, and of youth confronting old age and death.

In order to understand the character of Virginia more fully, this child-woman whose implicit sexuality is somehow linked with death, we may turn to Freud's earlier essay on "The Theme of the Three Caskets" (1913). There, Freud compares Bassanio's choice among the gold, silver, and lead caskets in *The Merchant of Venice* with Lear's choice among his three daughters. Freud links the lead casket, the youngest daughter, and the third fate, Atropos: "the third of the sisters is the Goddess of Death, Death itself" (SE 12:298). This third daughter can also be linked with the Goddess of Love, "who had once been identical with her" (SE 12:299), and with Apuleius's Psyche, who "has kept many traits that remind us of her relation with death. Her wedding is celebrated like a funeral, she has to descend into the underworld, and afterwards she sinks into a death-like sleep" (SE 12:300 n.). The figure can be identified by specific attributes, for "the fairest and best of women, who has taken the place of the Death-goddess, has kept certain characteristics that border on the uncanny [*unheimliche*]" (SE 12:300; GW 10:35). In particular, she may be pale, silent, and hidden or concealed; that is, she exhibits one or more traits that often symbolize death in dreams and in some fairy tales.

Wilde's Virginia exhibits several of these traits, as we have just seen. She disappears with the Ghost (whose ancient age is emphasized) into the Garden of Death to help him die and returns, momentarily silent, pale, bearing a casket. (The Ghost himself sleeps in a lead coffin [Wilde, 71].) Her first words after reappearing are, "Papa . . . I have been with the Ghost. He is dead" (Wilde, 83) and, in the narrative, her wedding is bracketed by the Ghost's funeral and by her visit to his grave when she returns from her honeymoon.[8] It is this conjunction of Virginia's virginal sexuality with the weird death of the wife-murdering Ghost which nearly makes her seem uncanny.

At one point in his 1919 essay, Freud broaches the subject of uncanny sexuality directly: "It often happens that neurotic men declare that they feel there is something uncanny about the female genital organs" (SE 17:245).[9] This is almost certainly an unacknowledged reference to "Notes upon a Case of Obsessional Neurosis," the case of the Rat Man (1909), which Freud had mentioned earlier in his essay (SE 17:239). In that case history Freud reports his patient as saying, "There were certain people, girls, who pleased me very much, and I had a very strong wish *to see them naked*. But in wishing this I had *an uncanny feeling, as though something must happen if I thought such things* . . . " (SE 10:162, Freud's italics). A related reaction appears in the later case history of the Wolf Man who recounted a childhood memory of chasing "a beautiful big butterfly with yellow stripes and large wings" until it landed on a flower and he was suddenly "seized with a dreadful fear of the creature, and ran away screaming" (SE 17:89). The explanation for his reaction, offered

"many months later," was that "the opening and shutting of the butterfly's wings while it was settled on the flower had given him an uncanny
feeling. It had looked, he said, like a woman opening her legs . . . " (SE
17:90).[10] Freud's reconstruction of male infantile sexual theories partly
explains this reaction. In his first apprehension of the female genitals, a
young boy finds the absence of a penis "an uncanny and intolerable idea"
(SE 11:95) leading to the conclusion that if the girl's penis is not there it
has been removed and, therefore, he fears that his own could likewise be
removed (SE 10:11 and n. 3).

If we connect these ideas we arrive at the concept of a female figure
who embodies sexuality and castration and death, a figure I would like
to call the Uncanny Woman. As both Goddess of Death and emblem of
castration, her specific manifestations may shift to emphasize one motif
or the other, but her final import involves them both. The absence or
"omission" of castration, the sexual "gap," replays in a different register
as the vacancy of death. One loss represents the other (they are reversible,
to some extent) on the basis of the common fear they evoke—that "(male)
nature abhors a vacuum."[11]

In Wilde's Virginia, therefore, we have a kind of archetypal figure,
one which Freud himself presented and analyzed elsewhere in his work.
But in "The 'Uncanny'," this figure is not allowed to appear directly in
the text; instead of dealing with Virginia as an Uncanny Woman, Freud
elides her in favor of the Ghost, whom he finds not-uncanny. There is
no mention of Virginia's experience with the Ghost or, indeed, of any
of several images and ideas that Freud thought noteworthy at other times.
Still, this oversight or omission would be little more than a curiosity,
taken by itself; it becomes something more than that when we realize
that Virginia is only one of several examples of the Uncanny Woman
whom Freud has ignored in the texts which he cites in his essay. This
Uncanny Woman, whose sexuality threatens castration and death, appears
prominently in several of Freud's other examples, but each time she is
effaced by some other feature of the text which Freud spotlights. Even
when Freud mentions her, her true nature is masked; in Herodotus's
story of Rhampsinitus, for example, Freud focuses his attention on a not-
uncanny severed arm rather than on the princess to whom the arm is left
(SE 17:246, 252).[12] But the details of the narrative clarify the princess's
role as an Uncanny Woman. Her father, attempting to catch the thief
who has been stealing his treasure, commands her to sleep with any man

who will tell her the cleverest and wickedest things he has done. When the thief thus reveals himself, the princess should grab him and detain him. The thief appears, reveals his identity to the princess, and then, as Freud notes, leaves her holding the amputated arm he has cleverly brought for the occasion. Freud's point in citing this text renders it, too, peripheral: a detached arm might well be an uncanny image but here, he says, it is not, because the viewpoint is that of the thief, not the princess, whose alarm we are not invited to imagine. Nonetheless, the princess is an Uncanny Woman to the extent that her sexuality is a temptation to certain death for the thief. The thief escapes by leaving a phallic arm with her instead of sleeping with her; this cleverness eventually wins him the hand of the princess and, by implication, a legitimate share of the (sexual) "treasure" which he had been stealing from the king's chamber.

In two other texts Freud cites, the Uncanny Woman plays a larger role although, once again, she eludes his notice. In discussing E. T. A. Hoffmann's *The Devil's Elixirs*, for example, Freud concentrates on the motif of the double (SE 17:233–4), which is unquestionably prominent in the novel.[13] But the careers of the evil monk Medardus and his double are haunted by variations of the Uncanny Woman. Early in his secular travels, Medardus confronts a witch who spooks his horse with an invisible dead body (Hoffmann, *Elixirs*, 86). Later, after Medardus's liaison with the evil Euphemia, she appears to him in a dream: "I saw Euphemia approaching me in voluptuous beauty. . . . She flung open her robe, and I shuddered with terror; her body had shrivelled to a skeleton, and innumerable serpents were writhing inside it, stretching their heads and their burning red tongues towards me" (Hoffmann, *Elixirs*, 245). Even the saintly Aurelia whom Medardus loves becomes a catalyst for symbolic castrations. In his first sexual attempt on her, Medardus is attacked by her protective brother who "tore madly at my neck with his teeth" (Hoffmann, *Elixirs*, 78). Later, the disguised Medardus goes mad and attacks Aurelia and, he believes, stabs her to death. In fact, however, he has stabbed himself (Hoffmann, *Elixirs*, 248).[14] Finally, as Aurelia takes her holy vows, Medardus's double (or is it Medardus?) leaps into the church and succeeds in stabbing her to death.

Part of Aurelia's uncanniness derives from her exact resemblance to a particular portrait of St. Rosalie.[15] Francesco, the dissolute painter of the portrait, gave it the face of Venus; when it was done, she seemed to look at him "with eyes full of voluptuous passion" (Hoffmann, *Elixirs*, 257).

He prayed hysterically for the figure to come to life until a woman who was "the living image of Venus" appeared in the flesh, bringing with her "a box [*Kiste*] full of jewels and money" (Hoffman, *Elixirs*, English, 258–9; German, 280). Later, when she died in childbirth,

Her neck and breast were disfigured by dark, ugly patches, and instead of her young and beautiful features they found themselves looking at a wrinkled, hideously distorted face with large, protruding eyes. . . . she had been in alliance with the devil. . . her beauty had been but a deceitful illusion produced by cursed witchcraft. (Hoffmann, *Elixirs*, 259)

These examples suggest an additional feature, a variability, in the figure of the Uncanny Woman. It seems that she may be uncanny in quite opposite ways, and that both of these modes are merely variations on Freud's narrative of male infantile sexual theory. If she is uncanny because she embodies a sexual "omission," because she appears to the infantile male observer to have been castrated, she is primarily perceived as a victim. It is his apprehension of this victim which leads the infantile male gazer to imagine his own vulnerability: if she has been castrated, so may he be. Furthermore, the offense which will earn him this punishment would be, precisely, his (visual) possession of the victim. This leads to a new development in the narrative of infantile male fantasy: the female victim may be promoted from an illustration, and then an occasion, of castration to its actual perpetrator. In this version of the fantasy, it is the Uncanny Woman who threatens the young male gazer with her own fate. She is the Medusa, once abused and punished, now vengeful.[16]

Just as the roles of the Uncanny Woman are reversible in this extended infantile narrative, so are those of the male gazer. His role initially shifts from that of passive observer to that of the potential victim of castration, either at the hands of the punitive father or at the hands of the vengeful woman. From this point a further elaboration is open to him: he may imitate the development of the Uncanny Woman and reverse himself from passive victim to active castrator: it is *he* who will castrate the woman.

Thus we are led to recognize two versions of the Uncanny Woman (victim and castrator) and two complementary versions of the male gazer who encounters her (victim and castrator). It only remains to point out that the "later" elaborations of the infantile male fantasy, those in which either the female victim or the male gazer become castrators, are essentially protective disguises intended to avoid the dangerous implications of the original, triangular configuration in which the male gazer must fear castration at the hands of the father.

In the two most comprehensive examples of the Uncanny Woman connected with Freud's essay, this fuller configuration is dramatized. It is the Uncanny Woman as victim who appears so strikingly in Wilhelm Hauff's "The Story of the Severed Hand."[17] Here, again, Freud passes over the most compelling elements of the story in order to fix on relatively minor ones. His reference to the severed hand (curiously, he omits the actual title of the story) is a disguise by displacement. The amputation, hardly described in Hauff's narrative, is Zaleukos's punishment for the murder which is the climax of the story and which presents an image arguably more disturbing, more profoundly uncanny, than any example Freud includes in his essay.

The key sequence begins when a mysterious man with a red cloak meets the physician-merchant Zaleukos on the Ponte Vecchio at midnight.[18] His sister has died and her foreign relatives have requested her body for the ancestral tomb; he wishes Zaleukos to sever her head so that his father can see his dead daughter once more. Zaleukos follows him into the bedroom where the girl lies:

Only the head of the corpse was visible, and it was so beautiful that I experienced involuntarily the deepest sympathy. Dark hair hung down in long plaits, the features were pale, the eyes closed. At first I made an incision into the skin, after the manner of surgeons when amputating a limb. I then took my sharpest knife, and with one stroke cut the throat. But oh, horror [*Schrecken*]! The dead opened her eyes, but immediately closed them again, and with a deep sigh she now seemed to breathe her last. At the same moment a stream of hot blood shot towards me from the wound. I was convinced that the poor creature had been killed by me. That she was dead there was no doubt, for there was no recovery from this wound. I stood for some minutes in painful anguish at what had happened. Had the "red-cloak" deceived me, or had his sister perhaps merely been apparently dead? The latter seemed to me more likely. But I dare not tell the brother of the deceased that perhaps a little less deliberate cut might have awakened her without killing her; therefore I wished to sever the head completely; but once more the dying woman groaned, stretched herself out in painful movements, and died.

Fright [*Schrecken*] overpowered me, and shuddering I hastened out of the room. (Hauff, English, 32; German, 42)

Escaping, Zaleukos finds the house dark and completely empty, the front door standing open. On the street he breathes more freely for he "had felt very strange inside the house [*denn in dem Haus war mir ganz unheimlich geworden*]" (Hauff, English, 33; German, 43). The next day he finds out that he has murdered the Governor's daughter, Bianca, "the loveliest flower in Florence," the day before her marriage. He is arrested; by a legal technicality he is allowed to sacrifice his possessions and one hand in exchange for his freedom.

Nearly all the facets of the Uncanny Woman which we have noticed elsewhere appear in combination here. The decapitation is itself a gruesome dramatization of symbolic castration and the legal technicality which saves Zaleukos from death is, in turn, its reversal, his own symbolic castration.[19] The story is a secondary elaboration of the "original" male infantile narrative, insofar as it is Zaleukos, the male gazer, who performs the castration. But the father is not absent. It is Bianca's fictional father (according to the man in the red cloak) who requires her castration; it is Bianca's real father, the Governor of Florence, who pursues Zaleukos until symbolic castration is imposed on him. As for Zaleukos, his enactment of the part of the male castrator clarifies the way that role develops from the simpler one of male gazer. In committing the decapitation, Zaleukos acts in behalf of one fantasy father; in suffering the consequent punishment of his own castration, he submits to the revenge of Bianca's true father. The implication is that the male castrator merely acts out another, attendant fantasy of the male gazer who, apprehending the castrated woman, must assume that it is the Father who has castrated her. In acting out the castration himself, he is identifying with the Father in order to avoid a similar fate and, by that very act, incurs the punishment he would avoid.

Bianca, the loveliest flower of Florence, also introduces two other, supporting motifs which are sometimes linked with the Uncanny Woman in Freud's literary sources. One of these is the motif of the treasure, or simply money, which symbolizes sexuality. Wilde's Virginia returned from her tryst with the Ghost bearing jewels in a small box, we noticed; in Herodotus's story of Rhampsinitus, the two brothers penetrate a sealed room (built by their father) in order to steal the King's treasure; in Hoffmann's *The Devil's Elixirs*, the monk Medardus begins his career of evil by stealing money from his half-brother double (Hoffmann, *Elixirs*, 46) and the elixirs of the title are kept in a little chest ("*Kistchen*") constructed by Satan (Hoffmann, *Elixirs*, English, 21–2; German, 31). In the case history of the Rat Man, too, it is a question of money, a small debt owed, which represents sexual issues in one of the Rat Man's more elaborately acted out obsessions (SE 10:168–73). We have already seen what a prime motive wealth is for the doctor-merchant Zaleukos, and how deeply it is involved in his castrating murder of Bianca and in his punishment (loss of property and hand); afterwards, he receives a "reward," an anonymous annuity, presumably from "red-cloak," in compensation for his action and his loss.

In connection with the theme of money and treasure, the related motif of the thief emerges with noticeable frequency in these texts. In Wilde's story, the topic appears in a predictably benign form: Virginia's father offers to return the jewels to the Canterville family, as if Virginia had "stolen" them by accepting them from the Ghost. The motif of theft makes minor appearances in *The Devil's Elixirs* and in the idea of an unpaid debt in the case history of the Rat Man, as we have just seen. But in the stories of Rhampsinitus and of "The Severed Hand" it is central. Freud calls the protagonist of the Rhampsinitus story "the master thief"; it is the stealing of the king's treasure which begins the plot and eventually elevates the thief to royal status. In Hauff's "The Story of the Severed Hand," theft assumes more discrete modes in the main events of the narrative, but those are consistently echoed by smaller, clearer incidents, such as Zaleukos's theft of the mysterious stranger's red cloak and the unexplained theft of his own papers (Hauff, 28–9, 35). When Zaleukos finishes telling the whole story to the band of his fellow traveling merchants, a sentinel reports horsemen in the distance, perhaps those of the terrible thief Orbasan, who attacks and robs caravans (Hauff, 38–9).

These motifs symbolically echo the central roles and events in the fantasy of castration. In their vocabulary, the Uncanny Woman is the victim whose phallic treasure has been stolen or she is the thief who steals a man's treasure. The male gazer is the horrified witness of the theft; the infantile castrator is the thief himself. Both of these supporting motifs appear in our last example of the Uncanny Woman where they enhance the most comprehensive and psychologically precise exploration of that figure in the jewel of Freud's collection, E. T. A. Hoffmann's "The Sandman."[20] In this story the Uncanny Woman makes her appearance in the form of the wooden automaton, Olympia, with whom the student Nathanael falls in love. Olympia, though ingeniously animated by her

"father," Professor Spalanzani, exhibits the telltale, morbid traits of silence, paleness, concealment, and statuesque immobility which mark the
figure of death in fairy tales and dreams. Although she, like Wilde's
Virginia, is an "only daughter" rather than a youngest daughter, she
possesses the extraordinary beauty which is a simple reversal of her true
significance. In addition, since Olympia is an automaton, that beauty
takes the specific mode of a disturbing perfection of form and movement,
a perfection which, like her name, alludes to its own superficiality.

Olympia's uncanniness is most apparent in the epiphany in which
Nathanael discovers her true nature. He is bringing her his mother's ring,
intending to propose to her, when he hears Professor Spalanzani and the
peddler Coppola fighting raucously over the doll. Coppola wrests the
figure away from Spalanzani, wounding him with it in the process, and
carries it down the stairs; Nathanael clearly sees "that in the deathly pale
waxen face of Olympia, there were no eyes, but merely black holes. She
was a lifeless doll" (Hoffmann, "Sandman," 163). Spalanzani picks up a
pair of bloody eyes from the floor and throws them at Nathanael, shouting
that they are Nathanael's eyes, which had been stolen from him. By
Freud's unsurprising reading of the eyes as castration symbols, here and
earlier in the story, Olympia recalls Hauff's Bianca in the way she fills
the role of the Uncanny Woman. Like Bianca, she has been castrated to
death and, in addition, is the occasion of the male gazer's castration.
Nathanael discovers Olympia's castration and then his own in quick
succession when he sees her eyes missing and then learns they are "his,"
lying on the floor in front of him.

Olympia thus offers a complex presentation of the Uncanny Woman.
The scene of her exposure offers the most comprehensive dramatization
of the motif we have yet seen and represents the narrative of infantile
male sexual theory in several particulars. The scene of her "kidnapping"
may not match the vivid horror of Bianca's decapitation, but she shares
several key attributes with Bianca. Like her, Olympia is the victim rather
than the perpetrator of castration and, like her, she suffers her fate at the
hands of her father(s).[21] Her castration, like Bianca's, inevitably leads to
that of the male gazer and so Nathanael pays the price with his eyes
which Zaleukos paid with his hand.

The appearance of the Uncanny Woman in the role of victim necessarily
clarifies another feature of the fantasy's basic structure, the identity of
the castrator. He is, of course, primarily the father. Only secondarily

does the castrator become either the male gazer, acting on his terror, or the Uncanny Woman herself, who embodies the male gazer's terror (projected and "turned around on the self"). In the simplest form of the fantasy, the male gazer beholds the Uncanny Woman who has been castrated by the father and concludes that he may be next.

This is the configuration which is played out more fully in Olympia's symbolic castration than in any other text Freud refers to in "The 'Uncanny.'" For once, the cast of characters is complete. Not only does the father commit the castration, but he does so in his double role of "good father" and "bad father," Coppola and Spalanzani, the split figures who represent the father's essential ambivalence and do so more clearly than the pair of fathers in Hauff. And just as the role of the father is more precisely specified, so too is the role of the male gazer. For Nathanael, unlike Hauff's Zaleukos, remains the gazer, not the castrator. His discovery of Olympia's castration quickly leads to his discovery of his own—which occurs exactly because he has witnessed the woman's castration. In his case as in Olympia's, it is the (double) father who performs the castration, who has stolen his eyes, which were also Olympia's. It is an advantage of Hoffmann's gothic romanticism that the castrations occur simultaneously (Olympia and Nathanael have only one pair of eyes between them, so to speak) and that, in addition, Nathanael discovers his own castration belatedly, after it has already happened, thus re-enacting the terror of the infantile male gazer who discovers that he is already, and has always been, vulnerable to castration.

It should thus seem odd that Olympia is allowed to break the barrier which excludes other Uncanny Women from the text of Freud's essay. Yet her victory is far from complete for, as she appears in "The 'Uncanny,'" Olympia is nearly unrecognizable in her true role. Freud adopts a policy of devaluing and effacing her by discounting her uncanniness, by muting the scene of her kidnapping in his summary of it, by shifting his emphasis from her to the castrating father, and by reducing her to a projection of Nathanael's "feminine attitude towards his father" (SE 17:232 n.). He argues that dolls which seem alive do not frighten children and, therefore, the story's uncanny effect must depend on its castration theme, not on Olympia (SE 17:233). His rendition of the scene of her kidnapping flattens out all its anxiety: "The student surprises the two Masters quarrelling over their handiwork. The optician carries off the wooden eyeless doll" (SE 17:229). His description of Nathanael's reaction to Olympia's exposure is based on an

error, as Neil Hertz has pointed out: Freud mistakenly claims that Nathanael recalls his father's death during his delirious reaction to Olympia's
exposure, thus shifting the emphasis from the Nathanael-Olympia confrontation to a Nathanael-Father confrontation.[22]

This shift is completed in Freud's complex footnote analyzing Nathanael's split fathers (Coppelius/Father; Coppola/Spalanzani) and describing Olympia as "nothing else than a materialization of Nathanael's
feminine attitude towards his father in his infancy" (SE 17:232 n.). It is
Freud's most successful defense against the Uncanny Woman, against the
need to recognize her. In this interpretation, Olympia disappears entirely
as a figure in her own right, leaving Nathanael to confront himself in
feminine guise, rather than an uncanny Olympia. Freud's interpretation
thus collapses the chronology of the infantile castration plot by conflating
the moment of the boy's apprehension of female castration with the later
moment of his apprehensive fear of castration. By translating the fantasy
into a confrontation only between the infantile male gazer and the castrating Father, Freud effectively eliminates the Uncanny Woman from
the scenario. She becomes the missing middle term, the "original" embodiment of castration who has, herself, been excised from the plot of
the fantasy and from the text of "The 'Uncanny'" as well. By eliminating
the Uncanny Woman, Freud has eliminated the source of danger from
the fantasy; there is now no longer either reason or occasion to fear the
castrating Father. Ironically, but not inappropriately, his method of eliminating the Uncanny Woman from the text of "The 'Uncanny'" has been
to perform a rhetorical castration upon the text itself, an amputation
worthy of the physician Zaleukos.

This metaphor of textual castration is a clue to the significance of the
Uncanny Woman in Freud's uncanny thoughts, though the figure is not
one which can be reduced to a simple, straightforward equivalence. Nonetheless, two features of the motif stand out prominently enough to suggest
that they might explain part of the figure's interest for Freud in May of
1919. One of these features is the Uncanny Woman's complex and ambiguous association of castration and death; the second is the precise *logic*
by which that association is constructed. Although the two are closely
connected, they need to be weighed separately.

As I mentioned earlier, Freud rewrote "The 'Uncanny'" between
drafts of *Beyond the Pleasure Principle*, which he began earlier in 1919
(Strachey, SE 17:218, 18:3). Several recent readers of "The 'Uncanny' "

have noticed the extent to which Freud banished or diminished the subject of death from the essay. As Sarah Kofman says,

Everything takes place as if Freud could not bear the importance of his discovery concerning the death instincts and as if "The 'Uncanny' "with its successive in-validations, its tortuous procedure, is a last effort to conceal "the return of the repressed" which emerges in the theory: an effort which once again proves the unacceptable nature of the theory of the death instincts.[23]

In addition to Freud's longstanding and well-known personal fear of death, the topic carries a theoretical charge in this context, for it is the theory of the death drive, as formulated in *Beyond the Pleasure Principle*, which finally displaces the first topography and libido theory as the *primary* focus of psychoanalysis.[24] It is in the spring of 1919 that Freud is beginning to capitalize on the theoretical fissures in his libido theory which first appeared, intellectually inconvenient and intractable, in his 1914 essay on narcissism. In an odd sense, perhaps, castration functions—in "The 'Uncanny' " and in the larger, secondary text of examples which surrounds it—as the representative of the libido theory being displaced, now its belated and problematic keystone. That this "confrontation" between two large movements of thought, libido theory (castration) and the second topography (the death drive), should choose the Uncanny Woman as its field is not, finally, surprising, for they had already met there, earlier in Freud's thinking, as we have seen.

A second reason for the invisible prominence of the Uncanny Woman might well be the particular *logic* which that figure implies, the logic of the infantile male fantasy which is the source of the Uncanny Woman in both her active and passive modes. It is the binary logic of presence and absence which structures that fantasy, the logic of the small male gazer who cannot imagine any possibility other than the presence or (potential) absence of the phallus. This is the mentality which Jean Laplanche calls "phallic logic," and which he describes as "an elementary logic, admitting of only two values . . . a logic of contradiction, of opposition, of yes or no."[25] We have seen, above, how thoroughly it operates in the infantile male fantasy of the castrated woman, and also how rich its elaborations are in those texts which feature the Uncanny Woman. It is also, however, the logic which dominates Freud's *other* text, the text which surrounds and brackets "The 'Uncanny,' " *Beyond the Pleasure Principle*. From the famous anecdote of Ernst's *Fort-da* game to the grand juxtaposition of Eros and Thanatos, *Beyond the Pleasure Principle* rematches binary opposites at every level. It is the rhetorical structure of this speculative text as well as its subject matter and, for these reasons, Freud's own mentality as he invents and composes it, before and after rewriting "The 'Uncanny.' "

Notes

1. Quoted by Theodor Reik at the November 15, 1911 meeting of the Vienna Psychoanalytic Society; Reik presented a paper "On Death and Sexuality" and was accepted into the society at the end of this meeting. See Herman Nunberg and Ernst Federn, eds., *Minutes of the Vienna Psychoanalytic Society*, trans. M. Nunberg (New York: International Universities Press, 1962–74), vol. 3, 310–9.
2. All references to Freud in English are to *The Standard Edition of the Complete Psychological Works of Sigmund Freud*, ed. and trans. James Strachey et al., 24 vols. (London: The Hogarth Press, 1953–74), cited as here in my text.
3. Samuel Weber, "The Sideshow, or: Remarks on a Canny Moment," *MLN* 88 (1973): 1105.
4. All references to Freud in German are to *Gesammelte Werke, chronologisch geordnet*, ed. Anna Freud et al., 18 vols. (London: Fischer, 1940–68), cited as here in my text. The Standard Edition renders "*besonderer Kern*" as "common core."
5. Although Freud offers no fewer than twelve formulations of a definition of the uncanny, quotes or paraphrases Ernst Jentsch's definitions six times, and offers his readers more than three pages of dictionary definitions, he is unable to construct a satisfactory definition of the uncanny in "The 'Uncanny.' " At one point he sees this clearly: "It may be true that the uncanny [*unheimlich*] is something which is secretly familiar [*heimlich-heimisch*], which has undergone repression and then returned from it, and that everything that is uncanny fulfils this condition. But the selection of material on this basis does not enable us to solve the problem of the uncanny. For our proposition is clearly not convertible—not everything that recalls repressed desires and surmounted modes of thinking . . . is on that account uncanny" (SE 17:245). I have attempted to redefine the uncanny in a forthcoming article, "Freud's Uncanny Text: Stealing the Letter."
6. Oscar Wilde, "The Canterville Ghost," in *The Complete Shorter Fiction of Oscar Wilde*, ed. Isobel Murray (Oxford: Oxford University Press, 1979), 59–87. Further references are identified parenthetically in my text.

7. See the long footnote which Freud added to *The Interpretation of Dreams* in 1919, in which Frau Dr. H. von Hug-Hellmuth's dream of offering her sexual "services" is recounted (SE 4:142 n. 3).

8. Wilde's story presents humorous versions of several other themes or images which are echoed in other texts Freud cites: the themes of doubling, of money (theft; inheritance), of uncanny mirror reflections, and of decapitation.

9. In this instance Freud associates the uncanny with the idea of the womb as one's first home: "This *unheimlich* place, however, is the entrance to the former *Heim* [home] of all human beings . . . " (SE 10:245); the same connection is treated in a 1909 addition to *The Interpretation of Dreams* which relates the "uncanny life before birth" to "the remarkable dread that many people have of being buried alive" (SE 5:400 n. 3).

10. The butterfly also suggested "a Roman V" and thus referred to the hour of five o'clock, the time of the patient's early (hypothesized) traumatic experiences of a primal scene (SE 17:37).

11. The sense of the womb as an *unheimlich Heim*, referred to in note 9 above, figures here, too, as it does in several key scenes in the texts I am examining: the gothic rooms in which confrontations with the Uncanny Woman take place can be both womb and grave.

12. Herodotus, *The History of Herodotus*, trans. David Grene (Chicago: University of Chicago Press, 1987). Further citations appear parenthetically in my text.

13. E. T. A. Hoffmann, *Die Elixiere des Teufels* (Frankfurt: Insel Verlag, 1978); *The Devil's Elixirs*, trans. Ronald Taylor (London: John Calder, 1963). Future references to both are cited parenthetically in my text. Jung mentioned this novel to Freud in his letter of March 11, 1909; see William McGuire, ed., *The Freud/Jung Letters*, trans. Ralph Manheim and R. F. C. Hull (Cambridge: Harvard University Press, 1988), 212–3.

14. There are somewhat bizarre similarities between Hoffmann's fictional scene and Sabina Spielrein's account of a physical conflict with Jung. See Aldo Carotenuto, *A Secret Symmetry: Sabina Spielrein between Jung and Freud*, trans. Arno Pomerans, John Shepley, and Krishna Winston (New York: Pantheon Books, 1982), 97.

15. Cf. Latin *rosalia*, the annual ceremony of hanging garlands of roses on tombs.

16. Allan Gardner Lloyd-Smith, commenting on Freud's treatment of women in "The 'Uncanny,' " notes the "historical situation to which Freud's own text points in its systematic obliteration of the significance of the female: tame, domesticated and silenced, yet carrying the power of mortality as well as sexual desire; one of the faces of the woman is Medusa's face, the *unheimlich* with the *heimlich*" (*Uncanny American Fiction: Medusa's Face* [London: Macmillan, 1989], 7–8).

17. Wilhelm Hauff, "Die Geschichte von der abgehauenen Hand," in *Sämtliche Märchen* (Munich: Winkler Verlag, 1970), 35–47; "The Story of the Cut-off Hand," in *Tales by Wilhelm Hauff*, trans. S. Mendel (London: George

Bell, 1886), 24–38. Further references to both are cited parenthetically in my text.

18. On the symbolism of the cloak see Theodor Reik, "On the Dream Symbolism of the Cloak," in *The Psychoanalytic Reader*, ed. Robert Fliess (New York: International Universities Press, 1948), 356–8. See also Freud's reference to "the 'red rag' of the sexual factor" in a letter to Lou Andreas-Salomé; see Ernst Pfeiffer, ed., *Sigmund Freud and Lou Andreas-Salomé: Letters*, trans. William and Elaine Robson-Scott (New York: Harcourt Brace Jovanovich, 1966), 83.

19. In his haste, Zaleukos also leaves behind his cap and instruments (Hauff, 33). The legal technicality depends on a precedent: since Zaleukos's crime is a repetition of an earlier one, his punishment will also repeat an earlier one (Hauff, 36–7).

20. E. T. A. Hoffmann, "The Sandman," in *Selected Writings of E. T. A. Hoffmann*, ed. and trans. Leonard J. Kent and Elizabeth C. Knight (Chicago: University of Chicago Press, 1969), vol. I, 137–67. Further references are cited parenthetically in my text.

21. In this respect she is a reversal of the far more usual figure of the Uncanny Woman as active castrator in fin-de-siècle imagery. See, for example, Bram Dijkstra, *Idols of Perversity: Fantasies of Feminine Evil in Fin-de-Siècle Culture* (New York: Oxford University Press, 1986), 352–401; Sander L. Gilman, *The Jew's Body* (New York: Routledge, 1991), 107–11; and Elaine Showalter, *Sexual Anarchy: Gender and Culture at the Fin de Siècle* (New York: Penguin Books, 1990), 144–68. Sarah Kofman treats Freud's attitude toward the castrated woman and the phallic mother in *The Enigma of Woman: Woman in Freud's Writing*, trans. Catherine Porter (Ithaca: Cornell University Press, 1985), especially 68–97.

22. Neil Hertz, "Freud and the Sandman," in *The End of the Line* (New York: Columbia University Press, 1985), 111.

23. Sarah Kofman, *Freud and Fiction*, trans. Sarah Wykes (Cambridge: Polity Press, 1991), 160–1.

24. On Freud's attitude toward death immediately after World War I, see, for example, Peter Gay, *Freud: A Life for Our Time* (New York: W. W. Norton, 1988), 394.

25. Jean Laplanche, *Problématiques II / Castration-Symbolisations* (Paris: Presses Universitaires de France, 1980), 178. My translation.

6. Freud and the Figure of Moses: The Moses of Freud

Harold P. Blum

Freud's identification with and studies of Moses are well known in both the psychoanalytic literature and the literature on art, the humanities, and religion. Following Freud's own writing, particularly on *Moses and Monotheism*, the literature on Freud and Moses has gradually expanded.

With recent and renewed attention to Freud's cultural interests and influence, the Moses leitmotiv in Freud's life and work warrants further consideration. This chapter will explore this theme, integrating the Moses of Michelangelo within Freud's documentary mosaic on this subject, from his family Bible and *Egyptian Dream Book* to his final Moses monograph. Moses had very special, indeed, uncanny significance for Freud in a way perhaps no other historic or legendary figure did. For Freud, Moses was a deeply personal, haunting preoccupation, an attachment and identification rooted in his Jewish heritage, a Biblical, historic, and legendary figure elaborated in his own mythopoetic fantasy. The ancient history he believed was embedded within the legend may now also be related to a concrete representation of a Moses-like Old Testament figure in Freud's early childhood.

In his autobiographic study, Freud asserted, "My deep engrossment in the Bible story (almost as soon as I learned the art of reading) had, as I recognized much later, an enduring effect upon the direction of my interest" (SE 20:8). In 1935, absorbed in his *Moses and Monotheism*, he added in a postscript,

...in 1912, I had already attempted in *Totem and Taboo* to make use of the newly discovered findings of analysis in order to investigate the origins of religion and morality. I now carried this work a stage further in two later essays: *The Future of an Illusion* and *Civilization and Its Discontents*. In *The Future of an Illusion,* I expressed an essentially negative valuation of religion. Later, I found a formula which did better justice to it: while granting that its power lies in the truth which it contains, I showed that that truth was not a material but a historical truth. (SE 20:72)

Freud's study of the Philippson Bible, with its Egyptian figures and its exposition of Moses as a great leader, liberator, and lawgiver was stimulated by both his father, Jacob Freud, and by his Hebrew teacher, Samuel Hammerschlag. Biblical names and personalities, Jacob and Samuel, Joseph and Moses, were part of Freud's heritage mediated through his socialization and education. Hammerschlag had succeeded Leopold Breuer (Josef Breuer's father) as head of the Jewish school where Freud most probably had his obligatory religious instruction. Freud wrote of Hammerschlag, "A spark from the same fire which animated the spirit of the great Jewish seers and prophets burned in him" (SE 9:255).

Considering Freud's identification with the Biblical patriarchs and prophets, and their supreme exemplification in Moses, it was of considerable interest to encounter (with Drs. E. Blum, E. Laible, and J. Sajner) a hitherto unnoticed statue of such a prophet in Freud's birthplace. Placed in the external rear of St. Mary's Church in Pribor (formerly called Freiberg when the Freuds resided there), the statue stood during the nineteenth century in the square of the little town. The statue resembles Moses, and the imposing figure appears to be wearing the breastplate of a high priest of Israel, a helmet with projections suggestive of horns, and to be writing on a stone tablet. The statue has now been determined to be, indeed, an Old Testament Hebrew prophet. The anonymous statue has been identified as Zacharius probably announcing St. Mary's birth (according to Dr. J. Sajner's inquiry of the Czechoslovakian monument authorities) and would have been in the same square with Catholic religious statues, including a regal statue of the Virgin. It is impossible to know what external and inner meaning this may have had for Freud, or his parents and nursemaid. For Freud, as a child, and again as an adolescent, this statue might well have represented or referred to Moses. Freud's later compelling attachment or "fixation" to the statue of Moses invites such speculation. The statuary in the square and in the church is intriguing in biographic associations. The statue of such a Hebrew prophet is probably rather rare in Moravia, a former center of Catholicism and devotion to the Virgin Mary.

Antecedent and parallel to his special preoccupation with the Moses statue, Freud was acquiring a great private collection of statuettes of antiquity. His Freiberg experience with religious statuary in the town and church and his assimilation of different identities, cultures, and languages may all be interrelated. Moses literally and figuratively is inside and outside the church, the sublime Hebrew prophet whom Freud visits, fears, and reveres in the (Freiberg) square and in church (the Church of St. Peter in Chains in Rome). By the time of his return to Freiberg in adolescence, Freud had been deeply influenced by the Philippson Bible exposition and Egyptian illustrations, and by ancient history and the classics. Screen memories of his childhood were activated in the context of his adolescent experience in Freiberg.

Jones noted that Moses represented a formidable father image as well as Freud himself.[1] Freud was probably familiar with reproductions of the Michelangelo statue from the plaster copy in the Vienna Academy of Art. On his very first trip to Rome in 1901, he went to see the Moses of Michelangelo. It is an awe-inspiring sculpture of artistic power, and grandeur. Freud, indeed, reacted to the statue with attraction, fascination, and wonder. He stated in a postcard to his wife that upon gazing at the statue he expected Moses to move at any moment. Then, proceeding toward the statue's later interpretation, he remarked, "I have come to understand the meaning of the statue by contemplating Michelangelo's intention."[2]

This was just the summer after his argument and break with Fliess and his overcoming his inhibition to enter the promised land of Rome. He visited the statue on all his visits to Rome, and Moses and Rome were rather inseparable. In Rome, 1912, he wrote to his wife that he was visiting Moses every day. Freud not only analyzed Moses, but he had a daily analytic session with Moses! Moses came to life, reborn as Freud's idealized self, object, and self-object, alter ego and ego ideal, replacing Fliess. Fliess and Moses were transference objects, while Freud was actually analyst and analysand. Fliess was the last mortal toward whom Freud had such an intensive, extensive transference relationship. When Freud relinquished Fliess, the sculptured Moses was further utilized as a concrete "living" presence, a partially externalized object and self-representation serving the remodeled internalization and consolidation of Freud's analytic ideals and identity.

In his writings, Freud described his deeply personal reaction to the Moses statue.

No piece of statuary has ever made a stronger impression on me than this. How often I have mounted the steep steps from the unlovely Corso Cavour to the lonely piazza where the deserted church stands and have essayed to support the angry scorn of the hero's glance? Sometimes I have crept cautiously out of the half gloom of the interior as though I myself belong to the mob upon whom his eye is turned—the mob which can hold fast no conviction, which has neither faith nor patience, and which rejoices when it has regained its illusory idols. (SE 13:213).

Freud had been then the apostle, regularly "going to church."

When Freud was writing his essay on the Moses statue Jones was visiting Rome, and Freud wrote to him: "Bring my deepest devotion to Moses, and write me about him." Jones replied, "My first pilgrimage the day after my arrival was to convey your greetings to Moses, and I think he unbent a little from his haughtiness. What a statue!"[3] Four dimensions of Moses converged for Freud in the larger than life sculpture, the historical Moses, the Moses of the Bible legend, the Moses depicted by Michelangelo, and the Moses of Freud. The personal dimension of Freud's relationship to Moses was almost explicitly autobiographical. It was a relationship which was maintained for a lifetime, but which also had its own development and vicissitudes. He identified with Moses on different levels of development, from childhood to old age, from global to selective attributes, from concrete image to abstract functions, influenced by analytic and life experience.

While Freud withers under the wrathful stare of old Brucke in the Non Vixit dream, it is extraordinary for him to really flinch and retreat from an angry glare of a person, let alone a statue (SE 4:422)! Jones sent Freud, at his request, photos taken from the lower edge of the Tables of the Law. For Freud prior interpretations of the statue and the artist's intent, by art historians, were open to complete contradictions. Freud analyzed this sculpture from almost every angle and point of view and proposed a sequence of movements that he presumed preceded the moment depicted by the statue. Freud noted that Moses was seated, clasping the upside down tablets carelessly under his right arm, the right forefinger clasping his beard, the imminent left foot movement, the face expressing a mixture of wrath, pain, and contempt. The inferences remain controversial, but the movements may significantly be regarded as projections of Freud's inner conflicts, feelings, and analytic journeys.[4] He laboriously, obsessively deconstructed and reconstructed the art work, its motive and meaning. Though he was interested in the creative artist as in his work on Leonardo, Freud was not primarily concerned here with Michelangelo, the creator, but with Moses—the lawgiver, leader, liberator, awesome prophet, and "creator of the Jewish people." It was as if Moses was almost a living heroic, idealized, immortal, and monumental figure. As a "double," Moses was the omnipotent protector and prophet with whom Freud identified, avoiding death, loss, rivalry, and narcissistic mortification.[5]

Freud was identified with Moses and Michelangelo, Pope Julius, his parents, and his Catholic nursemaid. Freud's brother Julius, who died in infancy, was a significant "revenant" associated with Rome. Pope Julius II had commissioned the Moses statue for his tomb in the city of Julius Caesar, so that Moses represents sibling as well as parent conflicts. Freud identified with Pope Julius who "desired to bring about single-handed what was not to happen for several centuries, and then only through the conjunction of many alien forces; and he worked alone, with impatience, . . . (SE 13:233). Julius and Moses were also linked in Freud's parapraxis concerning the name Julius Mosen.[6] (His maternal uncle, Julius, had died just one month before his brother Julius.) Freud's unconscious attitude toward Moses, as toward his father and brother, was ambivalent and conflicted. Surpassing ambition could be destructive and self-destructive.

Freud was fearful of the wrath of Moses for his incestuous, parricidal, and fratricidal wishes, fantasies of crime and punishment activated in his transference to Fliess. He was in high spirits, but his manifest behavior was more of the devoted pilgrim rather than the oedipal victor. Moses is invoked both as prohibition and as punishment for forbidden impulses and as protection against dire consequences. In this connection, it is noteworthy that Freud's description of the Moses of Michelangelo as frozen forever in his wrath omits the murderous, vengeful Moses of the Bible story. The sculpted, wrathful, retaliatory Moses is reminiscent of the stone Commendatore in *Don Giovanni*, one of Freud's favorite operas. The Biblical Moses was infuriated by the renegades who had returned to the worship of the golden calf and requested their execution after he had smashed the sacred stone Tablets in rage. Michelangelo probably depicted the Moses who had received the divine commandments again, and was reflecting celestial light on his second descent from Mt. Sinai. *Karan* in Hebrew, meaning "was radiant," was mistranslated as *keren*, "cornuate," horns.

Freud clearly preferred the restrained Moses of renunciation, with self-control, liberated from the sway of heated passions. Freud had noted the character change in Moses from the hot-tempered avenger who had earlier killed an Egyptian for the mistreatment of a Hebrew. Freud's father had referred to "the broken tablets of the law" in his Hebrew inscription and dedication to his son, when he presented the rebound family Bible to him on the occasion of Sigmund Freud's thirty-fifth birthday. Jacob Freud compared the new binding and covering of the Philippson Bible to the preservation of the Tablets. Freud, identified with his father, would later presume that the Tablets were indeed preserved because in his view they had never been broken by Moses in the first place. The Moses myth was recreated in Freud's image, and Freud's self and superego were transformed by successive and selective identifications with Moses.[7] The Tablets and Mosaic code may be regarded as inspiration for the later theory of the superego, its developmental origins, and relation to religion and culture.

Although Freud struggled with oedipal conflict and guilt because of his oedipal conquest of Rome, he gradually became secure and confident in his analytic identity and in his Moses role as patriarch of psychoanalysis. Transcending Michelangelo's magnificent graven image, Freud created a "new species of himself" as Moses through "analytic interpretation" and "reconstruction."

Freud proposed an historical development for the Michelangelo statue:

The Moses we have reconstructed will neither leap up nor cast the Tables from him. What we see before us is not the inception of a violent action but the remains of a movement that has already taken place. In his first transport of fury, Moses desired to act, to spring up and take vengeance and forget the Tables, but he has overcome the temptation, and he will now remain seated and still, in his frozen wrath and in his pain mingled with contempt. Nor will he throw away the Tables so that they will break on the stone, for it is on their especial account that he has controlled his anger; it was to preserve them that he kept his passion in check. In giving way to his rage and indignation, he had to neglect the Tables, and the hand which upheld them was withdrawn. They began to slide down and were in danger of being broken. This brought him to himself. He remembered his mission and for its sake renounced an indulgence of his feelings. His hand returned and saved the unsupported Tables before they had actually fallen to the ground... (SE 13:299–230)

"Michelangelo had placed a different Moses on the tomb of the Pope, one superior to the historical or traditional Moses. He had modified the theme of the broken tablet..." (SE 13:233). Freud "created" an exalted Moses through Michelangelo, identifying with the artist's creative interpretation of Moses in stone. He chose to interpret the reverse of those critics who assumed Michelangelo's Moses was about to rise and smash the Tablets, and he chose to not interpret the horns. His Moses was also neither the victorious horned conqueror of the totem bull-God described by Reik, nor the cuckold whose horns connote castration.[8]

It is interesting to note that Freud (1914) alluded to other artistic renditions of Moses, including that in an artist's birthplace: "Moreover, such deviations from the scriptural text were by no means unusual or disallowed to artists. A celebrated picture by Parmigiano possessed by his native town depicts Moses sitting on the top of a mountain and dashing the Tables to the ground,..." (SE 13:232).

Was the sculpture a depiction of a moment in the life of Freud and/or Moses, a study of character; a personal and historical crisis and a crisis in the psychoanalytic movement? Freud assumed that he corrected the questionable Biblical thesis that Moses had destroyed the Tables. The manifest statue represented the inner progressive mastery of infantile attitudes and irrational passions.[9]

Beyond his identification with Joseph the Son and interpreter of dreams, Freud had also become the father, the Moses-like founder and leader of the psychoanalytic "movement." Freud is the reverential son, but also the revolutionary son who has overturned established paradigms and traditions.[10] Emancipator from the tyranny of the infantile unconscious, he is simultaneously the rival leader of the mob upon whom Moses' eye is turned and the disappointed, rageful incarnation of Moses.[11]

At the time (1914) Freud wrote "The Moses of Michelangelo," he was identified with Moses in his restrained wrath over the bitter disappointment he experienced in Jung, Adler, and Stekel. The Moses essay just preceded his polemical "On the History of the Psychoanalytic Movement" (1914). He had written to Ferenczi, referring to the separation from Stekel, "At the moment, the situation in Vienna makes me feel more like the historical Moses than the Michelangelo one."[12] By contrast, in 1909 Freud had written to Jung, "If I am Moses, then you are Joshua and will take possession of the Promised Land of psychiatry, which I shall only be able to glimpse from afar."[13] Jung, Gentile apostle to the non-Jewish wider world, was also to be the prophet to psychiatry. Freud hoped for a binding analytic influence in psychiatry.

This same identification with Moses, seeing the Promised Land from afar, a Land he is forbidden to enter, can be found in the "Rome Dreams" and the dream of "My Son, the Myops" (SE 4:269). Rome was the forbidden city which Freud could enter only after his self-analysis—a city Freud associated with Moses and Jerusalem, with parents, brother, and nursemaid.

The totemic Moses interdicted and invited Freud's entry into the taboo Roman arena. Freud traversed the forbidden territory of the unconscious, with the attainment of inner freedom from infantile inhibition and prohibition.

Freud's attitude toward publication of his first Moses essay was also strange and uncomfortable. He was adamant about remaining anonymous, even when pressed by Jones and Ferenczi to identify himself. We know he had published "Screen Memories" in disguise, and this paper was also self-analytic autobiography. Freud was clearly ambivalent toward publication of his Moses paper and wrote to Jones, "Why disgrace Moses by putting my name on it?" (Jones, 1955:366).

The name deletions coincide with Freud's concern that his own name and discoveries were overlooked by Jung and others, and Freud's own change of his first name from Sigismund to Sigmund in his teen years. This name change appears to be related to Freud's adolescent and Jewish identity, and conflict over names and name effacement will reappear in *Moses and Monotheism* (SE 23).

To Jones and to Abraham he wrote, "It is only a joke."[14] Spruiell explicated Freud's "Moses of Michaelangeo" as a private joke and as a creative interpretation. He discussed Freud's extraordinary imagination and identification with Michelangelo and the creative artists and thinkers with whom Freud's own thought converged.[15] The joke is related to the hubris of the creator. Freud's fantasy murder of father, son, and brother could be benignly treated as a private joke.

Significantly, Freud actually began his first Moses paper on Christmas

Day, about seven months after *Totem and Taboo,* and in the same month as "On Narcissism" and "On the History of the Psychoanalytic Movement." He was then bitterly disappointed by Jung's defection and bigotry, and he identified with Moses exerting control over his own emotional turmoil.[16] Freud's identity and self-esteem had been assaulted, and just after his September 1913 quarrel with Jung he wrote to Abraham from Rome, "The Jew survives it." Freud would return to Moses on a new plane in his final years, facing Nazi anti-analytic and anti-Semitic policies. The Moses of Michelangelo was Freud's totem figure and "double." The identity conflict is clear in the essay's timing, and in the withholding of his name. His being an amateur in art history, uncertainty about his interpretation could hardly explain his anonymity. He had effaced his name from this Moses essay in noncompetitive deference to both Moses and Michelangelo, as if his name would replace the others. He also wished to withhold the essay's autobiographical character. Moses had tried to re-establish the monotheism of Akhenaten, and Akhenaten's name had been effaced by a reactionary Egyptian rebellion, just as Akhenaton had effaced his father's name and defaced his monuments. (Freud had fainted in Jung's presence during their disagreement over interpretation of Akhenaten's desecration of paternal monuments. This probably occurred in the same hotel room where he had argued with Fliess). Freud complained that Jung and Riklin wrote analytic articles without mentioning his name. He inferred that his own name and discoveries were to be effaced, a symbolic form of murder.[17]

The name and paternity issues are reminiscent of Freud's overlooking the role of Fliess in the theory of bisexuality and infantile sexuality. Fliess and other rivals vanished in the Non Vixit dream; Freud's associations led to his preoedipal ambivalently loved "playmates," his brother Julius, and nephew John, who were unconsciously deprived of existence. This could be the fate of Akhenaten, Moses, and Freud. But Moses endures in the "immortal" stone of Michelangelo, and the "immortal" stone Tablets described in the Bible. Freud's grandiose, victorious self is here identified with Moses, with hidden narcissistic as well as oedipal gratification. In citing *A Dream of Bismarck* by Hanns Sachs, Freud in 1900 noted the unconscious meaning of the "Biblical scene in which Moses struck water from a rock for the thirsting Children of Israel. . . . The prohibited seizing of the rod . . . , the production of fluid from its blow, the threat of death— in these we find all the principal factors of infantile masturbation united"

(SE 4:380). Moses was punished by being forbidden to enter the promised land; he was allowed only to see it. Bismarck's victorious dream represented erotic conquest, and Freud identified his father (who had the same birthday as Bismarck) and Moses with each other.

Freud also did not "disgrace" Moses by his submissive devotion to Moses, and by repression of the hostile side of his ambivalence. He resolved oedipal conflicts, and repaired narcissistic injuries and frustrations by his conscious and unconscious identification with Moses. He had associated in his Rome dreams to Moses, to the "via Dolorosa" of the indigent Jew, to Hannibal, the avenging foe of the Romans with whom Freud sympathized, and to Winckelmann, the archeologist, who entered Rome after agreeing with the Pope to become a converted Roman Catholic. Freud had renounced any presumed temptation to go to Rome to convert to Catholicism. He would not accept the anti-Semitic humiliation to which his father had submitted without protest. At the same time, "going to Church and worshipping graven images" was a disavowal and denigration of Moses, so that Freud incurred the wrath of Moses. Freud stated, "To my youthful mind Hannibal and Rome symbolized the conflict between the tenacity of Jewry and the organization of the Catholic church. And the increasing importance of the effects of the anti-Semitic movement upon our emotional life helped to fix the thoughts and feelings of those early days. Thus the wish to go to Rome had become in my dream-life a cloak and symbol for a number of other passionate wishes" (SE 4:196–97). Freud, the iconoclast, collected and venerated sculptures of antiquity which were ties to and departures from his Hebrew origins and classical views. The statue of Moses is similar to the "Moses-like" and mysterious statues that Freud had observed in Freiberg, and the statues of ancient deities which adorned Freud's study and desk. The Egyptian idols, condemned by Moses, also represented Moses. The statuettes on his desk had many meanings for Freud, including concrete representations of images and of the past in the present; loss and replacement; death and immortality.

After more than ten years of regular visits to "Moses," it took another ten years before Freud withdrew his anonymity in 1924, and thirteen years until he published, "a supplementary to 'The Moses of Michelangelo'." This paper was based upon a twelfth-century Moses statue which depicted Moses in just the poses which Freud had postulated as preceding Michelangelo's representation. Twenty years after writing "The Moses of Michelangelo", as he was preparing to begin his *Moses and Monotheism*, Freud wrote of the earlier essay, "My feeling for this piece of work is rather like that towards a lovechild. For three lonely September weeks in 1913 I stood everyday in the church in front of the statue, studied it, measured it, sketched it until I captured the understanding for it which I ventured to express in the essay only anonymously. Only much later did I legitimatize this non-analytical child" (SE 23:367).

Freud's association to an illicit love probably refers to both the unconsciously incestuous objects and temptations which Moses prohibits, and to his worshipful fear and love of Moses. Feminine identification, Moses as the primordial mother, and the omnipotent phallic mother who sets limits and imposes rules are not considered here. Freud actually "effaced" another name in this conection, a Moses figure who was a neighbor in Vienna. Theodore Herzl lived on Freud's street, and actually lived out a Moses dream by becoming the founder of modern political Zionism. Freud noted his attendance at Herzl's play, *The New Ghetto*, in a letter to Fliess (January 4, 1898), but omitted Herzl's name when he associated to the play in his published dream of "My Son, the Myops" (SE 4:442). Freud probably did not seek to meet Herzl, a Moses "double." He sent a copy of the *Interpretation of Dreams* to Herzl in 1902, hoping for a press review and referring to Herzl as "the poet and the fighter for the human rights of our people."[18]

Conflict over parenthood and origins, probably related to Freud's family romance, would again specifically focus upon Moses. I shall refer here to Freud's final work on Moses as it relates to the themes of this chapter. Freud undertook *Moses and Monotheism* as another unrestrained, murderous mob threatened a chaotic overthrow of civilized morality. Like his father and grandfather Jacob, he would have to emigrate, and like Moses, he anticipated the exodus from barbarism and bondage to the new promised land, England. This doubtless reactivated the confused, obscured exodus from Freiberg, the forbidden land of infancy. Aged and dying, Freud was doubtless also concerned with self and object loss and survival and with preservation of the corpus and tenets of psychoanalysis.

Freud had turned to Moses at moments of great inner and outer threat, associated with murderous aggression. He visited Moses as he arrived in Rome and departed from Fliess; he wrote his first Moses essay as he was enraged over the defection of Jung; he began *Moses and Monotheism* with all that he cherished imperiled and engulfed in social regression and primitive aggression. The *Moses and Monotheism* monograph was planned the month after Freud's books were burned by the Nazis. At a point of massive external and internal threats, it was a response precipitated by the burned books and the premonition of exodus and death. He was attacked from within by cancer and old age, and from without by the Nazis, with threats to humanity, and, particularly, to his family, the Jewish people, and psychoanalysts. Moses remained a figure of sublime stability and integrity, an omnipotent idealized parent who would always provide orientation and direction.

Freud's irregularly revised, piecemeal publication of *Moses and Monotheism* was again hesitant and protracted. He wrote two Prefaces and three chapters, suppressing publication and then publishing the first two chapters independently in *Imago*. His previously unpublished introduction has now been presented in illuminating historical context by Yerushalmi.[19] Concerned about the social, religious, and political implications of the work, *Moses and Monotheism* was also a deeply conflicted, personal, endeavor. He did not complete publication of this historically and scientifically controversial, dense, and disturbing monograph until he was safely in England. He expressed fears of bringing about a prohibition of psychoanalysis where it was previously tolerated, and thought that he would alienate many Jews by publication. He claimed Moses was originally Egyptian rather than Jewish, removing Moses and himself from Jewish descent. He then inferred that Jews had murdered Moses, analogous to the killing of Christ. Moses was once a murderer, himself murdered and immortalized in his work and accomplishment.

Ambivalent toward "Jewishness," the monograph was hardly a major repudiation of his Jewish heritage and identity. He averred that Mosaic influence had given preeminence to intellectual labors in the life of the Jewish people and helped to check brutality and the tendency to violence. The monograph was an elusive, tortuous expression of his analytic autobiography and Jewish identity and an exploration of group psychology. Why and how had the Jewish people been formed and survived as a group, and why were they the object of such relentless persecution? A central theme was that the Jewish people had a group identity and character, created and shaped by the man Moses. Within the many layers of meaning, his Moses studies are disguised self-revelations and explorations. Wallace noted that there was a wealth of information about Freud in *Moses and Monotheism* which cannot be exhausted in any single paper.[20]

Freud was also dealing with the traumatic present through the metaphor of the past, linked with the reconstruction of childhood trauma. The mass embrace of Hitler engendered a confrontation with Jewish identifications and identity, exposure to anti-Semitic, anti-analytic, dehumanizing attitudes, an exodus of Jews and analysts, and group psychological concerns with regression and massacre, and the question of reinstatement of morality after murder. The repressed trauma of the past had returned exerting negative contemporary influence, although possibly offering the mastery of destiny through insight.[21]

Freud's (unpublished) original subtitle was to have been *The Man, Moses: A Historical Novel,* and Freud, indeed, attempted to determine the historical truth within the legends and religious myths of Moses. The novel, like the statue, also portrayed the "Man, Moses." Freud attempted to ascertain the true identity of Moses (as he had also done for Shakespeare). Moses (as Shakespeare) is inferred to be of actual aristocratic origin, in a reversal of the humble parents of the family romance. Freud thought there were two historical Moses. The first "Egyptian" Moses, murdered by a Semitic primal horde, was condensed with a later Moses. Personal oedipal fantasy and guilt were replaced by an historic deed and group remorse. Freud, however, criticized the Jews for their refusal to admit this primal parricide. Freud implies collective Jewish guilt, and a need to confess, as if he here identified with the aggressor's depiction of the Jews as "Christ killers."

The complexities of Freud's Jewish identity are apparent, and in the deeply anti-Semitic culture in which he lived and worked, his Jewish identity was forged in his Jewish identifications and attachments but also in response to the anti-Semitic surround. His work on Moses depicts both sides of the ambivalence—his strong, positive Jewish identity and unconscious anti-Jewish attitudes in which the Jews are blamed for their persisting obstinate refusal to accept the Christian position and are blamed for their own misfortunes. Freud was probably the first person to recognize identification with the aggressor and, significantly, this was in connection with anti-Semitism. In his dream associations he recognized his identification with the minister who would not promote colleagues because they were Jewish. Freud treats the colleagues as though one were a simpleton and the other a criminal. He analyzed his defensive rationalizations which were used as a cover, similar to ministerial propaganda, to disguise the prejudice against Jewish professionals. Freud had been passed over for promotion to the equivalent of Associate Professor at the time he identified with the anti-Semitic aggressor, minister. This identification had many earlier determinants. It resurfaces as a return of the repressed. Freud turned to Moses at times of inner and outer crisis, but he recognized that he was taking Moses away from the Jewish people, declaring him to be a non-Jew at the time of their greatest peril from Nazi persecution. Freud's own ambivalent Jewish identity pointed to the importance of analyzing both idealization and denigration. However, the internalization of hidden anti-Semitic attitudes and the analysis of Jewish anti-Semitism emerge as subjects of great importance in the multi-dimensional interpretations of Freud studies of Moses. In this connection, Freud had observed in a letter to Arnold Zweig in August 1933, "Here a piece of opposition to one's own Jewishness may still be hiding cunningly. Our great master Moses was, afterall, a strong anti-Semite and made no secret of it."[22]

The Moses of Freud is, in the main, the austere, absolute moral prophet who has mastered ambivalence and demands instinctual renunciation. This Moses arouses external and internal opposition because of the heavy burden of guilt imposed by prohibition and renunciation and the need for self and social regulation. Moses and, later, Christ were not only revered but reviled, and Christian hostility to Christ and his moral precepts were projected onto the Jewish descendants of Moses as "Christ killers." The Christian anti-Semitism was facilitated by Jesus being a Jew and by the unconscious condensation of Moses and Jesus, representing the same omnipotent deified Jewish parent. Freud's Moses represented the underlying conflicts and their compromise solution in Freud's refusal to convert, assimilate, or conceal his Jewish identity.

The first Moses was a follower of the monotheism of the Pharaoh Akhenaten (circa, 1365 B.C). Moses inspired the monotheism of his own followers, leading them from an Egypt which reverted to polytheism (analogous to Freud's regarding the Christian Trinity as a regression to polytheism). The second Moses was assumed to derive from a fierce volcano God, Yahweh. In time the two leaders designated as Moses, as well as the God of Righteousness and the volcano God, were merged as the one God represented by Moses. Moses, the heroic lawgiver, is the representation of the austere ruler and imperious superego. Moses had a speech impediment, but God spoke directly through him. Moses was thus more than a messenger of God and was closer to an extension of omnipotent authority. Moses is consecrated and crucially changed for his divine mission of instinctual renunciation, and communal elevation of moral precepts; his submissive devotion permits grandiose identification with the Deity. The mute Moses articulates the divine word; and in this transformation the group acquires the word, and symbolic process. For Freud, Moses' speech impediment was further evidence that he was Egyptian and did not know Hebrew (or Yiddish). Moses, in Freud's disguised family romance, declared and was denied his specific Jewish roots, adopted and re-created in a new medium of a universal language rather than Hebrew or silent stone.

Freud reconstructed the origins of the Jewish people, and in the process, there was a disguised study of his own origins and his own family romance. There were Jacob and Philip, two father-figures, and he fantasied he was also Philip's son (cf. Philippson Bible); mother and nurse-maid of different cultures and religions; his father's two families; two half-brothers, and two sons since his playmate was also his father's grandson; and many similar complicated and confusing relationships. Freud even proposed two groups of Jews—one group having experienced "what may be properly termed as traumatic experience (the bondage and exodus) which the other was spared" (SE 23:79). The two groups of Jews and the two figures of Moses were probably in the process of formulation much earlier when Freud wrote, "Science would ignore me entirely during my lifetime; some decades later, someone else would infallibly come upon the same things—for which the time was not now ripe—would achieve recognition for them and bring me honor as a forerunner whose failure had been inevitable" (SE 14:22).

In connection with questions of identity, lineage, and allegiance, it is significant that Freud named his children through linkage with male heroes, with dividing lines of gender and religion. He named his sons for Christian men and his daughters for Jewish women. (His sons would be worldly men; his daughters, Jewish mothers). Freud did not discuss bisexual themes in his Moses papers which focus on father-son conflict. Mother-son conflict is conspicuously obscure, and women are conspicuous by their abscence. Moses as mother, particularly the omnipotent preoedipal mother, is hidden behind and within the great patriarchal image. Although the discussion of Moses as a maternal figure is beyond the scope of this chapter, it should be noted that Freud's need for concrete representation in the form of the Moses statue, the statuettes on his desk, and in his collection of antiquities refer to his own infantile past. They deal with origins, with his first objects, and with his ability to maintain contact with his roots. His first object relationships and identifications were primarily with his mother and then with her surrogates, his father and nursemaids. Moses, as Jewish and anti-Jewish, refers to the Jewish and Christian worlds in which Freud lived, beginning with his preoedipal years in Freiberg (Pribor), just as Moses also refers to the common bridge between the two religions. The first messages concerning rules and regulations, the dos and don'ts of early life, were transmitted by Freud's maternal caregivers and conveyed more elaborate communications in the mother-tongue. The church in Freiberg was a branch of the Roman Catholic church, and his later conflicts concerning visiting Rome may be presumed to be related to his earliest experiences with Jewish and Christian relationships from infancy onward. The need for concrete objects to master infantile loss and separation contributed to his becoming a collector, a sublimated compromise far removed from the unconsciously related addiction to cigars which led to his fatal oral cancer. In this connection, his passionate attitude toward his collection of antiquities, some of which he treated as though they were living, animate representations of lost objects, ghosts who had returned to life, and his addiction to cigars, fostered his creative inspiration through the safety and security of primary object relationships. Insofar as Moses is the paternal prophet who had created a people and shaped their vision and ideals, the omnipotent mother is hidden within the great father. The Jewish mother is not visible, and the birth of the nation derives from the paternal Moses, akin to Eve who does not give birth to Adam but who is born of Adam's rib.

Freud was identified with Old Testament prophets, and with diverse non-Hebrew heroes, e.g., Michelangelo and Leonardo, Sophocles and Shakespeare, and so forth. Freud's multiple identifications illuminate the contradictions and complexities, and the ambivalent themes which characterize *Moses and Monotheism*, and Jewish identity.

Freud's final monograph was a special extension of *Totem and Taboo*, which he also considered publishing anonymously. Judaism and Christianity were compared in relation to oedipal conflict and the acquisition of morality. Moses, representing the father religion of Judaism, is also a bridge between the two religions for whom the Ten Commandments are sacrosanct. Moses and the Tablets are sacred to both religions. As miraculous, supreme prophet and divine oracle, the voice and word of God, who alone had glimpsed God and glowed with celestial rays, Moses was a forbear of Christ as son and extension of God. (Moses meant child in Egyptian). Freud is the resurrected new Moses, the righteous redeemer whose truth will free tormented "souls." Freud traces the development of an internalized, abstract superego, tenuously autonomous from drive or social pressures. Archeological metaphors resurface, and actual history is to re-emerge from the buried past. The figure of Moses in stone was also a study in contradiction and ambivalence as well as developmental transformation. Freud's Moses was both non-Jewish and Jewish, history and legend, temperamental and tranquil, mortal and immortal. The supremacy of this primal father is re-established (through guilt and expiation), so that the principles of Moses will probably eventually prevail in distant time. Though Freud constructs his historic Moses, it is the mythic Moses and his tenets that transcend time, place, and person. For Freud, this idealized moral authority was also understood as fragile in humanity, subject to regressive alteration and defiant rebellion.

The Commandment forbidding deified graven images, i.e., idolatry, had inhibited sculpture and other artistic endeavor under literal interpretation of Mosaic law. The Commandments were written "forever" in stone, of divine origin, and inscription. And while Judaism is in its core a Mosaic religion, there are no Jewish monuments to Moses, so that the influence of Moses is through the "word"—internalization, psychic representation, and abstract symbolization. Development advances with verbalization and symbolic processes. Freud himself no longer venerated the Moses statue, but the invisible, internalized, ethical precepts of *Moses and Monotheism*. Significantly, Freud did not refer to his previous paper on the Moses statue. Freud wrote to A. Zweig, on December 16, 1934, "Moses being an Egyptian is not the essential point . . . but the fact that I was obliged to construct so imposing a statue on feet of clay so that any fool could topple it." Men and their monuments could be eradicated, and in a curious repetition of name effacement, he also omitted any reference to Abraham's pertinent paper on Akhenaton.[23] The name of God is too sacred to permit pronunciation in orthodox Judaism, but his

monotheistic spirit is regularly proclaimed in the traditional Mosaic blessing, "Hear, Israel, the Lord, Our God is One."

Freud's lifelong search for historical and psychological truth led to
propositions about human prehistory. As an historical antecedent deriv-
ing from Freud's infancy, the Biblical Moses complements and illuminates
Freud's identification with Moses and his particular attachment to the
Moses statue. His special relationship to Moses, and to his artistic representation, suggests the concretization of infantile fantasy. The Moses
statue can be linked to infantile memories associated with Freiberg, including the Freiberg statue of the Biblical prophet, and related monuments
and momentoes of childhood.

Freud attributed the covenant of circumcision to Moses, as well as the
second covenant of the Commandments (SE 23:27). Circumcision as a
symbolic token castration (rather than actual castration) facilitated acquisition of and deference to more progressively abstract rules and re-
straints. The commandments and covenants, the prohibition against idols,
and the internalization of an abstract, invisible divine Spirit representing
ethical perfection "forced upon the people an advance in intellectuality
which important enough in itself, opened the way, in addition, to the
appreciation of intellectual work and to further renunciations of instinct"
(SE 23:123). It should be noted here that the written commandments
assumed and demanded literacy of the "people of the book." The message,
and not the medium or messenger, was to be venerated. Moses was a
founding father with a new vision, "the idea of a single deity embracing
the whole world, who was not less loving than all powerful, who was
averse to all ceremonial and magic and set before man as their highest
aim a life in truth and justice . . . " (SE 23:50).

Freud's description of his relationship to the Moses statue has all the
fantasic awe, admiration, idealization, anxiety and intimidation, submission and rebellion, and concrete thinking associated with early childhood
experience. Moses later represented less the archaic than the mature superego, and more the renunciation of magic and mysticism, the voice of
reason, and insight which was Freud's legacy. Not effaced or replaced,
his discoveries and writings would endure, timeless.

On the day that Freud finished *Moses and Monotheism* he wrote his
last will and testament. Alluding to himself merging with Moses, the
dying Freud spoke through Volz "the exalted work of Moses was understood and carried through to begin with only feebly and scantily, till, in
the course of centuries, it penetrated more and more, and at length in

the great Prophets it met with like spirits who continued the lonely man's work" (SE 23:52).

Notes

1. Ernest Jones, *The Life and Work of Sigmund Freud,* 3 vols. (New York: Basic Books, 1953–7), 2: 364–66.

2. Jones, 2: 365.

3. Peter Gay, *Freud: A Life for Our Time* (New York: W. W. Norton, 1988), pp. 314–5.

4. R. Bremmer, "Freud and Michelangelo's Moses," *American Imago* 33 (1976): 60–75.

5. J. Glenn, "Narcissistic Aspects of Freud and His Doubles," and Mark Kanzer, "Freud and His Literary Doubles," in Mark Kanzer and J. Glenn, eds., *Freud and His Self-Analysis* (New York: Aronson, 1979), pp. 297–301 and pp. 285–96.

6. There may also have been a hidden reference to Frau Moser. The death of Julius had left a germ of guilt because of Freud's ill wishes toward his little brother. See Harold Blum, "The Prototype of Preoedipal Reconstruction," *Journal of the American Psychoanalytic Association* 25 (1977): 757–85.

7. Harold Blum, "The Forbidden Quest and the Analytic Idea," *Psychoanalytic Quarterly* 50 (1981): 535–56.

8. Theodor Reik, *Ritual: Psycho-Analytic Studies* (New York: International Universities Press, 1946).

9. Harry Trosman, "Toward a Psychoanalytic Iconography," *Psychoanalytic Quarterly* 55 (1986): 130–67.

10. Marthe Robert, *From Oedipus to Moses: Freud's Jewish Identity,* trans. Ralph Manheim (Garden City, NY: Anchor Books, 1976).

11. David Bakan, *Sigmund Freud and the Jewish Mystical Tradition* (New York: Van Nostrand, 1958).

12. Jones, op. cit., 2: 367.

13. William McGuire, ed., *The Freud/Jung Letters* (Princeton: Princeton University Press, 1974), pp. 196–97.

14. Jones, op. cit., 2: 366.

15. W. Spruiell, "The Joke in the Moses of Michelangelo," *Psychoanalytic Study of the Child* 40 (1985): 473–92.

16. Jones, op. cit., 2: 367.

17. Jones, 2: 317.

18. Peter Loewenberg, " 'Sigmund Freud as a Jew': A Study in Ambivalence and Courage," *Journal of the History of the Behavioral Sciences* 7 (1971): 363–69 as well as his "A Hidden Zionist Theme in Freud's 'My Son, the Myops...' Dream," *Journal of the History of Ideas* 31 (1970): 129–32.

19. Yosef Hayim Yerushalmi, *Freud's Moses: Judaism Terminable and Interminable* (New Haven: Yale University Press, 1991).

20. E. Wallace, "The Psychodynamic Determinants of Moses and Monotheism," *Psychiatry* 40 (1977): 79–87.
21. See Martin S. Bergmann, "Moses and the Evolution of Freud's Jewish Identity," *The Israeli Annals of Psychiatry and Related Disciplines* 14 (1976): 3–26 and K. Eissler, *Medical Orthodoxy and the Future of Psychoanalysis* (Detroit: Wayne State University Press, 1965).
22. *The Letters of Sigmund Freud and Arnold Zweig,* ed. Ernst L. Freud, trans. Elaine and William Robson-Scott (New York: Harcourt, Brace & World, 1970), p. 163.
23. L. Shengold, "A Parapraxis of Freud in Relation to Karl Abraham," in Kanzer and Glenn, op. cit., pp. 213–44.

7. Strategies of Persuasion: The Case of *Leonardo Da Vinci*

Jutta Birmele

"Leonardo is the Hamlet of art history, whom each of us must recreate for himself."[1] Kenneth Clark's characterization of Leonardo's enigmatic personality seems to represent as much of a problem for biographers of our time,[2] more than half a millennium after Leonardo's birth, as it did in 1939 when Clark's book was published, or, for that matter, for Leonardo's first biographer Giorgio Vasari, who was able to interview some of Leonardo's contemporaries for his 20-page treatise on the great artist.[3] Over the last century, the mystique surrounding Leonardo's personality intensified with the growing popularity of *Mona Lisa*, Leonardo's most famous picture, and possibly the most famous picture, ever. As Kenneth Clark once observed, "there are millions of people who know the name of only one picture—the *Mona Lisa*."[4]

It is hardly surprising that Freud felt compelled to apply the tools of his new science, psychoanalysis, to the biography of such a challenging personality as Leonardo's. The painter was a worthy subject for Freud's effort to unlock his inner secrets just as he had tried to analyze, ten years earlier in *The Interpretation of Dreams*, the enigmatic fictional character Hamlet, with whom Clark would compare the painter and who also figures at the very end[5] in Freud's *Leonardo* paper. But while the art historian aims at a better understanding of art through study of the artist's biographical data, Freud's foremost interest lies in the psychological make-up of the artist, of which the artistic product serves merely as a manifestation that guides or supports the analysis. Freud himself did not fail to emphasize that he was not an art expert and that the content matter of art held much greater interest for him than questions of form, style, and technique.[6] His copy of Marie Herzfeld's edition of Leonardo's *Trattato della Pittura,* in the London Library collection, reveals that Freud did not even bother to cut the book pages beyond Herzfeld's introductory essay and Leonardo's general statements on art and sciences (the first 65 out of 437 pages).[7] When Freud started to work on his *Leonardo* essay in 1909, the psychoanalytic community had for some time directed its attention to the subject of the artist and the creative process. Wilhelm Stekel had just finished his psychological study of the artist in *Dichtung und Neurose* (Poetry and Neurosis),[8] in which he proposed that every artist is a neurotic and that neurosis is the quintessential condition for all creative activity.[9] Sadger had recently come out with monographs on Conrad Ferdinand Meyer,[10] Nikolaus Lenau,[11] and Heinrich von Kleist.[12] Otto Rank's book on incest, dealing with a range of literary motives, was completed in 1906 and known to Freud when he wrote *Leonardo.*[13] Möbius had written an extensive study on the pathology of Goethe's fictional characters that emphasized that no person is free from "degenerate" elements, that only the degree of "Entartung" varied, and that "the writer naturally is attracted by the pathological" since it was more fascinating.[14] Schopenhauer (1899) and Nietzsche (1902) were other subjects of psychoanalytical studies by Möbius.

Freud himself had devoted a short essay to the subject of the poet, *Der Dichter und das Phantasieren,*[15] and his preoccupation with the fictional is evident in the *Gradiva* essay that preceded it. Even Freud's subsequent writing of the *Schreber* case can be interpreted as a further study of fiction since Freud based his analysis solely on texts and reconstructed Schreber's life as he had done Leonardo's, with some of the same psychological emphases (homosexuality, narcissism). Freud became the editor for a series of monographs, *Schriften zur angewandten Seelenkunde,* that issued mainly studies on literary topics and featured, besides Freud himself, authors such as C. G. Jung, Otto Rank, Isidor Sadger, Oskar Pfister, Max Graf, Franz Riklin, and Karl Abraham. In later years, Freud frequently returned to artists' biographies or literary topics to demonstrate the usefulness of psychoanalysis, e.g. in his essays on Goethe (1917), "The Uncanny" (1919), Dostoevsky (1928), Ibsen, and in his preface to Marie Bonaparte's *Edgar Allan Poe* (1933).

That the psychoanalytic community became fascinated with the artist is hardly astonishing. The men working in this discipline were, after all,

members of the *Bildungsbürgertum* (educated middle class) with its roots
in a humanist education that placed the highest value on familiarity with
the canon of cultural treasures, particularly with its men of letters. Freud's
biographers, above all Ernest Jones[16] and Peter Gay,[17] have pointed out
that, even for his time, Freud was unusually well versed in the humanities
and held the highest respect for writers. His own publications are full of
allusions and references to literary works and often read like fictional
writing themselves.[18] Freud's most often quoted author was Goethe.[19]
Anzieu points out that "for Freud the German culture is the culture to
which he belongs: the antique Mediterranean culture being the culture
of reference."[20] When Freud decided to write a kind of psychobiography
of an artist, he followed a pattern already established by his colleague
Sadger, and by choosing Leonardo as the subject, he located his study
ideally within his own cultural pluralism: it combined Freud's fondness
for Italy and its great artists of the Renaissance[21] with his own heritage
of German Classical and Romantic predilections, and it assured him an
interested readership. At the same time, in writing the Leonardo piece,
he succeeded in overcoming a personal obsession that had tormented him
for some years: his unresolved relationship with Fliess.[22] Having engaged
so many of his own interests and needs, he would, years later, confide
to Lou-Andreas Salomé that *Leonardo* was "the only beautiful thing I
have ever written."[23]

For Freud, the *Leonardo* essay may have been an ideal piece of writing
(Karl Abraham called it "elegant and perfect in its form"),[24] but scholarship has generally been less kind, and more attracted by its fallacies
than its validities. The story of Freud's use of a translation mistake, which
he obviously overlooked in several of his sources (Herzfeld, Merezkovsky, Solmi),[25] and which is crucial for his elaborate construct of linguistic
and hieroglyphic detective work, is well documented by now.[26] There is
reason to suggest that Freud did not see fit to correct his essay when the
mistake was pointed out,[27] and this has further contributed to dismiss
the entire essay as a failure.[28] These questions, however, need not be
reexamined here. The body of Freud's study, carefully constructed from
many angles and on several levels, and with a number of reinforcements
built in, does not automatically fall with the irrelevance of the Egyptian
discussion. The main thrust of the essay, as Freud intended it, i.e. as a
"medium for the presentation of a particular form of homosexuality,"[29]
is unaffected by this so-called *Geierphantasie*. Freud's rather fantastic, if

elegant, revelation of Leonardo's ultimate imbeddedness in Egyptian my-thology, via his assumed knowledge of Horapollo's interpretation of an Egyptian vulture legend,[30] would later provoke scholarly scrutiny and ultimate refutation. To some extent, this was foreseen by Freud himself, as my analysis will point out.

When Freud started to do the research and write the essay on *Leonardo,* psychoanalysis was still far from having attained the status of a recognized science. To be sure, the initial *Psychological Wednesday Society* of 1902 (with weekly reports in the Sunday edition of the *Neues Wiener Tageblatt*) had evolved into the *Vienna Psycho-Analytical Society* in 1908,[31] the same year the *First International Psycho-Analytical Congress* had taken place in Salzburg; protocols of meetings, a library, and professional journals like *Jahrbuch der Psychoanalyse* (1909), *Zentralblatt für Psychoanalyse* (1910), *Imago* (1911), and later on the *Internationale Zeitschrift für Psychoanalyse* all served to create the image of an academic discipline with institutional status. In 1909, in what Freud took as "the first official recognition of our endeavors,"[32] Freud was given an honorary doctorate at Clark University. But Freud's pioneering publication *The Interpretation of Dreams,* published in 1900, took six years to sell barely 350 copies, and its second edition did not come out until 1909. In his opening address to the *Second Psycho-Analytical Congress,* held in Nuremberg in March 1910, Freud spoke of the enormous resistance that the nascent psychoanalytic movement encountered: "Society will not be in a hurry to grant us authority. It is bound to offer us resistance, for we adopt a critical attitude towards it; we point out to it that it itself plays a great part in causing neuroses. Just as we make an individual our enemy by uncovering what is repressed in him, so society cannot respond with sympathy to a relentless exposure of its injurious effects and deficiencies. Because we destroy illusions, we are accused of endangering ideals."[33] One illusion that Freud proceeded to destroy was that of the "innocence" of children. In his *Three Essays on the Theory of Sexuality* (1905) his paper *On the Sexual Theories of Children* (1908), his *Five Lectures on Psycho-Analysis* at Clark University in the fall of 1909, immediately pre-ceding his work on *Leonardo,* and in his *Analysis of a Phobia in a Five-Year-Old Boy* (Little Hans), Freud makes the categorical claim that each child is born with sexual instincts and displays sexual activities from the start. He further proposed that the sexual encounters during early child-hood would be decisive for the shaping of adult sexuality. It is clear that

Freud's findings had enormous implications for such "deviant" sexual behavior as homosexual acts, a punishable criminal offense and one which bore high societal costs. In Germany, e.g., the scandalous court proceedings involving Count Philip Eulenburg, intimate friend of the Kaiser, and the unrelated case of the suicide of the head of the Krupp family, in response to an accusation of homosexuality, had kept the topic in the forefront of public discourse ever since all of Europe had followed the trial of Oscar Wilde in the 1890s. For the middle-class morality which prided itself on its sense of control and denial, homosexuality implied a decadent character, and it signaled an inexcusable loss of willpower to allow oneself to sink to the level of a woman. The fall of the Roman Empire was popularly attributed to the increase of homosexuality.

For Freud to pick up this topic was particularly problematic. Freud was very much aware of the fact that his new science carried, in addition to the burden of its unpopular truths, the stigma of being identified as "Jewish."[34] Vienna since 1895, with the election of an openly anti-Semitic municipal government that made anti-Semitism socially acceptable, had become a hostile environment for its Jewish intellectuals.[35] For the sake of helping his new science to gain universal acceptance, Freud could ill afford to present the touchy topic of homosexuality in such a way as to attract further hostility, particularly since "Jewish" already carried a taint of perverse, homosexual characteristics.[36] Under these circumstances, latching onto an icon of high culture revealed a sense for propitious tactics on Freud's part: *Leonardo* could make the particularly repellent theories on infantile sexuality more palatable to the medical community and the general readership.

The turn of the century witnessed in central Europe a revival of appreciation for the Renaissance and its artists. It became the rage of interior decorating in bourgeois households to display copies of the great masters.[37] Original art was displaced by reproduction, the authentic encounter with art by a new *voyeurism* of the bourgeois consumers.[38] In the German culture, the cult of the genius had particularly pronounced and deep roots, and during times of intellectual crisis served as an anchor against the onslaught of modern ideas. Thomas Mann's *Gladius dei* speaks to this phenomenon. Julius Langbehn, whose *Rembrandt als Erzieher* was immensely popular, with over 50 editions, had claimed Leonardo together with Shakespeare, Rembrandt, Bach, and Bismarck as the "heimliche Kaiser der Deutschen" (the secret emperors of the Germans).[39] The genius, in contrast to the intellectual (i.e. rootless, bloodless, decadent, Jewish, Dreyfussard) was characterized by creativity, idealism, depth, and originality. For centuries, Leonardo da Vinci was venerated beyond comparison in German culture. Winckelmann, Goethe, Kant, the Romantics, and more recently Jacob Burckhardt and Heinrich Wölfflin had marvelled at his vast talents and enormous range of scientific studies. Adolf Rosenberg, whose book on Leonardo is in Freud's London Library, has called him "den italienischen Doktor Faustus"[40] asserting that he aimed at the unattainable, and in this assessment echos a tradition of Leonardo legends from Vasari to Freud's time, which Freud accepts from the outset: the incompatibility of the artistic with the scientific endeavours which ultimately caused Leonardo to fail in both. This is e.g. Goethe's judgment in his essay *Antik und Modern* (which contrasts Raphael favorably with Leonardo)[41] before he reads Leonardo's *Trattato della Pittura* during his second Italian journey and on account of this reading develops an appreciation for Leonardo's intellectual pursuits. We can assume that Freud did not read Leonardo's writings since he left his copy uncut. Freud also seems to lack an appreciation for Leonardo's apprenticeship and working environment, in the *bottega* (art workshop) where no clear-cut division existed between theoretical and practical studies, between artistic and empirical inquiries. While we have come to understand Leonardo differently, it should not be overlooked that this is due in large measure to the rediscovery or reassembly of material that had gotten lost or dispersed. In 1965 important notebooks, lost since 1866, were found in the stacks of the National Library in Madrid. Leonardo's manuscripts are scattered all over Europe (Italy, England, France, Germany), and even today, the whereabouts of only seven out of thirteen thousand pages seems to be known.[42]

Between 1903 and 1906, Freud had come across a book that mentioned a curious "childhood memory" of Leonardo's that, it can be assumed for one so keenly alerted to childhood insights, must have stuck in his mind so that he could recall it a couple of years later when he treated a patient with a "similar constitution like Leonardo's but not his genius."[43] The book *Leonardo da Vinci* by Dmitri Merezkovsky was published in German in 1903, and in 1906 Freud listed the book among "ten good books" in answer to an inquiry from the bookseller and publisher Hugo Heller.[44] In October 1909, he set out to do the research, and on December 1, Freud gave a talk on Leonardo to the *Vienna Psycho-Analytical Society.*

In April of the following year his study was completed and, shortly thereafter, published in May.

Judging from Freud's markings in his books on Leonardo and the content of his essay, he seems to have drawn above all from Marie Herzfeld's introductory essay for her two editions of Leonardo's writings[45] and Merezkovsky's novel. Both sources were highly respectable and popular at the time. Herzfeld had already made a name for herself as a translator of Scandinavian authors, but in the wake of the general enthusiasm for the art of the Renaissance, she developed an expertise in that field. Her *Leonardo* books went through four editions, and she succeeded in engaging renowned scholars for her large two-volume book *Das Zeitalter der Renaissance*.[46]

While Herzfeld even now[47] has a reputation as a serious scholar, it is more difficult to appreciate from our perspective what Freud and his contemporaries saw in Merezkovsky. Freud's London Library contains no fewer than seven of Merezkovsky's novels, published between 1903 and 1927. Freud seems to have been in good company since Thomas Mann shared his admiration for Merezkovsky, calling him "der genialste Kritiker und Weltpsychologe seit Nietzsche" (the most ingenious critic and world psychologist since Nietzsche).[48] However, by the time the Russian author died, he had already outlived his popularity and is almost forgotten today. In all likelihood, his initial sympathizing with Pilsudski, Mussolini, and even Hitler had much to do with his fall from grace with the general public in the 1940s.[49] Yet, it should be remembered that in 1933 he was a candidate for the Nobel Prize in Literature, and his highly successful novels, in particular *Leonardo*, went through many editions and translations and are said to have influenced the genre of historical novels in Europe and in the United States.[50] The scholarship on Freud's *Leonardo* usually does not fail to point to Merezkovsky's low ranking as an artist (at present) and is puzzled about Freud's artistic taste. As is already apparent in his writings on Jensen's *Gradiva* and in his essay on *Daydreaming*, Freud acted as a scavenger in his use of fictional literature. With remarkable single-mindedness he appropriated only those features that suited his momentary scientific investigation and ignored others that the literary scholar often would have found much more rewarding but that interfered with Freud's intent. In spite of the numerous markings in Freud's edition of Merezkovsky's novel (there are 23 in total), a closer comparison with Freud's *Leonardo* will show that Freud made only limited use of Merezkovsky's fictional account of Leonardo's life.

To begin with, Freud is entirely uninterested in Merezkovsky's elaborately written historical backdrop for Leonardo's story that places the hero into a time of clashes between the newly discovered pagan culture and the institutionalized Christian doctrine. Freud's markings do not start until page 149 and are found only on those paragraphs that describe Leonardo's biography, particularly his behavior and his physical characteristics. Many of these passages, perhaps less colorful, can be found also in other accounts of Leonardo's life and are therefore not entirely products of Merezkovsky's fantasy. In Merezkovsky's portrayal, Leonardo is seen as a spiritual character who combines a "pagan" (i.e. joyful and self-affirming) perception of life with "Christian" (i.e. self-denying, compassionate) morality and is supposed to convey to the reader a vision of "the man of tomorrow"[51] and a glimpse of the new culture that would be the synthesis of Europe's pagan and Christian origins. Merezkovsky's vision is directed into the future, and he therefore frequently starts his chapters with quotes from Leonardo's prophesies and gives these also great emphasis in his protagonist's dialogues with his pupils. Freud's perspective is backward-looking, like that of a paleontologist. For Freud, the great painter's biography served a clinical purpose: as an analysand whose analysis allowed him to demonstrate the remarkable, still widely unknown or rejected, techniques of psychoanalysis in their ability to lay bare the innermost psychological conditions for a particular kind of homosexuality. While it is true that Freud saw his new science as a revolutionary tool in freeing people from the tyranny of their unconscious and in this sense shares Merezkovsky's (and Nietzsche's) view that the established culture in its understanding of human nature needed to be challenged and its mendacities mercilessly identified, he remained true to his training as a scientist, unaffected by Merezkovsky's sense of spiritual mission. While in Merezkovsky's eyes, Leonardo ultimately fails because of his political inequities, allowing himself to become a servant of the powerful, corrupt princes, Freud's Leonardo has no political dimension. Freud's portrayal of Leonardo concentrates solely on the childhood aspects, particularly Leonardo's attachment to his mother, and traces their powerful effects in adult life. The vision of moral and cultural regeneration—ultimately an "affirmation of spiritual Christianity as against the rationalist and godless West"[52]—which Merezkovsky aimed at introducing through his trilogy of novels (*Julian the Apostate, The Romance of Leonardo,* and *Peter and Aleksei*) completed in 1905, was much too metaphysical an aspiration for someone as rational and skeptical as Freud, whose philosophy was grounded in scientific empiricism.[53] Yet, quoting Merezkovsky and praising his intuitive understanding of some of Leonardo's character traits, i.e., making use of Merezkovsky's popularity, was entirely in keeping with Freud's attempt to break down the barriers of resistance to his scientific findings and also coincided with his own predilections.

Freud did not follow Merezkovsky in all his contentions on Leonardo's life, even if they could have substantiated Freud's own analysis, as can be seen by selecting an example. Based on the *Childhood Memory,* found in the books by Herzfeld, Solmi, and Merezkovsky (and possibly others), Freud's intention was to argue that an unusually intense relationship (erotic attachment) between Leonardo's mother Katharina and the infant and the absence of a disciplining male (in *Leonardo,* Freud consistently contrasts *mother* and *motherly* with the *male who is not seen in a nurturing role*)[54] in a critical phase had set the stage for a homosexual development and as an added bonus he would explain the curious smile on the *Mona Lisa.* Merezkovsky describes a memory of Leonardo's, now middle-aged, in which he recalls, while living with his grandfather, running back at night to his mother's house and climbing into her bed and feeling the warmth of her body.[55] A few pages later, he thinks back about Katharina's visit to him shortly before her death and again envisions himself as a young boy climbing into her bed and nestling against her.[56] This scene, as many other products of the author's fantasy, would have fitted nicely into Freud's concept but was ignored by Freud probably as too obviously fictional. Freud also differed from Merezkovsky in his view on Leonardo's seeming inability to finish his pictures: Merezkovsky regards it as an outcome of the painter's perfectionist drive, a Promethean defiance, rather than as a conflict between art and science. While Freud mentions Merezkovsky's argument politely ("valid as some of these excuses may be they still do not cover the whole state of affairs"),[57] he is aware that the writer, though insightful, lacks the necessary psychoanalytic training to see beyond the surfaces.[58] Freud also holds a different opinion about Leonardo's sexuality: in Merezkovsky's novel, the innuendos about Leonardo's being accused of sodomy are put into the mouth of a rather despicable character Cesare,[59] while the positive protagonist Giovanni dismisses the story as slander: "It is shameful that people delight in pulling the great into the gutter."[60] Rather, so it is said, Leonardo has "no time" for the diversion from his mission in life and therefore "keeps a distance from women."[61] Thus, Merezkovsky's Leonardo is deliberately depicted to invoke some aspects of the historical image of Christ, to which are added dionysian features based on Merezkovsky's reading of Nietzsche's *Zarathustra*. Freud, in contrast, treats Leonardo as he would a case study, and extracts from Merezkovsky's novel only those specific features that can be used for his analysis, which focuses on the infantile roots of Leonardo's sexual inclinations.

Besides the questions of why Freud chose Leonardo as a subject for his study on homosexuality and what sources he made use of, the structure and rhetoric of *Childhood Memory* can contribute to an understanding of Freud's strategy of persuasion.[62] To begin with, Freud does not give his study a subtitle, but in his introductory remarks he calls it modestly "ein biographischer Versuch" (a biographical experiment).[63] In similar fashion, for a later publication on Friedrich Hebbel (1920), his colleague Isidor Sadger chose the subtitle "ein psychoanalytischer Versuch" (a psychoanalytical experiment).[64] As he later stated in his brief essay *Constructions in Analysis*, the analyst's work compares with that of the archaeologist: "His work of construction, or, if it is preferred, of reconstruction, resembles to a great extent an archaeologist's excavation of some dwellingplace that has been destroyed and buried or of some ancient edifice. The two processes are in fact identical, except that the analyst works under better conditions and has more material at his command to assist him since what he is dealing with is not something destroyed but something that is still alive."[65] In his *Leonardo* essay, Freud repeatedly uses the word *übersetzen* (translate) in describing his task, for example: "... so that we may venture to translate the phantasy from its own special language into words that are generally understood. The translation is then seen to point to an erotic content."[66] Archaeologist and psychoanalyst discover and bring to light buried (repressed) material, often only fragments. But this represents only the first stage in a sequence of tasks which requires reconstruction and restoration, subsequently followed by interpretation and translation into common language.

Like Sadger in his psychobiography of Nikolaus Lenau (1909),[67] Freud begins with an apology and justification for this intrusion into the privacy of one of the *Großen des Menschengeschlechts:* even the great minds are

subjected to the laws (*Gesetze*) of nature. This essentially defensive stance
is given charm and elegance by Freud's literary style and allusions. Freud
further employs a depersonalized stance instead of injecting his own
person as the author by which, from the start, he creates legitimacy and
a barrier (status of scientific research) between his study and the potential
charge of indecent inquisitiveness. To further legitimate his undertaking
and to emphasize the common cultural bond with the reader, he quotes
Schiller: "das Strahlende zu schwärzen und das Erhabene in den Staub
zu ziehen" (to blacken the radiant and drag the sublime into the dust).
Indeed, the entire first paragraph has a Schillerian dramatic rhetoric,
evoking the rhythm of Schiller's philosophical poem *Nänie*, to which the
educated German reader would immediately feel an affinity. In Part II
he will repeat this justification upon mentioning the abhorrent topic of
Leonardo's homosexuality,[68] and in his conclusion in Part VI he returns
to the task of defending his analysis of Leonardo against the anticipated
reproach as being distasteful.

But rather than confronting the reader with the true subject of the
study from the outset, he prepares the stage for it (to lower the reader's
anticipated resistance) and engineers its approach gently to ease the reader
into a benevolent and cooperative mindset that will incline him or her to
look with sympathy on Freud's unfolding analysis, i.e. translation. Freud
takes the reader along on his expedition into new psychological territory
and allows him/her to participate in the psychoanalytical process. One
is reminded of Freud's advice for the author "who sets out to introduce
some branch of knowledge—or, to put it more modestly, some branch
of research—to an uninstructed public" in his later essay "Some Elementary Lessons in Psycho-Analysis":

It is possible to start off from what every reader knows (or thinks he knows) and
regards as self-evident, without in the first instance contradicting him. An opportunity will soon occur for drawing his attention to facts in the same field,
which, though they are known to him, he has so far neglected or insufficiently
appreciated. Beginning from these, one can introduce further facts to him of
which he has *no* knowledge and so prepare him for the necessity of going beyond
his earlier judgements, of seeking new points of view and of taking new hypotheses
into consideration. In this way one can get him to take a part in building up a
new theory about the subject and one can deal with his objections to it during
the actual course of the joint work. A method of this kind might well be called
genetic. It follows the path along which the investigator himself has travelled
earlier."[69]

Freud employs this *genetic* method from the very start of his *Leonardo* essay: Repeatedly and extensively he stresses the unquestioned greatness of Leonardo (an issue on which the reader would have no disagreement), describes movingly Leonardo's loneliness as the outcome of his estrangement from his contemporaries (which he leaves unexplained), and drops the first hint at Leonardo's homosexual nature without using the word by attributing feminine characteristics to him in increasing directness: "On the contrary, he was tall and well-proportioned; his features were of consummate beauty and his physical strength unusual; he was charming in his manner, supremely eloquent, and cheerful and amiable to everyone. He loved beauty in the things that surrounded him; he was fond of magnificent clothing and valued every refinement of living."[70] Lest the reader get the impression that Freud is implying that Leonardo is a dandy, he immediately elevates this enjoyment of earthly pleasures into the sphere of art criticism and diverts the reader's attention to a quote from the *Trattato* (it is the only one marked in Freud's largely uncut copy). Returning to Leonardo's character, he prepares the reader to accept a new viewpoint by introducing key words such as *unstet* (restless), *befremdlich* (strange), *Zeit vertrödeln* (idle away) to signify an unstable quality in Leonardo's constitution. This potentially damaging labeling is modified and deflected by references to the unstable time and the advent of a new epoch ("in an age which was beginning to replace the authority of the Church by that of antiquity and which was not yet familiar with any form of research not based on presuppositions"), for which Leonardo's experimental studies in the sciences were pioneering.[71]

At this point, having given a hint of Leonardo's switch from art to scientific investigation, characteristics such as "unfertig," "unvollendet" (unfinished), "Makel der Unstetigkeit" (flaw of restlessness) and "sich um das weitere Schicksal seiner Werke wenig kümmerte" (i.e. the theme of desertion)[72] are introduced, but relativized by ascribing these viewpoints to contemporary observers of Leonardo's, i.e. the author can still distance himself from any opinion, and he allows the reader to develop one him/herself. This strategy is evident in numerous instances throughout the essay.[73]

In following Freud's essay, the reader is not supposed to remain passive. As with the analysand, the psychoanalyst Freud needs to form a therapeutic alliance with his audience so that the unconscious material, hidden and repressed by society, can be identified and accepted. *Deu-*

tungsarbeit, i.e. the task of giving meaning, is as much a burden of the analysand or reader as it is the analyst's. At times, when Freud uses the first-person plural *wir*, he seemingly takes the reader into his confidence and emphasizes their common bond: "Let us rather therefore give a fair hearing for a while to the work of analysis, which indeed has not yet spoken its last word."[74]

But the meaning of *wir* can shift and it then denotes Freud and the psychoanalytic community. In those passages he simultaneously employs a casual, but authoritative, lecture style, which allows for no dissension from the scientific claims he is making: "We accept this process as proved whenever the history of a person's childhood—that is, the history of his mental development—shows that in childhood this over-powerful instinct was in the service of sexual interests."[75] Often, Freud shifts his text to a voice of authority higher than himself when he employs depersonalized subjects from which he claims to take his clues, such as e.g. *die Forschung* (research), *die Deutung* (interpretation), *die Sexualtheorien* (theories of sexuality), *die Mythologie* (mythology). In most instances, these excursions into psychoanalytic theory are prepared by everyday observations with which the reader who possesses common sense can identify: "Observation of men's daily lives shows us that most people succeed in directing . . ."[76]

In a few rare instances where Freud does not anticipate a challenge to his claim from the audience, he starts his argument with what he called "the dogmatic method of presentation"[77] by stating its conclusion first: "Indeed, the great Leonardo remained like a child for the whole of his life in more than one way; it is said that all great men are bound to retain some infantile part."[78] Freud typically proceeds from the general and familiar to the specific and controversial, by which method he puts Leonardo's peculiarities into perspective: "There is no doubt that the creative artist feels towards his works like a father. The effect which Leonardo's identification with his father had on his paintings was a fateful one. He created them and then cared no more about them, just as his father had not cared about him."[79] He varies this pattern at times, when he notes a particular phenomenon of Leonardo's life that he subsequently explains in general terms, substantiated by excursions into anthropology, mythology, and linguistics etc.: "On this view the scene with the vulture would not be a memory of Leonardo's but a phantasy, which he formed at a later date and transposed to his childhood. This is often the way in which childhood memories originate. Quite unlike conscious memories from the time of maturity, they are not fixed at the moment of being experienced and afterwards repeated . . . "[80]

By anticipating contrary arguments, questions, and objections, he minimizes or refutes their validity. In this way his reader is meant to become inoculated against later counterpersuasion: "We realize that we shall have to meet the objection that Leonardo's behaviour towards his pupils has nothing at all to do with sexual motives and that it allows no conclusions to be drawn about his particular sexual inclination. Against this we wish to submit with all caution . . . "[81]

It is obvious that Freud is completely in command of the organizational patterns in which his arguments are arranged. Repeatedly he points out the progression of his argument from *Ahnung* (conjecture) to *Bestätigung* (confirmation),[82] from *Andeutung* (hint) to *Klarheit* (clarity),[83] from *Wahrscheinlichkeit* (probability) to *Sicherheit* (certainty).[84] But a close reading also reveals that for Freud the state of *Ahnung* ("we begin to suspect the possibility that it was his mother who possessed the mysterious smile . . . ")[85] can suffice and be taken as proof for the development of his thesis. A telling sentence is one such as "*zu unserer Erwartung würde es am besten stimmen,*[86] wenn gerade die Vertiefung in die Züge der Monna Lisa Leonardo angeregt hätte, die Komposition der heilen Anna aus seiner Phantasie zu gestalten" (It would best agree with our expectations if it was the intensity of Leonardo's preoccupation with the features of Mona Lisa that stimulated him to create the composition of St. Anne out of his phantasy).[87] Freud seeks proof *selectively,* his expectation narrows the search for substantiation. As an initiated scientist, i.e. psychoanalyst, he trusts his intuition and expects the reader to set all reservations aside: "*Bei einer gewissen Vertiefung in dieses Bild* kommt es wie ein plötzliches Verständnis über den Beschauer . . . " (The standard edition unfortunately translates: "*after having studied* this picture for some time, it suddenly dawns on us . . . ", and thereby the sense of *going into depth,* of *loosing oneself in the picture* is lost).[88] Frank J. Sulloway in a recent study of Freud's case histories has noted that Freud "sought to turn the incompleteness and speculative nature of his case materials into a kind of rhetorical virtue."[89] The case of Leonardo provided the analyst with the scantiest of material (Freud retells the known childhood and adolescent biography in barely twenty-two lines, and as if to accentuate the minimal material he had to work with, he adds: "Das ist alles"—

that is all).[90] Freud's eloquence tends to screen a rather "unscientific" use of conjectures and suppositions as factual material. His assumption, for example, that Leonardo's mother was deserted and lonely gains legitimacy by repetition and subtle modification so that a phrase like "bei der armen, verlassenen, echten Mutter" (with the poor, deserted, real mother)[91] is eventually uncritically accepted by the reader. The ambivalent status of the presented material is accentuated by Freud's extensive use of the word "dürfen" (may, be permitted). As Muschg pointed out years ago, the word belongs to the "pet inventory" of the writer Freud, and denotes "a distancing" device, signifying confidence, and benevolence towards the audience, often found in traditional scientific discourse and as such implies an authoritative stance.[92] It can, however, also signal a measure of modesty and tentativeness. It can even reach a level of parody, as in "so darf man sich doch der Wahrscheinlichkeit anvertrauen" (we may place confidence in the probability)[93] when this quality is underlined by the word "scheinen" and variations thereof, as in "anscheinend" and "scheinbar" or "wahrscheinlich" (seem, seemingly, appear, apparently, probable, probably). The prominent use of the subjunctive and of double negatives further enhances the fluidity of the text. These stylistic devices all convey an unsettled quality of the argument and are designed to create a working alliance with the reader and thereby are able to result in the lowering of resistance.

In connection with the process of inversion (homosexuality) Freud often uses the word *arbeiten* (work) or references to *Leistung* (achievement) and *Fähigkeit* (ability), attributes held in high respect by his upper-middle-class audience subscribing to a meritocracy: "... that after his curiosity had been activated in infancy in the service of sexual interests he succeeded in sublimating the greater part of his libido into an urge for research."[94] Leonardo is given credit for having been able to live abstinent,[95] an achievement in the eyes of the educated readers ("die menschliche Kultur tragenden Schichten") who, Freud presumes, find sex disgusting and only subject themselves to it for procreational purposes, in contrast to the uncultivated lower strata of society ("roh gebliebenen, niedrigen Volksschichten").[96]

The reader finds him/herself being carried along in the incessant shifting of the narrative structure of Freud's analysis, from self-conscious disclaimers, justifications, and searches for solutions to sovereign lecturing on scientific findings, including medical terminology. Freud does not solely appeal to the reader's rationality but also to a willingness to co-operate intuitively. His writing technique becomes the message: "The endless analytic process of re-writing, or re-working the past is itself inscribed in the text, where the same ground is gone over and over, using repetition with slight differences to convey the layering, the complex texture of psychic reality."[97] Freud's task of digging out, uncovering, translating, of assigning meaning requires multiple perspectives, creativity, and an independence of mind (a quality in Leonardo that Freud obviously identified with): what seems a loathsome sexual *perversion* ("abscheuliche sexuelle Perversion") in "respectable society" can have its roots in a "scene of human beauty" ("menschlich schöne Szene").[98] Details too small for "anyone who was not a psycho-analyst" to attach importance to are "a manifestation of hidden mental processes" for the trained analyst.[99]

Much has been made of the obvious translation error of the Italian word "nibbio" for *Geier* or *vulture* and, assuming that Freud had knowledge of Maclagan's article of 1923, of his puzzling omission to correct this mistake in a later edition of this essay. Perhaps one can take a clue from Freud's *Leonardo* essay as to his willingness to entertain etymologically untenable lines of arguments if, in his eyes, they could lay claim to an "innere Wahrscheinlichkeit" (inner probability),[100] i.e. fit into his scheme: when accepting Merezkovsky's fictional story of Katharina's (Leonardo's mother) visit to her son shortly before her death, Freud comments: "This interpretation by the psychological novelist cannot be put to the proof, but it can claim *so much inner probability*, and is so much in harmony with all that we otherwise know of Leonardo's emotional activity, that I cannot refrain from accepting it as correct."[101] Freud could not refrain from accepting the fictional as factual because of its *innere Wahrscheinlichkeit*. The vulture with its Egyptian legendary roots, the hieroglyph for *mother* (vulture), and the resemblance of *Mut* (vulture-headed goddess with phallus) and *Mutter,* all these aspects fitted so superbly into Freud's overall scheme of Leonardo's infantile fixation on his over-affectionate mother that it presented too much of a temptation for Freud not to make use of them.[102] Just as Freud was selective in his use of fiction, in his attention to the historical and social context,[103] and in his interpretation of biographical data,[104] he made use of the Egyptian connection because it could claim the character of *innere Wahrscheinlichkeit* (being psychoanalytically correct?). Freud builds into his essay the

disclaimer: "I am far from over-estimating the certainty of these results."[105] Freud's goal was to stake out the limits of the use of psychoanalysis for biography, to demonstrate the methodology on an ideal case,
rather than claiming certainty for his biography of the historical Leonardo. Freud wanted to suggest an alternative reading of Leonardo's
personality at a time when, as Marie Herzfeld put it, "Leonardo der
Forscher, der Dichter, der Poet feiert in unseren Tagen seine Auferste-
hung aus dem Grab der Bibliotheken" (Leonardo, the explorer, writer,
poet, is celebrating his resurrection from the tomb of the libraries).[106]
Freud's attempt at giving new understanding to the enigma of the Renaissance artist did not prove to be a worse failure than other biographies,
as he himself pointed out: "And if in doing so we remain dissatisfied
with the degree of certainty which we achieve, we shall have to console
ourselves with the reflection that so many other studies of this great and
enigmatic man have met with no better fate."[107]

Notes

1. Kenneth Clark, *Leonardo da Vinci: An Account of his Development as an
   Artist* (New York: Macmillan, 1939).
2. The latest in a long series of biographies is Serge Bramly, *Leonardo. Discovering the Life of Leonardo Da Vinci*. Trans. Sîan Reynolds (New York:
   Harper Collins, 1991). Harry Trosman gives a survey of interpretations in
   the eighth chapter of his book *Freud and the Imaginative World* (Hillsdale,
   N.J.: Lawrence Erlbaum Associates, 1985).
3. Giorgio Vasari (1568), latest translation: *Lives of the Artists*, trans. Bull
   (Harmondsworth: Penguin, 1965).
4. Kenneth Clark, "Mona Lisa," *The Burlington Magazine*, Vol. 115 (March
   1973): 144–150.
5. Freud also chose to compare Leonardo with Goethe on account of their
   universal genius. "Ansprache im Frankfurter Goethe-Haus" (1930), Sigmund
   Freud, *Gesammelte Werke: Chronologisch Geordnet*, ed. Anna Freud, E.
   Bibring, W. Hoffer, E. Kris, and O. Isokower in collaboration with Marie
   Bonaparte, 19 vols. (Frankfurt a. M.: S. Fischer, 1952–1987) henceforth GW,
   14: 547–550; for ease of reference, the English translation is also noted in
   Standard Edition of the Complete Psychological Works of Sigmund Freud,
   ed. and trans. James Strachey in collaboration with Anna Freud, assisted by
   Alix Strachey and Alan Tyson, 24 vols. (London: Hogarth, 1955–1974),
   henceforth SE, 21: 208–212.
6. Freud, "Der Moses des Michelangelo," GW 10: 172–201.

7. Marie Herzfeld, ed., *Leonardo Da Vinci: Traktat von der Malerei* (Jena: E. Diederichs, 1909).

8. Wilhelm Stekel, *Dichtung und Neurose. Bausteine zur Psychologie des Künstlers und des Kunstwerkes* (Wiesbaden: J. F. Bergmann, 1909). Freud's copy, in his London Library, has an inscription from Jung.

9. Ibid., 5–6.

10. Isidor Sagder, *C. F. Meyer, eine psychographisch-psychologische Studie* (Wiesbaden: J. F. Bergmann, 1908).

11. Isidor Sadger, *Aus dem Liebesleben Nikolaus Lenaus* (Wien und Leipzig: Franz Deuticke, 1909).

12. Isidor Sadger, *Heinrich von Kleist. Eine pathographisch-psychologische Studie* (Wiesbaden: J. F. Bergmann, 1910).

13. Otto Rank, *Das Inzest-Motiv in Dichtung und Sage. Grundzüge einer Psychologie des dichterischen Schaffens* (Leipzig und Wien: Franz Deuticke, 1912). The dedication reads "Meinem hochverehrten Lehrer Prof. Dr. Sigmund Freud in Dankbarkeit gewidmet."

14. Paul Julius Möbius, *Über das Pathologische bei Goethe* (Leipzig: J. A. Barth, 1898), 15.

15. Sigmund Freud, "Der Dichter und das Phantasieren," *Neue Revue* I Nr. 10 (1908), 716–724. GW 7: 213–223; SE 9: 141–153.

16. Ernest Jones, *The Life and Work of Sigmund Freud*, 3 vols. (New York: Basic Books, 1953–1955).

17. Peter Gay, *Freud. A Life for Our Time* (New York: W. W. Norton, 1988).

18. Walter Muschg, "Freud als Schriftsteller," *Psychoanalystische Bewegung* 2, 467.

19. Peter Brückner, *Sigmund Freuds Privatlektüre* (Cologne: Horst, 1975).

20. Didier Anzieu, "The Place of Germanic Language and Culture in Freud's Discovery of Psychoanalysis between 1895 and 1900," *Journal for Psycho-Analysis* 67 (1986), 219–226.

21. See Peter Gay, *Freud*, 268.

22. Jones, Vol. II, 78, Letter to Jung, December 2, 1909.

23. Gay, *Freud*, 268.

24. Ibid., 269.

25. Marie Herzfeld, ed., *Leonardo Da Vinci. Der Denker, Forscher und Poet. Nach den veröffentlichten Handschriften.* Auswahl, Übersetzung und Einleitung von M. H., 2nd ed. (Jena: Eugen Diederichs, 1906). In Freud Library, with markings. Dmitry Sergewitsch Mereschkowski [Merezkovsky], *Leonardo Da Vinci: Ein Biographischer Roman aus der Wende des 15. Jahrhunderts.* Trans. Carl v. Guetschow (Leipzig: Schulze, 1903). In Freud Library with markings. Edmondo Solmi, *Leonardo Da Vinci.* Trans. Emmi Hirschberg (Berlin: E. Hofmann, 1909). In Freud Library, with markings, dated 1908.

26. The first to point this out was E. Maclagan, "Leonardo in the Consulting Room," *Burlington Magazine* 42:54–57. Meyer Schapiro, "Leonardo and

Freud: An Art Historical Study," *Journal of the History of Ideas*, (April 1956), 147–178. R. Richard Wohl, Harry Trosman, "A Retrospect of Freud's Leonardo. An Assessment of a Psychoanalytic Classic," *Psychiatry* XVIII (1955), 27–39. Kurt R. Eissler, *Leonardo Da Vinci: Psychoanalytic Notes on The Enigma* (New York: International Universities Press, 1961).

27. See Gay, *Freud*, 273.

28. Hans Ost, *Leonardo-Studien* (New York: de Gruyter, 1975), 86.

29. Heinz Kohut, "Beyond the Bounds of the Basic Rule. Some Recent Contributions to Applied Psychoanalysis," *Journal of the American Psychoanalytic Association* VIII (3)567–586 (572).

30. Liselotte Dieckmann, *Hieroglyphics. The History of a Literary Symbol* (St. Louis: Washington University Press, 1970), 45.

31. Jones, Vol. II, 8–9.

32. Ibid., 57.

33. "Die zukünftigen Chancen der Psychoanalytischen Therapie." GW 8:104–115 (111); SE 11: 141–151(147).

34. Freud wrote to Karl Abraham in a letter July 27, 1908: "Be assured, if my name were Oberhuber, my innovations would have found, despite it all, far less resistance."

35. Steven Beller, *Vienna and the Jews. 1867–1938. A Cultural History* (Cambridge: Cambridge University Press, 1989), 188–206.

36. See Sander L. Gilman, "Opera, Homosexuality, and Models of Disease: Richard Strauss's *Salome* in the Context of Images of Disease in the Fin de Siecle," *Disease and Representation. Images of Illness from Madness to Aids* (Ithaca: Cornell University Press, 1988), 155–181.

37. Hermann Bahr, Austrian literary critic, describes Theodor Mommsen's receiving room in Berlin: "Eine schöne volle Kopie nach Tizian und rings in Stichen die edelsten Wunder der Italiener, vom hageren Adel der Prärafaeliten aufwärts, und die klugen, wunderlichen, herb verführerischen Frauen des Leonardo und die reife Gnade des Tizianschen Bella. So wandelt Schönheit hier vom ersten Wunsch zur reichlichsten Erfüllung." *Der Antisemitismus. Ein internationales Interview* (Berlin: S. Fischer, 1894), 26.

38. Jochen Schmidt, *Die Geschichte des Genie-Gedankens in der deutschen Literatur, Philosophie und Politik, 1750–1945*, 2 vols. (Darmstadt: Wissenschaftliche Buchgesellschaft, 1985), vol. 2, 239.

39. Ibid., 190.

40. Adolf Rosenberg, *Leonardo da Vinci* (Bielefeld: Velhagen & Klasing, 1898), 1.

41. Goethe maintains in this essay, Leonardo "hatte sich, genau besehen, wirklich müde gedacht und sich allzusehr am Technischen abgearbeitet." *Gedenkausgabe der Werke, Briefe und Gespräche*, ed. Ernst Beutler (Zurich: Artemis, 1949), vol. 13, 845.

42. Bramly, 420–421.

43. Letter to Jung, Oct. 17, 1909.

44. SE 9: 245–247.
45. Herzfeld, *Leonardo Da Vinci. Der Denker, Forscher und Poet; Leonardo Da Vinci. Traktat von der Malerei*, ed. Herzfeld.
46. Marie Herzfeld, ed., *Das Zeitalter der Renaissance. Ausgewählte Quellen zur Geschichte der italienischen Kultur*, 2 vols. (Jena: E. Diederichs, 1910).
47. See *Österreichisches Biographisches Lexikon 1815–1950*, ed. Österreichische Akademie der Wissenschaften, Leo Santifaller, 2 vols. (Graz: Hermann Böhlaus, 1959).
48. Thomas Mann, *Gesammelte Werke in Zwölf Bänden* (Oldenburg: S. Fischer, 1960), Vol. 10, 596. See also Lilli Venohr, *Thomas Manns Verhältnis zur russischen Literatur*. Frankfurter Abhandlungen zur Slawistik (Meisenheim/Glan: Anton Hain); Manfred Dierks, *Studien zu Mythos und Psychologie bei Thomas Mann* (Bern: Francke, 1972), 70–78.
49. Heinrich Stammler, "Russian Metapolitics: Mereshowsky's Religious Understanding of the Historical Process," *California Slavic Studies* IX (1976), 123–138 (124).
50. Edith W. Clowes, "The Integration of Nietzsche's Ideas of History, Time and 'Higher Nature' in the Early Historical Novels of Dmitry Merezhkovsky," *Germano-Slavica* 3 (1981), 401–416, n. 30. Waclaw Lednicki, "D. S. Merezhkovsky," *The Russian Review* 1 (1942), 80–85.
51. Clowes, 406–407.
52. Nicholas V. Riasanovsky, *The Image of Peter the Great in Russian History and Thought* (New York: Oxford University Press, 1985), 231.
53. Gay, *Freud*, 118–119.
54. In his copy of J. J. Bachofen's *Das Mutterrecht*, Freud has marked the passage: "Der Vater ist stets eine juristische Fiction, die Mutter dagegen eine physische Thatsache." *Das Mutterrecht. Eine Untersuchung über die Gynaikokratie der alten Welt nach ihrer religiösen und rechtlichen Natur*, 2nd ed. (Basel: B. Schwabe, 1897), 9.
55. Merezkovsky, 367.
56. Ibid., 371.
57. GW 8: 132; SE 11: 66.
58. Minutes of the *Viennese Psychoanalytic Association*, February 13, 1907.
59. Merezkovsky, 164.
60. Ibid., 165 ("Es ist eine Schande, welche Freude die Menschen daran haben, Großes in den Schmutz zu ziehen.")
61. Ibid., 166 ("sich von den Frauen fern hält").
62. It is essential to work with the German text since the translation of the SE does not convey the often conditional, tentative, ambiguous, hesitant, and remote quality of Freud's style.
63. GW 8: 136; SE 11: 69.
64. Isidor Sadger, *Friedrich Hebbel. Ein Psychoanalytischer Versuch* (Leipzig, Franz Deuticke, 1920).
65. GW 16: 43–56; SE 23: 257–269.

66. "daß wir uns getrauen können, diese Phantasie aus der ihr eigentümlichen Sprache in gemeinverständliche Worte zu übersetzen. Die Übersetzung zielt dann aufs Erotische." GW 8:154; SE 11:85. Other examples of this kind: "We can now provide the following translation of the emphasis given to the vulture's tail in Leonardo's phantasy." (Die Hervorhebung des Geierschwanzes in der Phantasie Leonardos können wir nun so übersetzen), GW 8:168; SE 11:98. "We should have to translate it thus: it was through this erotic relationship with my mother that I became a homosexual" (Es erforderte die Übersetzung. Durch diese erotische Beziehung zur Mutter bin ich ein Homosexueller geworden). GW 8:177; SE 11, 106.

67. Isidor Sadger, *Aus dem Liebesleben Nicolaus Lenaus:* "Besitzt man das Recht, sich in das Intimste zweier Personen kühl kritisierend einzudrängen ... "). In his study on Heinrich von Kleist, Sadger started his apology with an homeric rhetoric: "Das Leben eines Dichters will ich heute schildern, dem gütige Götter ein reiches, mächtiges Genie ... "

68. GW 8:154; SE 11:86.

69. GW 17:141–147; SE 23:281–293.

70. "Er war vielmehr groß und ebenmäßig gewachsen, von vollendeter Schönheit des Gesichts und von ungewöhnlicher Körperkraft, bezaubernd in den Formen seines Umgangs, ein Meister der Rede, heiter und liebenswürdig gegen alle; er liebte die Schönheit auch an den Dingen, die ihn umgaben, trug gern prunkvolle Gewänder und schätzte jede Verfeinerung der Lebensführung." GW 8:130; SE 11:64.

71. GW 8:131; SE 11:65.

72. ibid.

73. Jones remarks on Freud's technique of persuasion: "His expositions succeed in persuading largely because they do not set out deliberately to do so. He divines with an unfailing understanding the difficulties in the mind of the reader, the exact nature of their criticism or opposition, and he can put all this into words more clearly than the reader himself." *Freud*, Vol. II, 209–210.

74. "Schenken wir darum lieber der analytischen Arbeit, die ja nocht nicht ihr letztes Wort gesprochen hat, für eine Weile gerechtes Gehör." GW 8:154; SE 11:86.

75. "Wir halten diesen Vorgang für erwiesen, wenn uns die Kindergeschichte, also die seelische Entwicklungsgeschichte, einer Person zeigt, daß zur Kinderzeit der übermächtige Trieb im Dienste sexueller Interessen stand." GW 8:145; SE 11:78.

76. "Die Beobachtung des täglichen Lebens der Menschen zeigt uns, daß es den meisten gelingt ... " ibid.

77. "Some Elementary Lessons in Psycho-Analysis," SE 23:281.

78. Der große Leonardo blieb überhaupt sein ganzes Leben über in manchen Stücken kindlich; man sagt, daß alle großen Männer etwas Infantiles bewahren müssen." GW 8:199; SE 11:127.

79. "Wer als Künstler schafft, der fühlt sich gegen seine Werke gewiß auch als Vater. Für Leonardos Schaffen als Maler hatte die Identifizierung mit dem Vater eine verhängnisvolle Folge. Er schuf sie und kümmerte sich nicht mehr um sie, wie sein Vater sich nicht um ihn bekümmert hatte." GW 8:192; SE 11:121.

80. "Jene Szene mit dem Geier wird nicht eine Erinnerung Leonardos sein, sondern eine Phantasie, die er sich später gebildet und in seine Kindheit versetzt hat. Die Kindheitserinnerungen der Menschen haben oft keine andere Herkunft; sie werden überhaupt nicht, wie die bewußten Erinnerungen aus der Zeit der Reife, vom Erlebnis an fixiert und wiederholt..." GW 8:152; SE 11:82.

81. "Wir wissen, daß wir der Einwendung zu begegnen haben, das Verhalten Leonardos gegen seine Schüler habe mit geschlechtlichen Motiven überhaupt nichts zu tun und gestatte keinen Schluß auf seine sexuelle Eigenart. Dagegen wollen wir mit aller Vorsicht geltend machen..." GW 8:172; SE 11:101.

82. GW 8:186; SE 11:114.

83. GW 8:182; SE 11:110.

84. GW 8, 158; SE 11, 89.

85. "wir beginnen die Möglichkeit zu ahnen, daß seine Mutter das geheimnisvolle Lächeln besessen..." GW 8:183; SE 11:111.

86. Italics my own.

87. Ibid. Another example of Freud's preconceptions: "Es steht im besten Einklang mit der Deutung der Geierphantasie, wenn mindestens drei Jahre, vielleicht fünf, von Leonardos Leben verflossen waren, ehe er seine einsame Mutter gegen ein Elternpaar vertauschen konnte." ("It fits best with the interpretation of the vulture fantasy if...") GW 8:160; SE 11:91.

88. Italics added, GW 8:184; SE 11:112.

89. Frank J. Sulloway, "Reassessing Freud's Case Histories. The Social Construction of Psychoanalysis," ISIS 82 (1991), 245–275, 265.

90. GW 8:149; SE 11:81.

91. GW 8:159; SE 11:91.

92. Walter Muschg, "Freud als Schriftsteller," Psychoanalytische Bewegung II (1930), 467–511 (476).

93. GW 8:171; SE 11:101.

94. "... daß es ihm nach infantiler Betätigung der Wißbegierde im Dienste sexueller Interessen dann gelungen ist, den größeren Anteil seiner Libido in Forscherdrang zu sublimieren." GW 8:148; SE 11:80.

95. GW 8:204–205; SE 11:132.

96. GW 8:166; SE 11:96–97.

97. Leslie Dick, "Notes on Freud and Writing," Women: A Cultural Review 1 (1990), 256–260, 259.

98. GW 8:155; SE 11:86.

99. GW 8:190; SE 11:119.

100. GW 8:175; SE 11:104.
101. "Erweisbar ist diese Deutung des seelenkundigen Romanschreibers nicht, aber sie kann auf so viel *innere Wahrscheinlichkeit* Anspruch machen, stimmt so gut zu allem, was wir sonst von Leonardos Gefühlsbetätigung wissen, daß ich mich nicht enthalten kann, sie als richtig anzuerkennen." Ibid., italics added.
102. see also Alan Bass, "On the History of Mistranslation and the Psychoanalytic Movement," in Joseph F. Graham, ed., *Difference in Translation* (Ithaca: Cornell University Press, 1985), 102–141.
103. See Meyer Schapiro, 158.
104. R. Richard Wohl, Harry Trosman, 39.
105. GW 8:207; SE 11:134.
106. Herzfeld, *Leonardo Da Vinci. Der Denker, Forscher und Poet.*
107. GW 8:153; SE 11:85. Significant in this regard is Freud's double marking of the following statement in Ernst Grosse, *Die Anfänge der Kunst* (Freiburg i. B. and Leipzig: J. C. B. Mohr, 1894), p. 7: "Wenn man verlangen sollte, daß sie (die Kunstwissenschaft) irgend eine Erscheinung ihres Gebietes in allen Einzelheiten bis auf den Grund erkläre, so stellt man an sie eine Forderung, welche keine Wissenschaft zu erfüllen vermag." (If one were to demand that art history explain a phenomenon in its field in all detail to its roots, one would require something which no science is able to fulfill).

8. Chiasmatic Reading, Aporetic History: Freud's *Macbeth*

Ned Lukacher

In his wartime notes, Heidegger remarks that "the drive of animality and the *ratio* of humanity become identical" in the epoch of modernity that begins with Descartes, ends with Nietzsche, and includes, in one of its more minor episodes, the history of psychoanalysis.[1] Philosophy draws to a close as the question of Being, the question of fundamental causes and origins, becomes completely erased. The consideration of drive, instinct, and natural forces comes, at this defining moment of philosophy's closure, to an ominous end by fully covering up the abyss of the unthought origins of time, space, matter, and energy. In any putative "postmodern" recovery of the meaning of the question of Being, psychoanalysis would presumably play no part. For Heidegger, Freud's thinking is contained within the nihilism of the metaphysical-technological epoch. What I want to consider here is an instance of Freud's thinking that may force us to reconsider Heidegger's account of the historical destiny of psychoanalysis.

At the end of the war, Heidegger concludes his "Letter on Humanism" by suggesting that we reconsider Aristotle's ideas on the relation of poetry and history: "But Aristotle's words in the *Poetics,* although they have scarcely been pondered, are still valid—that poetic composition [*das Dichten*] is truer than the exploration of beings."[2] Aristotle's remarks in chapter 9 of *The Poetics* on the superiority of the universality of poetry over the particularity of history would thus indicate to Heidegger the possibility of another beginning, a new reading of the *logos* that turns to the *energeia* in thinking that is not ruled by the logic of scientific method.

Heidegger decries the reductive empiricism of psychoanalysis in his *Zollikon Seminars* of the 1960s and tries to clarify the relation between Binswanger's and Boss's *rapprochement* between the analytics of *Dasein* and the ontical nature of Freud's metapsychology. While Heidegger is concerned with the ontical-ontological difference that divides and complicates our understanding of all phenomena, Freud makes assumptions (*Unterstellung, suppositio*) about phenomena that enable him to determine their "causal connection" (*Kausalzusammenhang*).[3] Such leveling presumptions about the nature of phenomena are, for Heidegger, characteristic of the scientific-technical forgetting of the meaning of Being. *Poiesis,* by Aristotle's reckoning, proceeds otherwise than by the ontical exploration of beings. Rather than returning to the unthought beginnings of Greek philosophy, psychoanalysis would mark the end of an exhausted epoch that insisted on thinking presence as representation, thus forgetting the question of the presentation itself.

What I shall consider here is whether Freud's reading of *Macbeth* is indeed as averse to the ontological, universal, and thus specifically poetic elements of Shakespeare's writing as Heidegger's formulations would lead one to believe. As we will see, Freud sees such exclusions as marking the specificity of psychoanalysis, whose historicity and scientificity he sees as a decided advance over the universalizing pretensions of philosophy.

More precisely, what I want to consider is the way Freud and Heidegger coincide, or rather, pass into greatest proximity to one another in the course of their very different trajectories. The crossing or chiasmus I wish to construct here will be organized around the differing meanings Freud and Heidegger give to the word *Versagung,* "frustration," "refusal," "denial," and, more exactly, around the differences *where* Freud and Heidegger situate that which resists, refuses, denies, "speaks against" (*ver-sagen*) the thinker-analyst's will to truth. *Sagen* ("saying") is one of Heidegger's fundamental words, for it names the ways in which what lies beyond Being, what lies undiscoverable within the *Abgrund,* the abyss into which the origins of space and time fall, nevertheless finds its way to us, makes us *Its* own, appropriates us in the *Ereignis,* the abyssal event of appropriation in which something entirely other, wholly imponderable, seizes time, space, matter, energy, and human being itself. "Saying" announces this anxious evangile. As one might expect, Freud situates that which brings reading, interpretation, and analysis to a halt somewhere between the empirical and the transcendental, whereas Heideggerian *Ver-*

sagung is located, not within the realms of historicity and the ontical, but within the impenetrable concealments within the ontological order itself. Both Freud and Heidegger reach liminal points beyond which one can proceed no further, but these points are situated in very different orders of experience and thought. Their thinking meets despite (and indeed because of) the decisive countermovements that govern their respective projects. Though their ideas move in very different directions, they cross at the chiasmatic point that they both name *Versagung*.

Versagung, then, is another word for "aporia," the impasse, the *a-poros*, the absent opening, beyond which one cannot proceed. Aporia, writes Aristotle, is "an equality between contrary reasonings [that] would seem to be a cause of perplexity; for it is when we reflect on both sides of a question and find everything alike to be in keeping with either course that we are perplexed which of the two we are to do."[4] And aporia can be located virtually anywhere: in the fork in the path that blocks the hunter's pursuit of his prey, or in philosopher's effort to trace the cause of an effect to either sensation or reflection. Aporia will define the shape of Freud's reading of *Macbeth* as well as of the relation of Freud to Heidegger. Chiasmus *and* aporia describe this relation because, while these two thinkers cross at the point named *Versagung*, and while the lines representing their thought appear, in a two-dimensional model, to meet, these lines forming the chiasmus, when considered in three-dimensional space-time, are at very different levels. Aporia names the unbridgeable gap that separates them, while chiasmus names the non-identical point of their crossing.

For Aristotle, the relation of poetry to history is above all characterized by the question of possibility: "the difference lies in the fact that the historian speaks of what has happened, the poet of the kind of thing that *can* happen."[5] Rather than being opposed to one another, what *has* happened and what *can* happen can be one and the same: "for there is nothing to prevent some of the things that have happened from being the kind of thing that can happen."[6] If poetry is "a more philosophical and serious business than history," it is because of its concern, not with what "particular" persons have done, but with the universality that inheres in determining "what kind of person is likely to do or say certain kinds of things, according to probability or necessity." Aristotle never actually says that poetry is "truer" than history, as Heidegger implies. What is important for Aristotle is that poetry deals with the structures that link certain kinds of speech and action to certain kinds of people, and that those structures can be revealed as simply probable, or, more significantly, they can be universal, "truer" in Heidegger's sense. What an immense distance separates the probable from the necessary! It is not simply the *mimesis* of what *can* happen but of what *must* happen that defines poetry's genuine universality.

While Heidegger pushes Aristotle's emphasis toward the necessity of poetic universality, Freud would reorient poetic mimesis toward historical particularity. Therein lies at once their chiasmatic proximity and their aporetic separation. The question that joins and separates them concerns the very possibility of poetic universality. Freud conceives of psychoanalysis as an avowedly *anti*-philosophical practice. Heidegger conceives of his project as rather a post-philosophical one and insists that psychoanalysis remains locked within the presuppositions of Cartesian modernity. Freud's reading of, or rather his response to, *Macbeth* will allow us to displace both of these characterizations. Heidegger conceives of the primordial *Versagung* that meets us when we confront the abyssal *Seinsfrage* as the leitmotif of the post-philosophical era, the epoch after the *Gestell* or "set-up" of Cartesian modernity, the epoch of poetic thinking that turns instead on the question of the *Ereignis*. Freud situates the *Versagung* within his theory of drives and instincts (*Trieblehre*) and sees it as an intractable resistance within the animality of Cartesian *ratio*. Heidegger, however, sees it not in terms of our bodily existence but rather as the basis of our relation to language. For Freud, the unthinkable thing that thwarts the will, the resistance that *der Trieb* cannot overcome or tolerate, the frustration that makes us fall ill, lies within the depth of our nature. For Heidegger, the depth of our nature itself lies beyond *phusis*, beyond the transformations of matter and energy. He discerns a still more primordial act of poetic making (*poiesis*) underlying the coming-to-being of the physical universe itself. It is precisely such sublimity that Freud is determined to forswear. We will have to determine, then, to what extent Freud himself either achieves a certain postphilosophicality or, inversely, succumbs to a certain Enlightenment reductionism; and, likewise, to what extent Heidegger's putative step beyond the metaphysical-technological determination of the meaning of Being either provides cover for the most conventional idealizations, or whether *Gelassenheit*, the "releasement" of the will to power, ever gets beyond the organicity of animal will and cunning.

• • •

Reading *Macbeth* is a double frustration for Freud, or more precisely, the frustrated reading of a double frustration (*Versagung*). The frustration comes at once from the external world, the world of nature and history, and the internal psychological world of desire and repression. And the frustration does not stop for Freud with the experience of Macbeth and his Queen, it spills over into the reader's experience as well and disrupts the hermeneutic expectation of a fusion of interpretive horizons. "Those Wrecked by Success," which is the second and most substantial section of "Some Character-Types Met With in Psycho-Analytic Work," begins by focusing on the word *Versagung* and on the ego's struggle with its own internal frustrations, which is also a struggle with conscience:

Psycho-analytic work has furnished us with the thesis that people fall ill of a neurosis as a result of *frustration*. What is meant is the frustration of the satisfaction of their libidinal wishes, and some digression is necessary in order to make the thesis intelligible. For a neurosis to be generated there must be a conflict between a person's libidinal wishes and the part of his personality we call his ego, which is the expression of his instinct of self-preservation and which also includes his *ideals* of his personality. A pathogenic conflict of this kind takes place only when the libido tries to follow paths and aims which the ego has long since overcome and condemned and has therefore prohibited for ever. . . . [7]

Versagung is the factor or catalyst that precipitates a neurotic conflict by unveiling the double temporality of a divided subject. When a person falls ill "precisely when a deeply-rooted and long-cherished wish has come to fulfilment," "there can be no question," Freud remarks, "that there is a causal connection [*dem ursächlichen Zusammenhange*]." The rest of the essay tries to situate that causality, and always without success. When one is finally forced to decide whether it is an internal or external frustration that has brought about an illness, one is forced to make a decision about the relation of mind, motion, and matter. The nosological question is finally less remote from the ontological question than it might appear at first glance. What underlies the potentiality for conflict within the ego? What makes it possible for the realization of a primordial wish to trigger a division within the ego in its present state of development? What makes it possible for the ego to internalize both the ideals to which it aspires and the menacing judgments of conscience? What I want to trace is the way Freud forswears these philosophical questions even as his thinking everywhere leads to them.

"It seems to me impossible to come to any decision," writes Freud of what he regards as Shakespeare's mysterious suppression of all "signs [*Anzeichen*] of a deeper motivation that will make [Lady Macbeth's collapse] more humanly intelligible to us" (SE 14:320; GW 10:375). In the discussion of *Macbeth* in this 1915 paper, Freud is emphatic about Shakespeare's concealment of the secrets underlying the protagonists' frustrations. While this concealment creates, for Freud, a desirable aesthetic effect in *Richard III*, where Shakespeare engages our critical reflection simply by withholding "the secret springs" of Richard's actions, in *Macbeth* Shakespeare actually "breaks the causal connection" (*die causale Verknüpfung aufhebt*). Lady Macbeth's collapse, Freud will argue, is intimately linked to Shakespeare's manipulation of the play's timeline. By reconstructing the timeline, Freud will decipher the etiology of the illness of the Macbeths. But by so doing (and this is the interesting point), Freud is responding to the aesthetic universality that Shakespeare's manipulations create by reducing that universality to a singular, idiosyncratic case history. Freud's interest is principally in Shakespeare's gestures of evasion in *Macbeth*. The task of psychoanalysis is to fill in the blanks that artists must create in order to produce aesthetic universality. In that sense, psychoanalysis is an avowedly anti-aesthetic mode of reading.

"Those Wrecked by Success," the essay's second section, follows a section entitled "Exceptions," which concerns those whose illness is linked to a congenital injury and who consequently regard themselves as "exceptions" whose lives have a special logic, and whose literary exemplar is the hunchback Richard III. Lady Macbeth and the ill-fated Rebecca in Ibsen's *Rosmersholm* are adduced in "Those Wrecked by Success." The third and final section of the essay, "Criminality from a Sense of Guilt," is a brief reflection on the Oedipal dimensions of these illnesses.

Freud also elaborates some of the material on *Macbeth* in his contemporaneous *Introductory Lectures on Psycho-Analysis* at the University of Vienna, the first of which he delivered in the fall of 1915. It is toward the end of his fifth lecture, on "Difficulties and First Approaches" to dream interpretation, that Freud turns to this play in connection with what he calls the inaccessibility of the "essence of dreams" (SE 15:97). *Macbeth* is linked in Freud's thinking with impasse and the inability to proceed.

The interpretive impasse is not specific to the reading of literary texts, but pertains to clinical understanding as well. It is in his 1912 paper, "Types of Onset of Neurosis" ("Uber neurotische Erkrankungstypen"), that Freud first uses the term *Versagung*, "frustration," to organize his argument about the opposing claims of internal and external casuality: "The most obvious, the most easily discoverable and the most intelligible precipitating cause of the onset of neurotic illness lies in that external factor which may generally be described as *frustration*. The subject was healthy so long as his need for love was satisfied by a real object in the external world; he becomes neurotic as soon as this object is withdrawn from him without a substitute taking its place" (SE 12:231). Freud wants to address only the question of the cause of the illness and not its form. All the elements of Freud's reading of *Macbeth* are already in place in this essay. While in this essay, cases that are triggered by external frustration are clearly separate from those caused by "an internal change," the text of *Macbeth* will prevent Freud from any longer differentiating these two orders of nosogenesis. There are in fact four types of causality, which Freud does not want to insist on since different types of exciting cause can sometimes be discerned within a single illness: "the erection [*Aufstellung*] of these four types cannot lay claim to any high theoretical value; they are merely different ways [*Wege*] of establishing a particular pathogenic constellation in the mental economy [*seelischen Haushalt*]" (SE 12:237; GW 8:329). They are only ways of separating different conjunctions between the disposition or organization of the ego and its experiences. An external frustration will not cause the onset of neurosis for a subject who is able to renounce the demand for instinctual gratification or who is able to sublimate its libidinal drive or otherwise "elude the frustration." Internal states (e.g. libidinal fixations, the quantity of libido) are exacerbated or become retroactively triggered by certain external events, and the ego either adjusts to these realignments of its internal and external worlds or it falls ill.

Freud's guiding impulse in this essay is to avoid any formal theoretical model and to limit his account only to "impressions arrived at empirically" (*empirisch gewonnener Eindrücke*). This phrase from the essay's opening line is echoed in the concluding sentence: "Psycho-analysis has warned us that we must give up the unfruitful contrast [*unfruchtbaren Gegensatz*] between external and internal factors, of experience and constitution [*Schicksal und Konstitution*], and has taught us that we shall

invariably find the cause of an onset of neurotic illness in a particular
psychical situation, which can be brought about in a variety of ways"
(SE 12:238; GW 8:330). Theoretical barrenness and the barrenness of the
Macbeths are, as we shall soon see, never far apart in Freud's thinking.
Against the barrenness that one encounters in the effort to achieve theoretical insight or resolution, Freud poses only the concrete particularity
of the empirical, which is apparently fruitful insofar as it enables therapy
to be effective. Freud's hypothesis on childlessness in *Macbeth* already
looms on the horizon. For Freud, *Macbeth* is the tragedy of having fallen
victim to the barren antithesis of theoretical resolution. There are, in
effect, two separate impasses to be dealt with here: on the one hand, that
between inside and outside, and on the other hand, that between the
theoretical effort to decide between inside and outside and the empirical
effort to describe the particular genealogy of the case at hand. The inside
and outside lie, as it were, inside the question of inside/outside; which
is another way of saying that psychoanalysis defines itself as precisely
the refusal to go down the path that leads to the kind of gratification we
might call theoretical. "Die Psychoanalyse hat uns gemahnt," has warned
us to abandon, *aufzugeben,* to give up, to offer, to sacrifice, but sacrifice
what? A barren antithesis? Hardly something we should have to be persuaded to renounce, unless, of course, it were also something Freud
desired. To unfold the dynamic of Freud's reading of *Macbeth* is to unfold
the dynamic that accounts for the specificity of psychoanalysis itself, and
that would thus account for the generativity and what we might call the
dynastic drive of analysis. It is as though, in order to realize itself,
to become itself, psychoanalysis would have first to renounce philosophy, to abandon the drive to pose the most fundamental questions,
or, inversely, to pose fundamental philosophical questions as precisely
something to be prohibited, refused, denied, disavowed absolutely. Psychoanalysis is thus first and foremost the refusal of theory; it is the
response to the frustration, the *Versagung,* that the external world presents to the psychoanalytic ego par excellence, namely, that of Sigmund
Freud, which manages to take its satisfaction otherwise by becoming
psychoanalysis, which is to say, by becoming Sigmund Freud. Psychoanalysis speaks for empiricism against theory insofar as it speaks on behalf
of the instinct of renunciation rather than of satisfaction. But this simply
begs the question of the theory implicit in empiricism itself. It thus tries
to present a middle course between the extreme solutions exemplified by

the first two nosogenetic types: the first which lacks the power to renounce a now impossible demand for satisfaction from an absent object,
and the second which cannot learn to desire the still present object otherwise, in a new manner. Psychoanalysis both invents a new object *and*
learns to desire it otherwise.

Psychoanalysis imagines that it has disavowed theory. But what of the
place of literature? Where does *Macbeth* intervene in Freud's struggle to
prevent his empirical impressions from being lost in the barrenness of
theoretical reflection? It intervenes as a *via negativa*, as the exemplary
case of Shakespearean aporia, of the impairment of the text itself, whose
elisions make it impossible to read the nosogenesis of Lady Macbeth's
collapse. It is in the interval between the 1912 essay on the "Types of
Onset of Neurosis" and the 1915 discussions of the play that Freud begins
to study the play. In a letter of 17 July 1914 to Sandor Ferenczi, Freud
writes: "I have begun to study *Macbeth* which has long tormented me
without my having been able to find a solution. How curious it is that
I passed the theme over to Jones years ago, and now here I am so to
speak taking it back. There are dark forces at work in the play."[8] Ernest
Jones, who cites this passage from the still unpublished correspondence
between Freud and Ferenczi, makes no comment concerning having had
this theme passed to him and then having it taken back, nor does he
allude to *Macbeth* in his book *Hamlet and Oedipus* (1949). The question
of Freud's heirs, of Ferenczi's tragic end, and of Jones's role, are all
doubtless at work here and form significant elements in defining the
dynastic drive of psychoanalysis. The play seems always to have been
caught up in Freud's thinking with the questions of productivity and
survival, with the most elemental struggles between the life and death
drives. Jones also cites a letter from Freud to Oskar Pfister in 1910
concerning Freud's fear of becoming unproductive, his fear of a "day
when thoughts cease to flow and the proper words won't come," a fear
that brings Freud to a secret prayer and a quotation from *Macbeth:* "I
secretly pray: no infirmity, no paralysis of one's powers through bodily
distress. We'll die with harness on, as King Macbeth said."[9] Freud is thus
taking rather tragic airs, for this line from the play, "At least we'll die
with harness on our back" (5.5.52),[10] concludes Macbeth's defiant response to the news of his wife's death and of the fast approaching army
of Malcolm and Macduff. But the whole point of Jones's narrative is to
suggest that Freud achieved fame precisely by *not* struggling toward it.

While Freud did become famous after World War I, Jones insists that Freud's work was never predicated by an external cause but was exclusively motivated by inner impulses: "he did nothing in order to achieve fame; it was an incidental consequence of the work he was doing from other motives." It is to this end that Jones cites a letter from Freud to Marie Bonaparte: "Surely we write first of all to satisfy something within ourselves, not for other people. Of course when others recognize one's efforts it increases the inner gratification, but nevertheless we write in the first place for ourselves, following an inner impulse." Jones's effort to purify Freud's reputation from any contaminating traces of externality and of a mere straining after effect is a strangely anxious effort to contain the instabilities that Jones sensed were at work here. What is significant is not the transparency of Jones's effort at containment, but rather his intuitive sense that the play somehow provided Freud with a focus for his most searching meditation on the modalities of inside and outside.

Versagung, inside/outside, *Macbeth,* the specificity of analysis: let us begin to think the inner logic that joins these elements in Freud's thinking. Here is Freud in his lectures from the winter of 1915–16 on the obscurity shrouding the origin of dreams that remains after one has considered the internal and external stimuli:

Where the rest of the dream comes from remains obscure.

Let us notice, however, one peculiarity of dream-life which comes to light in this study of the effects of stimuli. Dreams do not simply reproduce the stimulus; they work it over, they make allusions to it, they include it in some context, they replace it by something else. This is a side of the dreamwork which is bound to interest us since it may perhaps bring us nearer to the essence of dreams [*das Wesen des Traumes*]. When a person constructs some thing as a result of a stimulus, the stimulus need not on that account exhaust the whole of the work. Shakespeare's *Macbeth,* for instance, was a *pièce d'occasion* composed to celebrate the accession of the king who first united the crowns of three kingdoms. But does this immediate historical occasion cover the content of the tragedy? Does it explain its greatnesses and its enigmas? It may be that the external and internal stimuli, too, impinging on the sleeper, are only the *instigators* of the dream and will accordingly betray nothing to us of its essence. (SE 15:96)

Like the mysterious mycelium out of which the dream-wish rises in *The Interpretation of Dreams* (SE 5:525), *Macbeth* here names something like the final veil covering the dream-work's most fundamental content. The very elements of obscurity and undecidability that Freud finds so interesting in thinking about the origin of dreams or in reading *Macbeth* would be intolerable in clinical experience, where a certain strategic decisiveness would be essential. The liminal ontological concealments of *Macbeth* and the language of dreams present absolute resistances, frustrations that cannot be eluded. Psychoanalysis crosses from this realm into the order of practical reason by sacrificing the thought of these dark forces. Philosophy lacks this power of instinctual renunciation, this psychoanalytic power to sacrifice the thought of that which lies beyond the internal and external stimuli. *Macbeth* becomes the proper name for the sacrificial moment within psychoanalysis itself; it names the renunciation, on the part of analysis, ever to speak of the most fundamental philosophical questions of origins and ends. Two paragraphs after the above passage, Freud makes the characteristic link to philosophy and to its imagined rebuke of psychoanalytic thinking: "We have nothing to expect from philosophy except that it will once again haughtily point out to us the intellectual inferiority of the object of our study" (15:98). Philosophy, we can assume, would not, in Freud's estimation, be capable of accounting for the impasses of *Macbeth*, even though the tragedy of *Macbeth* might prove to be the tragedy of philosophy, or more precisely, literature as the tragedy of philosophy's rigid fixations and exclusions. Psychoanalysis accounts for *Macbeth* precisely by *not* accounting for it, and by adapting to the external frustration and refusal that one experiences in reading by placing a value on what cannot be read.

The irreducible factor in practice is the palpable experience of the patient's libido, which is at once so incontrovertible and difficult to measure, and which Freud calls "the quantitative factor":

All the other factors—frustration, fixation, developmental inhibition—remain ineffective unless they affect a certain amount of libido and bring about a damming-up of libido to a certain height. It is true that we are unable to measure this amount of libido which seems to us indispensable for a pathogenic effect; we can only postulate it after the resulting illness has started. [...] it is not a question of an *absolute* quantity, but of the relation between the quota of libido in operation and quantity of libido which the individual ego is able to deal with— that is, to hold under tension [*in Spannung erhalten*], to sublimate or to employ directly. (SE 12:236; GW 8:328)

Here the most profound questions concerning the deepest levels of intentionality, agency, and the will are present only insofar as they are excluded. It is not the quantity of will/libido but the relational structure in which such quantity is deployed or activated. Where Heidegger would discuss the division or difference within the will itself, and Lacan would turn to the difference between the division between the subject of the signifier (i.e. the unconscious subject) and the subject of the signified (i.e. the subject of self-reflection), Freud refuses even to consider the preconditions necessary for the absolute applicability of this relative quantity; that is, for the universality of this particularity. For Freud, the ultimate resistance lies within the empirical itself and thus constitutes, in effect, its theoretical moment, which Freud admits only under the negative sign of *Versagung*. Freud wants to insist that there is no way to exceed *phusis* or the empirical, even while he is forced in the same breath to admit that, within the realm of the empirical will, there are resistances and concealments that do not, properly speaking, belong to the order of nature. While Freud uses *Versagung* to name those resistances *within* the empirical, Heidegger would insist that such resistances open onto a genuinely "other scene," one that is properly the domain of *poiesis* and post-philosophical thinking.

At those enigmatic points of crossing between the universality of theory and the particularity of psychoanalytic practice, Freud sees that which is unreadable and unanalyzable in his patients' experience under the sign of *Macbeth*, and more particularly, he sees Lady Macbeth as the figure who haunts the essence of analysis from its margins. Freud argues both that it is necessary and impossible to distinguish internal from external frustrations, and that the absolute factor is in fact a relative one; and more exactly, it is the relation between pent-up libido and the amount of libido the ego can tolerate. The reading of *Macbeth* is the obscure supplement to the clear determinations of "Types of Onset of Neurosis."

Versagung, frustration, names the relation between libidinal quantity and the libidinal apparatus itself, and more precisely, the impasses that arise in the functioning of the apparatus once too great a strain has been placed upon it. The whole of "Some Character-Types Met With in Psycho-Analytic Work" is directed toward the elaboration of the modes and meanings of *Versagung*, which thus functions as a liminal or horizontal term insofar as it names both the oppositional terms and the difference that separates them and puts them into play. Summing up his analyses of Lady Macbeth and Ibsen's Rebecca, Freud makes even clearer what has been evident from the outset: that *Versagung* is another word for *Gewissen*, "Conscience":

Psycho-analytic work teaches that the forces of conscience [*Gewissenskräfte*] which induce illness in consequence of success, instead of, as normally, in consequence of frustration [*Versagung*], are closely connected with the Oedipus-complex, the relation to father and mother—as perhaps, indeed, is our sense of guilt in general. (SE 14:331; GW 10:389)

In "Types of Onset of Neurosis," Freud had already remarked that, "if we apply ethical standards [*mit ethischen Maßstabe*]: we see people falling ill just as often when they discard an ideal as when they seek to attain it" (SE 12:234; GW 8:326). What is remarkable is that these very diverse modes are modes of *Versagung*, which is to say, both are cases of conscience, cases where, whether the impasse originated in the internal or external worlds, the demands of conscience make it impossible for the ego to act and thus bring the ego to a crisis by the onset of an illness.

As a matter of intellectual history, psychoanalysis may finally appear as yet another chapter, however important, in the very ancient history of conscience. Freud's psychoanalytic redefinition of *das Gewissen* is an effort at a radical de-idealization of our understanding of a moral reality. In this sense, Freud no less than Heidegger is a figure in the post-Hegelian dismantling of the notion of a moral reality outside the historicity of concrete human existence. Freud's intervention in this tradition is extremely important, and it begins in earnest during the years between 1912 and 1915, and continues to intensify throughout the 1920s and 30s, culminating in *Civilization and Its Discontents* (1930) and *Moses and Monotheism* (1938). I tell the rest of this story elsewhere.[11] Let me note here only that Heidegger's account of the "silent voice of conscience" in *Being and Time* already points to his later concerns with the *Versagung* that characterizes the relation of language to the human. The imposition of the logic of the signifier upon the human being, the internalization of authority figures, the call of language upon the human: such Lacanian, Freudian, or Heideggerian notions sever conscience from the onto-theological tradition. They do so without, however, being able to put paid to the question of conscience. Even Freud finds himself confronting the question of the transcendental preconditions for the existence of conscience in *Civilization and Its Discontents*. It is my concern here only to link the early stages of Freud's reflections on conscience to his reading of *Macbeth*.

That Lady Macbeth's collapse is a case of conscience is a critical commonplace whose fundamental significance Freud enables us better to grasp. That Freud had pondered the meaning of *Macbeth* for a very long time is evident from the fact that in the first edition of *The Interpretation of Dreams* (1900) Freud already noted in passing that *Macbeth* is about the contrast between the curse of childlessness and natural succession (SE 4:266). What is most original, and perhaps most problematic, about Freud's reading of the play is its conjunction between the crisis of conscience and the question of childlessness.

In the *Introductory Lectures*, Freud referred to *Macbeth*'s content or *Inhalt*. In the second part of "Some Character-Types," he refers to the chronology of the plot of the play as its *Stoff*, its primordial stuff or materiality. The plausibility and, more exactly, the manipulation of chronology is decisive to Freud's reading. The typological expectations of Freud's examination of "character-types" are differentiated along lines which cases of conscience have always followed; and they finally boil down to the greater or lesser tension brought on by the relation between quantity to the degree of resistance of the ego structures in which that quantity circulates. Freud's crucial point is that Shakespeare, in what Freud regards as a psychoanalytic concealment that is crucial to the production of a truly masterful aesthetic effect, condenses radically the timeline as he found it in Holinshed's *Chronicle*, where ten years elapse between the murder of Duncan and the other crimes committed by the Macbeths. There would have been plenty of time, argues Freud, for the royal couple to confront the terrible ironies that fate has dealt them, time for the extremity of their will to dynastic power to be agonizingly thwarted by the affliction of childlessness. Shakespeare's manipulation of the timeline is thus read by Freud as pointing to what is most essential to understanding the characterological issues defining the historical Queen, about whom Holinshed has no details whatsoever to offer. By thus uncoupling Lady Macbeth's collapse from the historical timeline, Shakespeare forced all of our attention to the inner workings of Lady Macbeth's character, and therein lies the key to his artistic genius, which is bought, precisely, at the price of eliding what, for psychoanalysis, remains the essential element.

The play is thus defined by an essential contradiction: "the contradiction remains that though so many subtle interrelations in the plot [*Stückes*], and between it and its occasion, point to a common origin in the theme of childlessness, nevertheless the economy of time in the tragedy expressly precludes [*ausdrücklich ablehnt*] a development of character from any motives but those inherent in the action itself [*aus anderen als den innerlichsten Motiven*]" (SE 14:322; GW 10:378). The "economy of time" (*die zeitliche Ökonomie*) conceals the external dimension of the fatal *Versagung* within the enigma of Lady Macbeth's inner motivations. The play's aesthetic effect is produced at the price of sacrificing the external factor of childlessness behind the layers of obscurity that are produced by Shakespeare's decision to compress Holinshed's timeline. The work of the *große Dichter*, "the great poet" like Shakespeare, inheres essentially in this *Ablehnung*, this "omission" or "exclusion," which is proper to tragedy, and which works precisely by situating the structure of frustration or *Versagung* within the play's language and structure. And, as Freud had remarked à propos of *Richard III*, this evasion of the spectator's power of critical reflection only serves to strengthen our identification with the hero. The evasion of a concrete genealogy of Lady Macbeth's illness is precisely the element that universalizes her experience and makes it possible for her dilemma to engage our intellectual attention. Of course, Freud's notion of childlessness as a largely external motive begs the question of the liminality of the very notion of childlessness. Freud reminds us that Holinshed himself says nothing about childlessness but simply leaves "warrant enough—both time and occasion—for this probable motivation."

"What, however, these motives can have been which in so short a space of time [*so kurzer Zeit*] could turn the hesitating, ambitious man into an unbridled tyrant, and his steely-hearted instigator into a sick woman gnawed by remorse, it is, in my view, impossible to guess [*erraten*]." The onset of the illness becomes the play's crucial element precisely by virtue of its being concealed behind "a triple obscurity of the bad preservation of the text, the unknown intention of the dramatist, and the hidden purport of the legend [*Sage*]." And while all these obstacles "overwhelm us [. . .] and paralyse our thinking [*Denken*]," analysis nevertheless tries "to grasp this effect" (*diese Wirkung* [. . .] *zu begreifen*)." Within the play's *Sage*, within the *Sagen*, the "saying," of its "legend" lies the *Versagung*, and what one grasps is finally only this irremovable obstacle.

Reading the play is, for Freud, like swimming upstream against the rushing current of events that, in Shakespeare's handling of the plot, seem to "crowd breathlessly on one another." Freud cites J. Darmstetter's introduction to his 1887 edition of play to confirm this impression, which is of course a commonplace in *Macbeth* criticism, and Freud might just as easily have cited Hazlitt, Coleridge, or A. W. Schlegel. But Freud has something to say about the play that is unique to him, and that is that the play's compression is finally *un*justifiable, regardless the aesthetic effect produced: "the sacrifice of common probability" is "justified [*rechtfertigen*] only when it merely interferes with probability, and not when it breaks the causal connection" (*die kausale Verknüpfung aufhebt*). Here we have the clearest definition of what amounts to an *Aufhebung* of *Versagung*, a sublating, elevating, preserving, and negating transformation of what resists analysis and that works by removing itself from the realm of what Freud calls "natural time" (*die natürliche Zeitfolge*), thus "breaking" the link to time, and, instead of merely "leaving the time-duration indeterminate [*der Zeitablauf unbestimmt gelassen wäre*], expressly limited it to a few days" (SE 14:323; GW 10:379). Freud linked *Macbeth* in his *Introductory Lectures* to a causal network that lies hidden beneath the internal and external "instigators" of the dream. Here we glimpse the dynamic of hiding and concealment as it works itself out in the way the play itself eludes the solutions to the very questions posed by the onset of the illness. What Freud has intuited, however indirectly or partially, is that something about time intervenes to block the realization of the human being's will to power. While he will not, à la Heidegger, trace the time question back to its primordial mystery, Freud does recognize that the question of "temporal economy" bears within it the most resistant *Versagung*.

Freud also insists here, and at greater length than in his lectures, on *Macbeth* as a *pièce d'occasion*. Freud is particularly interested in the "remarkable analogies" between the plot of the Macbeth legend and the accession in 1603 of James VI of Scotland to the English throne as a result of the childlessness of the Queen who had put his mother, Mary Stuart, to death:

The "virginal" Elizabeth, of whom it was rumored that she had never been capable of childbearing and who had once described her self as "a barren stock," in an anguished outcry at the news of James's birth, was obliged by this very childlessness of hers to make the Scottish king her successor. And he was the son of the Mary Stuart whose execution she, though reluctantly, had ordered, and who, in spite of the clouding of their relations by political concerns, was nevertheless of her blood and might be called her guest. (SE 14:320)

Freud reads the play as Shakespeare's confirmation of the lesson of James's accession, demonstrating "the curse of unfruitfulness and the blessings of continuous generation." Macbeth's desire "to found a dynasty," even though the Witches have foretold that Banquo is the father of kings, is what Freud thinks is "overlooked if Shakespeare's play is regarded only as a tragedy of ambition." The link between Elizabeth and Lady Macbeth (even Elizabeth as a figure who conjoins both Macbeths), even to the point of seeing Mary's execution as the paradigm for Duncan's murder, is incontrovertible. And Freud might have proceeded even further by adding that the royal performance of *Macbeth* before James I in 1606 made this *pièce d'occasion* a veritable psychoanalytic allegory of Tudor-Stuart relations.

The historical allegory of Macbeth's "fruitless crown" (3.1) is Freud's crucial piece of evidence in support of his thesis on the role of childlessness in the play. Freud is positing in effect a double historical proof of childlessness, for he is saying not only that Shakespeare was addressing the most immediate dynamic of royal power, but that Holinshed's account also suggests, however circumspectly, that childlessness was a factor in the transformation of the Macbeths. After remarking that Macbeth's reign was exemplary in its contribution to the well-being of the "public weal of his subjects," Holinshed adds that Macbeth's ability to govern "the realm for the space of ten years in equal justice [. . .] was but the counterfeit zeal of equity showed by him, partly against his natural inclination, to purchase thereby the favor of the people."[12] Holinshed focuses, however, not on childlessness but on Macbeth's guilty conscience. The above passage continues: "Shortly after, he began to show what he was, instead of equity practicing cruelty. For the prick of conscience (as it chanceth ever in tyrants and such as attain to any estate by unrighteous means) caused in him ever to fear lest he should be served of the same cup as he had ministered to his predecessor." Holinshed's emphasis on the division in Macbeth's character, a "counterfeit zeal of equity" concealing an unrighteous cruelty, all of which is inscribed under the heading of the harrowing persistence of "the prick of conscience," which is so decisive to Shakespeare's elaboration of the legend, was clearly for Freud inadequate to explain the onset of the Macbeths' tragic demise. It is as though for Freud "the prick of conscience," the fear of death, and the recognition of the unarrestable cycle of violence to which their crimes have given rise, were somehow not enough to explain Macbeth's collapse into brutality and his wife's madness. Holinshed, by the way, does not at all develop the character of Lady Macbeth. Freud is simply projecting back into the legend what is specific to Shakespeare's own singular fusion of Lady Macbeth and elements of Elizabeth's historical dilemma. This is no oversight or misunderstanding on Freud's part but rather what he regarded as a necessary effort "to grasp" the unstated element in the legend and in Shakespeare's elaboration of it that might account for the fact that, at a particular time and in a particular manner, the prick of conscience no longer simply menaces or even tortures but actually destroys the subject.

Freud's reading of *Macbeth* situates the psychoanalytic "event" in the aporia or impasse between the inner motives, the ravages of conscience, and the external historical obstacles to dynastic ambition, like childlessness or an opposing army. What is singular about Freud's reading is precisely its insistence on the empirical component, on precisely that which exceeds the psychological or cognitive experience of the subject, exceeds it to the extent that it remains largely unsaid and perhaps unsayable. It is in this very general sense that Freud understands the difference between psychoanalysis and philosophy. Freud's reading of the play is itself an important component in his intervention in the history of conscience, important in that it redirects thinking away from the psychological and spiritual element in conscience and turns instead to the material events and conditions that are essential precipitating agents. Freud is thus himself compelled to try "to grasp the psychological mechanism" that explains the illness without ever being able "to come to a decision" vis-à-vis the relative roles of libidinal quantity, ego-structures, and "actual external alterations in circumstances": "Analytic work has no difficulty in showing us that it is forces of conscience [*Gewissensmächte*] which forbid the person to gain the long-hoped-for advantage [*Gewinn*] from the fortunate change in reality. It is a difficult task, however, to discover the essence and the origin of these judging and punishing tendencies, which so often surprise us by their existence where we do not expect to find them" (SE 14:318; GW 10:372–73). Freud continues Hegel's historicization of conscience by showing that certain *Tendenzen* are realized while others are not. What Freud wants to resist, however, is the philosophical or dialectical appropriation of particularity into any kind of universality, the transformation of this particular case, this relative set of connections, into any universal element whatsoever. Freud expressly wishes *not* to idealize or spiritualize the operations of conscience.

What we must consider now are the lengths to which Freud will go in trying to resist what he construes as a philosophical gesture. The extremities to which his aversion to philosophy can lead him may themselves enact a surreptitious spirituality in Freud's own thinking, perhaps driven by a dynastic component in the will no less irresistible than philosophy itself.

The nosogenetic types employ a new vocabulary that, while it appears to demystify the old notion of conscience as the trace of an onto-theological moral order, finally reminds us how enigmatic the operations of conscience still remain. For Freud, a case of conscience necessarily entails a pathological element, and that is what he calls *Versagung*, which is "closely connected with the Oedipus-complex, the relation to father and mother—as perhaps, indeed, is all our sense of guilt in general" (SE 14:331). And *Versagung*, Freud discovers, has an aporetic structure that cannot be reduced to either empirical or psychological, outer or inner, causality. Freud himself, in effect, is driven by his own case of conscience to acknowledge the paralyzing impasse that confronts him and to adduce, however reconditely or in opposition to received ideas, an incontrovertible material element in an otherwise psychological structure, just as, conversely, he introduces psychological elements into otherwise material causalities. Philosophy would lie in the extremity to which either the empirical or the psychological might finally be taken, the idealizing extremity that can befall the material as well as spiritual elements in any etiology.

Shakespeare was, of course, present, along with Sophocles and Wilhelm Fliess, at the birth of psychoanalysis in October 1897, where it is precisely Hamlet's line, "Thus conscience does make cowards of us all," which Freud interprets to mean that it is Oedipal guilt that causes the Prince's downfall. In the case of *Hamlet* the onset of the illness is once again inconceivable without the change in external circumstances, i.e. Old Hamlet's murder and returning Ghost. But more important to Freud's thinking, it is inconceivable without Shakespeare's intuitive knowledge of unconscious structures. *Hamlet* appears to yield its secrets to Freud more readily than does *Macbeth*, though Freud never in fact devoted the kind of critical attention to *Hamlet* that he did to *Macbeth*. Freud adduces the death of Shakespeare's own father as a possible historical factor in triggering the pale, sickly cast of the son's unconscious guilt, and thus the invention of Hamlet. If the circumstances surrounding James I's accession are crucial to *Macbeth*, Freud has only the biography of the man from Stratford to rely on in reading *Hamlet*. In 1915–16, Freud still believed that the man from Stratford wrote the plays of Shakespeare. Thomas Looney would soon convince him otherwise. What we might now be able better to grasp is that the arguments put forth in "Types of Nosogenesis" and "Some Character-Types Met With in Analytic Work" go far toward explaining how it is possible that Freud could have been persuaded by the Oxfordians.

Peter Gay's recent essay, "Freud and the Man from Stratford," explains Freud's embarrassing, yet revealing, adherence to Looney's theory that Edward de Vere, the Seventeenth Earl of Oxford (1550–1604) authored the plays, as a psychological phenomenon largely attributable to, of all things, Freud's impatience in the face of insoluble problems: "his patience grew shorter as well, particularly as he repeatedly set dates for his probable demise. This, too, is why when he was getting old he entered into the two most eccentric commitments of his life, both revisionist in the extreme—the identification of Moses as an Egyptian and of Shakespeare as the earl of Oxford."[3] Freud discovered Looney's *Shakespeare Identified* (1920) in 1926 and remained an Oxfordian until his death. The discussions of *Macbeth* (1915–16) thus present us with a Freud fully on the aporetic horns of a dilemma, which he will, in a kind of psychological desperation, resolve in the last ten or so years of his life by, in effect, impaling himself on those horns by posing two apparently ill-founded theories. What Gay calls "Freud's impatient compulsion to tackle enigmas" is at full tilt in the discussion of *Macbeth*. It is thus significant that, as Gay points out, the only passage Freud underlined in Darmstetter's introduction to the 1887 Garnier edition of the play concerns Lady Macbeth's "*inexplicable contradictions.*"[4] While early Freud psychologizes *Hamlet* into Shakespeare's psychobiography (the man from Stratford), middle Freud suffers the irresolvable impasse of *Macbeth* where both internal and external factors lead into dark enigmas about the origin and essence of conscience, and late Freud abandons the evidence to embrace the Seventeenth Earl of Oxford.

Listen to his letter of 2 April 1937 to Arnold Zweig:

We will have a lot to discuss about Shakespeare. I do not know what still attracts you to the man of Stratford. He seems to have nothing at all to justify his claim, whereas Oxford has almost everything. It is quite inconceivable to me that Shakespeare should have got everything secondhand—Hamlet's neurosis, Lear's madness, Macbeth's defiance and the character of Lady Macbeth, Othello's jealousy, etc. It almost irritates me that you should support the notion.[15]

Zweig had earlier offered, in an apparently conciliatory gesture, a kind of theoretical compromise where he conceded that Oxford, though not the author of the plays, nevertheless exerted strong influence on the man from Stratford: "Certainly Oxford had a profound influence on Sh., indeed regenerated him, as it were. [. . .] He is, however, not the author of Sh.'s works, but the begetter."[16] Coming, as it does, in response to Zweig's reasonable suggestion, Freud's intransigence on this question becomes unmistakable. This is no mere pique or fiat on Freud's part, but rather the necessary resolution to something Freud experienced as unbearable aporia and crippling irresolution. And the basic element in Freud's final reflections appears to be, in this letter to Zweig, the incontrovertibility of the evidence and its apparently overwhelming quantity. That Freud resolved this question, which was always essential to his psychoanalysis of culture, in what is simply the wrong way is not something that can be dismissed as mere impatience, a sort of hasty placing of one's bet before the final throw of the dice. It is incredibly important to Freud's contribution to the history of conscience, of moral reasoning, and of the origins of moral law that he decided that Edward de Vere "has almost everything" to justify his claim and that the man from Stratford "has nothing at all," and it is incredibly important that he decided that the doctrine of conscience and instinctual renunciation originated in the thinking, not of a Jew, but of an Egyptian. Moses and Shakespeare are, as Gay recognizes, the proper names of different stages in the same history, the ancient and modern history of conscience. That both theses are incorrect and misleading is something that psychoanalysis must account for.

What clearer testimony could there be to Freud's relentless determination to dismantle the subtle and not so subtle theological-metaphysical assumptions and arguments that have always governed the philosophy of conscience and the law! Psychoanalysis thinks itself anti-philosophical in precisely this regard, that it does *not* regard guilt solely as the result of an internal relation or structure but as a transformation involving an external *Versagung* as well. It is as though Freud were being overly vigilant in fending off the philosophical or inward solution. That he finally settled upon Edward de Vere and the Egyptian Moses suggests the desperation that at last overcame Freud's ability to bear with undecidability. The man from Stratford is quintessentially the poet-dramatist of conscience, whose voices reinvent the dark tangle from which conscience is spun. Freud was not a literary scholar and cannot be expected to pursue all lines of inquiry. But something so much larger than that clearly comes into view. The choice of Vere as author of the plays is an emphatic and definitive judgment on the nature of conscience itself, and above all a judgment on the relationality, the relativity that Shakespearean conscience measures out between the realm of unconscious structures and the world of chance and history. In deciding that the man from Stratford has "nothing at all" to do with the plays, Freud is saying that only a man who had a firsthand knowledge of power and of the intricate psychological structures of life at Court could have written those poetic histories of the new individualist, subjectivist-modernist, experience of conscience. Freud simply reached a point where it became as difficult to accept Shakespeare's moral-poetic reinvention of the world as it had been earlier to accept Holinshed's moral reading of the downfall of the Macbeths. Freud must finally posit an external, historical experience, some empirical factor, in order to explain the shape of law and conscience. Freud wants to avoid the pitfalls of philosophy and in so doing falls into one of the deepest.

Freud found an external pretext for Mosaic law in the monotheism of Akhenaton and a pretext for Shakespeare's poetry of conscience in the biography of Edward de Vere. This is not the result of impatience but of long and sustained reflection, and it doubtless produced some relief as well by shuffling off the mortal coil of aporetic reading. Suddenly, Shakespeare's plays seem comfortably situated in some historicist referentiality where the aesthetico-political high jinks of the European aristocracy clearly take precedence over the power of poetic imagination. Freud's hyper-realism finally begins to resemble the most idealizing effort to have the last word and to utter the originary names of the meaning of being. The interdiction against philosophy appears as a ruse to divert attention from the secret philosophical agenda of psychoanalysis itself.

Childlessness in *Macbeth* is thus a significant step on Freud's way to becoming an Oxfordian. The relation of internal and external motives in the onset of an illness or in the production of the plays of Shake-speare or in the historical origin of the instinctual renunciation of the Jews, is Freud's defense against idealizing conscience, his way of de-transcendentalizing the history of conscience. But this very expectation that there must necessarily be a relational structure is itself an idealizing residue within Freud's own thinking and one that he automatically univ-ersalizes. Freud simply found the disequilibrium between imagination and experience in the case of the man from Stratford too unstable, too irregular to be believed. And so it might have been expected that the implicit idealism that absolutizes the relative difference would take the form of the explicit idealism of a belief in the aristocratic lineage of Europe's greatest poet.

Is there something in the order of experience that lies beyond the order of nature? Freud says "no," while Heidegger insists that something does remain of a poetic act that defines the emergence of nature itself, defines it even as the character of the act itself continues to withdraw into the abyss of time. Freud's *Versagung* lies within *phusis* itself; and *Macbeth* is the name of one its vanishing points. Freud accounts for the play's aesthetic nature only insofar as he is convinced that the artist must conceal the particular relational structure in the process of creating the effect of a universalizing identification between his protagonists and their audi-ence. Freud's thinking would thus imply that the universality of poetry which, for Aristotle, brought it closer to philosophy and further from history, was an aesthetic device rather than an analytic structure. In this case, psychoanalysis and poetry would be in countermovement to each other, crossing chiastically in Shakespeare, Goethe, or in Diderot's re-flection on the incest motif in *Rameau's Nephew*. Could we not read Freud's reading of *Macbeth* as a radically historicist one that, in its zeal to differentiate itself from the idealizing conventions of philosophy, ends up foreclosing a most material element, namely the power, the will, of *poiesis* itself? And is not such a foreclosure the very mark of an idealism? Freud joined the Oxfordians in a rather perverse act of revenge upon his own precursors. Freud's version of the Nietzschean-Heraclitean revenge against time takes the form of revenge against Moses and Shakespeare, against the two major efforts in Western culture to poetically reinvent conscience and the moral law. Moses the Jew, *Der Mann Moses*, and "the man from Stratford," are locutions that betray Freud's deep rivalry with any mere mortal; if these men anticipated, equaled, or surpassed him, then surely they must have been gods, or, which is nearly the same thing, Egyptian or English princes. Psychoanalysis's denial of its philosophical-dynastic will to power is at the same time the key to understanding how that power works. There is still, as Heidegger recognizes, the metaphysical-technological will to truth as empirically grounded and manifest, but there is also in Freud, however concealed or sublimated, a subversive act of *poiesis*, a motion that gives form to an act that marks a divergence or difference from natural motion. The Earl of Oxford and Moses the Egyptian reveal the extent to which Freud's apparent empiricism betrays an unmistakably idealist coloring.

By the time of "Neurosis and Psychosis" (1924), Freud appears to have reduced *Versagung* to a purely external causality; but now there appears a new complication: the unreadability of conscience:

There always remains as a common feature in the etiology both of the psychoneuroses and the psychoses the factor of frustration—the lack of fulfilment of one of those eternal uncontrollable childhood wishes [*ewig unbezwungenen Kindheitswünsche*] that are so deeply rooted in our composition, phylogenetically ordained as it is. In the last resort this frustration is always an outer one; in the individual case it may proceed from that internal institution (in the super-ego) which has taken over the part played by the demands of reality. Now the pathogenic effect depends on whether, in the tension of such a conflict, the ego remains true in its allegiance to the outer world and endeavours to subjugate the *id*, or whether it allows itself to be overwhelmed by the *id* and thus torn away from reality. In this apparently simple situation, however, a complication is introduced by the existence of the super-ego, which, in some connection not yet clear to us, combines in itself influences from the *id* as well as from the outer world, and is to some extent an ideal prototype of that state towards which all the ego's endeavours are bending, the reconciliation [*die Versöhnung*] of its manifold allegiances. (SE 19:151; GW 13:390)

Conscience thus appears as a kind of pre-originary pathology, a kind of homeopathic complication that is introduced precisely in order to protect the ego from any future onslaughts of the id. Freud's last decade is an effort to salvage his second *Trieblehre* (the opposition of Eros and Thanatos) and to prevent it from collapsing into an idealism. Conscience becomes another name for that which frustrates Freud's effort to ground behavior in *der Trieb*.

In " 'A Child Is Being Beaten' " (1919) Freud again turns to *Macbeth* at the very moment he senses that the putative duality of ego drives and sexual drives seems to dissolve away: "As is well known, all the signs [*Kennzeichen*], on which we are accustomed to base our distinctions, tend to melt into one another as we come nearer to the source" (SE 17:187; GW 12:207). What follows suggests that Freud sees himself in the place of Macbeth and Banquo as they hear the enigmatic promise of the Weird Sisters, who, having uttered their seeming paradoxes, vanish into the air. "The earth hath bubbles, as the water has," says Banquo, "And these are of them"; to which Macbeth responds, "and what seem'd corporal,/ Melted as breath into the wind" (3.1.79–82). Like the mysterious thing called "conscience," the Witches are the origin of an utterance whose binding, incontestable power to foretell the shape of things disrupts all human expectations of natural law even as it melts away. Language as a bubble on the earth, the unreadable "stuff" that would appear to go even deeper than the materiality of *phusis:* "So perhaps like the promise [*Verheissung*] of the weird sisters to Banquo: not clearly sexual, not in itself sadistic [i.e. ego drives], but yet the *Stoff* from which both will later come" (SE 17:187; GW 12:207). The play turns around the irreducible asymmetry between *being* king and *being father* of kings, between, in Freud's idiom, the ego and sexual drives, Thanatos and Eros. It is as though there is a conscience in the very ground of things, beyond the scope of human sensation but nevertheless palpable and active. The promise of language is also the work of necessity, Aristotle's *ananke*, the domain of poetic universality and philosophy. This is precisely the domain that Freud fears and is determined not to enter, and his writing stages the various ways he succeeds in resisting temptation. The imbrication, in the beating phantasy, of sadistic and sexual elements is for Freud an occasion to replay this primordial struggle between nature and its other, and between psychoanalysis and philosophy. The strange place where they cross is always in Freud's mind linked to *Macbeth*.

In the above passage Freud referred to conscience as "the ideal prototype" (*ein Idealvorbild*) because it tries to reconcile (in advance of any conflict) the struggle in the ego between the opposing drive mechanisms. And this is exactly how he speaks of the almost hermaphroditic fusion of the Macbeths into one dynamic figure. Freud remarks in "Some Character-Types" that "It is a difficult task to discover the essence and origin of these judging and punishing trends; which so often surprise us by their existence where we do not expect to find them." Referring to a recent study by Ludwig Jekels, Freud suggests that Macbeth and his Queen may in fact be "like two disunited parts of a single psychical individuality, and it may be that they are both copied from a single prototype [*Nachbilder eines einzigen Vorbildes*]" (SE 14:324; GW 10:380). Freud cites several incidents, and there are many more besides, where something *said* by Macbeth becomes something *experienced* by Lady Macbeth: "Thus what he feared in his pangs of conscience is fulfilled in her: she is incarnate remorse after the deed, he incarnate defiance." The Macbeths would be the *Nachbilder*, the divided after-images of the tension within conscience. Of the prototype, the "single psychical individuality" from which they were presumably drawn, Freud says nothing. But would not such an extraordinary case of conscience have to be drawn from the author's own experience? We can conclude only that, in the following years, Freud must have decided that such an experience lay beyond the capacity of the man from Stratford.

The question Freud does not ask is of course the question that Heidegger finds most compelling; for the *Versagung* of conscience, the strange promise and mystery it withholds, is not the negativity that Freud experiences but rather the promise of a still withheld secret of the fourth side of time, that in which past, present, and future are themselves contained. For Freud *Versagung* is a negative limit; for Heidegger it is the first step toward the thought of the *Ereignis*.

"More original than man," writes Heidegger in the late 1920s, "is the finitude of Dasein in him."[7] What Heidegger calls "the inner function of the law itself for Dasein"[8] becomes, by the mid-1930s, the site of an irresistible *Versagung*. Following the debacle of the Rectorship of 1933–34, when Heidegger, to the amazement of friends and colleagues, espoused Nazi ideology with astonishing fervor, he began writing (in a major effort of intellectual reinvention) what is now being called his greatest work besides *Being and Time*. Published for the first time in 1989, the *Beiträge zur Philosophie (Vom Ereignis)* is as much concerned with recognizing limitations as *Being and Time* was with trying to overcome them. It is in this context that the words *Versagung* and *Verweigerung* (refusal, denial) become central to Heidegger's new thought of the *Ereignis*: "The *Ereignis* as the deferring *Versagung* and therein as the maturation of 'time,' the greatness of the harvest and the immensity of the giving [*Verschenkung*], and in *truth* as *clearing* [*Lichtung*] for the *self-concealing* [*Sichverbergen*]."[9] *Versagung* is nothing less for Heidegger than the "inner necessity" (*die innigste Nötigung*) of the *Ereignis* and the mainspring of Its donation of time and space.

Versagung in Heidegger thinks the transcendental conditions of the abyssal ground of *Versagung* in Freud, while *Versagung* in Freud particularizes, historicizes the idealizing tendencies in Heideggerian *Versagung*. While some students of Freud and Heidegger will inevitably conclude that, in an era of Heidegger, Carl Schmitt, and Alfred Bäumler, Freud's intrepid avoidance of philosophy will always stand him in good stead, others might also see philosophy as precisely what proves irresistible to Freud as well, and, if not philosophy, then certainly the uncircumventible *Versagung* that lies on the poetic margins and in the unsounded depths of nature. The aporetic history that joins and separates Freud and Heidegger nevertheless holds them, in their differing positions, in relation to the moral law of their epoch. And while they traverse the history of conscience at radically different trajectories, they cross in their shared sense of the need to reinvent our relation to language and the law. Heidegger's opposition to psychoanalysis and Freud's anti-philosophical exhortations may prove still more wide-ranging and fundamental as yet more of both authors' writings are made available.

Notes

1. Martin Heidegger, "Overcoming Metaphysics," in *The End of Philosophy*, trans. Joan Stambaugh (New York: Harper & Row, 1973), 106.
2. Martin Heidegger, "Letter on Humanism," in *Basic Writings*, ed. David Farrell Krell (New York: Harper & Row, 1977), 240; "Brief über den 'Humanismus,' " in *Wegmarken*, ed. Friedrich-Wilhelm von Herrmann, *Gesamtausgabe*, Vol. 9 (Frankfurt a. M.: Vittorio Klostermann, 1976), 363.
3. Martin Heidegger, *Zollikoner Seminare: Protokolle-Gespräche-Briefe*, ed. Medard Boss (Frankfurt a. M.: Vittorio Klostermann, 1987), 233–34.
4. Aristotle, *Topics*, in *Complete Works*, ed. Jonathan Barnes, 2 vols. (Princeton: Princeton University Press, 1984), 1:245 (Book 8 [145b]).
5. Aristotle, *Poetics*, trans. Gerald Else (Ann Arbor: University of Michigan Press, 1970), 32–33.
6. Aristotle, *Poetics*, 34.
7. Sigmund Freud, "Some Character-Types Met With in Psycho-Analytic Work," in SE 14:316; Subsequent references to this edition are indicated by SE. References to Freud's German text are to: Sigmund Freud, *Gesammelte Werke*, ed. Marie Bonaparte, Anna Freud, et al., 18 vols. (Frankfurt a. M.:

S. Fischer, 1952–77), 10:370. Subsequent references to this edition are in-dicated by GW

8. In Ernest Jones, *The Life and Work of Sigmund Freud*, 3 vols. (New York: Basic Books, 1953–57), 2:372.
9. In Jones, *Life and Work of Sigmund Freud*, 2:397.
10. All references are to *Macbeth*, ed. Kenneth Muir (New York: Methuen, 1984).
11. In *Scenes from a History of Conscience* (forthcoming).
12. *Shakespeare's Holinshed: Holinshed's Chronicle (1587)*, ed. Richard Hosley (New York: Capricon, 1968), 19–20.
13. Peter Gay, *Reading Freud* (New Haven: Yale University Press, 1990), 44.
14. Gay, *Reading Freud*, 48.
15. *The Letters of Sigmund Freud and Arnold Zweig*, ed. Ernest L. Freud, trans. Elaine and William Robson-Scott (New York: Harcourt Brace Jovanovich, 1970), 140.
16. Ibid., 138.
17. Martin Heidegger, *Kant and the Problem of Metaphysics*, trans. Richard Taft (Bloomington: Indiana University Press, 1990), 156.
18. Heidegger, *Kant and the Problem of Metaphysics*, 175.
19. Martin Heidegger, *Beiträge zur Philosophie (Vom Ereignis)*, ed. Friedrich-Wilhelm von Herrmann, in *Gesamtausgabe*, vol. 65 (Frankfurt a. M.: Vittorio Klostermann, 1989), 268. (Italics appear in the original.) Also see pages 22, 29, 113, 240–41, 384–85, 388, 411.

9. Freud v. Freud: Freud's Readings of Daniel Paul Schreber's *Denkwürdigkeiten eines Nervenkranken*

Jay Geller

Till near the nucleus [*Kern*] we come upon memories which the patient disavows even in reproducing them—Sigmund Freud, "Psychotherapy of Hysteria"

Before beginning his analysis of Daniel Paul Schreber's *Denkwürdigkeiten eines Nervenkranken* (Memoirs of My Nervous Illness)[1] Sigmund Freud admonishes his "readers [first] to make themselves acquainted with the book."[2] Despite this advice, virtually all subsequent interpretations of Schreber's dementia have been based upon Freud's selective citations in his "Psychoanalytic Notes on an Autobiographical Account of a Case of Paranoia (Dementia Paranoides)."[3] Displaced by Freud's case study, Schreber's text became thereby the "most-quoted unread book of the twentieth century."[4] This chapter, however, takes Freud's advice quite literally: it reads the markings and marginalia he made in his own copy of the *Denkwürdigkeiten* against the rhetorical strategies by which he constructed his case study. By analyzing the conflicts between those two narratives, this paper reconsiders the methods and motivations of Freud's "Psychoanalytic Notes."

In his copy Freud fixes upon a passage about which his marginalia, the case study, and Schreber's memoirs all pivot. After describing the series of events which led to his mental collapse, Schreber writes: "I must now discuss... what in my opinion is the tendency innate in the Order of the World, according to which under certain circumstances the

'*Entmannung*' (transformation into a woman) of a human being . . . must result . . . " (S44). Freud double underlines this first appearance of *Entmannung* in the memoirs and writes in the margins *Kern der Sache*, the heart of the matter. The revelation of the *Kern der Sache* is the climax of a quest for sources, symptoms, and significance undertaken in the margins of Freud's copy. His comment also anticipates *Entmannung*'s central role in the case study. Finally this initial mention of *Entmannung* concludes Schreber's cosmological and biographical contextualization of his illness as well as heralds the central portion of his memoirs: the ensuing depiction of that "*Nervenkrankheit.*"

The matter of each of these three narratives hinges upon the core meaning of *Entmannung*—yet, as Freud had written of the etiology of hysteria, "It can happen that there is more than one nucleus" (*Kern;* SE 2:290). The contrasting strategies of the translators of the *Standard Edition* of Freud's works and of the translators of the *Memoirs* mark the opposing fields of meaning which converge on *Entmannung*. Strachey et al. read this term as "emasculation" and correlate it explicitly with both physical and figurative castration. "Emasculation" evokes the castration complex, the matrix of childhood phantasies and theories which leads to the recognition of sexual difference and the interpellation of the child into normative structures of symbolic differences. The "emasculated" Schreber is presented as a devirilized victim of phantasized sexual persecution. By contrast, Macalpine and Hunter, by opting for "unmanning," literalize a more figurative translation of the term in order, on the one hand, to emphasize *Entmannung*'s connection with Schreber's transformation into a reproductive woman and, on the other hand, to deemphasize its connotation of "sterilization." The choice of "unmanning," by privileging women's necessary activity, here the female-specific capacity to reproduce, questions the authority of castration as the determinant of difference. The "unmanned" Schreber, for Macalpine and Hunter, is a pregnant Redeemer.[5] "Emasculation" and "unmanning" converge on *Entmannung* in Schreber's text; so do the oppositions between universal theory and normative structures, male epistemology and the female body, homosexuality and heterosexuality, the hegemony of German Christian culture and Jewish identity. Schreber embraces these contradictory representations.[6]

But, as the heart of Freud's matter and possessed by such conflicting meanings, *Entmannung* threatens to undermine not only Freud's interpretation of the Schreber case but also the authority of psychoanalysis and even his self-identity. Freud's deployment of *Entmannung* in "Psychoanalytic Notes," particularly his separation of Schreber's "emasculation" from his pregnancy phantasies, endeavors both to constrain the overdetermination of the term and to elide the mixture of personal concerns and competing theories betrayed by that polysemy. When the divergent strands and curious silences which sometimes characterize Freud's marginal notes to Schreber's discussion of *Entmannung* are read against his emphasis in "Psychoanalytic Notes" upon "emasculation," more seems to be at work than the manifest motivations of the study: an interpretation of Schreber's delusion, an explanation of paranoia, and the promotion of psychoanalysis and its theory. Other matters that may have compromised either Freud's narrative or himself[7]—the roles of bodies and women, homosexual and ethnic identifications—also occupy the margins of his copy. Freud's marginalia contested and conditioned a case study that sought to conceal its own heterogeneous origins.

After examining how Freud constructed "Psychoanalytic Notes" about the core of "emasculation," this chapter explores the alternative etiologies and troubling identifications that arose in Freud's annotations only later to be secreted in the case study. Particular focus is then placed upon how Freud's neglect of Schreber's vision of the "unmanned" Eternal Jew both in print and in the margins suggests a relationship between the "emasculated" Schreber's problems with his sexual identity and the circumcised Freud's own concerns about his ethnic identity.[8] *Entmannung* reproduces a Jewish difference Freud would disavow.

Entmannung: From the Court to Castration

Freud first read the *Denkwürdigkeiten*[9] in the wake of his discovery of the role of castration in psychosexual development.[10] He had concluded that castration, as little boy's theory and as paternal threat, was necessary to the recognition of sexual difference, the resolution of the Oedipus complex, and the formation of gendered identity, both normal and pathological. And an analysis of the *Denkwürdigkeiten,* since it explicitly discussed fathers, homosexuality, and castration/emasculation, offered him an ideal forum not just for explaining paranoia but also for presenting the truth and efficacy of psychoanalytic theory and method in general.[11]

In "Psychoanalytic Notes" Freud contours his narrative of Schreber's case about two foci: "emasculation" and its necessary concomitant, Schreber's father. Oriented by these topoi, Freud generates an interpretation of Schreber's delusional system in which "emasculation" represents both the key delusion and the key to the germ of his illness: "The enormous significance of homosexuality for paranoia is confirmed by the central emasculation fantasy."[12] Schreber's paranoia, he concludes, originated in the castration complex,[13] the consequent homosexual feelings toward his father, and their repression.

Freud opens his portrayal of Schreber's "Case History" (section 1) with a brief summary from the Royal Superior Country Court:[14] "He believed he has a mission to redeem the world and to restore it to its lost state of bliss. This, however, he could only bring about if he were first transformed from a man into a woman" (SE 12:16, S475). The soteriological and gender-crossing strands of the delusions delineated by the Court and echoed in the medical reports then become the guidelines for Freud's initial selection of citations. For the Court, Schreber's belief in his Redeemer role and not his transformation into a woman is primary; further, these delusional topoi are originally interconnected. But in his ensuing presentation of Schreber's system Freud shifts the Court's evaluations of the religious and gender components as well as its understanding of their relationship to one another. Once the initial depiction of Schreber's delusions is completed Freud asserts the opposite, "That the emasculation phantasy was of a primary nature and originally independent of the Redeemer idea" (SE 12:20).[15] Freud's claim here also indicates a more important change in the meaning of Schreber's delusions. That is, his gender switch attains in Freud's presentation a more sexual significance: his delusion that he had been transformed into a woman becomes a phantasy of emasculation (*Entmannungsphantasie*).

Freud's preference for "emasculation" (*Entmannung*) over "transformed into a woman" follows from his recent determination of the castration complex. The consequent emphasis on "emasculation" determines Schreber as a man who has been demeaned, who has lost his manliness, who has been overcome by homosexual affect. This choice all but obviates Schreber's avowed rationale for his transformation into a woman: the reproduction of the all-but-destroyed human race. Freud emphasizes instead an emasculated Schreber who is a resistant victim to a "sexual delusion of persecution" (SE 12:18). This Schreber, reduced to playing the part of a prostitute or "female wanton" (*weiblichen Dirne;* SE 12:48), looks upon his transformation not as a blessing but as a "disgrace" (*Schmach, Schimpf;* SE 12:33, 48). This deemphasis upon Schreber's acceptance of his gender transformation had already been implicit in Freud's selection of the Court excerpt as a summary statement; it omitted Schreber's impregnation by God to repopulate the world. Further, in describing Schreber's situation almost solely in terms of *Entmannung* Freud ignores Schreber's use of the term. When Schreber employs *Entmannung,* it is usually in conjunction with a parenthetical phrase that he added to clarify its meaning: "(transformed into a woman) [(*Verwandlung in ein Weib*)]" (S44). Freud inverts that formulation: "the idea of being transformed into a woman (that is, of being emasculated)" (SE 12:18). Schreber does not assume a new gender identity; rather in Freud's account normative sexual difference has been rendered problematic as Schreber becomes a feminized man.[16] *Entmannung* signifies his castration and not transformation (cf. SE 12:56).

The role of the Redeemer also undergoes a subtle shift of significance in Freud's depiction: from his saving relation with the world to his favored relation with God. This alteration allows Freud to emphasize the feminine aspect of the Redeemer's relation with the deity. Hence after Freud lays out the "Case History" he sets forth his project of elucidating Schreber's delusion: "In Schreber's system the two principal elements of his delusion (his transformation into a woman and his favored relation to God) are united in his assumption of a feminine attitude towards God. It will be a necessary part of our task to show that there is an essential *genetic* relation between these two elements" (SE 12:34). In this formulation the relationship among the elements of Schreber's delusional system as determined by both the Court and the doctors has been transformed: the transformation into a woman is not just the formal cause for redemption, a mere albeit bizarre accident; rather, now understood as emasculation, it has become the final cause as well. Schreber becomes Redeemer in order to redeem his desire to be emasculated. And his emasculation is the realization of a wish: his assumption of a feminine attitude toward God.

In the next section of his case study Freud argues how Schreber's deluded emasculation, as the icon and index of the castration complex, would mediate the "essential genetic" relationship between Schreber's "transformation into a woman and his favored relation to God." However, prior to concluding the "Case History," Freud proffers an image that exemplifies how "emasculation" dominates all aspects of his argument. Freud adds that either he demonstrates the nature of this relationship, "Or else our attempts at elucidating Schreber's delusions will leave us in the absurd position described in Kant's famous simile in the *Critique of Pure Reason:*—we shall be like a man holding a sieve under a he-goat while someone else milks it" (SE 12:34). By referring to this passage from Kant, Freud potentially identifies himself with an "incautious listener" who offers "absurd answers" to the propounder, here Schreber, of a question that "is absurd in itself and calls for an answer where none is required."[17] The logical implication then is that if Schreber's delusions are meaningless, Freud's interpretation is equally and embarrassingly so. But Freud is also evoking a rhetorical, if not strictly logical, implication. If Schreber's delusions have a meaning—and the meaningfulness of symptoms is presupposed by psychoanalysis—then the "essential genetic relation" theorized by Freud is the key to that meaning.[18] The context of Kant's simile further supports Freud's rhetorical intent: Kant is giving his "nominal definition of truth [as] the agreement of knowledge with its object." Freud, too, is making such claims about psychoanalytic theory and its objects: the neuroses and psychoses.

Yet for all of its desired rhetorical effects, Freud's choice of image is very curious. This gender-bending figure underscores the significance of understanding Schreber's gender transformation as emasculation. Thus in this simile Schreber assumes the position of one who cognitively mistakes the he-goat for a she-goat and—this is implicit to the notion of milking a male—physically emasculates him by pulling on his penis. The implications of this image for Freud and psychoanalysis are perhaps even more striking. On the one hand, it foregrounds emasculation as primary for his specific task of interpreting Schreber's delusions and for the general project of psychoanalysis: namely, the essential genetic role of the castration complex. On the other hand, it suggests that if Freud is unable to locate the etiology of Schreber's dementia, then Freud (and psychoanalytic theory), like the psychotic Schreber, would be unable to recognize appropriate sexual identities and their development. Rather than providing a theory which can explain all of the vicissitudes of sexual difference, psychoanalysis would fall victim to its own misrecognitions. Consequently, the significance of Freud's ensuing attempts at interpreting Schreber's delusional system extends beyond resolving his particular case or even generating a general theory of paranoia. What is at stake is the universality of the castration complex and normative sexual difference which it maintains.

A Compelling Case for the Father

Having apparently milked the *Denkwürdigkeiten* of all the pertinent facts, Freud proceeds to secure their meaning. In his "Attempts at Interpretation" (section 2), Freud undertakes a series of brilliant rhetorical moves: including the insertion of new material and the strategic omission of old material from Schreber's text. Finally he reveals that Schreber's psychosis was an effect of his defense against the return of his repressed passive homosexual feelings toward his father. By the time Freud presents this conclusion, his compelling attempts render his interpretation—and the truth of psychoanalysis—seemingly self-evident.

First, Freud sets up the necessary conditions for his own efforts at interpretation. He had already undertaken a polemical differentiation of psychoanalysis from psychiatry with regard to the understanding of psychosis (SE 12:17–18, cf. 43).[19] At the beginning of the second section Freud praises the previous interpreters of Schreber's delusional utterances—C. G. Jung and Schreber himself. The mention of Jung reinforces the authority of psychoanalytic interpretation over psychiatric. It was as the author of a treatise on psychosis—and Schreber—*Psychology of Dementia Praecox*, which Freud here describes as providing a "brilliant example" (SE 12:35) in the interpretation of psychosis, that the psychiatrist Jung was so warmly brought into the fold in 1907.[20] Freud then proceeds to demonstrate the efficacy of the psychoanalytic method for interpreting such data. Satisfied that he can generate just as viable interpretations as did those other practitioners, Freud wishes to distinguish himself (and psychoanalysis) from them. They are, according to Freud, caught up in Schreber's delusional effects without investigating the exciting causes. He also applies this diagnosis to another member of his psychoanalytic circle: Alfred Adler. Schreber's feminization and his depictions of submission and domination evoked for Freud Adler's theory of the masculine protest.[21] Yet if the phenomenon of protest seems to confirm empirically Adler's theoretical counter to Freud's etiological primacy of sexuality, within Freud's case study Adler's theory is subordinated to the role of footnote, and his conclusions are shown to invert the causal sequence. Schreber's protests against his feminization come amid his dementia; they do not initiate it (SE 12:42 & n2).

While bemoaning the absence of sufficient information on Schreber's family to provide an explanation for his illness (SE 12:37, cf. 12:12, 45–46),[22] Freud returns to the case history to seek out those causes. Yet, he returns neither to the wealth of Schreber citations he produced in the first part of his paper nor to the medical reports, which he also excerpted. Rather, to help determine the source of Schreber's dementia Freud "now mention[s] a further element in the case history to which sufficient weight is not given in the reports, although the patient himself has done all he can to put it in the foreground. I refer to Schreber's relation to his first physician, Geheimrat Prof. Flechsig of Leipzig" (SE 12:38). Flechsig had been the presiding physician during Schreber's first breakdown in 1884–85, and it was to Flechsig that Schreber returned following the onset of the second attack.[23] With the emergence of Flechsig into the foreground of his presentation, Freud prepares the way for Schreber's father. But first, after juxtaposing Schreber's persecution phantasies about Flechsig both to a reiteration of his reverie of being a woman submitting to intercourse and to his statement of gratitude for Flechsig's earlier efforts, Freud boldly asserts: "The exciting cause [of his collapse], then, was an outburst of homosexual libido; the object of this libido was probably from the very first his physician, Flechsig; and his struggles against this libidinal impulse produced the conflict which gave rise to the pathological phenomenon" (SE 12:43). Freud moves to quell the "storm of [anticipated] remonstrances and objections" (SE 12:43) to these claims with a series of not-previously-cited passages from the *Denkwürdigkeiten*, including Schreber's fears of sexual abuse and his assertion that "what especially determined [his] mental breakdown" was a night with six nocturnal emissions (S44, SE 12:45).

Amid this parrying with imagined interlocutors Freud addresses the issue of why at that particular moment Schreber became subject to a serious mental illness. Initially, Freud suggests that the fifty-one-year-old Schreber may have attained his "climacteric" and by implication the end of his capacity to reproduce (SE 12:46). This curious resort to somatic rather than psychological causality will return in another guise once Schreber's concerns about reproduction can be safely nested in the father-complex and separated from any necessary connection with his transformation into a woman (cf. SE 12:57–58). But at this juncture of Freud's narrative, discussion of Schreber's delusions of impregnation is avoided because of their connection in the *Denkwürdigkeiten* to *Entmannung* and because Schreber's father has not yet assumed the central role he is destined for. Consequently, the matter is aborted.

Freud then returns to answer the doubts of his imagined opponents about the role of Flechsig in the sudden emergence of Schreber's paranoia. And here the father makes a brief, anticipatory appearance. While details from the *Denkwürdigkeiten* may quiet questions about the etiology of Schreber's personal pathology, Schreber's particular object of desire, his physician, presents a problem. His choice of Flechsig threatens to mark as potentially perverse one of the fundamental relationships in a masculinist society governed by a regime of (medical) expertise: that of the male patient with his doctor. The transformation of Schreber's friendly relations with Flechsig into their opposite, Freud suggests, may be explained by the "transference" (SE 12:47). By invoking the transferential relationship between doctor and patient, Freud calls upon his own variant of the classic dramatic device *deus ex machina:* the *pater ex machina.* Flechsig thus becomes a surrogate for someone who is not there: the dead father. And here Freud quotes from Schreber's report to the Court: "The memory of my father and my brother . . . is as sacred [*heilig*] to me as . . . " (SE 12:47; cit. S442; the ellipses are Freud's). The dead father silences all objections: "We shall therefore raise no further objections that the exciting cause of the illness was the appearance in him of a feminine (that is a passive homosexual) wish-phantasy, which took as its object the figure of his physician" (SE 12:47).

After this apparent conclusion Freud, rather than leaping to a discussion of the genetic mechanism of paranoia, makes a leap of faith; that is, he discusses the displacement of Schreber's affections from Flechsig to God. When the dead father returns, his irreplaceability must be secured. Only after showing both that the particular characteristics of Schreber's God are compatible with the information Freud has available about Schreber's father (and fathers in general) and that another member of the series of God-identified figures, the sun, can despite German grammar (*die Sonne*) be a symbolic father[24] substitute does Freud write: "Thus in the case of Schreber we find ourselves once again upon the familiar ground of the father-complex" (SE 12:55).

Once the father is firmly in place as the sun of Schreber's delusional system, the various strands of delusional material become accessories—

like the ray-like ribbons with which Schreber used to adorn himself as he would prance half naked in front of the mirror (cf. S280, 429)[25]—to his relationship with his father. Consequently, the tie between Schreber's transformation into a woman and his being impregnated by God for the reproduction of the race arises from its earlier relegation to a footnote (SE 12:32n1; cit. S4n1) and submits to the law of the patronym: Schreber desires to continue the family name. Since Schreber's marriage had been childless and since he may have attained his climacteric, the "family line threatened to die out. . . . [Hence] Schreber may have formed a phantasy that if he had been a woman he would have managed the business of having children more successfully; and he may thus have found his way back into the feminine attitude towards his father" (SE 12:58). Similarly, once both "emasculation" and the desire to reproduce are embraced by the father-complex, Schreber's phantasies of world catastrophe, which in the *Denkwürdigkeiten* are tied to both unmanning and reproduction, can be disentangled from that particular knot and then positioned within the general theory of paranoia (SE 12:68–71).

Freud provides a compelling argument; all of its threads, like so many Schreberian "sun's rays . . . nerve-fibers . . . spermatozoa" (*Sonnenstrahlen, Nervenfasern, und Samenfäden;* SE 12:78), seem to converge on the equation of God and father. Freud has apparently deflected all of the posed objections to his argument. And he has engaged his readers in a quest narrative which requires a successful resolution. Moreover, Freud quotes so extensively from the *Denkwürdigkeiten*—he emphasizes that all of his interpretations are based upon verbatim quotations (SE 12:11)— and expresses such apparent respect for Schreber's intelligence (cf. SE 12:35, 79)[26] that his Schreber and the Schreber of the memoirs seem to be coextensive. Psychoanalytic theory and the facts of the case appear adequate to one another.

Freud's Ellipsis and Alternative Etiologies

The force of Freud's presentation is illustrated by an encounter I had with several colleagues, who had just completed reading Freud's paper. They expressed their anger toward Schreber over his virtual neglect of his wife in the *Memoirs*. In their conflation of Freud's quote-laden depiction of Schreber with the narrator of the *Denkwürdigkeiten*, Ottilie

Sabine Schreber fell into Freud's ellipsis. That is, when, as discussed above, Freud prepares to shift from Schreber's relationship with Flechsig to that with God and thereby to the identification of God with his father, he cites a passage from Schreber's appeal to the Court: "The memory of my father and my brother . . . is as sacred [*heilig*] to me as . . ." (S442, SE 12:47). Beyond providing rather weak evidence for Freud's hypothesis of the transference at work in Schreber's relationship with Flechsig, the passage associates the father with sacrality—with divinity. (Schreber never explicitly makes this connection in his published memoirs.) In addition to preparing the reader for the apotheosis of the father, Freud also omits a reference to Schreber's wife. The full passage reads: "The memory of my father and my brother *as well as the honor* [die Ehre] *of my wife* is as sacred to me as *to anyone in similar circumstances who has the reputation* [der gute Ruf] *of his near relatives at heart*" (S442; italics added).

Omission of Schreber's concern for his wife's honor and reputation is reasonable within the specific context in which Freud cited this passage. Within the larger contexts of his argument for the role of the father and castration complexes as well as homosexuality in paranoia the omission of Schreber's wife might also be understandable. Beyond responding to specific narrative and theoretical demands,[27] the restored ellipsis also suggests that like the Kantian simile even Freud's punctuation underscores the significance of "emasculation" by functioning as a performative symbol of castration: it cuts out the castrated one, woman. But this ellipsis doesn't merely figure, in the words of Jacques Derrida, a "double invagination";[28] it acts as such. *Entmannung*, which according to Schreber, but not Freud, "consisted in the (external) male genitals (scrotum and penis) being retracted into the body" (S73), as it were folds back upon itself. That is, this hole in Freud's text through which Schreber's own text appears leads not only to the *Denkwürdigkeiten* but to Freud's marginalia. In order to understand the role of the ellipsis, it becomes necessary to draw on more than the elided passage. Freud's other text on Schreber, his marginalia to the *Denkwürdigkeiten*, offers another interpretive perspective both on the ellipsis and the passage which frames it. Beyond insight into Freud's strategy of citation, pursuing the implications of this ellipsis and its frame[29] provides access to the myriad of concerns which constellate about Freud's preoccupation with *Entmannung*. Bringing the *Denkwürdigkeiten* and Freud's accompanying marginalia to bear on Freud's discourse of "emasculation" unmans it.

Jealousy

Specifically, by omitting Schreber's wife, Freud also effaces alternative etiologies of Schreber's psychosis. Although "emasculation" and its implications—father complex, homosexual wish-phantasies and their repression, delusions of persecution, narcissism—dominate the construction of Freud's narrative, his marginalia call attention to other possible etiological factors and/or symptoms of Schreber's paranoia that are largely ignored in the case study. At the top of the page (S36) in which Schreber records his reverie about being a woman enjoying intercourse Freud writes: "Aetiologie d[er] Erkrank[un]g." Such a comment is consistent with the case study; however, this reverie is not the only passage on the page which caught Freud's attention. He doubly emphasizes the first few lines of that page, which read: "My wife felt even more sincere gratitude and worshipped Professor Flechsig as the man who had restored her husband to her; for this reason she kept his picture on her desk for many years." In the case study Freud cites this passage initially to demonstrate that Schreber had long been married (SE 12:12) and later to exemplify "the original cordiality of [Schreber's] feelings towards the physician who had treated him so successfully" (SE 12:42). But in the margins of the *Denkwürdigkeiten* Freud writes "Eifersucht" (jealousy). Jealousy certainly plays a significant role in the initial interpretation of the Schreber Case that he communicated to Jung:[30]

I have fathomed the secret. The case is easily reduced to its nuclear complex. His wife falls in love with the doctor and keeps his picture on her writing-desk for years. He too, of course, but in the woman's case there are disappointments, attempts to have children are unsuccessful; a conflict develops; he ought to hate Flechsig as his rival, but loves him thanks to his predisposition and the transference from his first illness. The infantile situation is now complete, and soon his father emerges behind Flechsig.

Although the presence of Schreber's wife is not obscured in this letter by an ellipsis, even here the manner in which Freud presents this material certainly detracts from any possible role for Schreber's relationship with his wife in the etiology of his illness. Nonetheless, Freud apparently did not wish to give fodder to his opponents or even broach the possibility of a nonmale mediator between Schreber and his father by even discussing the wife's catalytic role.[31]

Syphilis

Schreber's relationship with his wife may have provided still another contributing cause of his dementia, and the key to this alternative also appeared on the page that Freud crowned with "Aetiologie d[er] Erkrank[un]g" (36). On that page Freud jots down "Kindlos" next to Schreber's regret about "the repeated disappointment of our hope of being blessed with children." Both in the marginalia and in the case study Schreber's childlessness is emphasized. While Freud did not have access to the medical reports of Schreber's first institutionalization which connect his wife's miscarriages with possible syphilitic infection,[32] it was a truism of the time to suspect syphilis in cases of repeated miscarriages or stillbirths.[33] Did Freud surmise that Schreber may have suffered from some organic ailment like syphilis?

Freud quotes Dr. Weber's testimony (SE 12:13) that Schreber complained of *Hirnerweichung* when he committed himself the second time. At the time softening of the brain was a frequent euphemism for syphilis-caused progressive paralysis.[34] Similarly, many of the "miracles" which Schreber's body underwent find themselves described in the medical textbooks of the time as indications of constitutional syphilis.[35] What Freud considers to be Schreber's identification with a prostitute—he writes "Prostitut" in the margin next to Schreber's fear that his "body, after the intended transformation into a female being, was to suffer some sexual abuse, particularly as there had even been some talk for some time of my being thrown to the Asylum attendants for this purpose" (S98; cf. SE 12:48)—could be just as much a reaction to the acquisition of syphilis from a prostitute as to his own reputed and repudiated homosexuality. Freud also emphasizes in the margin Schreber's account of how he built a wall to protect God's realms against "an advancing yellow tide: I related this to the peril of a syphilitic epidemic" (S74). Schreber's syphilis or his fear of having syphilis could both elucidate Schreber's insistence on the connection between "emasculation" and reproduction as well as undercut Freud's theory of Schreber's climacteric. While neither an organic complaint nor a phobic reaction would necessarily contradict Freud's interpretation, they would not support it either. Is Freud fearful of history repeating itself? Just as a family history of syphilis placed a shadow over his exemplary case of psychoneurotic hysteria, namely Dora,[36] syphilis or the fear of syphilis[37] may have colored the etiology and symptomatology of Freud's paradigmatic paranoid psychotic. This question cannot be definitively answered. None of Freud's letters of the time even broaches the possibility. Still, some fifteen years later in *Inhibitions, Symptoms, and Anxiety* (1926; SE 20:148), Freud connects syphilis—or rather syphilophobia—with castration in such a way as to recall the case of Daniel Paul Schreber: "Thus, for instance, a man may retain his fear of castration in the guise of a syphilophobia, after he has come to know that it is no longer customary to castrate people for indulging their sexual lusts, but that, on the other hand, severe diseases may overtake anyone who thus gives way to his instincts."

Incest

It is not only the ellipsis that secretes an alternative cause for Schreber's dementia; its frame does as well. The "passage in which the patient sets these doubts [about Flechsig's surrogacy] at rest: 'The memory of my father and brother . . . ' " (SE 12:47) seems self-evidently to anticipate Freud's eventual conclusion of the importance of the father-complex— and to foreclose Schreber's possible incest with a sister as a possible etiological factor. But first, following the intrepid Freud's "prolonged search through the pages of the *Denkwürdigkeiten* [until he] came at last upon" this passage restores those doubts—if not necessarily about the transferential relationship or the father-complex,[38] then certainly about Freud's selection of quotes. The *Denkwürdigkeiten* seemed to provide for Freud clear confirmation of the truth of psychoanalysis's discoveries about the castration and father-complexes. Thus, as soon as the sun is mentioned Freud connects it with the father by remarking, "Sonne als Symbol Gottes Vaters" (sun as symbol of God the Father; top of S9, cf. S139n65). And adjoining Schreber's discussion of the state of blessedness achieved after death, Freud writes, "die Seligkeit (todtes Vater[s])" (the blessedness [of the dead father]; top of S12). The latter annotation would seem to be the product of Freud's second reading of the text, however, since Freud claims to have had no knowledge of Schreber's family prior to reading the *Denkwürdigkeiten*. Moreover, the first suggestion that Schreber's father was in fact dead at the time of his son's illness occurs some eighty-four pages later. There Schreber refers to "his father's soul" (S96, cf. S115).[39] This passage also happens to be the first time in the published memoirs that Schreber mentions his father—as Freud himself noted in the margin: "erstes Auftreten" (first appearance).[40]

Freud's clear awareness of the earlier appearance of the dead father in the *Denkwürdigkeiten* renders dubious his claim to have had to undertake a prolonged search to discover the dead father.[41] Consequently, Freud's selection of the latter passage about the "memory of his father *and brother*" (italics added) suggests that it was as important to introduce the brother as it was the father. The emergence of the brother manifestly served at least two functions; less evident is a third. First, his appearance allowed Flechsig to be positioned within the family constellation as the brother (cf. SE 12:50) after Schreber breaks off his (transferential) identification of Flechsig with God in order to allow his father alone to assume that position.[42] Second, it allowed Freud to evoke once again the connection of Schreber and homosexuality by implying Schreber's possible homosexual feelings toward his brother. The latter rationale for resurrecting the dead brother may have had an added motivation: it also "breaks off" the pursuit of the role of incest in the etiology of Schreber's illness. That is, just before Freud begins the discussion in which Schreber's father and brother make their first appearance he attempts to understand Schreber's feminine attitude toward God. To that end he pursues the "thread" of soul murder[43] to Schreber's invocation of Byron's *Manfred*. When Schreber mentions Manfred in his memoirs (S20) Freud queries in the margin "Schwesterinzest?" (sister incest); however, in the case study Freud remarks that the "essence" (*der Kern*) of the poem is *Geschwisterinzest*, which is translated as "incestuous relation between a brother and a sister" (SE 12:44).[44] By opting for the more familiar term, Freud chose a more sexually ambivalent term, since *Geschwisterinzest* need not be exclusively heterosexual. Although Schreber had four sisters, Freud does not pursue the possibility—can not, because, as he remarks in a phrase evocative of castration: "And here our thread breaks off short" (reißt . . . ab, SE 12:44)—at which point Freud follows another line that takes him to Schreber's brother and homosexuality. The lack of biographical data may be responsible for the abrupt end of his speculations. How much family information Dr. Stegmann made available to Freud is unknown, although it is reasonable to assume that the issue of *Der Freund der Schreber-Vereine*, celebrating the centenary of Schreber père's birth, that Freud received (cf. SE 12:51n1), would have mentioned all of his children. Freud may be both resisting brother-sister incest as a competing explanation as well as reinforcing the importance of Schreber's homo-sexuality, because for Freud, the *Kern* lies elsewhere—in "emasculation."

Der Kern der Sache

Freud explored alternative etiologies or contributing causes of Schreber's paranoia—jealousy, syphilis, incest—in the margins of the *Denkwür-digkeiten*. Women's acts, their bodies, and "their" diseases threaten the explanatory authority of the castration complex in all cases, not just Schreber's. But these alternatives never surface as such in the case study. In "Psychoanalytic Notes" "emasculation" remained the primary de-lusion and the key to Freud's understanding of the causes of Schreber's dementia. Yet when Freud's response to Schreber's discussion of "*Ent-mannung*" is pursued along the margins of his copy, certain aporia appear that may affect the understanding of his study. Freud's marginalia respond to an *Entmannung* whose conflicting meanings threaten to undermine its own central role. The "heart," the "nucleus" (*Kern*) of Schreber's case and of psychoanalysis seems to be split. Unwritten annotations that appear like cracks in his commentary—empty margins amid the plethora of notation—signal a shift in the significance of "emasculation." The object of analysis begins to incite Freud's subjective identifications and evoke his social situation. *Entmannung* divides the analyst from himself,[45] and Freud emerges as an emasculated Jew.

When *Entmannung* first appears in the *Denkwürdigkeiten* (S45), Freud, as already mentioned, double underlines the term and writes "Kern der Sache" in the margin. But placed against this assertion and the nar-rative trajectory in which it is situated, his later responses to Schreber's discussion of *Entmannung* appear aporetic. The *Kern der Sache* had emerged as the climax of a narrative seeking sources and sexual references. In lieu of biographical detail—partial responsibility for which belongs to prepublication censorship[46]—Freud sought in Schreber's literary refer-ences possible sources of Schreber's delusions. When Schreber mentions a work of literature the margins of Freud's copy read "Quelle" (source; cf. S8n3, 17n10, 20n13; also cf. S91) or "Reaktion auf Lektüre" (reaction to reading; S7n2). When the middle name "Fürchtegott" repeatedly ap-pears in Schreber's genealogy of his and Flechsig's families, Freud queries: "Leipzig? [Christian Fürchtegott] Gellert? Hinweis auf Quelle" (indication of source; S24). In these literary allusions Freud also sought clues to reconstruct the psychosexual source of Schreber's illness. Thus, as noted above, Freud queries "Schwesterinzest?" following the mention of *Manfred*.

Freud also attended to more explicitly sexual references. Anticipating the revelation of the *Kern der Sache* Freud had underlined, emphasized in the margins, and/or annotated all suggestions of sexuality or phantasies of feminization ("w. Ph."[= "weibliche Phantasie"]; cf. S4n1). Thus he heavily emphasizes Schreber's self-comparison with the Virgin Mary and underlines his comparison of male sperm with divine nerves. After Schreber describes divine nerves, Freud notes "Ursprüngl[iche] sexuelle Natur der Nerven" (top of S7). Freud exclaims "secret! sexuell" next to the censored passage "on the essential nature of soul murder or, so to speak, its technique" (S28). Schreber's reverie about how nice it would be "to be a woman submitting to the act of copulation" is double emphasized and marked "fem[inine/inisierende] Ph[antasie]" (S36). And just prior to the first mention of *Entmannung*, Freud doubly emphasizes Schreber's description of his night of six emissions. Freud also notes in the margin and at the top of the page, "Homosex[ualität]!" and "Beweis d[er] Homosex[ualität]" (proof of homosexuality), respectively (S44).[47]

All of these passages are cited in the case study, yet all are deformed by the requirements of the soon to be revealed "Kern der Sache": *Entmannung* and its consequential homosexuality. Thus, for example, when Freud invokes Schreber's self-comparison with the Virgin Mary, Freud refers to her as "God's wife" (SE 12:32) and not, as Schreber describes her, the mother of Jesus Christ. Where Schreber's designation clearly emphasizes her reproductive capacity, Freud's terminology privileges (conjugal) sexuality. In other words, Freud again severs the connection between Schreber's transformation into a woman and reproduction in order to maintain the authority of castration.

"It Can Happen That There Is More Than One Nucleus" (Kern; SE 2:290)

Just as the narrative of Freud's marginalia reaches a climax with the revelation of the *Kern der Sache*, the emergence of " '*Entmannung*' (*Verwandlung in ein Weib*)" at the end of Schreber's chapter four both concludes Schreber's own history of his illness up to his collapse and heralds the central portion of his memoirs. The recognition of this "tendency innate to the Order of the World" (S45), i.e., of being " 'unmanned' (transformed into a woman)' "—as well as the other symptoms he mentions here, inner voices and compulsive thinking—marks a shift in the narrative. All that had preceded provided a frame and a series of contexts for the depiction of his "*Nervenkrankheit.*" Chapter five begins the account of his mental illness. Schreber describes voices from outside, obsessive thinking, and the struggle for domination among nationalist-religious groupings of souls, consisting of Catholics and Germans, (baptized) Jews and Slavs. He then proceeds with his vision of the end of the world and in its wake the necessary transformation of the last man into a woman in order to save the order of the world. According to this vision (*Vision*),

Perhaps God was also able to withdraw partially or totally the warmth of the sun from a star doomed to perish . . . ; this would throw new light on the problem of the Ice Age. . . . In such an event, in order to maintain the species, one single human being was spared—perhaps the relatively most moral—called by the voices that talk to me the "*Eternal Jew.*" This appellation has therefore a somewhat different sense from that underlying the legend of the same name of the Jew Ahasver; one is automatically reminded of the legends of Noah, Deucalion and Pyrrha, etc. Perhaps the legend of the founding of Rome belongs here also. . . . The Eternal Jew (in the sense described) had to be *unmanned* (transformed into a woman) to be able to bear children. The process of unmanning consisted in the (external) male genitals (scrotum and penis) being retracted into the body and the internal sexual organs being at the same time transformed into the corresponding female sexual organs, a process which might have been completed in a sleep lasting hundreds of years. . . . A regression occurred therefore, or a reversal of that developmental process which occurs in the human embryo in the fourth or fifth month of pregnancy, according to whether nature intends the future child to be of male or female sex. It is well known that in the first months of pregnancy the rudiments of both sexes are laid down and the characteristics of the sex which is not developed remain as rudimentary organs at a lower stage of development. . . . I have myself twice experienced (for a short time) the miracle of unmanning on my own body, as already mentioned in footnote 1 . . . (S53–54)

Most curiously, in this first, and indeed most extensive, discussion of the rationale for and technique of *Entmannung* to follow its revelation as the *Kern der Sache*, Freud's copy is unmarked. Freud does underline the tie of "moral decay" (*sittliche Fäulnis*) and "nervousness" (*Nervosität*) to the destruction of the world (S52 and n29). This connection reappears in the case study to confirm Freud's notion that moral repugnance toward homosexuality is one of the motors for repression (cf. SE 12:30–31 and n). Freud also marks the appearance of the gods Ariman and Ormuzd as sort of gender toggles: the former "emasculating" the Eternal Jew/Schreber, the latter restoring his masculinity (S54). And Freud notes how those miraculously created human forms which Schreber calls "fleeting-improvised-men" (*flüchtig hingemachte Männer*) take care of the Eternal Jew (S54). Both the gods and the "fleeting-improvised-men" are also discussed in the case study—although Freud only cites from among their other appearances in the *Denkwürdigkeiten*. Thus, while the rationales and delusions that frame the vision are noted, the entire discussion of the Eternal Jew, his "emasculation," its purpose, the procedure, the tie to embryology, is ignored both in the margins and in the case study. Instead when Freud focuses upon Schreber's phantasies of world catastrophe, Freud invokes (SE 12:68–69) other mentions of world destruction (S71, 73, 91). He does mention the glaciation of the world, but without providing a page reference.

Why would Freud, who up until this chapter had been anything but reluctant to mark up his copy of the *Denkwürdigkeiten*, ignore what appeared to confirm the significance of *Entmannung*? Several possibilities suggest themselves.[48] For instance, *Entmannung* is not identified with *Kastration*, an act of cutting or loss—according to Schreber the penis is as it were preserved, only invaginated. Second, Freud may have found the embryological argument of innate androgeny or bisexuality (asexuality) problematic on several grounds. Freud had repudiated heredity as the sole determinant of sexuality.[49] In a development related to this theoretical concern, Freud is beginning to argue at this time against theories of repression (and psychosis is an effect of repression) based on bisexuality, whether by Adler who does appear in the case study (see above) or by his former friend and confidante Wilhelm Fliess.[50] Fliess, in particular, had adopted the embryological argument in order to ground bisexuality in biology.[51]

The Fliess connection suggests a third and perhaps more significant rationale for the empty margins: Freud was disavowing his lingering homosexual affect for Fliess[52] and consequent fear that he too had been "emasculated." Although Fliess is never explicitly mentioned in the case study nor in the marginalia, the editors of the *Standard Edition* note the continuing influence of Fliess's theory of periodicity (SE 12:46n1) when

Freud curiously emphasizes Schreber's age. More pertinent, Fliess had embodied for Freud the connection between paranoia and homosexuality. In a 1908 letter to Jung, Freud wrote "My one-time friend Fliess developed a dreadful case of paranoia after throwing off his affection for me, which was undoubtedly considerable. I owe this idea [of paranoia caused by the repression of homosexuality] to him, i.e., to his behavior."[53] Hence it is not surprising that while engaged on the Schreber Case Freud would re-encounter his allegedly worked-through homosexual affect toward Fliess. After returning from the trip during which he read the *Denkwürdigkeiten* Freud wrote to Ferenczi that "since the case of Fliess, with whose overcoming you just saw me occupied, this need [for intimacy with colleagues like Ferenczi] has died out in me. A piece of homosexual charge has been withdrawn and utilized for the enlargement of my own ego. I have succeeded where the paranoiac fails."[54] Fliess returns in the letter announcing the completion of the "Psychoanalytic Notes": "Fliess—you [i.e., Ferenczi] were so curious about that—I have now overcome. Adler is a little Fliess redivivus, just as paranoid."[55]

Although the earlier letter to Ferenczi suggests that Freud's homosexual affect toward Fliess had been "overcome" prior to preparing his "Psychological Notes," a letter to Jung written two days after the later letter questions that impression. The Jung letter also puts in doubt whether that affect was indeed ever overcome.[56] Speaking of his "fleetingly improvised" *(flüchtig hingemacht)* work—an intentional reference to Schreber—Freud comments: "I am unable to judge its objective worth as was possible with earlier papers, because in working on it I have had to fight off complexes within myself (Fliess)."[57] Perhaps the fear that the allegedly worked-through affect was merely repressed and that the distinction between his own work and that of the paranoiac may not be so clear-cut motivated the silent margins just as it seemed to motivate his famous conclusion to "Psychoanalytic Notes." After asserting that he arrived at his theory of projection prior to reading the *Denkwürdigkeiten*, Freud half facetiously poses a question to those who come after: "It remains for the future to decide whether there is more delusion in my theory than I should like to admit, or whether there is more truth in Schreber's delusion than other people are as yet prepared to believe" (SE 12:79). Concerns about his interchangeability or identification with paranoid, repressed homosexuals are clearly evident in Freud's encounter with Schreber.

The necessary connection between impregnation and "emasculation" in Schreber's "vision" presented another problem for Freud. As discussed above, Freud severs reproduction from its context and delays the mention of this wish-phantasy until the conclusion of his explication of the causes of Schreber's delusions. There he ties the childless Schreber's phantasy of becoming a childbearing woman to his desire as the apparently only surviving son to extend the family line despite having reached his purported climacteric. Hence the desire to reproduce, to provide a (grand)son for his father, becomes yet another expression of his feminine attitude toward his father. Opponents might argue instead that the delusion of "emasculation" is a logical outgrowth of the necessity for the last man to reproduce humanity: how else could it be reborn? More pointed, to have cited this passage may have undercut both the genetic role of "emasculation" and its indexical relationship to castration; it may have undercut castration, the function of which is to produce subjects, not reproduce them.

In addition to the theoretical, personal, and rhetorical reasons for avoiding this passage, ethnic and political reasons may also be at play. Schreber's vision of the Eternal Jew suggests an anti-Semitic dimension to his delusions. The figure of the Eternal Jew has obvious negative connotations for Schreber; hence to justify the moral stature of his visionary creation, he adds that "This appellation has therefore a somewhat different sense from that underlying the legend of the same name of the Jew Ahasver." Freud is quite aware of this aspect of Schreber. In Schreber's earlier discussion of the chosenness of the Germans (S14), Freud writes in the margin "chauvin." And bearing perhaps additional testimony to Freud's sensitivity to anti-Semitism and anti-Semitic representations,[58] the only nonexplicitly castrationlike hypochondriacal symptom that Freud underlines in Schreber's chapter about "Bodily integrity damaged by miracles" is the "Jew's stomach" (*Judenmagen*) that replaced Schreber's "healthy, natural" one (S151).[59] Calling attention to Schreber's tendency toward anti-Semitism would have confirmed the role of the castration complex in Schreber's dementia. Only a year earlier in a famous footnote to his 1909 "Analysis of a Phobia in a Five-Year-Old Boy,"[60] Freud had noted that:

The castration complex is the deepest unconscious root of anti-Semitism; for even in the nursery little boys hear that a Jew has something cut off his penis—a piece of his penis, they think—and this gives them a right to despise Jews. And there is no stronger unconscious root for the same sense of superiority over women. Weininger . . . in a chapter [of *Sex and Character*] that has attracted much attention, treated Jews and women with equal hostility and overwhelmed them with the same insults. Being a neurotic, Weininger was completely under the sway of his infantile complexes; and from that standpoint [that is, when under the sway of infantile complexes] what is common to Jews and women is their relation to the castration complex.

For the neurotic (and the psychotic) the circumcised Jew is "emasculated."

Yet to assert any connection between anti-Semitism and Schreber's paranoia would have had a number of negative consequences. First, Freud desires to construct a universal theory, and to tie psychosis to the particularities of German politics rather than to universal human development would undercut his intentions. Second, for the Jewish Freud to call attention to Schreber's anti-Semitism might be perceived as special pleading and would undermine his authority as a spokesperson for science. Combining these first two concerns is a third feared consequence: that discussion of this passage would confirm the allegation that psychoanalysis was a "Jewish national affair"[61] and not a universal science. Finally, for Freud to call attention to an "emasculated" Eternal Jew would have recalled the "emasculation" of all male Jews—their circumcision. Any discussion would have contributed to the regnant association of Jews with effeminacy and deviant sexuality, on the one hand, and with mental illness, on the other.[62] It may also have reinforced an identification with the emasculated that the Jewish Freud had been endeavoring to disavow.

Freud's inability—refusal?—to recognize Schreber's identification with the Eternal Jew[63] further substantiates this contention. Freud's marginalia distance Schreber from such an identification by situating his assumption of a redemptive role, his "Grösse[nwahn]" (megalomania) in a later passage. There Schreber wears a Christlike *Strahlenkron* (crown of rays; S76) and is called the *Geisterseher* (seer of spirits; S77, which Freud underlines). Finally, when in the "Psychoanalytic Notes" Freud allows Schreber's text to testify to the connection between unmanning and reproduction, he draws from a much later passage (S293) and situates it in a footnote (SE 12:48n1).[64] Since, as suggested above, Freud was concerned about a certain affinity with Schreber, Schreber's identification with a non-Jewish Eternal Jew, may have drawn him and Freud, who also identified himself with a variety of Jewish and non-Jewish cultural heroes,[65] closer together. Ultimately, by refusing to recognize Schreber's identification with the Eternal Jew, Freud substitutes an "emasculated" Schreber for an "unmanned" Jew.

Charles Bernheimer has recently shown how castration not only provided a theory for Freud's understanding of fetishism, but how castration had also become a fetish for Freud's understanding of theory.[66] A fetish is an overvalued symbolic substitute which simultaneously disavows and acknowledges the sexual difference instituted by the resolution of the castration complex. If castration is a fetish, for what does it symbolically substitute? This study has shown how the "heart of the matter" *Entmannung*, which Freud reads as an icon and index for the castration complex, dominated both Freud's narrative construction of "Psychoanalytic Notes" and his reading practices of the *Denkwürdigkeiten*. The polyvalence of *Entmannung* undercut Freud's rhetoric of "emasculation." By situating Freud's case study against both Schreber's text and Freud's marginalia, this paper examined how alternative etiologies and threatening identifications along the margins of Freud's copy often contested the authority of "emasculation" (castration) as an explanatory principle of individual development and a structuring principle of social relations. The most striking of these contestations—Freud's silence about the "unmanning" of the Eternal Jew—may indeed reflect a certain fetishistic logic. Whereas Freud's jottings elsewhere in the *Denkwürdigkeiten* demonstrate a cognizance of a certain anti-Semitic tendency in Schreber's delusions, Freud ignores the site where castration and a Jewish referent converge. Freud's fetishized theory may well be a symbolic substitute for his disavowal and acknowledgment of an ethnic difference that in early twentieth-century Europe would have questioned the scientific claims of psychoanalytic theory and jeopardized the professional status of the psychoanalytic movement.

Notes

Sigmund Freud Copyrights graciously permitted this chapter's employ of Sigmund Freud's marginalia to the *Denkwürdigkeiten;* © 1993 A. W. Freud et al. I also thank Keith Davies, librarian of the Freud Museum, Michael Molnar, the Museum's researcher, and Sander Gilman for their aid in deciphering Freud's annotations, as well as Ned Lukacher for his comments at a crucial moment in the composition of this chapter. The research for this chapter was conducted under the auspices of the NEH Seminar, "Freud and the Culture of His Time," led by Sander L. Gilman at the Freud Museum, London, England, 24 June–8 August 1991.]

1. Ed. Samuel M. Weber (Frankfurt/M: Ullstein, 1973; orig. Leipzig: Oswald Mutze, 1903). Eng. tr. Ida Macalpine and Richard A. Hunter (Cambridge: Harvard, 1988; orig. 1955). All citations follow the pagination of the 1903 edition and are preceded by S.

2. "Psychoanalytic Notes on an Autobiographical Account of a Case of Paranoia (Dementia Paranoides)," in Vol. 12 of *The Standard Edition of the Complete Psychological Works of Sigmund Freud*, tr. and ed. James Strachey et al. (London: The Hogarth Press, 1958), 11. (Hereafter SE) All German passages are from "Psychoanalytische Bemerkungen über einen autobiographisch beschriebenen Fall von Paranoia (Dementia paranoides)," in Freud, *Zwang, Paranoia und Perversion*, Vol. 7 of *Studienausgabe*, ed. A. Mitscherlich et al. (Frankfurt/M: Fischer, 1982), 133–203.

3. Until recently: the early work of Franz Baumeyer, "Der Fall Schreber," *Psyche* 9 (1955):513–36; William G. Niederland, *The Schreber Case* (New York: Quadrangle, 1974; includes articles from 1951 to 1972); and Morton Schatzman, *Soul Murder: Persecution in the Family* (New York: Random House, 1973), aside, the appearance of Han Israëls's 1980 University of Amsterdam thesis, *Schreber, vader en zoon* (Schreber: Father and Son) [Eng. ed. by Israëls: Madison, CT: International Universities Press, 1989], which drew on then East German archive material, Schreber family mementos, and a close reading of the *Denkwürdigkeiten*, marked the turning point. A brief survey of Schreber interpretation in the wake of Freud appears in the editors' introduction to D. B. Allison, (E.) Prado de Oliveira, M. S. Roberts, A. S. Weiss (eds.), *Psychosis and Sexual Identity. Toward a Post-Analytic View of the Schreber Case* (Albany: SUNY Press, 1988).

4. W. Kendrick, "God Must Be Crazy," *Voice Literary Supplement* (May 1990):33.

5. Cf. Macalpine and Hunter, "Notes," in *Memoirs*, 361.

6. On the role of these oppositions in the *Denkwürdigkeiten*, see my "The Unmanning of the Wandering Jew," *American Imago* 49 (1992):227–62.

7. Cf. Peter Gay, *Freud: A Life for Our Time* (New York: Norton, 1988), 267, 277–84.

8. The question of Freud's Jewish identity and identifications has become very much at issue of late. Against Peter Gay's depiction of Freud the *godless* Jew (cf. *A Godless Jew: Freud, Atheism, and the Making of Psychoanalysis* [New Haven: Yale University Press, 1987]), Yosef Hayim Yerushalmi (*Freud's Moses. Judaism Terminable and Interminable* [New Haven: Yale University

Press, 1991]), and Sander L. Gilman ("The Struggle of Psychiatry with Psychoanalysis: Who Won?" *Critical Inquiry* 13 [1987]:293–313), in particular, have explored the manifold ways in which Freud's Jewishness impinged upon the formation of psychoanalysis, both theoretically and institutionally. These works have restored the proper emphasis onto the noun: Freud the godless *Jew*.

9. Freud mentions possessing a copy of the *Denkwürdigkeiten* in his 22 April 1910 letter to Jung; William McGuire (ed.), *The Freud/Jung Letters*, tr. R. Manheim and R. F. C. Hull (Cambridge: Harvard, 1988), 311 (#187F). He began to read it while traveling in Italy during the summer of 1910 with Ferenczi.

10. Freud worked out the implications for psychoanalysis of his recognition of the importance of castration in "On the Sexual Theories of Children" (1908; SE 9:205–19), "Analysis of a Phobia in a Five-Year-Old Boy" (= "Little Hans"; 1909; SE 10:1–147); and *Leonardo da Vinci and a Memory of His Childhood* (1910; SE 11:57–137). Also see Freud's letters to Jung of 21 June 1908 and 21 November 1909; *Freud/Jung Letters*, 159 (#99F), 265–66 (#163F). Cf. Charles Bernheimer, " 'Castration' as Fetish," *Paragraph* 14 (1991): 1–9; and Schatzman, *Soul Murder*.

11. After working on his analysis of Schreber's paranoia throughout fall 1910, Freud announced on 16 December in letters to two of his closest junior colleagues, the Hungarian psychoanalyst Sandor Ferenczi and the Berlin psychoanalyst Karl Abraham, that he had completed the case study. The following summer Freud published it in *Jahrbuch für psychoanalytische und psychopathologische Forschungen* 3, 1. Cf. "Editor's Note" to "Psychoanalytic Notes," SE 12:3.

12. Freud's letter to Jung, 31 October 1910; *Freud/Jung Letters*, 369 (#218F).

13. Although in the case study Freud does not explicitly make this connection, the castration complex is implicit to Freud's discussion of the relationship between Schreber's wish-phantasy of becoming a woman and his infantile resistance toward and eventual acceptance of the father's threat of castration (SE 12:56). While working on his analysis of Schreber, Freud wrote to Jung that "The castration complex is only too evident" (31 October 1910; *Freud/Jung Letters*, 369 [#218F]).

14. Schreber included in his *Denkwürdigkeiten* the medical and legal documentation generated by the Court hearing which allowed him to return home after a nine-year institutionalization.

15. While the case study decenters the role of religion in Schreber's delusion, Freud took great delight in Schreber's implicit skepticism of normative Christianity. For example, in his introduction Schreber broaches the "unanswerable" questions of Christianity such as "how did God come to be?" (in the margins Freud writes "religiöse Zweifel"; S2), doubts the literal sense of certain dogmas like the Sonship of Jesus (which Freud emphasizes; S3) and the truth of others like resurrection and eternal damnation ("Kritik festge-

halten"; S3). Next to the discussion of the "fleeting-improvised-men" Freud writes "Erklärung Aufersteh[un]g" (S4n1). These and other such passages (cf. S8) may have sustained Freud's judgment that "in the Redeemer of to-day much remains of the doubter of yesterday" (SE 12:24).

16. It may quite legitimately be argued that at times Freud contends that woman is nothing other than a castrated man. However, in Schreber's case, since the castration is delusional, sexual difference is both threatening and threatened.

17. Immanuel Kant, *Critique of Pure Reason,* tr. Norman Kemp Smith (New York: St. Martin's Press, 1965; orig. 1929), 97 (A58, B83).

18. Another rhetorical effect of this passage is to represent Freud as a risk-taker, thereby preparing the reader to engage the ensuing narrative of Freud's attempts at interpretation as an adventure story with a happy ending.

19. The desired supersession of the older discipline by psychoanalysis is no less evident in Freud's marginalia to the *Denkwürdigkeiten*. In a number of passages where Schreber critiques psychiatry or psychiatrists Freud notes in the margins "Bravo" (S59, 79 n42, 82).

20. By taking on the Schreber Case, Freud was perhaps undercutting his heir apparent Jung. In their correspondence of the time, however, Freud and Jung seem very much to be enjoying themselves in sharing Schreberisms; there does not seem to be any overt hostility; cf. *Freud/Jung Letters,* 307–380 (#186J–225F; 17 April–18 December 1910). Still, Jung was ever-sensitive to Freud's reception of the Dementia Praecox essay [Gay, *Freud,* 199], and Gay holds that after the appearance of "Psychological Notes" that their breakup was inevitable. Moreover, after the breakup Jung would return to Schreber (in "On Psychological Understanding," 1914) and endeavor to one-up Freud. Cf. C. G. Jung, *The Psychogenesis of Mental Disease,* Vol. 3 of *The Collected Works of C. G. Jung,* ed. H. Read et al., tr. R. F. C. Hull (Princeton: Princeton University Press, 1982; orig. 1960), 179–93.

21. And on occasion Freud notes in the margins of his copy of the *Denkwür-digkeiten* "Protest" (cf. S57).

22. Freud asserts that he can base his interpretation almost exclusively on his reading of the *Denkwürdigkeiten* because of the nature of paranoia. Since paranoiacs "possess the peculiarity of betraying (in a distorted form, it is true) precisely those things which other neurotics keep hidden as a secret... it follows that this is precisely a disorder in which a written report or a printed case history can take the place of a personal acquaintance with the patient" (SE 12:9). He does receive information from Arnold Georg Stegmann, a psychiatrist from Schreber's hometown of Dresden, although Freud did not incorporate all of it into his narrative; cf. SE 12:6n1 (on omitting knowledge of Schreber's third illness), 46, 51.

23. The *Denkwürdigkeiten* chronicles this second attack.

24. Freud writes: "In this instance symbolism overrides grammatical gender—at least so far as German goes, for in most other languages the sun is masculine" (SE 12:54).

25. Cf. Baumeyer, "Der Fall Schreber," 518: "Juli 1898. Dasselbe Verhalten. Oft nackt in seinem Zimmer vor einem Spiegel lachend und schreiend mit bunten Bändern geschmückt."

26. On 31 October 1910 Freud writes to Jung of "our dear and ingenious friend Schreber"; *Freud/Jung Letters,* 368 (#218F).

27. Although Schreber's concern about his wife's honor could easily be evoked in support of Freud's argument about Schreber's anxiety over the *Schmach* and *Schimpf* which homosexuality entails.

28. Cf. Jacques Derrida, "Living On: Border Lines," in Harold Bloom et al., *Deconstruction and Criticism* (New York: Seabury Press, 1979), 100ff.

29. Technically one cannot speak of an ellipsis without the presence of either an antecedent or subsequent or, frequently, both an antecedent and subsequent citation. Moreover, the meaning of an ellipsis—of anything—cannot be determined without consideration of its borders, both within the text and between texts.

30. 1 October 1910; *Freud/Jung Letters,* 358 (#214F).

31. Yet considering Freud's discussion of jealousy as one of the permutations of the paranoiac's repressed sentence "I (a man) love him" (cf. SE 12:63–64) Schreber's jealousy may well have supported Freud's argument.

32. Baumeyer, "Der Fall Schreber," 514.

33. Jill Harsin, "Syphilis, Wives, and Physicians: Medical Ethics and the Family in Late Nineteenth-Century France," *French Historical Studies* 16, 1 (Spring 1989): 72–95, here 87.

34. Emil Kraepelin, *Psychiatrie. Ein Lehrbuch für Studierende und Aertze,* 6th ed., 2 vols. (Leipzig: Johann Ambrosius Barth, 1899) 2:604.

35. Cf. Gerd Busse, *Schreber, Freud, und die Suche nach dem Vater. Über die realitätsschaffende Kraft einer wissenschaftlichen Hypothese* (Frankfurt/M: Peter Lang, 1991). In "The Unmanning of the Wandering Jew" I undertake an extensive analysis of how the trope of syphilis infects the *Denkwürdigkeiten.*

36. Cf. Sander Gilman, *The Jew's Body* (New York: Routledge, 1991), 81–87.

37. As the nineteenth century drew to a close, the European bourgeoisie were terror-stricken before the "venereal peril"; cf. Alain Corbin, *Women for Hire. Prostitution and Sexuality in France after 1850,* tr. Alan Sheridan (Cambridge: Harvard University Press, 1990), esp. 261–75; and Jay Geller, "Blood Sin: Syphilis and the Construction of Jewish Identity," *Fault Line* 1 (1992): 21–48.

38. Yet besides this appearance and the latter invocation of his father's memory there is only one other reference to Schreber's father in the published text: Schreber mentions reading his father's *Ärztlichen Zimmergymnastick* (Medical Indoor Gymnastics), which Freud greets with an "also!" (S166). As has been pointed out by many for a figure who plays such a major function in Freud's etiological scenario, Schreber's father appears to play a rather minor role in the *Denkwürdigkeiten.*

39. Thus this suggestion occurs way before the passage on 442 which Freud claims was discovered after a prolonged search.

40. This passage is not cited in Freud's text. Actually on 51 Schreber parenthetically refers to a still earlier mention of his father: presumably in the *Denkwürdigkeiten*'s omitted third chapter.

41. For Freud to have discussed this paper trail would have also undercut the rhetorical function of evoking a "prolonged search": the narrative of a quest engaged the readers vicariously in the scientific adventure of hypothesis and confirmation. That narrative helped quiet those who assumed that Freud already had the answer and had not followed his own advice to read Schreber's memoirs.

42. The eventual splitting off of God from Flechsig is, like Schreber's splitting of God into higher and lower persona, a function of paranoia's decomposing tendencies and not of intrinsic differences between figures. "They were all duplications of one and the same important relationship" (SE 12:50). Yet as Gerd Busse has reminded me (correspondence, 4 October 1991), while Freud notes at the bottom of a discussion of God's "irregular policy" toward Schreber, "Erheb[un]g des Verfolg[un]gswahn zu Gott [und] Gott identif[iziert] mit Flechsig" (sublimation of persecution delusion to God and God identified with Flechsig; S62), and annotates "Bravo! Identific[ation]" next to a passage (S82) which demonstrated in "Psychoanalytic Notes," that for Schreber, Flechsig and God "were ideas belonging to the same class" (SE 12:49), Freud never explicitly states that Flechsig was *identified* with God. Indeed, the discussion of paranoia's characteristic decomposition of identifications and condensations implies that Flechsig and God were always distinct figures (SE 12:49–59).

43. Macalpine and Hunter describe "soul murder" as "the most obscure issue in the Memoirs" ("Notes," 359). It refers to the advantage or influence exercised by one person over another; "illness, particularly nervous illness, is caused when the soul leaves the body temporarily, or is under another's influence" (ibid.).

44. Freud also refers to the presence of "Schwesterinzest"—not *Geschwisterinzest*—in *Manfred* in his 31 October 1910 letter to Jung (*Freud/Jung Letters*, 369 [#218F]).

45. *Entmannung*'s only previous appearances in Freud's collected works also manifested a conflicted Freud and the heart of a different matter. In the original edition of *Interpretation of Dreams*, Freud asserts that "Zeus emasculated [*entmannt*] his father [Kronos] and made himself ruler in his place" (SE 4:256). In both *The Psychopathology of Everyday Life* (SE 6:218 and n) and a 1909 note to the *Interpretation*, Freud corrects, with qualifications, his original assertion: "Or so [Zeus] is reported to have done according to some myths. According to others, emasculation [*Entmannung*] was only carried out by Kronos on his father Uranus" (SE 4:256n1). Ned Lukacher, "K(Ch)ronosology," *Sub-Stance* 25 (1980): 55–73, has thoroughly elaborated

the implications of Freud's parapraxis, albeit without specific reference to *Entmannung*. Freud is concerned here with more than exemplifying the neglect of filial piety. In addition to providing evidence of Freud's resistance to a theory of castration (cf. Jean Laplanche, "La castration, ses précurseurs et son destin," *Bulletin de Psychologie* 311, 27 [1973–74]: 635), "the omission of reference to Kronos's role as castrator and the repetition of his role as castrated inscribes in Freud's text the concealed fulfillment of his [i.e., Freud's] desire to castrate the father and possess the mother" (cit. "K[Ch]ronosology," 67). Freud's self-analysis had yet another side: the incorporation of the fault, here figured by emasculation, of the father; cf. Marie Balmary, *Psychoanalyzing Psychoanalysis. Freud and the Hidden Fault of the Father*, tr. Ned Lukacher (Baltimore: Johns Hopkins Press, 1982; orig. 1979).

46. For example, when Schreber is about to enlarge upon his few hints about the essential nature of soul murder, a parenthetical remark appears: "(the passage which follows is unfit for publication)" (S28). Moreover, chapter three's discussion of Schreber's family was excised. The removal of these sections leads Freud to lament that "in working upon the case of Schreber I have had a policy of restraint forced on me by the circumstance that the opposition to his publishing the *Denkwürdigkeiten* was so far effective as to withhold a considerable portion of the material from our knowledge—the portion, too, which would in all probability have thrown the most important light upon the case" (SE 12:37). For this and other reasons, Freud has often been faulted for not trying to contact Schreber—who was still alive when Freud began writing the case study—his family, or his doctors. However, the correspondence with Jung shows a Freud desirous of making inquiries. On 1 October 1910 Freud writes to Jung: "Since the man [i.e., Schreber] is still alive, I was thinking of asking him for certain information (e.g., when he got married) and for permission to work on his story. But perhaps that would be risky. What do you think?" (*Freud/Jung Letters*, 358 [#214F]). Jung does not seem to have responded.

47. In a 1911 addition to *Interpretation of Dreams* (SE 5:392–94), Freud cites a long passage from Otto Rank's 1911 "Zum Thema der Zahnreizträume," *Zentralblatt der Psychoanalyse* 1, in which dental dreams accompanied by nocturnal emissions are tied to auto-eroticism or, at most, "a slight tendency toward homosexuality."

48. Professor Valerie Greenberg in private correspondence, suggests a fourth: "Freud might have been in such complete agreement with parts of a text that his concentration did not permit interrupting to make marks. [W]e know he was engrossed by many texts that he did not mark at all." It is indeed possible that Freud was so engrossed in this one page (S53) that his pen remained silent; however, the silence belies his marking practices in this text. For example, on this page rife with biblical, classical, and literary references, even "Quelle," the sign of Freud's ongoing concern with possible sources for Schreber's delusions (cf. S8n3, 17n10, 20n13, 91), is missing.

49. Cf. Gilman, "Who Won?"
50. Cf. Freud's later works, "From the History of an Infantile Neurosis" (SE 17:110–11, on Adler), "A Child Is Being Beaten" (SE 17:200–201, on Adler and Fliess), and "Analysis: Terminable and Interminable" (SE 23:251, on Fliess).
51. Cf. Wilhelm Fliess, *Die Beziehungen zwischen Nase und weiblichen Geschlechtsorganen: In ihrer biologischen Bedeutung dargestellt* (Leipzig/Vienna: Franz Deuticke, 1897), 223.
52. Cf. Gay, *Freud*, 86–87, 204, 274–76.
53. 17 February 1908; *Freud/Jung Letters*, 121 (#70F).
54. Freud to Ferenczi, 6 October 1910; cit. Gay, *Freud*, 275.
55. Freud to Ferenczi, 16 December 1910; cit. Gay, *Freud*, 274.
56. As Freud's fainting scene in November 1912 in Munich would testify; cf. Gay, *Freud*, 275.
57. 18 December 1910; *Freud/Jung Letters*, 379, 380 (#225F).
58. Freud may well have been familiar with the alleged problems of Jewish digestion, anchored empirically perhaps in the tendency of Ashkenazim to contract ileitis, but more a function of the abject fascination which Jewish dietary law had for non-Jews; compare the appetitive theory of Judaism proffered by one of the favorite authors of Freud's youth: Ludwig Feuerbach.
59. Another neglected aspect of Schreber's illness is his hypochondria. Both Schreber and his doctors give considerable weight to his hypochondriacal symptoms. Freud does cite Dr. Weber's list of these symptoms (esp. SE 12:13). Freud also mentions that Schreber developed an "enormous number of delusional ideas of a hypochondriacal nature," and then adds in a footnote that he "shall not consider any theory of paranoia trustworthy unless it also covers the hypochondriacal symptoms by which that disorder is almost invariably accompanied" (SE 12:56 and n3). But Freud fails to follow through. In his copy of the *Denkwürdigkeiten* Freud too emphasizes a number of passages. For example, where Schreber notes that the body changes described in chapter eleven are for him the most vivid and certain of all of his experiences Freud writes "Beziehung zur Hypochondrie" (S150n68). As might be expected Freud is most struck by the "miracles" related to "emasculation": Freud underlines the word *Entmannung* and notes "Kastration Komplex" next to the ensuing description of changes to Schreber's sex organs and of the removal of single hairs from his beard and moustache (S149). But none of this material makes its way into the case study. Why does Freud not address this material? Surely psychoanalysis would have no difficulty analogizing Schreber's delusional organ losses with castration. Did Freud fear that by focusing on the body, even the delusional one, he would be transgressing the confines of medical psychiatry? Or did he fear that Schreber's body language would transgress the gendered boundaries of nosological classification and be diagnosed as the "female malady" of hysteria? Such a diagnosis would invalidate both his own diagnosis of paranoia and the

concomitant theory of its mechanism. Further, although Freud had essayed the existence of male hysteria in the 1880s, the adverse professional response to his proposal dampened his interest in the matter. On this last matter, cf. Gay, *Freud*, 53–54.

60. SE 10:36n; cf. *Leonardo da Vinci and a Memory of His Childhood*, SE 11:95–96n.

61. Freud discusses his fears that psychoanalysis is perceived as a Jewish science in a letter to Karl Abraham, 3 May 1908, in *A Psycho-Analytic Dialogue: The Letters of Sigmund Freud and Karl Abraham, 1907–1926*, ed. H. Abraham and E. Freud, tr. B. Marsh and H. Abraham (London: The Hogarth Press, 1965), 34.

62. On this association, cf. the prolific work of Sander Gilman, e.g., "Sigmund Freud and the Sexologists: A Second Reading," in this volume. Also see my *The Nose Job: Freud and the Feminized Jew* (Albany: SUNY Press, forthcoming); and "(G)nos(e)ology: The Cultural Construction of the Other," in *People of the Body. Jews and Judaism from an Embodied Perspective*, ed. H. Eilberg-Schwartz (Albany: SUNY Press, 1992). On Freud's efforts to counter or suppress the association, cf. Gilman, "Who Won?" and my "Paleontological View of the *Leitfossil* Circumcision: Freud's Study of Religion," *Modern Judaism* 13, 1 (1993).

63. In "(G)nos(e)ology" and more fully in "The Unmanning of the Wandering Jew" I demonstrate such an identification.

64. Prior to signaling the importance of *Entmannung*, Freud places in a footnote, without commentary, an earlier citation (from S4n1) in which Schreber's having female genitals and being impregnated by God are conjoined.

65. Cf. Gay, *Freud*, passim.

66. Bernheimer, " 'Castration' as fetish."

10. Freud's Pompeian Fantasy

Peter L. Rudnytsky

Delusions and Dreams in Jensen's "Gradiva" (1907), although one of Freud's least famous works, is undoubtedly far better known than the novel it anatomizes, Wilhelm Jensen's *Gradiva: A Pompeian Fantasy* (1903). This reversal of the customary relation between primary and secondary texts invites the reader of Freud's interpretation of Jensen to assume a postmodern stance. Despite its intricate web of themes and images, Jensen's tale of the archeologist Norbert Hanold's mysterious attraction to a relief depicting a young woman with an unusual gait is formally naive and employs the convention of an omniscient narrator. Freud's appropriation of Jensen's novel as a parable of psychoanalysis, by contrast, paradoxically at once enhances and distorts its meanings and imposes a subjective frame that transforms an unsophisticated text into a radically unstable and self-reflexive one. After Freud, every reading of *Gradiva* becomes a double reading, in which there is no position of absolute knowledge or mastery but only a series of more or less adequate transferential investments in the reading and writing process.[1]

Delusions and Dreams—a title I shall use to distinguish Freud's *Gradiva* from Jensen's—stems from the halcyon days of the psychoanalytic movement. Although it was almost certainly Wilhelm Stekel and not, as is generally believed, C. G. Jung who first drew Freud's attention to *Gradiva*,[2] much of the confidence that Freud exudes in *Delusions and Dreams* derives from his having secured the support of a band of like-minded adherents, to which Jung was the latest and most distinguished recruit. Basking in Jung's praise of the work as "magnificent," Freud expatiated in a letter on May 26, 1907: "this little book was written on sunny days and I myself derived great pleasure from it.... To tell the truth, a statement such as yours means more to me than the approval of a whole medical congress."[3]

The frame of mind in which Freud wrote *Delusions and Dreams* is further attested by its opening words: "A group of men who regarded it as a settled fact that the essential riddles of dreaming have been solved by the author of the present work..." (*SE* 9:7). In the exaltation of a peak moment, Freud wraps himself in the mantle of third-person authority, asserts the findings of his magnum opus to be a "settled fact," and appeals for confirmation to the "group of men" who formed the nucleus of what in 1908 would become known as the Vienna Psychoanalytic Society. Thus, one crucial dimension of Freud's transference in *Delusions and Dreams* is to his followers in the psychoanalytic movement, and to Jung in particular, and is marked by its appearance at a moment when the "sunny days" of collaboration were untroubled by the clouds of dissension that would soon dim the horizon.

A second transferential dimension in *Delusions and Dreams* arises from Freud's relation to Jensen's text, and by extension to literature as a whole. Just as in 1906 Freud began to gather the fruits of his heroic early labors and his professional life was at its most harmonious, so *Delusions and Dreams* shows him at the height of his optimism concerning the relations between psychoanalysis and literature. *Delusions and Dreams* is Freud's first extended venture in applied analysis, and it remains his most ambitious and detailed exegesis of a literary work. In the same way that Freud's original 1901 title for the Dora case, *Dreams and Hysteria*, published in 1905 as *Fragment of an Analysis of a Case of Hysteria*, signaled his intention to synthesize his achievements in *Studies on Hysteria* (1895) and *The Interpretation of Dreams* (1900), so in *Delusions and Dreams* Freud defends and illustrates his findings on dreams, sexuality, and the nature of the therapeutic process.

Extending a line of argument begun in *The Interpretation of Dreams*, Freud opens *Delusions and Dreams* by disdaining "the reproaches of strict science" and proclaiming himself "a partisan of antiquity and superstition" (*SE* 9:7) in upholding the meaningfulness of dreams. Again referring to himself in the third person, he enlists imaginative writers as being "on the same side as the ancients, as the superstitious public and as the author of *The Interpretation of Dreams*" (p. 8).[4] In unabashedly championing imaginative as opposed to scientific truth, *Delusions and*

Dreams is at the opposite pole from a work such as *The Future of an Illusion* (1927), in which Freud aligns psychoanalysis with the natural sciences in its fidelity to the reality principle and antipathy to all forms of illusion, aesthetic as well as religious. Although this shift in part reflects an evolution between Freud's earlier and later writings, it expresses at bottom an unresolved dialectical tension in his thought.

Freud's enthusiasm for literature in *Delusions and Dreams* leads him to hail the creative writer as one who has "from time immemorial been the precursor of science, and so too of scientific psychology" (*SE* 9:44). Invoking one of his talismanic quotations from *Hamlet*, Freud affirms that the testimony of writers is to be "prized highly, for they are apt to know a whole host of things of which our philosophy has not yet let us dream" (p. 8). So radically does Freud adhere to this conviction that he elevates *Gradiva* to the status of a clinical case history. Conceding that he has proceeded as though Norbert Hanold and Zoe Bertgang "were real people and not the author's creations," Freud defends this apparent naïveté—akin to that of the Romantic tradition of Shakespeare criticism descended from Maurice Morgann—by arguing that "all [Jensen's] descriptions are so faithfully copied from reality that we should not object if *Gradiva* were described not as a phantasy but as a psychiatric study" (p. 41). He adds: "Thus the creative writer cannot evade the psychiatrist nor the psychiatrist the creative writer, and the poetic treatment of a psychiatric theme can turn out to be correct without any sacrifice of its beauty" (p. 44).

But if the psychiatrist and the creative writer cannot evade each other, and the latter can be clinically accurate, this carries the subversive implication that Freud's psychiatric study may be no more than a fantasy. In intimating this possibility, *Delusions and Dreams* summons a specter that haunts all Freud's writings. As early as *Studies on Hysteria* he avers that "it still strikes me myself as strange that the case histories I write should read like short stories and that, as one might say, they lack the serious stamp of science";[5] and the original title for his valedictory *Moses and Monotheism* (1939) was *The Man Moses: A Historical Novel*. In reading Jensen's novel as a case history, Freud assimilates it to the paradigms generated in *Studies on Hysteria*. Zoe Bertgang's cure of Norbert Hanold's delusion "shows a far-reaching similarity—no, a complete agreement in its essence—with a therapeutic method which was introduced into medical practice in 1895 by Dr. Josef Breuer and myself" (*SE*

9:89). In *Studies on Hysteria* Freud optimistically contends that, just as individual symptoms disappear after they have been abreacted through language, so "it is only with the last word of the analysis that the whole clinical picture vanishes" (*SE* 2:299). In *Delusions and Dreams,* despite his intervening recognition of the dynamics of transference in the Dora case, Freud writes of Norbert Hanold: "The disorder vanishes while being traced back to its origin; analysis, too, brings simultaneous cure" (*SE* 9:89). One may surmise that Freud, having experienced his first major setback as a therapist, chronicled in a narrative that he himself stigmatized as fragmentary, found in the closure provided by *Gradiva* a reassuring coherence that harkened back to his own earlier work. In both *Studies on Hysteria* and *Delusions and Dreams* Freud uses the word "vanishes" (*schwindet*)[6] to convey his magical belief that when the analysis reaches its "last word" the "clinical picture" disappears, as it were, in a puff of smoke.

The difficulty of distinguishing between fictional and clinical writing closely links *Delusions and Dreams* not only to *Studies on Hysteria* but also to the Schreber case and the essay on Leonardo. Although he believes his interpretations of *Gradiva* to be well founded, Freud nonetheless muses whether it is not "rather we who have slipped into this charming poetic story a secret meaning very far from its author's intentions" (*SE* 9:43), and admits that it might be so. Similarly, at the end of the Schreber case (1911) Freud leaves it to the future to decide "whether there is more delusion in my theory than I should like to admit, or whether there is more truth in Schreber's delusion than other people are as yet prepared to believe."[7] In *Leonardo da Vinci and a Memory of His Childhood* (1910) Freud confesses that even his supporters may deem that he has "merely written a psychoanalytic novel," and adds that "I am far from over-estimating the certainty of these results."[8]

Freud rings every possible change on the dialectical interplay between fiction and case history in *Studies on Hysteria, Delusions and Dreams, Leonardo,* and the Schreber case. In *Studies on Hysteria* he writes case histories that read like short stories; in *Delusions and Dreams* he reads Jensen's novel as though it were a case history; in *Leonardo* he writes what amounts to a psychobiographical novel about a historical figure; and he bases his so-called case history of Schreber solely on his reading of the latter's *Memoirs of My Nervous Illness* (1903). (The Schreber case might thus be better described as a work of literary criticism.) Any attempt to maintain sharp ontological distinctions between the pure and applied uses of psychoanalysis breaks down in the face of Freud's own highly equivocal practice.

The contention that *Delusions and Dreams, Leonardo,* and the Schreber case constitute enactments of a single continuous reading and writing process can be further scrutinized thanks to the circumstance that in all three instances the Freud Museum in London possesses the original books belonging to Freud, with markings in his hand. Although an exhaustive analysis of Freud's marginalia to *Gradiva,* to say nothing of the other sources in question, is beyond the scope of this chapter, some brief observations will suffice to make my point.[9]

On the penultimate page of his copy of *Gradiva,* which is heavily annotated throughout in green pencil, Freud notes that the word *"Verschüttung"* (burial) is the *"symbolischer Kern"* (symbolic nucleus) of the whole story. In his discussion of psychotherapy in *Studies on Hysteria,* Freud had previously used *"verschütten"* to warn the physician lest he inadvertently "bury" a memory that the patient is seeking to recall (*SE* 2:292; *GW* 1:297). Thus, when he encountered the same word in Jensen, it must have been with a shock of recognition, which underlies his sweeping assertion that *Gradiva* shows a "complete agreement" with the ideas that he and Breuer had already expounded in *Studies on Hysteria.* Echoing Jensen but also his own earlier formulation, Freud reiterates in *Delusions and Dreams* that there is "no better analogy for repression, by which something in the mind is at once made inaccessible and preserved, than burial [*Verschüttung*] of the sort to which Pompeii fell a victim" (*SE* 9:40; *GW* 7:77).[10]

Like *"verschütten,"* Freud's phrase *"symbolischer Kern"* is charged with significance. In *Studies on Hysteria,* Freud strives to penetrate to the "heart of the matter" (*Kern der Sache; SE* 2:126; *GW* 1:186) in the case of Katharina and asserts in his discussion of psychotherapy that memories are organized around a "pathogenic nucleus" (*pathogenen Kern; SE* 2:289; *GW* 1:292). Later, during the period 1907–12, Freud embarks on a quest to find a *Kernkomplex*—a core or nuclear complex— of the neuroses, which he gradually comes to equate with the Oedipus complex, so that he is able to proclaim in *Totem and Taboo* (1912–13): "We have arrived at the point of regarding a child's relation to his parents, dominated as it is by incestuous longings, as the nuclear complex of the neuroses."[11] In his copy of *Memoirs of My Nervous Illness,* moreover,

Freud annotates Schreber's reference to his fantasies of emasculation as the *"Kern der Sache."*[12] Similarly, wherever he comes across a source for the content of Schreber's delusions Freud writes *"Quelle"* in the margins, just as he does in *Gradiva*, where the word refers to the etiology of Norbert Hanold's delusions. Thus, whether the text deals with a real or a fictional character, Freud's way of reading is identical, and the analyses he goes on to frame reflect this indeterminacy.

The principal subtext for *Leonardo da Vinci and a Memory of His Childhood* is Dmitri Sergeyevich Merezkovsky's *Leonardo da Vinci: A Biographical Novel from the Turn of the Fifteenth Century*, written in Russian and read by Freud in a 1903 German translation. Freud's copy of Merezhkovsky has no annotations, but only occasional lines penciled in the margin. The most salient fact is that Freud based his study of Leonardo on a biographical novel, so that when he admits that he may have written only a "psychoanalytic novel," he is simply placing his work in its proper generic context. What is more, Freud's notorious mistranslation of the Italian word for "kite" (*nibio*) as "vulture" in his exegesis of Leonardo's childhood memory occurs in the German translation of Merezhkovsky, and is thus a culturally determined and not a personal lapse on Freud's part.

Although there are no annotations, it remains revealing to see which passages attract Freud's notice. Of only three marked with double lines, all are in chapter 11, "The Wings Will Come." Two have to do with Leonardo's mother and her smile; the third recounts his memory of the bird that visited him in his cradle. I quote the first passage:

Leonardo remembered his mother. Especially vivid to him was her tender, mysterious [*geheimnisvolles*], and rougish smile, which stood out oddly from her sad, severe, beautiful face. One day in Florence in the museum of the Medici garden of San Marco he found a small copper statue of Cybele, the ancient goddess of the earth, which had been excavated from a small Etruscan city in Arezzo. The features of its face showed the same smile that belonged to the young peasant woman from Vinci, his mother.[13]

The most controversial aspect of Freud's procedure in *Leonardo* is that he moves from the known—the smile of the *Mona Lisa*—to the unknown—speculations about Leonardo's childhood memories: "we begin to suspect the possibility that it was his mother who possessed the mysterious [*geheimnisvolle*] smile—the smile that he had lost and that fascinated him so when he found it again in the Florentine lady" (*SE* 11:111; *GW* 8:183). Freud's reconstruction of Leonardo's childhood is highly conjectural, but, as the iteration of "mysterious" attests, it is grounded in his reading of Merezkovsky, whom he cites in a note to this passage, adding that Merezkovsky's depiction of Leonardo's childhood differs in essential respects from his own, based on an analysis of the vulture fantasy.

Freud's assumptions in *Delusions and Dreams* are identical to those to which he adheres three years later in *Leonardo*. Not only does he regard Norbert Hanold and Zoe Bertgang as real people, but he traces the origin of Hanold's fixation on the statue of Gradiva to childhood experiences: "For there can be no doubt that even in her childhood the girl showed the same peculiarity of a graceful gait, with her toes almost perpendicularly raised as she stepped along; and it was because it represented that same gait that an ancient marble relief acquired such great importance for Norbert Hanold" (*SE* 9:46). Merezkovsky's description of Leonardo's discovering a statue in a museum that reminds him of his mother's smile uncannily parallels Jensen's story, which opens with Hanold's mysterious attraction to a bas-relief he sees in a museum in Rome, of which he obtains a plaster-cast copy to hang on the wall of his study. Since Freud's knowledge about the historical figure of Leonardo is mediated by textuality and contaminated by fictional elements, it does no more than reverse the equation for him to look upon fictional characters as though they were living beings and to impute to them an empirical history.[14]

In keeping with the double reading required by *Delusions and Dreams*, Freud's conflation of real and fictional characters reenacts the central problem faced by Norbert Hanold in Jensen's story. Hanold is smitten by the bas-relief because it seems to have been taken "from life" and the grace of the represented movement gives the impression of "imparting life" (*PF*, p. 4) to the relief. But when he seeks to find a contemporary woman whose gait resembles that of the statue, whose folded dress is pulled up slightly and trailing right foot touches the ground almost vertically, Hanold at first fails and regretfully concludes that this manner of walking "had been created by the imagination or arbitrary act of the sculptor and did not correspond to reality" (p. 11). However, on one occasion, after awakening from a dream, he catches a glimpse of a woman walking in this fashion through the street of his northern German university town and, still dressed in his night clothes, rushes after her in vain. Finally, in the last sentence of the novel, after Hanold has recognized the apparition of Gradiva he encountered at Pompeii to be his childhood friend Zoe Bertgang and won her consent to marry him, she gratifies his desire and strikes the requisite pose: "raising her dress slightly with her left hand, Gradiva *rediviva* Zoe Bertgang, viewed by him with dreamily observant eyes, crossed with her calmly buoyant walk, through the sunlight, over the stepping-stones, to the other side of the street" (pp. 117–18). In his copy of Jensen, Freud annotates this passage: *"Erotik! Aufnahme der Phantasie-Versöhnung"* (Erotic! Acceptance of the fantasy-reconciliation).

Hanold's confusion between reality and fantasy is equally one between life and death. When he arrives in Pompeii on a journey unconsciously motivated, as he belatedly realizes, by a quest to find the woman of whom he thought he had caught a glimpse in his native town, and who he dreamed had been buried in the eruption of Mount Vesuvius in 79 A.D., he becomes convinced that dead spirits return to life at noon: "Then something came forth everywhere without movement and a soundless speech began; then the sun dissolved the tomb-like rigidity of the old stones, a glowing thrill passed through them, the dead awoke, and Pompeii began to live again" (*PF*, p. 45). Precisely at noon, Hanold beholds the apparition of Gradiva, walking in her inimitable fashion, and addresses her first in Greek and then in Latin, before she wryly tells him he must use German if he wishes to be understood. After she disappears, Hanold is bewildered by the "physical manifestation of a being like Gradiva, dead and alive at the same time, although the latter was true only at the noon hour of spirits" (p. 64).

The theme of reality and fantasy again converges with that of life and death when Hanold buys a brooch from the innkeeper at the remote Albergo del Sole—the name of which links it to the sun imagery throughout the story—in the belief that it had been worn by a young woman, the original of Zoe-Gradiva, one of a pair of lovers who had been buried together near the Forum by the eruption of Vesuvius. Just then he sees in an open window of the inn an asphodel branch covered with white flowers—the same flower of death he had given at noon to Gradiva— and "without needing any logical connection, it rushed through his mind, at the sight of the grave-flower, that it was an attestation of the genuineness of his new possession" (*PF*, p. 78). Hanold's mistaken inference exemplifies Freud's original definition of transference in *Studies on Hysteria* as a "false connection" (*SE* 2:302), and in *Delusions and Dreams* Freud explains Hanold's delusion concerning the brooch by saying that he "transferred [*überträgt*] his conviction that Gradiva lived in the house to other impressions which he had received in the house" (*SE* 9:79; *GW* 7:107). Subsequently, when Hanold recognizes the woman he has met in Pompeii as Zoe Bertgang, she observes that it is strange "that a person must die to become alive again, but for archaeologists that is of course necessary" (*PF*, p. 110).

The intertwined problems of distinguishing what is alive from what is dead and what is real from what is fictional, central both to Jensen's story and to Freud's analysis, bring *Delusions and Dreams* into close connection with Freud's later and far more famous paper, "The 'Uncanny' " (1919). Observing that the appearance of a living Gradiva in Pompeii initially bewilders the reader no less than it does Norbert Hanold, Freud notes that Jensen, "who has called his story a 'phantasy,' has found no occasion so far for informing us whether he intends to leave us in our world . . . or whether he intends to transport us to another and imaginary world, in which spirits and ghosts are given reality" (*SE* 9:17). He goes on to cite Shakespeare's ambiguous exploitation of supernatural phenomena in *Hamlet* and *Macbeth*. Similarly, in "The 'Uncanny,' " Freud states with reference to E. T. A. Hoffmann's "The Sand-Man" (1816) that "the writer creates a kind of uncertainty in us in the beginning by not letting us know, no doubt purposely, whether he is taking us into the real world or into a purely fantastic one of his own creation";[15] and he again adduces Shakespeare's use of supernatural agents in *Hamlet* and *Macbeth*.

This parallel movement of thought suggests that *Delusions and Dreams* prefigures "The 'Uncanny,' " and "The 'Uncanny' " retroactively supplements *Delusions and Dreams*. In "The 'Uncanny' " Freud distinguishes between two causes of eeriness—repressed complexes and superseded thought processes. His paper is largely a polemical effort to debunk the second hypothesis, which he equates with Ernst Jentsch's derivation of the uncanny from intellectual uncertainty, though by the end Freud admits that "these two classes of uncanny experience are not always sharply distinguishable" and "an uncanny effect is often and easily produced when the distinction between fantasy and reality is wiped away, when something real appears before us which we have previously taken for fantasy" (*SE* 17:249, 244). Thus, this second definition of the uncanny, a suppressed element in his own text, returns to subvert Freud's ostensible argument. Although Freud nowhere mentions Jensen in "The 'Uncanny,' " his description of the confusion between fantasy and reality precisely glosses the action of *Gradiva*.

For theoretical purposes, it is useful to correlate the two sources of the uncanny—repressed complexes and superseded thought processes—with Freud's distinction between primary and secondary repression.[16] Secondary repression pertains to ideas and memories that can in principle be remembered and put into words, whereas primary repression pertains to infantile memories that can only be recaptured as moods or states of being. Christopher Bollas refers to these existential memories of maternal holding (or its lack) as the "unthought known."[17]

This distinction between primary and secondary repression can in turn be applied to Jensen's *Gradiva*, where from the beginning Norbert Hanold is disoriented by moods he cannot understand. On the one hand, there is his mysterious attraction to the statue of Gradiva; on the other, his reiterated sense of loss and something missing in his life. Seeing from his window a caged canary, which actually belongs to Zoe, Norbert was "moved by a feeling that he, too, lacked a nameless something" (*PF*, p. 20). Throughout his Italian journey Norbert is irritated by the billing and cooing of honeymooning couples from Germany, and upon arriving in Pompeii his mood is further soured by the houseflies he associates with these couples. "He felt that he was out of sorts because he lacked something without being able to explain what, and this ill-humour he took everywhere with him" (p. 35); and again, "even nature was unable to offer him what he lacked in his surroundings and within himself" (p. 36).

As in his commentary on Hoffmann's "Sand-Man," where he seeks to play down the importance of the episode involving the mechanical doll Olympia so as to sidestep Jentsch's derivation of the uncanny from uncertainty about whether or not something is animate, so in his discussion of Jensen's novel Freud concentrates on the oedipal level of repressed wishes but leaves out all mention of moods or states of being. (Freud, of course, is writing in 1906, but it is still revealing to see what he includes and excludes.) He brings out the theme of sexual jealousy in Norbert Hanold's fantasy that Gradiva has been buried in the embrace of a rival, but it emerges most clearly in Freud's elucidation of Zoe's attraction to

Norbert. Zoe was raised only by her father, an absent-minded zoologist, and she found in Norbert Hanold a man who, like him, was "absorbed by science and held apart by it from life and from Zoe. Thus it was made possible for her to remain faithful in her unfaithfulness—to find her father once more in her loved one" (*SE* 9:33).

Freud's oedipal analysis of the characters is surely convincing as far as it goes, but it leaves out important aspects of Jensen's novel. In particular, Freud glosses over the fact that Zoe has lost her mother and never mentions that Norbert is also a double orphan. Jensen writes that Norbert Hanold "already at birth had been hedged in by the grating with which family tradition, by education and predestination, had surrounded him" as the only son of a university professor. He had "clung loyally" to the task of exalting his father's name "even after the early deaths of his parents had left him absolutely alone." He passed his university examinations brilliantly, but could take no pleasure in aesthetic objects or human emotions. "That beside these objects from the distant past, the present still existed around him, he felt only in the most shadowy way; for his feelings marble and bronze were not dead, but rather the only really vital thing which expressed the purpose and value of human life" (*PF*, pp. 18–19).

If we follow Freud and look upon Norbert Hanold as a real person, the confusions of life and death and of reality and fantasy in his attraction to Gradiva can be attributed to what Harry Guntrip would call his schizoid condition.[18] His early parental losses and the consequent absence of nurturing are the sources of his nameless lack and longing. As James W. Hamilton has written, "archeology, as the science which deals with the relics of the past, serves as a symbolic representation of the lost object which is incorporated and becomes a 'frozen introject,' "[19] from which Norbert is unable to break free in order to invest his emotional energy in a living woman. In other words, his inner sense of lifelessness is the consequence of an incomplete work of mourning. Finally, after meeting Zoe, "with the prospect of recovering the lost object in the outer world, he can begin to give up or decathect the internal representation or introject—archaeology."[20]

Another aspect of Jensen's novel not dealt with by Freud is the aggression manifested in Norbert Hanold's irrational hatred of flies. There is likewise an incident in which he slaps Zoe's hand to see whether she is real. Insofar as Freud considers aggression at all, he regards it as an expression of "man's inevitable duty in love-making" (*SE* 9:38), as when near the end of the story Norbert uses an imaginary fly on Zoe's face as a pretext for pressing his lips on hers. But the aggression exhibited by Hanold may have other sources than masculine sexuality. In particular, as the work of John Bowlby has demonstrated, anger and longing are inevitable components of the reaction to bereavement, especially an early one. Of a patient who had lost his mother at the age of five and could not express his grief, Bowlby writes: "although immobilized, both his love and his anger had remained directed towards the recovery of the dead mother. Thus, locked in the service of a hopeless cause, they had been lost to the developing personality. With loss of his mother had gone loss also of his feeling life."[21] Bowlby's account of this patient applies verbatim to Norbert Hanold.

If we add the contributions of object relations theory to a classical analytic perspective, we can heuristically posit three superimposed levels of pathology in Norbert Hanold's character: (1) oedipal sexuality, involving rivalry with other males and repressed desire for the woman (the level delineated by Freud); (2) a preoedipal hostility toward women and life, indicative of an internalized image of the bad mother and an aggressive persecutory ego (the level brought into view by W. R. D. Fairbairn's work);[22] and (3) a regressed or schizoid ego, the inner sense of nonexistence due to the deaths of his parents and the absence of love (the level probed by Guntrip). From this final vantage point, Gradiva becomes a tale of death and rebirth, or what Michael Balint would call the achievement of a "new beginning" through psychoanalytic therapy.[23] Both Zoe and Norbert are phantoms recalled to life through the power of love. As the happily united pair stroll hand in hand through the streets of Pompeii, "the whole excavated city seemed overwhelmed, not with pumice and ashes, but with pearls and diamonds, by the beneficent rainstorm"; and Zoe's eyes shone over "her childhood friend who had, in a way, also been excavated from the ashes [Verschüttung]" (PF, p. 117; Urban and Cremerius, eds., p. 85).

Although the preoedipal dimensions of Gradiva uncovered by object relations theory enhance Freud's oedipal reading, they remain within the confines of traditional assumptions about character. Thus, to the three levels of analysis governed by a metaphysics of presence, I would propose also a Lacanian and a Derridean approach to the text.[24] Jensen's story is Lacanian in its stress on the role played by names and signifiers. Hanold's choice of the name Gradiva ("the girl who steps along") for the statue that obsesses him is determined not simply by its appearance but also by his unconscious memory of the name Bertgang. As Freud explains, "that very name turns out to have been a derivative—indeed a translation—of the repressed surname of the girl he had loved in childhood which he was supposed to have forgotten" (*SE* 9:38). Moreover, the name Zoe means "life," and is thus part of the ironic counterpoint of life and death throughout the work. When Norbert Hanold encounters Zoe in Pompeii without recognizing her, he says that her name "sounds to me like a bitter mockery." She replies: "I have long accustomed myself to being dead" (*PF*, p. 71). As Maud Mannoni has insisted from a Lacanian standpoint, analysts should construe fantasy "not as the image or trace of an experience lived through, but rather as a word lost."[25]

Mannoni's reference to a trace leads us from a Lacanian to a Derridean reading of *Gradiva*. Norbert Hanold goes to Pompeii in search of "traces" of his beloved, "and that in a literal sense—for with her unusual gait, she must have left behind in the ashes a foot-print different from all the others" (*PF*, p. 47). The motif of the trace is bound up with the collapse of the distinction between the original and copy in Jensen's novel. In his analysis, Freud draws attention to two implausible elements of the plot: first, where Jensen "makes the young archaeologist come upon what is undoubtedly an ancient relief but which so closely resembles a person living long afterwards"; and second, "where he makes the young man meet the living woman precisely in Pompeii, for the dead woman had been placed there only by his imagination, and the journey to Pompeii had in fact carried him away from the living woman, whom he had just seen in the street of the town in which he lived" (*SE* 9:41–42). Although this second coincidence can be ascribed to chance, Freud continues, the first—"the far-reaching resemblance between the sculpture and the live girl"—seems "to spring from the author's arbitrary decision." But if the relief of Gradiva mysteriously resembles the living Zoe, the reason is that Jensen—notwithstanding his aesthetic naïveté—has staged a postmodern reversal of the usual metaphysical relations between life and art, so that it is rather the living woman who imitates her inanimate double, as when in the final sentence she becomes "Gradiva *rediviva*."

Jensen's collapse of the distinction between life and art, original and copy, is strikingly glossed by a passage in Hoffmann's "Sand-Man," in which the belatedly introduced narrator explains his reasons for having first presented his protagonist through a series of letters: "Perhaps, like a good portrait painter, I may succeed in depicting Nathanael in such a way that you will recognize it as a good likeness without being acquainted with the original, and will feel as if you had very often seen him with your own bodily eyes. Perhaps, too, you will then believe that nothing is more wonderful, nothing more fantastic, than real life."[26] Even life—Zoe—is hollowed out by the signifier and not knowable outside the trace. And Freud, in his clinical fictions, like a good portrait painter, depicts likenesses we can recognize without being acquainted with the originals. No less than Norbert Hanold, moreover, Freud kept a replica of Gradiva (cast from the statue in the Vatican Museum) in his study, so that even today we can verify her appearance or purchase a simulacrum for our own walls. There are, then, a range of possible psychoanalytic readings of *Gradiva*—oedipal, preoedipal, Lacanian, deconstructionist. To these should be added a feminist critique, since Gradiva's status as the fetishized object of a male gaze is taken for granted both by Jensen's text and by all the above modes of interpretation.[27]

Both in *Delusions and Dreams* and "The 'Uncanny,' " Freud highlights the issue of repressed complexes and neglects intellectual uncertainty or superseded thought processes. But, as Jentsch argued, the latter actually holds the key to the uncanny. I think it was resisted by Freud on subjective grounds because he could not come to terms with his own magical belief in the omnipotence of thoughts. As I have documented in *Freud and Oedipus,* a dread of the power of his own thoughts was instilled in Freud by the premature death of his younger brother Julius—his first rival for his mother's love—when Freud was less than two years of age.[28]

The effects of the fulfillment in reality of Freud's infantile death wishes against Julius are exhibited in the recurrent theme of the revenant in his life and writings. In *Delusions and Dreams,* Freud seeks to account for the "mental cobweb" that caused Norbert Hanold to believe that he was conversing at noon with the ghost of Gradiva—a delusion that, as Freud says, justifies Jensen's calling his story a "Pompeian fantasy." Freud points out that "the belief in spirits and ghosts and the return of the dead . . . is far from having disappeared among educated people," and offers an exemplary anecdote:

A man who has grown rational and sceptical, even, may be ashamed to discover how easily he may for a moment return to a belief in spirits under the combined impact of strong emotion and perplexity. I know of a doctor who had once lost one of his women patients suffering from Graves' disease [exophthalmic goiter], and who could not get rid of a faint suspicion that he might have contributed to the unhappy outcome by a thoughtless prescription. One day, several years later, a girl entered his consulting-room, who, in spite of all his efforts, he could not help recognizing as the dead one. He could only frame a single thought: "So after all it's true that the dead can come back to life." His dread did not give way to shame till the girl introduced herself as the sister of the one who had died of the same disease as she herself was suffering from. The victims of Graves' disease, as has often been observed, have a marked facial resemblance to one another; and in this case this typical likeness was reinforced by a family one. The doctor to whom this occurred was, however, none other than myself; so I have a personal reason for not disputing the clinical possibility of Norbert Hanold's temporary delusion that Gradiva had come back to life. (*SE* 9:71–72)

Freud compellingly presents his ideas not through description or exposition but through an embedded narrative, which is itself uncanny in the way that it first solicits the reader's belief in spirits, then undercuts it, and finally produces a genuinely eerie effect through the revelation that Freud is himself the guilt-ridden protagonist.

In "The 'Uncanny,'" Freud returns to the experience of the uncanny as it is "associated with the omnipotence of thoughts, the prompt fulfillment of wishes and with the return of the dead." This concatenation of themes parallels *Delusions and Dreams,* and Freud continues:

We—or our primitive forefathers—once believed that these possibilities were realities, and were convinced that they actually happened. Nowadays we no longer believe in them, we have *surmounted* these modes of thought; but we do not feel quite sure of our new beliefs, and the old ones still exist within us ready to seize upon any confirmation. As soon as something *actually happens* in our lives which seems to confirm the old, discarded beliefs we get a feeling of the uncanny; it is as though we were making a judgement something like this: "So, after all, it is *true* that one can kill a person by the mere wish!" or, "So the dead *do* live on and appear on the scene of their former activities!" and so on. (*SE* 17:247–48)

The exclamations voiced impersonally in "The 'Uncanny'" echo Freud's autobiographical confession in *Delusions and Dreams,* as the original German passages clearly show: "Also ist es doch wahr, daß man einen anderen durch den bloßen Wunsch töten kann, daß die Toten weiterleben";[29] "es sei doch wahr, daß die Toten wiederkommen können" (*GW* 7:99). Near the end of the story, Norbert Hanold reflects that he had "mitigating grounds for his madness in for two days considering

Gradiva a resurrection [*Rediviva*]" (*SE* 9:109–10; Urban and Cremerius, eds., p. 81). Similarly, in a 1910 letter to Ferenczi, Freud discloses that the defections of Adler and Stekel constitute for him reenactments of the rupture of his friendship with Wilhelm Fliess: "Adler is a little Fliess redivivus. . . . Stekel, as appendage to him, is at least called Wilhelm."[30] Freud's compulsive viewing of his life in terms of such repetitive patterns is rooted in infantile determinants, particularly the death of Julius, the prototype of Fliess and all his other male friends and rivals. In view of his early history, Freud indeed had "a personal reason for not disputing the clinical possibility of Norbert Hanold's temporary delusion that Gradiva had come back to life."

Freud's reading of Jensen's text, then, is filtered through his identification with Norbert Hanold, the archeologist-protagonist in search of a lost object. As is well known, Freud was himself a noted collector of antiquities and frequently compared psychoanalysis to archeology in its quest to reconstruct the past. But his transference to *Gradiva* takes place on multiple levels simultaneously. In reading the novel as a clinical case history, Freud proposes that it depicts not only the origins of Norbert's delusion but also its cure, a process in which Zoe Bertgang plays the part of analyst. Thus, Zoe-Gradiva provides a further magnet for Freud's identification in his capacity as therapist, though she, unlike other analysts, is also Norbert's original love object and thus permitted to gratify his transference love in reality. Implicit here is a noteworthy reversal that casts the male Norbert as patient, and the female Zoe as analyst. Freud specifically diagnoses Norbert Hanold's malady as a "*hysterical* delusion" (*SE* 9:45n) and assimilates Jensen's "imaginary case" to those patients "medically treated in real life" by Breuer, Charcot, and Janet, as well as by himself in the Dora case (p. 54). Freud does not draw attention to this inversion of conventional gender roles, but his silence eloquently testifies that he took for granted that women could be analysts and did not succumb to the temptation to define hysteria as an essentially feminine discourse.

Beyond his identification with the two main characters, Freud exhibits a transference to Wilhelm Jensen as the author of this Pompeian fantasy. His attachment is, however, ambivalent, as the striking metamorphosis in Freud's estimation of Jensen's literary merits attests. In *Delusions and Dreams*, Freud reveres Jensen as a genius, seriously comparing him to Shakespeare not only in his deployment of supernatural elements but also in the way he grounds the plot on an implausible premise, where the alleged resemblance is to *King Lear*. In Freud's first blush of enthusiasm, Jensen can do no wrong. He "never introduces a single idle or unintentional feature into his story" (*SE* 9:68), and even the dreams are wholly believable. By his 1912 postcript, written the year after Jensen's death, Freud has begun to have second thoughts. He refers condescendingly to writers like "our Wilhelm Jensen" who are "in the habit of giving themselves over to their imagination in a simple-minded [*naiver*] joy in creating" (p. 94; *GW* 7:123). Finally, in his *Autobiographical Study*, Freud dismisses *Gradiva* as a story that "has no particular merit in itself,"[31] notwithstanding its utility for his psychoanalytic purposes. If, in his euphoria at the burgeoning international recognition of the psychoanalytic movement and discovery of literary confirmation for his ideas, Freud at first overestimated the worth of *Gradiva*, his later disparagement likewise seems correspondingly exaggerated. But this ambivalence, characteristic of all encounters with a double,[32] attests that Freud's deepest transference is not to Jensen as author, but to literature itself as the uncanny twin of psychoanalysis.

Freud sent a copy of *Delusions and Dreams* to the elderly Jensen, who was flattered by his attentions, and followed it with a request for information that he hoped would corroborate his theories about the biographical genesis of *Gradiva*. After reading two other stories recommended by Jung, "The Red Umbrella" and "In the Gothic House," collected in *Superior Powers* (1892), Freud speculated in a letter to Jung on November 24, 1907 that either "Jensen actually had a sister who died young or... never had a sister and transformed a playmate into the sister he had always longed for."[33] Freud interpreted these three stories, culminating in *Gradiva*, as a cycle depicting the loss and refinding of an object. What Freud learned from Jensen, who, despite Freud's complaints to the contrary in the 1912 postscript (due in all likelihood to his emotionally charged sense of disappointment in the author), answered his intimate queries with unfailing courtesy, dazzlingly confirmed his reconstructions: "No. I never had a sister or any other blood-relation. But 'The Red Umbrella,' to be sure, is woven together from my own life-memories, from my first youthful love for a dear girl friend of childhood who grew up with me and died of tuberculosis at age 18; and from the essence of a young woman with whom, many years later, I came into friendly relations and who likewise was snatched away by sudden death" (quoted in Urban and

Cremerius, eds. p. 15; my translation). Thus, object loss and recovery indeed played a decisive role in the genesis of Jensen's art. But Jensen neglected to add that he had lost his mother when he was thirteen and his father when he was eighteen.[34] Hence Freud divined even more truly than he knew, and his reading of *Gradiva* lays bare the inexhaustible overdetermination of aesthetic creativity and our own transferential responses to it.

Notes

1. I use "transferential" broadly to mean governed by unconscious anticipatory ideas. Although transference occurs in its purest form in the clinical setting, psychoanalysis holds it to be a ubiquitous phenomenon in life that is operative in all our personal relationships and our encounters with aesthetic objects. See Sigmund Freud, "The Dynamics of Transference" (1912), in *The Standard Edition of the Complete Psychological Works*, ed. and tr. James Strachey et al., 24 vols. (London: Hogarth Press, 1953–74), 12:99–108, esp. p. 100. All English quotations from Freud will be to the *Standard Edition*, with volume and page numbers indicated parenthetically by the abbreviation *SE*. All German references to Freud will be to *Gesammelte Werke*, ed. Anna Freud et al., 18 vols. (London: Imago, 1941–68), and indicated parenthetically by the abbreviation *GW*. Quotations from *Gradiva* will be to Wilhelm Jensen, *Gradiva: A Pompeiian Fantasy*, tr. H. M. Downey (New York: Moffat, Yard, and Co., 1918), and will be indicated parenthetically by the abbreviation *PF*. I have read *Gradiva: Ein pompejanisches Phantasiestück* in the edition of Sigmund Freud, *Der Wahn und die Träume in W. Jensens "Gradiva" mit dem Text der Erzählung von Wilhelm Jensen*, ed. Bernd Urban and Johannes Cremerius (Frankfurt am Main: Fischer, 1981). References to this work will also be included parenthetically in the text.
2. The assumption that Jung first alerted Freud to *Gradiva* originates with Ernest Jones (*The Life and Work of Sigmund Freud*, Vol. 2 [New York: Basic Books, 1955], p. 382), and has been echoed by virtually all subsequent commentators, including James Strachey in the *Standard Edition*. However, as William McGuire has observed, the Freud-Jung correspondence "casts no light" (*The Freud/Jung Letters: The Correspondence between Sigmund Freud and C. G. Jung*, ed. W. McGuire, tr. Ralph Manheim and R. F. C. Hull [Princeton: Princeton University Press, 1974], p. 45) on Jones's claim, which is rather called in doubt both by the fact that neither Jung nor Freud ever indicates that Jung had mentioned the work to Freud and the fact that Freud wrote *Gradiva* in the summer of 1906 before his first meeting with Jung. The case for Stekel's influence hinges on a passage in *The Dreams of Creative*

Writers (Die Träume der Dichter: Eine vergleichende Untersuchung der un-bewussten Triebkräfte bei Dichtern, Neurotikern und Verbrechern [Wies-baden, J. F. Bergmann, 1912], p. 14), in which he states that he had written to Jensen to ask whether he had been aware of *The Interpretation of Dreams* before writing *Gradiva*, and received a negative answer. In the final section of *Delusions and Dreams* (*SE* 7:7–95, p. 91), Freud refers to an unspecified member of his circle who had contacted Jensen with this question, adding that this was the same individual cited at the outset of the work, whom he credits with having introduced him to *Gradiva* (p. 9). This interlocking series of allusions warrants the conclusion that the anonymous colleague who first sought to apply Freud's method to *Gradiva* was Stekel rather than Jung.

3. McGuire, ed., *The Freud/Jung Letters*, pp. 51–52.

4. In Freud's German text, the word *Verfasser*, or scientific author, contrasts with *Dichter*, or creative writer. See *Der Wahn und die Träume in W. Jensens "Gradiva," GW* 7:31–125, p. 32.

5. Sigmund Freud and Josef Breuer, *Studies on Hysteria, SE* 2:160.

6. Sigmund Freud and Josef Breuer, *Studien über Hysterie, GW* 1:77–312, p. 304; and, for *Der Wahn und die Träume, GW* 7:118.

7. S. Freud, *Psycho-Analytic Notes on an Autobiographical Account of a Case of Paranoia, SE* 12:9–82, p. 79.

8. S. Freud, *Leonardo da Vinci and a Memory of His Childhood, SE* 11:63–137, p. 134.

9. A preliminary assessment of Freud's marginalia to *Gradiva* is offered by Edward Timms, "Freud's Library and His Private Reading," in E. Timms and Naomi Segal, eds., *Freud in Exile: Psychoanalysis and Its Vicissitudes* (New Haven: Yale University Press, 1988), pp. 65–79. The edition in Freud's library is Wilhelm Jensen, *Gradiva* (Dresden: C. Reissner, 1903).

10. The word "*Verschüttung*" recurs in Freud's comparison of repression to the "burial" of Pompeii in the case of the Rat Man. See S. Freud, *Notes upon a Case of Obsessional Neurosis* (1909), *SE* 10:155–249, p. 176; and *Bemerkungen über einen Fall von Zwangsneurose, GW* 7:381–463, p. 400.

11. S. Freud, *Totem and Taboo, SE* 13:1–161, p. 17.

12. Daniel Paul Schreber, *Denkwürdigkeiten eines Nervenkranken* (Leipzig: Oswald Muße, 1903), p. 45.

13. D. S. Mereschkowski [Merezhkovsky], *Leonardo da Vinci: Ein biographisches Roman aus der Wende des 15. Jahrhunderts* (Leipzig: Schulze, 1903), p. 366. Translated from the Russian. The passage quoted in the text is my translation from the German.

14. To give the matter one more twist, Max Schur (*Freud: Living and Dying* [New York: International Universities Press, 1972]) quotes from a letter written by Freud to Martha Bernays in 1882: "You don't seem to know how observant I am. Do you remember how in our walk with Minna along the *Beethovengang* you kept going aside to pull up your stockings? It is bold of

me to mention it, but I hope you won't mind." Freud adds that the foot of the Venus de Milo could cover two of Martha's. Schur comments: "Could the memory of this episode including the name *Beethovengang* (so similar to Bertgang) and the comparison between Martha's foot and that of the Venus de Milo have been an added determinant for Freud's interest in the Gradiva story?" (p. 248).

15. S. Freud, "The 'Uncanny,' " *SE* 17:219–56, p. 230.

16. See S. Freud, "Repression," *SE* 14:146–58.

17. See Christopher Bollas, *The Shadow of the Object: Psychoanalysis of the Unthought Known* (New York: Columbia University Press, 1987).

18. See Harry Guntrip, *Schizoid Phenomena, Object Relations, and the Self* (London: Hogarth Press, 1968).

19. James W. Hamilton, "Jensen's *Gradiva:* A Further Interpretation," *American Imago*, 30 (1973), 380–412, p. 384.

20. Hamilton, "Jensen's *Gradiva:* A Further Interpretation," p. 398.

21. John Bowlby, "Childhood Mourning and Its Implications for Psychiatry" (1961), in *The Making and Breaking of Affectional Bonds* (London: Tavistock/Routledge, 1989), pp. 44–66, p. 56.

22. See W. R. D. Fairbairn, *Psychoanalytic Studies of the Personality* (London: Routledge and Kegan Paul, 1952).

23. See Michael Balint, "Character Analysis and New Beginning" (1932), in *Primary Love and Psycho-Analytic Technique* (London: Maresfield Library, 1985), pp. 159–73.

24. An excellent postmodern analysis of *Gradiva* is offered by Sarah Kofman in *Freud and Fiction* (1974), tr. S. Wykes (London: Polity Press, 1991), pp. 83–117.

25. Maud Mannoni, *The Child, His "Illness," and the Others* (1967), translated from the French (New York: Pantheon, 1976), p. 44.

26. E. T. A. Hoffmann, "The Sand-Man," translated from the German, in *The Best Tales of Hoffmann*, ed. E. F. Bleiler (New York: Dover, 1967), pp. 183–214, p. 196.

27. I am grateful to Maureen Turim for calling attention to my own complicity in this occlusion when I presented this paper to the Group for the Application of Psychology at the University of Florida. The concept of the fetish applies with particular aptness to Hanold's obsession with female feet, but can be understood not only in the phallic terms delineated by Freud but also preoedipally as an attempt to cling to a representation of the prematurely lost maternal breast.

28. See Peter L. Rudnytsky, *Freud and Oedipus* (New York: Columbia University Press, 1987), pp. 18–23.

29. S. Freud, "Das Unheimliche," in *GW* 12:229–68, p. 262.

30. Quoted in Peter Gay, *Freud: A Life for Our Time* (New York: Norton, 1988), p. 274.

31. S. Freud, *An Autobiographical Study,* in *SE* 20:7–74, p. 65.
32. See Otto Rank, *The Double* (1914), tr. Harry Tucker (Chapel Hill: University of North Carolina Press, 1971).
33. McGuire, ed., *The Freud/Jung Letters,* p. 100.
34. See Hamilton, "Jensen's *Gradiva:* A Further Interpretation," p. 410.

11. "A Piece of the Logical Thread . . . ":[1] Freud and Physics

Valerie D. Greenberg

Discussions of Freud as a scientist generally presume a biological model of science,[2] although they may include references to physical concepts, to studies by Hermann von Helmholtz that might today be called biophysics, or to Gustav Theodor Fechner's "psychophysics" which Freud credited with influencing his work. I propose that the influence of classical physics may have played a more significant role in Freud's early thinking than is usually acknowledged. Accordingly, our picture of the development of psychoanalysis may require inclusion of a further dimension: the thinking characteristic of a mathematical science which asked different questions of the world and explored those questions with methods different from the contemporary biological sciences. Physics, which Newton had established as the model for science per se, was toward the end of the nineteenth century on the verge of developments (discovery of the quantum, relativity) that by the 1920s were to establish it even in the public eye as the paradigm science. There is evidence that for Freud physics became and remained a kind of scientific superego, functioning perhaps above all as a model of rigorous logic.[3]

In his biography of Freud, Ernest Jones notes without comment that in the summer semester of 1875 while Freud was a student at the University of Vienna, he took one extra physics class beyond those required by the medical curriculum.[4] Freud's program of physics courses at the university consisted all together of four courses—two courses in the winter semester of 1874–75 (Freud's third semester) and two the following semester. The first two courses were "Magnetism, Electricity and Heat," and "Theory of Magnetic Forces"; the second two were "Optics," and "Theory of Heat Conduction."[5] All four courses were taught by the same professor: Josef Stefan (1835–93), who at that time was director of the Institute of Physics at the university, and secretary of the Mathematical-Physical Section of the Imperial Academy of Sciences in Vienna. Stefan also played a prominent role as a dean (1869–70) and Rector (1876–77) of the university.[6] Stefan was considered a brilliant theoretical and experimental physicist, and, significantly for the student Sigmund Freud, a profoundly influential teacher. One observer reported that Stefan was "unexcelled as a lecturer."[7] Stefan's most illustrious student was Ludwig Boltzmann who was to be become one of the greatest names in theoretical physics. Boltzmann's eulogy of his old teacher at the time of Stefan's death includes a description of Stefan's exceptional qualities as a teacher and of the "magic" of his influence on his students.[8]

According to the record of Freud's grades on his high school comprehensive exams, he was outstanding in physics.[9] Thus it is not surprising that he wrote to Eduard Silberstein in early 1875 of his plans to transfer to the University of Berlin in 1875–76 to attend the lectures of the great physicist/physiologists Helmholtz and Du Bois-Reymond.[10] While nothing came of this plan, it nevertheless shows Freud's strong and continuing interest in these subjects while he was taking Stefan's courses. Freud's letters to Silberstein show how pronounced this interest was.[11] A telling example is the long letter devoted entirely to describing Freud's encounter with the ideas and the person of empiricist philosopher Franz Brentano. Brentano was an advocate of applying the methods and standards of the natural sciences to philosophy and psychology. The young student was deeply influenced by the charismatic Brentano, although Freud at the same time maintained some critical distance, particularly to Brentano's theism. With his friend as a sounding board, Freud tries to come to grips with the idea that Newtonian laws seem to support Brentano's arguments for the existence of God.[12] Freud wrote of Brentano: "His great distinction is that he abhors all glib phrases, all emotionality, and all intolerance of other views. He demonstrates the existence of God with as little bias and as much precision as another might argue the advantage of the wave over the emission theory."[13] The "another" whom Freud had in mind as standing for precision and lack of bias would have been Josef Stefan, whose course on optics Freud was taking at the time he wrote this letter and whose demonstration of the superiority of the wave theory of light had apparently impressed Freud enough to serve as a model. Optics, known for "the exactness of its measurements and the accessible mathematical regularities of its phenomena,"[14] proved so fascinating to Freud that he planned to study it on his own during the summer break of 1875. Nothing came of the plan, although he had tried to arrange for Silberstein to buy him a copy of Helmholtz's *Handbook of Physiological Optics* if a cheap, used copy could be found.

Freud's imagination seems to have been excited by his class on heat conduction where he would have learned the theories of Clausius, including the idea, derived from the Second Law of Thermodynamics, of entropy, or the irreversible tendency toward degradation of matter and energy resulting in a uniform state. Freud interprets tongue in cheek for Silberstein what the ultimate state of the universe is likely to be, adding the implication that, therefore, all energy-consuming, heat-generating effort ought to be eschewed as contributing to a premature end. He pictures a permanent and permanently uniform springtime with "neither war nor murder, nor new discovery nor cravings for women's emancipation," where the result of any exertion will be that you are "a killer of yourself and the whole universe: . . . transforming a living force into heat and [unable to] change it back."[15] Freud explains that this state is derived from a mathematical formula which is thus responsible for the unpleasant situation of knowing one's ultimate fate. In devoting the better part of a long letter to imagined ultimate consequences of entropy, Freud is aiming for humorous effect for the sake of entertaining his friend. Nevertheless, his very preoccupation with it shows a certain fascination and his conclusion reveals a different kind of involvement: "This phenomenon, incidentally, is not uncommon, and I have been told that D. Nussbaumer, Brühl's assistant, whom you may remember, has used it to good scientific effect."[16] The word "incidentally" ("übrigens") alerts us to its implied opposite meaning: introducing an idea with "incidentally" suggests that it is really the more significant concern of the writer. The tone has without transition switched from ironic to serious, indicating Freud's actual continuing speculations about the concepts of physical science.

If we compare work reported in the 1870s by Freud's mentors in the biological sciences with work reported by Stefan we must conclude that, at least as represented by the research of these scientists, physics was significantly more advanced in rigor of investigation, experimentation, and analysis. Looking back upon this period, one author wrote in a book published in 1896 that "physics experiences the strongest epistemological drive of all the natural sciences: no other natural science is as little satisfied as physics with the mere arrangement of facts; none is so determined to go beyond them to their connection through basic laws; none is so committed to carefully constructed exact theories."[17] Beyond this perception of physics as theory, there is no doubt that by this time experimental physics had the benefit of a consistent and finely honed discursive framework in which to discover, formulate, and transmit its results.

In his discussion of Freud's draft of a scientific psychology (the "Project" of 1895), Sulloway advances the common notion that it is characterized by "reductionism" to the laws of physics and chemistry. This is not meant to be a negative comment by Sulloway who supports the central importance of the "Project" in Freud's oeuvre and in the history of psychoanalysis. Further, Sulloway supports the tracing of conceptual ties from the "Project" to the work of Freud's teachers Brücke and Meynert, as well as to the traditions of Hebart and Fechner.[18] I would like to take issue with the common usage of the term "reductionism" and suggest that in the case of Freud's internalization of physics, it signifies something more like "rigor." I would also like to take issue with the caliber of some of the work of Ernst Brücke, despite the fact that Freud gave Brücke as a scientist and mentor enormous credit for his influence and his example.

In 1872 the Reports of the Imperial Academy of Sciences contained lengthy papers by Freud's future mentors Brücke, and Brücke's assistant, Sigmund Exner, as well as by Josef Stefan. By juxtaposing these papers we can compare the most advanced methods in a biological science (physiology in the case of Brücke and Exner) with those of physics. Stefan's paper, "Investigations of heat conduction in gases,"[19] is a model of precision, logic, and lucidity. It goes without saying that results are expressed in equations, thus also that symbols such as Greek or Latin letters stand for such factors as temperature, distance, or conductivity. This symbolic language is absent in Brücke's paper which consists entirely of narrative. Stefan's strictures include such a precise limit to an experimental observation that it must be performed within the first three seconds of the experiment in order for results to be valid. He records this limitation as one of the possible sources of error in his investigation. In fact, Stefan attends to several possible sources of error that have to do with the external conditions of time, temperature, and behavior of materials under which his experiments are performed. His primary method of calculation of properties is to hold one value constant while altering, or allowing one or two others to vary. Having found a minimum value for conductivity, he is concerned with establishing an upper, or maximum value, at least in theory. In order to do this, his calculations take into consideration loss or gain of heat from the container and the surrounding air, the mathematical ratio of temperature increase to conduction capacity, and many other factors.

The precision of Stefan's work does not indicate that it was ahead of its time. For example, in another paper in the same volume, "On the dynamic theory of the diffusion of gases,"[20] Stefan, like other investigators, rejects the notion that the mass of atoms might produce "forces," and depends instead upon the effects of the pervasive "ether" for explanation. In addition to the above-mentioned features of the first paper, this paper is marked by rhetorical strategies to involve the reader. For example, after a careful and convincing review of one theory, Stefan interjects the information that a variation in proportion showed the basic hypothesis to be unfounded. For the moment the reader is caught off balance and told as much as: no matter how good this stuff may sound, I [the narrator] can find holes in it and you [the reader] had better follow my every step closely if you want to avoid such analytical pitfalls. In general, the defining logical procedure is the "if . . . then" sequence: "If one understands the repulsion between molecules as a force that has an effect over a distance, even if a limited distance, then the diameter of a molecule signifies that distance of two homogeneous molecules in which their relative velocity is destroyed and reversed during a central collision" (338).

Sigmund Exner's paper in the same volume, "Further studies on the structure of the olfactory mucous membrane in vertebrates,"[21] is similar to Freud's first publications—an anatomical study based on observations during dissection. In particular, the author is attempting to establish boundaries and origins, beginnings and ending of nerves. The report is not of an experiment, but a careful descriptive topography. Exner seems sensitive to the metaphorical implications of language use, apologizing ("wenn ich mich so ausdrücken darf"[16]) for his use of the term "roots" for fibrillous, hair-like extensions into cells which may not be "roots" at all. A historical, personal narrative, Exner's story is written in a style that is open and accessible to the reader. Exner is also sensitive to the potential disturbance of results by faulty techniques. For example, he expresses the belief that whether or not the nuclei of cells appear granulated or homogenous will depend upon how carefully they are handled. Exner's investigation is a thoughtful one that arrives cautiously at a modest conclusion, making a tiny addition to knowledge of the function of sensory nerves in full and acknowledged awareness of the limits of techniques and conditions of observation. This paper is an early version of the kind of pre-psychological investigation Freud was to carry out and also of the later preoccupation of Freud and other investigators with the nature of sense perception.

Brücke's paper "Studies on carbohydrates and the manner in which they are digested and absorbed"[22] is of particular interest because of its extreme contrast with the modest caution of Exner and with the precision of Stefan. The great professor, associate of Helmholtz and Du Bois-Reymond, in whose laboratory Freud was to work for six years (1876–82), and who found in the young medical student a devoted assistant and acolyte, produced in this paper a lengthy study that fails to meet basic methodological standards that were accepted at that time and continue to prevail now. Lacking any logical thread, the narrative is difficult to follow. There is no attempt at structured argument. Although this is an experimental account (as opposed to Exner's descriptive paper), it does not include mathematical expression of results. In fact, the idea of quantification itself is lacking, meaning that the paper lacks persuasive power. Brücke writes, for example: "... the precipitate of which is dissolved again in *a little* water..." (132); or "... even in a *rather* concentrated solution only after *relatively long* boiling [results in] an *insignificant* precipitate..."; or "a *generous* precipitate"; or a "*considerable* amount" (137); or "a *significant surplus*," and "I made *a few* quantitative attempts. ..." Brücke is equally careless about time. He writes: "I extracted... but *only as long as I could expect to get* a filtrate without starch" (142). His experiment consisted of feeding starch paste to dogs who were then killed and the contents of their digestive tracts examined. Brücke begins his procedure with "*a series* of dogs." "*In some cases*" they were given wheat meal instead of starch paste. *Within one to five hours* after taking the food, *some* were killed with curare, *others* by being bled to death. (No mention is made of any possible influence on the outcome of the experiment of the different methods of killing the dogs.) "*Some* of the experiments were carried out *a long time ago, the rest in the course of the years 1871 and 1872. Generally speaking,* with one exception explained below, all results were in agreement" (144; my italics). More than lack of precision, this kind of report fails the test of repeatability, without which the experiment has no value as science. There is no way another researcher can use such a report to duplicate and thus to test and verify the results. If it cannot be duplicated, it cannot lead to generalizations, hypotheses, theories, or laws. Brücke's account shows how imperative it was to apply to the other sciences the standards prevailing in the best of physical experiments. After a lengthy discussion of some results of tests with saliva, Brücke inserts a footnote explaining that while otherwise all his experiments were conducted on dogs, those with saliva used human saliva (151)—this after a reader will have followed a discussion dealing exclusively with results in dogs. By standards prevailing in other scientific publications of the Imperial Academy in 1872, this adds up to shoddy work. Finally, a last example having to do with Brücke's metaphors: he writes that "the ferment is obviously present [in the stomach] permanently, since it will certainly rarely be cleaned with the perfection with which a milkmaid cleans her bowls so that the milk will not sour in them" (155). Considering the capacity of metaphor to reveal an otherwise unacknowledged truth, we may interpret this quaint and imprecise image as standing for the quality of Brücke's paper as a whole, which may possibly stand for the general state of experimental physiology at this juncture.

In the Reports of the Imperial Academy of Sciences of the following year, 1873, we find a paper by Stefan, "Experiments on evaporation."[23] I would like to focus on Stefan's experimental methods and his analysis shortly before he became Freud's teacher, in order to review the kind of thinking that may have had an influence on the excellent student of physics. If we disregard the proportion of natural language to mathematics in the text, which today has changed in favor of mathematics, we can find no other fundamental difference between the physics paper of Stefan's in 1873 and a physics paper today. Naturally, topics will have changed, as the state of knowledge has changed, but the format of the argument and the standards of analysis are clearly recognizable as modern physics. Stefan opens by explaining that previous experiments have not led to results that could have been expressed as new physical laws. The error has been that the experiments were not conducted under controlled variable conditions expressible in sufficiently simple mathematical form. "The lack of a precise theoretical concept of the nature of the evaporation process was also a handicap for the experimental development of the theory of evaporation" (385). That is to say that theory and experiment are interdependent. An experiment without a theoretical basis is meaningless; likewise theory must eventually be supported by experiment. Stefan, who was outstanding as an experimenter *and* as a theorist, would have stressed this interdependence in class, laying the foundation, perhaps, in the young Freud's fertile mind for his future commitment to the natural and necessary interdependence of theory and practice. Stefan continues in his introductory section by explaining that despite his positive results, the experiments will have to be repeated many times "in order that ... the numerical values of the new constants for the nature of the vapors can achieve the necessary certainty" (385). In addition, the experiments will have to be extended to many other kinds of liquids. With transparent logic and persuasive rhetoric, Stefan sets out the questions, problems, and results. In contrast to Brücke, Stefan takes into consideration the influence of all possible variations in the conditions of the experiment and expresses them mathematically, if possible. The text is structured around repeated questioning of his own and others' results. Of one conclusion he writes: "This is correct within the limits of experiments carried out up to this point, but it need not be correct for all cases" (407). Or again he writes: "If such experiments are to provide comparable results, then they must naturally be carried out under equivalent conditions" (417). With regard to some irregularities in an otherwise constant series of mathematical ratios (of experimental results), Stefan explains that they can only be interpreted as errors in the observations. We understand that this is the stance of the superior scientific investigator of the time—aware of the fallibility of the observer. Toward the end of his paper, having reviewed some earlier experimenters' results, Stefan writes: "According to this, the result found by me contradicts many earlier experiments. This is, however, not the case" (418). He shows that those earlier experiments tested only the temperature variable and not the nature of the gas involved. Although his experiment, Stefan asserts, leaves no doubt as to the influence of the nature of the gas, nevertheless it seemed desirable to test his results by yet another kind of experiment (one he had described at the beginning of the paper). Stefan's reasoning process is so convincing, his rhetorical control of the text (and thus of readers' responses) so masterly, that his papers provide enjoyment of the text beyond the stimulation of the ideas. One might say that the text exceeds the limits of late nineteenth-century physical knowledge by its rhetorical power, its logical coherence, and intellectual scrupulousness. Readers of Freud's texts might recognize in these terms also an approximate description of the effects of his most closely reasoned writings.

If we were to examine the 1875 volume of the Reports of the Imperial Academy of Sciences (published in 1876) we would find, in addition to contributions by Stefan and Brücke, papers by Sigmund Exner and Freud's later much-admired friend and mentor, Ernst Fleischl (von Marxow). Fleischl's papers have to do with electrical stimulation of nerves, and show thoughtful and meticulous experimental procedures and measurements.[24] Exner's paper, "On seeing movement and the theory of the compound eye,"[25] begins with a deconstruction of Helmholtz's generally accepted distinction between "sensation" and "perception." Exner shows that these are mutually contradictory terms which can no longer be useful or heuristic in modern physiology, but which must nevertheless remain in use until the new science has developed its own set of terms. Thus Exner once again (see above) sets an example as a scientist who reflects upon problems of language and representation in science. While largely anecdotal, his account of optical experiments includes careful microscopic observations and measurements. Given the limits of apparatus and implements, Exner seems to have carried out a thorough investigation. One must conclude, however, that the biological science in which Freud would be involved remained largely descriptive in the 1870s, a state of affairs which would be reflected in the earliest papers Freud wrote, beginning with the publication in 1877 of the results of his first study of the nervous system of the petromyzon.

When Freud fled to London from Vienna in 1938, he brought part of his library with him. The choice of volumes to be rescued under those conditions is significant. Among them are Rudolf Clausius's classic *The Mechanical Theory of Heat* (2nd ed., 1876) which established the foundations of thermodynamics (an earlier edition of which may have been one of Freud's student texts and a source of his ideas on entropy), four volumes of lectures and essays by Helmholtz (three bear Freud's signature and dates in 1882 and 1883; the fourth was a gift from Wilhelm Fließ in 1892), and a copy of the 1911 edition of *The Grammar of Science* by British scientist Karl Pearson which Freud read on the recommendation of Ernest Jones.[26] Freud's markings in his copy of *The Grammar of Science* help to make the connections between the intellectual impetus Freud received from physics as a student, and features of some of his early writings.

Pearson (1857–1936) was founder of the twentieth-century science of statistics. He was a multi-talented researcher who mastered and contributed to more than one field, including physics, applied mathematics, mechanics, and later eugenics. His book, *The Grammar of Science*, first published in 1892, "influenced the scientific thought of an entire generation."[27] Pearson's view, like that of Austrian physicist Ernst Mach, was that "all science is description and not explanation"; it is no more than a kind of "shorthand description, an economy of thought."[28] This is an interpretive stance that places Pearson (and Mach) at a great distance from positivism, or Newtonian physics. Freud marked the margin of his copy next to the above definitions of science. He also marked the following passages: "In truth, the field of science is much more consciousness than an external world. . . . [an] interpreter of conceptions rather than . . . investigator of a 'natural law' . . . science still considers the whole contents of the mind to be ultimately based on sense-impressions" (52). These views remained of interest to Freud who earlier had also read and been drawn to Mach's ideas. Of particular relevance, however, are Freud's marks in Pearson's chapter on space and time. Pearson's thinking on space and time is considered to have anticipated relativity (as it was first enunciated by Einstein in an article published in 1905).

Pearson defines space as "a mode of perception—the order in which our perceptive faculty presents coexistence to us" (191). Time is also a mode of perception:

As space marks the coexistence of perceptions at an epoch of time—we measure the breadth of our field—so time marks the progression of perceptions at a position in space—we measure the length of our field. The combination of the two modes, or change of position with change of time, is *motion*, the fundamental manner in which phenomena are in conception presented to us.

If we had solely the power of peceiving coexisting things, our perception might be wide, but it would fall far short of its actuality. The power of "perceiving things apart" by progression or sequence is an essential feature of conscious life, if not of existence. Without this time-mode of perception the only sciences possible would be those which deal with the order or relationship of coexisting things, with number, position, and measurement . . . (208–9)

Freud's interest is supported by his marginal marking at a footnote that reads: "Our notion of 'being' is essentially associated with space and time, and it may well be questioned whether it is intelligible to use the word except in association with these modes of perception" (207).

I would like to suggest that, among other things, the discourse of experimental physics may have meant for Freud the addition of a mode of time to his perception of the phenomena he was investigating.[29] We saw that the biological (physiological) investigations that were characterized by precision and intellectual rigor were the descriptive investigations. Freud's own earliest articles were descriptive rather than experimental. They show the same precision we noted in articles by Exner and Fleischl, in addition to some stylistic features of Freud's, such as a certain flippancy of tone, and even humor—reminiscent of the kind of rhetorical control Stefan had exercised in his articles. This applies in particular to Freud's magistral, eighty-six-page study, "On the spinal ganglia and spinal cord of the petromyzon."[30] His scholarly exactitude included, for example, an exhaustive coverage of the literature on the problem he was investigating. He would show how in some cases preconceptions had directed prior investigations, leading to errors in interpretation. His own dissections were characterized by the utmost precision with regard to timing, choice of solutions, and unprejudiced observation. But they remained primarily reports that marked "the coexistence of perceptions at an epoch of time" (Pearson above). By its nature, the anatomical study necessarily "deal[s] with the order or relationship of coexisting things." It necessarily lacks the dimension of sequence in time, in contrast to the course of an experiment which follows changes over time. The report of an experiment is set up to reflect a step-by-step procedure (whether nor not the experiment followed the order reported). The impressive experiments carried out by Josef Stefan for his students in the classroom, and those described in his articles would naturally have followed a space-time model—"the combination of the two modes, or change of position with change of time."

At one point in his long petromyzon article, however, Freud's narrative slips into a narrative of motion. He chooses verbs that tell a story of action and development, that add the experimental feature of time to the static description. It is as if his language took the bit in its teeth and dashed ahead in spite of the rider. These are also the paragraphs that interject humor—an especially unusual feature in a scientific article. The author seems to be pressing against the boundaries of the descriptive article form and testing its limits.

Nevertheless, when he wrote a descriptive topography of hysteria in his "Psychotherapy of Hysteria" section of the *Studies on Hysteria* (1895), Freud remained in the spatial mode familiar from his early studies of the anatomy of the nervous system. He presents a complex, multidimensional morphology, stratified around a "pathogenic nucleus."[31] No matter how intricate the imagery becomes, it remains a description of relations in space. Whole passages read like his reports of dissections of the nervous systems of creatures such as the petromyzon or the river crab:[32] "[i]t contains nodal points at which two or more threads meet and thereafter proceed as one; and as a rule several threads which run independently, or which are connected at various points by side-paths, debouch into the nucleus. To put this in other words, it is very remarkable how often a symptom is determined in several ways, is 'overdetermined.' "[33] By this evidence, we must conclude that the notion of "overdetermination" arises from the anatomical appearance of multiple nerve strands entering a nucleus.

Later in 1895 Freud composed the "Project," possibly with the intention of providing a more satisfactory theoretical foundation for the *Studies on Hysteria*.[34] Though it has received significantly less attention than Freud's other works, the "Project" is said to mark the origins of some of the most important later developments in psychoanalysis.[35] In contrast to *Studies on Hysteria*, the "Project" is characterized by the addition of time as the operative discourse which means conceptualizing in the manner of an experiment rather than an anatomical description and produces an analysis that does greater justice to the complexity of the object of investigation. An agenda directly from physics is set in the brief introductory statement:

The intention is to furnish a psychology that shall be a natural science: that is, to represent psychical processes as quantitatively determinate states of specifiable material particles, thus making those processes perspicuous and free from contradiction. Two principal ideas are involved: [1] What distinguishes activity from rest is to be regarded as Q, subject to the general laws of motion. (2) The neurones are to be taken as the material particles.[36]

The definition of the external world, to which neurones react, is derived from the worldview of physics: "... there is no question but that the external world is the origin of all major quantities of energy, since, according to the discoveries of physics, it consists of powerful masses which are in violent motion and which transmit their motion."[37] Freud's central hypothesis is that memory and perception are activated in two different neuronal systems—the first being impermeable and altered by the passing through of a certain quantity of excitation, the second being permeable and unaltered. Thus the elaborate edifice of theory of how the mind works is erected upon a system that is dynamic, continually in process and subjected to changes measurable in quantities that vary in proportion to one another.

The most critical problem for Freud is the relationship between "quality" and "quantity": how to explain consciousness which is unaware of the quantifiable neuronal activities, Consciousness supplies "qualities," whereas science only recognizes quantities. How, Freud asks, is quantity transformed into quality? His answer is "time," that is, periodicity in the transfer of impulses to one system of neurones:

I can see only one way out of the difficulty: a revision of our fundamental hypothesis about the passage of Qn. So far I have regarded it only as the transference of Qn from one neurone to another. But it must have still another characteristic, of a temporal nature; for the mechanics of the physicists have allowed this temporal characteristic to the other motions of masses in the external world as well. I speak of this as *period* for short.[38]

That is to say time has entered both as sequences of events and relationships, in an account like a physical experiment, and as an explanatory feature of the theory—the key, in fact, that allows the theory to function at all. Freud makes his debt to physics obvious, but even if he never mentioned physics, the influence of the experimental method and the influence of time as explanation would testify to the pervasive presence.[39]

Freud believes that the "periods" he extrapolates are governed by the "general laws of motion." His hypothesis assumes "that the w neurons are incapable of receiving Qn, but that instead they appropriate the *period* of the excitation and that this state of theirs of being affected by period while they are filled with the minimum of Qn is the *fundamental basis of consciousness*" (my italics). Now follows an hypothesis that links Freud's thinking in 1895 to the marks he made around 1912 in Pearson's text:

Where do these differences of *period* spring from? Everything points to the sense-organs, whose qualities seem to be represented precisely by different periods of neuronal motion. The sense-organs act not only as Q-screens, like all nerve-ending apparatuses, but also as *sieves;* for they allow the stimulus through from only certain processes with a particular period.[40]

Sense organs acting like "screens" or "sieves" for the entry of impressions to the mind at certain regulated intervals of progression or sequence is a notion that comes very close to Pearson's views (above p. 24), and shows the staying power of such concepts—from 1895 to at least 1912—in Freud's attention.

To explain *defense* or *repression,* Freud introduces the idea that a neuronal system can be "taught biologically" to seek to reproduce a state which marked the cessation of pain. "With the expression *taught biologically* we have introduced a new basis of explanation, which should have independent validity, even though it does not exclude, but rather calls for, a recourse to mechanical principles (quantitative factors)."[41] On this basis Freud builds the idea that logical thought processes depend upon biological rules, and thus logical faults consist in "the non-observance of the *biological rules* for the passage of thought." The biological rules "can be transposed directly into the rules of logic," which explains the disturbance of the intellect at encountering logical contradictions, and the intellectual pleasure in logic without contradiction.[42] Freud has thus subsumed the logic of physics into the physics of the mind—a notion that raises more questions than it answers. (There is, after all, more than one kind of logic, which suggests the possibility of a relationship between logics and cultural history.)

Finally, the segment of the "Project" that carries us most obviously into the future evolution of psychoanalysis is the discussion of the origin of the ego. It remains, in the context of the "Project," a quantitative discussion that proposes a ratio between increase in the level of cathexis and expansion of the ego on the one hand, and decrease in the level of cathexis and narrowing of the ego on the other. Such an explanation suggests an analogy to the relationships between substances, such as different gases, measured mathematically in a physical experiment. It reflects, among other things, the discourse of physics as Freud knew it and had learned it already as a young man.

Before concluding, I would like to refer again to a psychoanalytic theory on which my argument rests: without our necessarily recognizing or acknowledging it, an admired model may be internalized as a superego. Such was the case with Freud and physics. By way of evidence, I shall point to several (among many) references to physics in Freud's texts. *An Autobiographical Study* of 1925 contains a discussion of the place of defining concepts in the sciences. In contradiction to the conventional wisdom, Freud maintains that sharply defined concepts are at home not in the natural sciences—where they are, in fact, impossible—but in the non-scientific fields. Therefore it is to be expected that psychoanalysis also will continue to evolve its theories without producing final definitions of its basic concepts. "Zoology and Botany did not start from correct and adequate definitions of an animal and a plant; to this very day biology has been unable to give any certain meaning to the concept of life. *And even physics* would never have made any advance if it had had to wait until its concepts of matter, force, gravitation, and so on, had reached the desirable degree of clarity and precision" (my italics).[43] The words "and even physics" tell us that in Freud's mind there is a continuum of the scientific, reaching its apotheosis in physics. The importance of this becomes clear when we remember to what extent Freud, throughout his career, presents psychoanalysis as a science. Later, in "The Question of Lay Analysis" (1926), Freud uses physics as an analogy when explaining why the science of psychoanalysis should not be considered a medical specialty.[44] More significantly, in "The Future of an Illusion" (1927), when predicting that psychoanalysis is likely to be subjected to attack as a result of its founder's critique of religion, Freud explains that it has already withstood many storms and must be exposed to his one as well. "In point of fact psycho-analysis is a method of research, an impartial instrument, like the infinitesimal calculus, as it were. If a physicist were to discover with the latter's help that after a certain time the earth would be destroyed, we would nevertheless hesitate to attribute destructive tendencies to the calculus itself and therefore to proscribe it."[45] Here, in more sophisticated terms, is a replay of the ideas that had impressed Freud as a student fifty years before, and of his account of them (in the letter to Silberstein of April 28, 1875) that separates the sober mathematical and physical operations from the ideas about the end of the world. This is obviously a deeply meaningful comparison for Freud. Physics becomes thereby the ultimate provider of legitimacy for the new science: physics lends psychoanalysis its prestige. The presumption implicit in these texts is that no reader could question the legitimacy of physics, its power, its value, or its claim to respect.

Toward the end of Freud's life, physics continues to play a prominent role in his thinking. In the "Outline of Psychoanalysis," (1938)[46] however, another dimension has entered the comparison of psychology to physics. Psychology is like physics because its object of investigation—the "psychic apparatus"—is also "spatially extended," and shares other qualities with the objects of physics. These qualities mean that psychology rests on the same basis "as every other natural science, e.g. as physics," and thus requires that we discover something else behind the qualities accessible to our powers of perception. Freud speculates that this something else is probably closer to reality. We can never reach it, however,

since it is evident that everything new that we have inferred must nevertheless be translated back into the language of our perceptions, from which it is simply impossible for us to free ourselves. But herein lies the very nature and limitation of our science. It is as though we were to say in physics: "If we could see clearly enough we should find that what appears to be a solid body is made up of particles of such and such a shape and size and occupying such and such relative positions."

We can try to increase the capacity of our senses through various technical aids, but the end result will be the same. "Reality will always remain 'unknowable.'" The most we can hope for is "insight into connections and dependent relations which are present in the external world, which can somehow be reliably reproduced or reflected in the internal world of our thought..." (196). "[W]e make use of... methods just as a physicist makes use of experiment" (197). This neo-Kantian description approximates closely a description in an essay written by the discoverer of the quantum, Max Planck, in the first decade of the twentieth century.[47] It reflects the mindset of mainstream physicists at that time. But Freud adds yet another layer of distance from the extrapolated "reality"—language. We can get no further than the reproduction of the language in which our perceptions are expressed. This insight takes Freud up to the era of quantum mechanics (beginning in the late 1920s) by suggesting, as Bohr and Heisenberg did, that we are trapped within the limits of our language.

A few years earlier, in his public letter of 1932 to Albert Einstein on the subject "Why War?" Freud makes a suggestion about their two sciences that takes him up to contemporary discussions of the cultural and historical contingency of science. "It may perhaps seem to you [i.e. Einstein] as though our theories [i.e. psychoanalysis] are a kind of mythology. . . . But does not every science come in the end to a kind of mythology like this? Cannot the same be said today of your own Physics?"[48] It is a testimony to the scope and flexibility of Freud's thinking that his nearly life-long focus on physics as the paradigm science, serving to politically justify and scientifically buttress psychoanalysis, could lead him from a positivist stress on the solidity, power, and legitimacy of physics to the suggestion that, like all endeavors of the human mind, physics cannot exceed the limits set by language and by the inherent human propensity for myth-making.

Notes

1. In the *Studies on Hysteria* Freud used this phrase twice in his prescription for successful therapeutic strategies. *Standard Edition of the Complete Psychological Works of Sigmund Freud,* ed. and trans. J. Stachey, A. Freud. A. Strachey, and A. Tyson, 24 vols. (London: Hogarth, 1955–74). (Referred to in the notes as SE), here, 2:292 and 294. For the German original see Sigmund Freud, *Gesammelte Werke,* 19 vols. (Frankfurt am Main: S. Fischer, 1952–87). (Referred to in the notes as GW), here 1:297 and 299.

2. A leading example is Frank J. Sulloway, *Freud, Biologist of the Mind* (New York: Basic Books, 1979).

3. I am concerned with methods and discourses, or modes of description, not with concepts of nineteenth-century physics, such as the principle of constancy, or conservation of energy and the role they played in the evolution of psychoanalysis. The role of concepts has been explored by other authors, for example Erwin H. Ackerknecht, "Geschichtliches zur Theorie der psychischen Energie," *Schweizer Archiv für Neurochirurgie und Psychiatrie* 135(1984):181–85; Robert Galatzer-Levy, "Perspective on the Regulatory Principles of Mental Functioning," *Psychoanalysis and Contemporary Thought* 6(1983):255–89; Willem van Hoorn, "Psychoanalysis, Romanticism and Biology," *Storia e Critica della Psicologia* 3(June 1982):5–25; and Edwin R. Wallace IV, "A Critical Reappraisal of Certain Freudian Tenets," *The Psychiatric Forum* 5(Winter 1976):38–45.

4. Ernest Jones, *The Life and Work of Sigmund Freud,* 3 vols. (New York: Basic Books, 1953), 1:37.

5. Siegfried Bernfeld and Suzanne Cassirer Bernfeld, *Bausteine der Freud-Biographik,* ed. and trans. Else Grubrich-Simitis (Frankfurt am Main: Suhrkamp, 1981), 179. My translation.

6. Information on Stefan is from the article by Walter Böhm in the *Dictionary of Scientific Biography,* editor in chief Charles Coulston Gillespie (New York: Scribner's, 1970–80), 13:10–11. (Referred to in notes as DSB.) And from

Almanach der Kaiserlichen Akademie der Wissenschaften (Vienna: Tempsky, 1893) 43:252–57; F. Herneck, "Wiener Physik vor 100 Jahren," in *Physikalische Blätter*, 17 (October 1961):460–61; A. v. Obermayer, *Zur Erinnerung an Josef Stefan* (Vienna and Leipzig: Wilhelm Braumüller, 1893); Christa Jungnickel and Russell McCormmach, *Intellectual Mastery of Nature. Theoretical Physics from Ohm to Einstein*, 2 vols. (Chicago and London: University of Chicago Press, 1986); and Engelbert Broda, *Ludwig Boltzmann. Man. Physicist. Philosopher*, trans. Larry Gay and the author (Woodbridge, Conn.: Ox Bow Press, 1983).

7. Letter from James Moser to Heinrich Hertz, March 21, 1890, as quoted by Jungnickel and McCormmach in *Intellectual Mastery of Nature*, 2:184.

8. Ludwig Boltzmann, *Populäre Schriften* (Leipzig: Barth, 1905), 101. My translation. For a knowledgeable discussion in English of Boltzmann's life, career, and importance, see Broda, *Ludwig Boltzmann*.

9. Sigmund Freud, *Jugendbriefe an Eduard Silberstein 1871–1881*, ed. Walter Boehlich (Frankfurt am Main: S. Fischer, 1989). (Referred to in notes as JB.) For the translation see *The Letters of Sigmund Freud to Eduard Silberstein 1871–1881*, ed. Walter Boehlich, trans. Arnold J. Pomerans (Cambridge, Mass.: Harvard University Press, 1990). (Referred to in notes as ES.)

10. Letter to Silberstein of January 24, 1875. Freud also wanted to attend Rudolf Virchow's lectures. (JB, 98; ES, 84.)

11. William J. McGrath writes: "The detailed letters Freud wrote to Silberstein during the 1874–75 academic year indicate that he was beginning to lay down the intellectual foundations for his scientific approach to psychology." *Freud's Discovery of Psychoanalysis. The Politics of Hysteria* (Ithaca and London: Cornell University Press, 1986), 100.

12. Letter of April 11, 1875. JB, 126; ES, 111.

13. Letter of March 15, 1875. JB, 118; ES, 104.

14. Jungnickel and McCormmach, *Intellectual Mastery of Nature*, 2:105.

15. Letter of April 28, 1875. JB, 129; ES, 114.

16. Ibid. JB, 130; ES, 115.

17. Paul Volkmann, *Erkenntnistheoretische Grundzüge der Naturwissenschaften und ihre Beziehungen zum Geistesleben der Gegenwart. Allgemein wissenschaftliche Vorträge* (Leipzig, 1896; 2nd ed. Leipzig and Berlin: B. G. Teubner, 1910). As quoted in Jungnickel and McCormmach, *Intellectual Mastery of Nature*, 2:145.

18. Sulloway, *Freud, Biologist of the Mind*, 131 and 116, n. 8.

19. "Untersuchungen über die Wärmeleitung in Gasen," *Sitzungsberichte der Kaiserlichen Adademie der Wissenschaften, Mathematisch-Naturwissenschaftliche Classe*, Abtheilung 2, 65 (1872):45–69. Translations of all scientific papers are mine.

20. "Über die dynamische Theorie der Diffusion der Gase," *Sitzungsberichte*, Abtheilung 2, 65(1872):323–63.

21. "Weitere Studien über die Structur der Riechschleimhaut bei Wirbelthieren," *Sitzungsberichte*, Abtheilung 3, 65(1872):7–41.

22. "Studien über die Kohlehydrate und über die Art wie sie verdaut und aufgesaugt werden," *Sitzungsberichte*, Abtheilung 3, 65(1872):126–61.

23. "Versuche über die Verdampfung," *Sitzungsberichte*, Abtheilung 2, 68(1873):385–423.

24. "Über die Graduirung elektrischer Inductions-Apparate," *Sitzungsberichte*, Abtheilung 3, 72(1875):41–44; and "Untersuchungen über die Gesetze der Nervenerregung. I. Abhandlung: Über die Lehre vom Anschwellen der Reize im Nerven," *Sitzungsberichte*, Abtheilung 3, 72(1875):393–406.

25. "Über das Sehen von Bewegungen und die Theorie des zusammengesetzten Auges," *Sitzungsberichte*, Abtheilung 3, 72(1875):156–91.

26. For the opportunity to examine these and other volumes in Freud's library I am indebted to the National Endowment for the Humanities for a grant to participate in the 1991 summer seminar in London, "Freud and the Culture of His Time," directed by Professor Sander Gilman. I am also very grateful to the staff at the Freud Museum in London, in particular Director Erica Davies, Librarian Keith Davies, and Director of Research Michael Molnar, for their assistance and for their generosity in making themselves and the museum's resources available to visiting scholars.

27. Information on Pearson is from the article by Churchill Eisenhart, DSB 10:447–73, here 448.

28. *The Grammar of Science*, 3rd ed. (London: Adam and Charles Black, 1911), viii and v.

29. I do not mean to refer here to Darwinian evolutionary time, but rather to time as perception of synchronic processes. See below, n. 39.

30. "Über Spinalganglien und Rückenmark des Petromyzon," *Sitzungsberichte*, Abtheilung 3, 78(1878):81–167. (Published in 1879.)

31. SE 2:255–305, here 289; GW 1:252–312, here 292.

32. The article on the river crab is "Über den Bau der Nervenfasern und Nervenzellen beim Flusskrebs," *Sitzungsberichte*, Abtheilung 3, 85(1882):9–46.

33. SE 2:290; GW 1:294.

34. I use James Strachey's title "Project" as shorthand. Freud did not supply a title to the manuscript which was written rapidly under conditions of great intellectual ferment and stress, and sent off in a letter to Fließ. Freud refers to it in one letter (April 27, 1895) as "Psychology for the neurologist." (GW, Nachtragsband:375). Isabel F. Knight assesses the "Project" as a reaction to Freud's dissatisfaction with Breuer's theoretical chapter in the *Studies on Hysteria*. She argues that it is the theoretical foundation that Freud believed ought to have been provided for the *Studies*, but could not be because of Breuer's limitations. ("Freud's 'Project': A Theory for *Studies on Hysteria*, *Journal of the History of the Behavioral Sciences* 20 [October 1984]:340–58.)

35. See, for example, the editorial introduction to the "Project" in SE 1:290–93 and GW Nachtragsband:382–85, as well as the extensive footnotes in both

editions which draw out relationships to Freud's later work. Of the studies on the "Project," one which I find particularly stimulating for its language-centered reading is "Psychoanalysis and natural science: Freud's 1895 *Project* revisited," by John Friedman and James Alexander, *The International Review of Psychoanalysis* 10(1983):303–18.

36. SE 1:295; GW Nachtragsband:387. I have used the Standard Edition translation, although I disagree with two points: (1) "perspicuous" is too stilted a term for Freud's "anschaulich" which is a word that plays a specific role in the history of science and means something more like "plastic," or visualizable, imaginable; (2) in the last line the definite article "the" preceding "material particles" is not in Freud's original text.

37. SE 1:304; GW Nachtragsband:397.

38. SE 1:310; GW Nachtragsband:402.

39. Time also enters the "Project" in the form of the idea of biological evolution. But this is an entirely distinct concept, providing not a shift in perceptual mode, but rather—in Freud's view—supplying the history and reasons for various functions.

40. SE 1:310; GW Nachtragsband:402–3.

41. SE 1:322; GW Nachtragsband:415.

42. SE 1:386; GW Nachtragsband:476.

43. SE 20:3–74, here 58; "Selbstdarstellung" in GW 14:31–96, here 84–85. I have used the Standard Edition translation with the exception of the words "And even physics" which I substituted for Strachey's "Physics itself, indeed," because I find my version clearer and more accurate. Freud draws the same analogies in the "Outline of Psychoanalysis" (1938), "Abriß der Psychoanalyse," GW 17:63–138.

44. SE 20:179–258, here 252 and 254 (this is the "Postscript," written in 1927); "Nachwort zur 'Frage der Laienanalyse,' " GW 14:207–96, here 289 and 291.

45. SE 21:1–56, here 36–37; "Die Zukunft einer Illusion," GW 14:323–80, here 360.

46. SE 23:141–207; "Abriß der Psychoanalyse," GW 17:63–138.

47. "Die Einheit des Physikalischen Weltbildes" (1908), in Max Planck, *Physikalische Abhandlungen und Vorträge,* 3 vols. (Brunswick: Vieweg, 1958), 3:6–29; and in English, "The Unity of the Physical World-Picture," trans. Ann Toulmin, in *Physical Reality: Philosophical Essays on Twentieth-Century Physics,* ed. Stephen Toulmin (New York: Harper and Row, 1970), 1–27.

48. SE 22:195–215, here 211; "Warum Krieg?" GW 16:11–27, here 22.

12. The Bizarre Chair: A Slant on Freud's Light Reading in the 1930s

Michael Molnar

She [Mathilde Freud] explained to me that S. F. had a habit of reading in a very peculiar and uncomfortable body position. He was leaning in this chair, in some sort of diagonal position, one of his legs slung over the arm of the chair, the book held high and his head unsupported. The rather bizarre form of the chair I designed is to be explained as an attempt to maintain this habitual posture and to make it more comfortable.[1]

"A Diagonal Position"

Freud's armchair now stands empty in the middle of his study at 20 Maresfield Gardens. It is reminiscent of a Henry Moore figure—a broad seat with a narrow back topped by a small protruberant headrest. Two arms curve gracefully round the imagined sitter.

Felix Augenfeld designed it in about 1930 but it is not known how long before that time Freud had been in the habit of adopting the reading position he describes. The posture would not have allowed Freud to take notes without swiveling round to sit upright at the desk, probably it was therefore the position he assumed for his private reading.

Looking at the empty chair today, it would be difficult to deduce that posture. Looking at the surrounding books in Freud's library it would be almost as difficult to say which books he chose to read for pleasure. The library at 20 Maresfield Gardens contains virtually all the books he chose to rescue from Vienna. But this does not necessarily mean that its catalog alone will include an accurate guide to his lighter reading, even if we supplement it with the listing of those books that he chose to sell in Vienna, and which ended up in New York. In the intervening years numerous books, which Freud is known to have possessed, have been lost, lent or given away. Many of the books constitute a professional, working library. Some were clearly gifts from visitors or colleagues, hence not purposefully acquired. Some are uncut. [2]

Moreover, the Freud Museum also houses a parallel library, namely those books left by Anna Freud (and this also includes books that belonged to other members of the household). It contains a large number of books published before 1939; clearly neither library was hermetically sealed and books may well have passed from one to the other. Given the closeness of their relationship during the 1930s, it is more than likely that Anna and her father may often have been reading the same books.

Jones writes: "In later years, and especially when suffering, Freud turned a good deal to lighter reading," and he cites some examples of such books, including Agatha Christie and Dorothy L. Sayers. [3] Neither of these can be found in Freud's library at Maresfield Gardens, but there are two books by Dorothy L. Sayers among Anna Freud's books. Since Freud left no record of his light reading this subject can only be tackled haphazardly. Here I shall pick a few examples of his non-professional reading during his final years, based mainly on scattered comments. Without expecting that any firm conclusions can be drawn from such an unsystematic survey, I can only hope it may offer at least the imprint of a reader's body in the cracked leather of his armchair.

Light reading has no purpose or end except transient pleasure and the problem of such pleasures is that they may leave no observable trace, whereas, when dealing with books that provided Freud with ideas, it is always possible to follow migrating or transmuting concepts. But occasionally Freud does give his reactions to his light reading in his correspondence. A letter of November 27, 1932, to Arnold Zweig offers one of Freud's most complete comments of this type. [4] Two paragraphs are devoted to his immediate reaction to Zweig's latest novel, *De Vriendt kehrt heim*, which Freud had read straight through within a day or two of receiving the author's first bound copy. He praised the novel's richness of material, its sharp, objective descriptions and its masterly historical background; also he commented on a salient feature of the plot, namely the absence of women. But, most interestingly, he draws attention to the character of the British agent, Irmin, as Zweig's representative within the narrative and as the reader's point of reference, his friend and guide.

The hero of Zweig's book, the Dutch poet de Vriendt, a naive, scholarly Jew living in Jerusalem attempts to mediate politically between Arabs and Palestinian Jews (and on a personal level too, since he is in love with a pupil of his, an Arab boy). Both the Jewish zealots and the hard-line Arabs are out for his blood, but it is a Zionist settler in Palestine who eventually assassinates him. De Vriendt's friend, the clever, sympathetic British agent Irmin, is left to deal with the case, without arousing either of the populations to riot.

Evidently Freud's interest in this book is at a number of levels. At this period both he and Zweig were deeply concerned by clashes between Arabs and Jews in Palestine and by the uncompromising stance of the extreme Zionists. At another level Freud had a friendly and fatherly interest in Arnold Zweig. This did not mean he refrained from criticism for that reason, but it does increase the vital element of transference, to which he himself drew attention. In highlighting the key role of Irmin, Freud was indicating that the affections of both writer and reader must be engaged in the work, in this case through transference upon a sympathetic figure. However, it was at another level that Freud's own interest was most deeply engaged in this book, namely through his curiosity to discover its factual background: "Strangely enough my attention is attracted most potently this time by what in a dream I would call 'day residues.' Surely you have not invented in every detail your de Vriendt and other figures and events."[5]

A few months later another book is subjected to a similar questioning. On April 3, 1933, Freud met the Scottish writer Norman Douglas (1868–1952), who was visiting Vienna with his friend Bryher, the poet H. D.'s protector and patron. Having read and enjoyed Douglas's *Old Calabria*, Freud wrote to the author to point out an instance of possible confused identities, between Frederick Barbarossa and his grandson Frederick II. "This brings out my pedantry. I cannot reconcile it [Barbarossa in Venosa and his contact with a sultan] with my knowledge of Rotbart. I cannot believe that he was in Southern Italy or Sicily or that he was the friend of a Mohammedan." Frederick II, he suggested, as legendary creator of a new German Reich, was an avatar of Adolf Hitler: " ... so the past always glimmers through the very latest moment in time."[6]

This presents a further example of Freud as historical unmasker attempting to unravel confused historical identities—a practice that had particularly embroiled him during the mid-1930s owing to his research on *Moses and Monotheism*. The fact that the traces of day-residues were the primary fascination in the reading of Zweig's book indicates that the joys of psychoanalysis might outweigh whatever literary pleasures the text offered. (The phrasing of the letter to Zweig does not necessarily imply that the book engaged him greatly at an aesthetic level.)

In his reactions to Zweig and Douglas, Freud chose to stress the fascination of detecting overlapping identities and also the element of reader transference. These are two quite separate levels of involvement; the former demands a certain distancing from the narrative and the latter a degree of self-abandon to it. Both are in effect substitutions, but exchanging characters within the narrative for their historical equivalents is an intellectual operation whilst the transference of reader upon fictional mediator presupposes empathy.

Freud enjoyed the two books mentioned, but there is no evidence they were favorites of his. He is, however, clearly enthusiastic about another book that he recommended to others as "delightful," "charming" and "quite unusually beautiful."[7] This was Thornton Wilder's *The Bridge of San Luis Rey,* a novella that recounts the collapse of a bridge in Peru, surrounding that event with widening ripples of significance as it works backwards through the lives of the victims, until the whole story is lapped in a universal moral: "There is a land of the living and a land of the dead, and the bridge is love, the only survival, the only meaning . . . "[8]

One aspect that may well have appealed to Freud is fairly evident. The book appeared in 1927, the same year as *The Future of an Illusion,* and Freud could hardly have failed to appreciate the forlorn attempt by one of the book's protagonists, Brother Juniper, to prove God's existence by statistical methods. After tabulating the virtues and vices of all the inhabitants of a village struck by the plague, the unfortunate monk finds that, by comparison with the survivors, "the dead were five times more worth saving . . . "[9] Whereupon the author concludes: "The discrepancy between faith and the facts is greater than is generally assumed."[10]

But "charm" evidently involves more than intellectual assent or even appreciation of the book's wit. And here it cannot be a matter of transference upon any single protagonist, for there are a number of interwoven plots with none predominating. If transference does indeed come into play, then it is not so much upon character as upon a certain authorial tone of voice. In this instance it could be characterized by its humor and humanity, and by a fading of the individual story into a universal perspective. The narrative blends into a philosophical reflection upon the world; the overall tone is in some respects nearer to that of the eighteenth-century Enlightenment than to the critical realism of the late nineteenth and early twentieth centuries.

However it is clearly specific to this work and not Wilder's authorial persona in general for Freud took a great dislike to one of his succeeding novels. On October 13, 1935, when Wilder paid a visit on Freud, Freud told him: "I could not read your latest book [*Heaven's My Destination*]— I threw it away [. . .] Why should you treat of an American fanatic; that cannot be treated poetically."[11] But why, one might ask, should a novel be constrained by "the poetical"? Perhaps Freud was contrasting the successful *Dichtung* of *The Bridge of San Luis Rey* with the "unpoetical" *Wahrheit* of its successor. Yet his comment remains quirky: it may, in part, be a further instance of his notorious anti-Americanism, aroused by the hero's religious fanaticism and reinforced by his nationality.

Wilder reported Freud's comment in English, and Freud's term "poetically" (given the context) presumably corresponds to "dichterisch" rather than "poetisch." But another book that delighted Freud at this period offers an extreme example of poetical (elegiac) prose; this is Marie Bonaparte's *Topsy, Chow-Chow au poil d'or*. Again the work is by a close acquaintance and in this case the factor of sympathy or transference may well be predominant in accounting for Freud's evident appreciation of the book, for it lacks any of the more complex literary features that characterize Zweig's or Wilder's novels.

On receiving the manuscript Freud wrote:

I love it; it is so movingly real and true. It is, of course, not an analytic work, but the analyst's search for truth and knowledge can be perceived behind this creation. It really gives the reasons why one can love with such a strange depth an animal like Topsy or (Jo-fi): its affection without any ambivalency, the simplicity of its life free from the almost unbearable conflict with civilization, the beauty of an existence complete in itself. And in spite of the alien nature of its organic development nevertheless a feeling of intimate relationship—an undeniable sense of belonging together—exists between us.[12]

Here Freud offers "reality" and "truth" as reasons for the book's attraction, though implying that these are of value in this context as expressions, as well as sources, of love. But reality and truth are of particular significance in this particular book, as far as Freud was concerned, for in effect it is his own story.

Marie Bonaparte wrote the book between May 1935 and June 1936. It was prompted by Topsy's sickness—a cancerous tumor in the dog's mouth which threatened to kill it. The book is written in short episodes, in effect prose poems, each a meditation on some aspect of the dog's imminent death. "The verdict on Topsy has been delivered: there is a lympho-sarcoma beneath her lip which is once again beginning to swell, a tumor which will grow, spread, proliferate, burst open, stifle her, condemn her to die the most terrible of all deaths within a few months."[13] The author, watching the creature, extrapolates from her sickness to the human condition: "Topsy, Topsy, death is approaching! but you are happier than I am for you do not think of it. [. . .] you can teach me by showing that you know better than us humans that life is but the present moment in which we are alive and nothing else."[14]

In a certain respect this book cannot be considered mere light reading, or even just reading, since Freud in fact made himself a co-writer of the work, together with Anna, by translating it and having it published in May 1939. For Freud its autobiographical connotations were self-evident. His adoption of the book signified some sort of hope or faith. The translation helped see him through the dark days after the Anschluss, when he had no patients and was unable to concentrate for any length of time on *Moses*. Topsy's cancer was in fact cured by X-rays at the Institut Curie in Paris. When Freud's cancer turned out to be inoperable in 1939, Marie Bonaparte brought over the radiologist who had cured Topsy to treat Freud.[15]

Dying, Freud was reading about dying. Topsy was not the only instance. Max Schur mentions his enthusiasm for Rachel Berdach's *Der Kaiser, die Waisen und der Tod* in December 1938.[16] And, as both Schur and Jones point out, the last book Freud is known to have read was *La Peau de Chagrin*—Balzac's allegorical fantasy, the story of a pact with the devil and of a life diminishing as the wild-ass's skin of the title gradually shrinks with each of its possessor's wishes. On finishing it Freud remarked: "This was the proper book for me to read; it deals with shrinking and starvation."[17]

That a dying man should find a book about dying suitable indicates a peculiar counterbalance between personal experience and the narrative. By this time Freud was probably no longer reading sprawled across the chair as before, but would have been recumbent on a bed in the garden or in his study. It may be assumed that by this time his attitude towards reading had entered a final phase in which most of the concerns of the living carried little weight.

" . . . to Maintain This Habitual Posture . . . "

Taste in reading may be defined negatively: what Freud did *not* read, or respond to, is also of some interest.

In a letter of October 25, 1937, to the poet Victor Wittkowski who had sent him a book, Freud wrote: "Thank you very much for the gift of your poems. I suspect that they are very beautiful but for many years now I have been unable to enjoy lyric poetry."[18] It should be added that the fact he was no longer able to enjoy it, did not, strictly speaking, mean he did not read it at all. Before the American poet H. D. came to him for analysis in early 1933 Freud actually asked to read her poems. But he added apologetically that this was not in order to appreciate or criticize them: "I am a bad judge on poetry especially in a foreign language. I wanted to get a glimpse of your personality as an introduction to making your personal acquaintance."[19]

Freud's unease about lyrical poetry in particular may stem from his sense of it as virtually unmediated emotion. About 30 years previously, he wrote: "Lyric poetry serves the purpose, more than anything, of giving vent to intense feelings of many sorts—just as was at one time the case with dancing."[20] Judging both from his library and his habit of quotation, Freud never much appreciated lyrical poetry. His poetical citations originate in a limited repertoire of poets, Goethe, Schiller or Heine, and they tend to carry non-lyrical (aphoristic, jocular or philosophical) messages. Two fragmentary pastiches of Freud's own, one from a letter to Silberstein, the other to Fliess, are both mock-heroic in tone.[21] Molded by his education in the classics and an early admiration for Milton, his taste in poetry seems to have been primarily in favor of syntactic weight and semantic density rather than for the wayward gleam of the lyrical.

There was, however, one Viennese poet whose dramatic work possesses an almost Miltonic gravity and this was Freud's near contemporary, Richard Beer-Hofmann (1866–1945). In a letter congratulating him on his 70th birthday, Freud stated his regret that they were not better acquainted: " . . . you should not conclude that I have remained indifferent towards the majestic beauty of your writing [*Dichtung*]. I have indeed gained the impression from things I have heard about you that you and I must share many significant points of agreement. But life sped by in the breathless excitement of demanding work and now that I enjoy more leisure there is not much of me left over."²²

For many years Beer-Hofmann had been working on a cycle of Biblical verse dramas. Of one of these, *Jaákobs Traum*, Max Schur wrote: "I knew that Freud was particularly fond of this play, but I had not realized that he saw himself as having 'struggled with the Angel,' or that he had used this metaphor, along with those of the inner tyrant and the cancer, to describe the force of his drive toward making new discoveries decades before he had read *Jacob's Dream* [. . .] or met its author."²³

The play is a preface to a cycle of three plays "The History of King David": it relates how David's ancestor Jaákob, the gentle son favored by his mother Rebekah over the hunter son Edom, steals their father Isaac's blessing. Jaákob then becomes Israel—he who wrestled with God. In Beer-Hofmann's play, Jaákob challenges the archangels who act as intermediaries for God, insisting on speaking directly to God. This demand is granted, but because he thereby becomes God's chosen, God will not spare him future suffering.

In the play Beer-Hofmann examines the theme of blood in a specifically Jewish context. After God has promised Jaákob that his line will be eternal, Samáel, the tempter, says to him:

> selig
> Mischt sich mit jungen Völkern altes Blut!
> Und ihres Schicksals dürfen sie vergessen—
> Nur dir bleibt ewig—was dich traf—bewusst..
> Sie können wohl gedenken ihrer Ahnen..
> Du—Volk, das nicht vergessen darf—du musst!
> Es schleift dich Gott mit sich durch alle Zeiten . . . ²⁴

(blissfully/Old blood mingles with young races!/And permits them to forget their fate—/Only you must remain eternally conscious of your lot ../They may, if they like, think of their forefathers ../You—people that cannot forget—you must!/God drags you with him down the ages . . .)

Leaving aside the mythical transference upon the figure of Jaákob that Schur mentions, it is evident that Freud's admiration for Beer-Hofmann's work also presents another aspect of his fascination with the mystery of

Jewishness. Where, in *Bilanz der deutschen Judenheit 1933* and *De Vriendt kehrt heim*, Arnold Zweig had examined the political and social situation of Jews in Germany and Palestine, Beer-Hofmann in his *Theater zu König David* explored the mystical roots of Jewish culture. This was a theme of the utmost importance for Freud in the 1930s. Just as Arthur Schnitzler could be read as a concealed Doppelgänger to the *Studies in Hysteria* or the "Dora" case, so Beer-Hofmann may be heard as one of the background voices to *Moses and Monotheism.*

Beer-Hofmann had risen to fame with the publication of his *Schlaflied für Miriam* (1897), a cradle song for his daughter. Its final stanza has intonations that are both Rilkean *avant la lettre* (the poem was to become one of Rilke's favorites) and not incompatible with certain Freudian concepts, for one could read "blood" here in terms of instincts and acquired characteristics:

> Schläfst du, Mirjam—Mirjam, mein Kind,
> Ufer nur sind wir, und tief in uns rinnt
> Blut von Gewesenen—zu Kommenden rollts,
> Blut unsrer Väter, voll Unruh und Stolz.
> In uns sind Alle. Wer fühlt sich allein?
> Du bist ihr Leben—ihr Leben ist dein—
> Mirjam, mein Leben, mein Kind—schlaf ein!

(Are you sleeping, Miriam—Miriam, my child,/We are but river banks, and deep in us flows/Blood from the past—it rolls to the future,/Our fathers' blood, filled with commotion and pride./All are within us. Who feels alone?/You are their life—their life is yours—/Miriam, my life, my child—go to sleep!)

Yet there is a curious silence around Rilke. Even if the unnamed companion mentioned in "On Transience" is in fact Rilke, this would not change the case, since the shadowy poet in that essay serves as little more than a foil to Freud's meditation. This is surprising in view of their long acquaintance, for Freud had met Rilke on several occasions and during the First World War there was even the prospect of Rilke entering analysis with Freud.[25] It is all the more surprising in view of Rilke's stature, of which Freud was well aware—he speaks of "the great poet" in his obituary for Lou Andreas-Salomé. Ernst Freud idolized Rilke and Anna Freud possessed virtually all his works in her library, including a volume of his *Buch der Bilder* bearing Rilke's handwritten dedication to

her. However, there is no Rilke in Freud's library. One would expect
that he must have read something of his work at some time. But I have
yet to come across any evidence of this in his letters or elsewhere, and
whether he did actually read the work and refrained from comment or
simply did not choose to read it (which sounds highly unlikely), in either
case this silence is curious.

It is, however, less surprising during Freud's unpoetical final decade.
Though he had more time for reading, illness often deprived him of the
concentration and patience to spare for embarking on literary adventures.
The intellectual effort demanded by new and unusual work ought not to
be underestimated. If Freud chose not to broaden his literary horizons
in the 1930s he could not have considered it a high priority at his time
of life, or dying, to read work that was obscure or uncongenial. Nevertheless he remained well aware of what was going on in art and literature.
Apart from his own children, his analysands, his numerous literary cor-
respondents and his visitors during this period were all able to keep him
in touch with new developments.

During the course of H. D.'s psychoanalysis in 1933 and 1934, various
writers were discussed, including D. H. Lawrence and Ezra Pound who
both played an important role in her life. "The Professor knew the name,
Ezra Pound. He said he had seen an article, but could not pretend to
follow it."[26] Freud's modesty may be taken at face value, for there is no
evidence he was making any especial effort to follow modern literary
theory or movements. But the opportunities were obviously not lacking.
On September 15, 1935, for example, Freud was visited by the writer
Willy Haas, who had belonged to Kafka's circle in Prague and who was
to edit Kafka's letters.[27] The meeting can only be mentioned as a hypothetical intersection; I find no sign before or after that Freud knew of,
or read, Kafka. A month later, on October 13, 1935, Thornton Wilder
visited Freud. On that occasion Freud spoke of Franz Werfel, Stefan and
Arnold Zweig's failed attempts to incorporate psychoanalysis into the
novel. Wilder retorted that Joyce had already done this successfully in
Ulysses.[28] This book is not, however, to be found either in Freud's or
Anna's library. So if Freud failed to read Kafka, Joyce, Pound, or, say,
Proust, Virginia Woolf or T. S. Eliot, then it was probably not for lack
of knowledge, but rather a matter of taste and choice. And this may also
have been partly because "there is not much of me left over."

• • •

Freud's tributes to artists as the discoverers of the unconscious went side by side with a certain antipathy to those like Dostoevsky who seemed too greatly in its power. The display of unconscious forces was in itself no grounds for literary pleasure nor any guarantee of excellence; he rejected surrealism and slighted *Gradiva* as a work of art. It is not surprising he should have enjoyed Goethe rather than Hölderlin, Mann rather than Kafka, Beer-Hofmann rather than Rilke. Perhaps Freud's seeming indifference to Rilke or Joyce was a reaction against the disruption of subjectivity or the subjection of intellect to perception he may have glimpsed in them. A sense of disorder afflicting poetry or narration may have inspired the same aversion as mental disorder. In an extraordinary letter to István Hollós in 1928 he wrote:

I finally admitted to myself that [. . .] I did not like these sick people, that I was angry with them at finding them so far from myself and everything human. A curious type of intolerance which of course makes me unfit to be a psychiatrist.

In the course of time I have ceased to find myself interesting, which is of course analytically incorrect. [. . .] is it the result of an ever more clearly discernible partisanship for the primacy of the intellect, the expression of a hostility towards the id?[29]

In his study of Freud's reading, Peter Brückner concludes: "Perhaps, for anyone who knew how to preserve their understanding and their hopes, reading books was once an 'attitude towards the world': an attempt *to withstand the power of the world.*"[30] That argues turning the world's image against its influence, using literary language against the language of power like the petrifying mirror-shield of Perseus. This combative model of reading fails to account for reading as an experiment of the self or a ludic venture or as a form of interaction and projective identification. Patrick Mahoney has stressed the extraordinary responsiveness of Freud the writer to his audience, whether in the lecture hall or at the writing desk.[31] In the lecturer or writer responsiveness requires constant attention: in a reader it may demand a form of abandon.

If the intellect asserts its primacy too insistently, it may foreclose on emotional or poetical effects. It is true that the Teutonic root of the verb "to read" had the sense of taking control. But the word is also cognate with riddle. This brief survey remains too random to provide more than a glimpse of some of Freud's reading and non-reading in his later years.

I cannot therefore end with any satisfactory conclusion about his range or technique. In place of a summary I can only offer this emblem of a particular attitude to reading—the image of Freud twisted into a strange posture that combines abandon and concentration, sprawled across his armchair yet with his head upright, a book held up in front of his face.

Notes

1. Felix Augenfeld–Dr. Hans Lobner. February 8, 1974 (Copy: Freud Museum).
2. The catalog of Freud's library, compiled by J. Keith Davies, is now awaiting publication.
   On the background of the library in London, see: Dorothea Hecken and Steve Neufeld, *Reassembling Freud's Library*, Freud Museum (London, 1986. Typescript: Notes added by J. K. Davies, 1988).
   A bibliography of Freud's collection of books on archaeology can be found in: Wendy Botting and J. Keith Davies, "Freud's Library and an Appendix of Texts Related to Antiquities," in Lynn Gamwell and Richard Wells (Eds.), *Sigmund Freud and Art* (Binghampton: SUNY, 1989) pp. 184–192)
   For a listing of Freud's books sold by Heinrich Hinterberger, see: K. R. Eissler, "Bericht über die sich in den Vereinigten Staaten befindenden Bücher aus S. Freuds Bibliothek," *Jahrbuch der Psychoanalyse* 11 (1975) pp. 10–50.
3. Ernest Jones, *Sigmund Freud: Life and Work* Vol. III (London: Hogarth, 1980 [1957]) p. 458.
4. Freud–Arnold Zweig. November 27, 1932, in Ernst L. Freud (Ed.: Translated by Professor and Mrs. W. D. Robson-Scott), *The Letters of Sigmund Freud and Arnold Zweig* (London: Hogarth, 1970 [1968]).
5. Ibid.
6. Freud–Norman Douglas. April 10, 1933, in Mark Holloway, *Norman Douglas. A Biography* (London: Secker & Warburg, 1976) pp. 399–400.
7. "...jenes reizendes Buches *The Bridge of San Luis Rey*...(Freud–Arnold Zweig. October, 14, 1935. Typescript copy: Archive of Sigmund Freud Copyrights, Colchester).
   "Thornton Wilder *The Bridge of San Luis Rey* müsst Ihr lesen, es ist etwas ganz ungewöhnlich schönes." (Freud–Ernst and Lucie Freud. October, 16, 1928. Ms: Library of Congress).
8. Thornton Wilder, *The Bridge of San Luis Rey* (London: Longmans, 1964 [1927]) p. 140.
9. Ibid. p. 127.
10. Ibid. p. 128.
11. Linda Simon, *Thornton Wilder: His World* (Garden City, N.Y.: Doubleday, 1979) pp. 118–19.

12. Freud–Marie Bonaparte, in Jones, op. cit. pp. 225–26.

13. Marie Bonaparte, *Topsy, Chow-Chow au poil d'or* (Paris: Denoël et Steele, 1937) p. 17. (My translation.)

14. Ibid. p. 69. (My translation.)

15. Michael Molnar (Ed.), *The Diary of Sigmund Freud 1929–1939* (New York: Scribner's, 1992) pp. 233, 257, 260.

16. Max Schur, *Freud: Living and Dying* (London: Hogarth, 1972) pp. 514–17.

17. Ibid. p. 528. There is no edition of *La Peau de Chagrin* in Freud's own library. However, there is a copy among Anna Freud's books.

18. Freud–Victor Wittkowski. October 25, 1937 [Copy: Freud Museum] ("Ich danke Ihnen sehr für das Geschenk Ihrer Gedichte. Ich vermute, dass sie sehr schön sind, aber ich kann Lyrik seit langen Jahren nicht mehr geniessen.")

19. H. D., *Tribute to Freud* (Manchester: Carcarnet, 1985 [1970]) p. 190.

20. "Psychopathic Characters on the Stage" SE 7:306.

21. Walter Boehlich (Ed.) *Sigmund Freud: Jugendbriefe an Eduard Silberstein 1871–1881* (Frankfurt/Main: Fischer, 1989) p. 215. Poem to Fliess on the birth of his son, in Max Schur, op. cit. p. 546.

22. Freud–Richard Beer-Hofmann. July 10, 1936, in Ernst and Lucie Freud (Eds.) *Sigmund Freud: Briefe 1873–1939* (Frankfurt/Main: Fischer, 1980). (My translation.)

23. Max Schur, op. cit. p. 208.

24. Richard Beer-Hofmann, *Jaákobs Traum* (Berlin: Fischer, 1920) p. 142.

25. H. Lehmann, "A Conversation between Freud and Rilke," *Psychoanalytic Quarterly* 35 (1966) pp. 423–27.

Freud was, of course, well aware of Rilke. They had first met, through Lou Andreas-Salomé, at the 1913 Munich Congress. After his final visit to the Freuds in December 1915, at a time when he was crushed by his military service in the War Archive in Vienna, Rilke wrote: "... öfters war ich daran, mir durch eine Aussprache mit Ihnen aus der Verschüttung zu helfen. Aber schliesslich überwog der Entschluss, die Sache allein durchzumachen, soweit einem eben noch ein trüber Satz Alleinseins bleibt. Wenn ich es nach und nach zu etwas Fassung bringe, so frag ich mich sicher bei Ihnen an und komme; ich weiss, das wird gut sein." (Rilke–Freud. February 17, 1916. Copy: Freud Museum). Nothing came of this hope.

26. H. D., op. cit. p. 181.

27. Molnar, op. cit. p. 190.

28. Ibid. p. 191.

29. Freud–Hollós. April 10, 1928, in ibid. p. 278.

30. Peter Brückner, *Sigmund Freuds Privatlektüre* (Cologne: Verlag Rolf Horst, 1975) p. 148. ("Vielleicht war das Lesen von Büchern für jeden, der sich

seinen Verstand und seine Hoffnungen zu bewahren wusste, einmal ein 'Verhalten zur Welt': ein Versuch, *der Macht der Welt zu widerstehen.*") (My translation.)

31. Patrick J. Mahoney, *Freud as a Writer* (New Haven and London: Yale University Press, 1987 [2nd expanded edition]) pp. 54–71.

13. On the Sources of *Moses and Monotheism*

Ritchie Robertson

Moses and Monotheism is related to a wide range of prior texts, many of which could be called sources of various kinds. Limitations of space and knowledge oblige me to deal only with three. First, since the book is presented as an amateur's incursion into Biblical scholarship, the most obvious sources would be those scholarly works on the Old Testament that Freud drew on when planning and writing it. However, we also need to know how Freud used them and in what spirit he approached them; and for this we need to consider Freud's view of the historical process that connected Old Testament times with the twentieth century, and the sources from which, at an early age, he derived this conception of history. Secondly, we may note how far Freud's familiarity with classic German literature affected the composition of *Moses and Monotheism*. And thirdly, we may consider *Moses and Monotheism* as a text launched against rival texts, and in particular against an alternative theory of monotheism which Freud knew of and detested.

There are of course many other intertextual relationships that have been or could be investigated. One could regard the Bible itself as a source and try to describe the status it had for Freud, as neither a fully sacred nor a fully secular text; this would mean examining the edition of the Bible by Ludwig Philippson, with parallel Hebrew and German texts and a German commentary drawing heavily on Talmudic and subsequent exegeses, that Freud read in childhood, and considering how the text was mediated by Philippson's Enlightenment convictions, his respect for the Talmud and his belief in the historicity even of the Creation narrative.[1]

More diffusely, one could inquire into the general climate of opinion, in which the idea that Moses was an Egyptian turns out to have been widespread before Freud advanced it.[2] And one could consider also Freud's reliance not only on his own psychoanalytic theories but on those developed by his followers: Otto Rank's *The Myth of the Birth of the Hero*, which Freud acknowledges, and Karl Abraham's argument that Jewish monotheism originated in Egypt. This argument, closely anticipating Freud's, was put forward in 1912 in an article in *Imago* which Freud edited and discussed with Abraham, yet in *Moses and Monotheism* Freud makes no reference to it, perhaps because he felt that Abraham had subsequently treated him disloyally.[3]

Although this chapter is not primarily an interpretation of *Moses and Monotheism*, one can hardly ignore the interpretations that have so far been proposed. These range from the narrowly personal to the broadly cultural. Since Freud surmises that the Jews killed Moses, the text has inevitably been interpreted as expressing Freud's oedipal hostility towards his father.[4] This would be difficult to dispute, yet such interpretations have surely long since lost their power to illuminate. More interesting is a recent interpretation in which Freud's emphasis on the murder of Moses is taken as a disguise for his ambivalence towards his mother, who is symbolically represented by the monotheistic religion.[5] When family dynamics are combined with cultural pressures, the text can be read as a symbolic rejection of the Galician origins of Freud's father.[6] It has also been seen as expressing Freud's ambivalence towards Judaism and Jewishness in general.[7] I have myself tried to interpret it as a meditation on the underlying paradoxes of Jewish identity, and on how doctrines (including that of psychoanalysis) may survive despite temporary oblivion.[8] Accordingly, I am inclined to find more plausible those interpretations that are furthest from "vulgar Freudianism" and make *Moses and Monotheism* above all an articulation of the cultural forces whose conflicting pressures Freud registered; and later in this chapter I shall suggest another such interpretation.

I

As an amateur in Biblical study, Freud has to position himself in relation to the professionals. His unease is sometimes evident in tensions between his main text and his footnotes. In his main text he speaks with due respect of "the sober historical researches of the present day" (SE 23:33). In his footnotes, however, he denies that professional Biblical scholars have any special claim to objectivity, and he does so with a sometimes biting irony that itself affronts the norms of academic discourse. In one footnote he admits that "in dealing so autocratically and arbitrarily with Biblical tradition—bringing it up to confirm my views when it suits me and unhesitatingly rejecting it when it contradicts me—I am exposing myself to serious methodological criticism"; but the irony behind this statement becomes clear when he adds: "Certainty is in any case unattainable and moreover it may be said that every other writer on the subject has adopted the same procedure" (SE 23:27n.). Later in the text, Freud points out that it is wrong to seek monocausal explanations, since every event is multiply determined; in a footnote, he rejects the possible misinterpretation that every explanation must contain some truth, and adds: "Our thought has upheld its liberty to discover dependent relations and connections to which there is nothing corresponding in reality; and it clearly sets a very high value on this gift, since it makes such copious use of it both inside and outside of science" (SE 23:108n.). Thus Freud attacks the authority of scholarship, asserts his own freedom of inquiry, and intimates that he is actually more self-critical than the professional scholars.

Freud's own approach is illustrated by his comments dating from 1934, on Hugo Gressmann's *Mose und seine Zeit* (*Moses and His Age*), which have recently been quoted by Y. H. Yerushalmi from the manuscript draft of *Moses and Monotheism* kept in the Library of Congress. Gressmann argued that the Israelites must have crossed the Gulf of Aqaba, not the Red Sea, because the former region is volcanic and a well-timed volcanic eruption could explain how the Egyptians were drowned by a tidal wave after the Israelites had crossed safely.[9] Freud dismisses this explanation as "only a historical novel, no more certain than the one constructed by us," on the grounds that the adoption of a new religion could hardly be attributed to a volcanic phenomenon and that in any case the phenomenon Gressmann hypothesized was barely possible.[10]

However, Freud was not so critical of sources when they happened to suit his own preferences. The most striking instance is his adoption of Ernst Sellin's argument that Moses was killed by his followers. Sellin wanted to prove that Moses offered the Israelites a monotheism which they rejected. He tried to support this hypothesis by an interpretation, which later scholarship has agreed to be idiosyncratic and untenable, of the text of Hosea.[11] Freud remarks: "Sellin's hypothesis cannot be called fantastic—it is probable enough" (SE 23:47). Probable in what sense? Not because Sellin's interpretative method was watertight (something Freud could hardly have established in any case), but because Freud found the conclusion intrinsically probable in view of its correspondence to the theory of primal parricide. Similarly, in *Totem and Taboo* Freud gratefully adopted Robertson Smith's argument that the totem meal formed an integral part of the totemic system, although (as Freud admits, SE 23:132) this argument was founded on a single piece of evidence concerning the actions of some Saracens in the fourth century A.D.[12]

In his account of the Pharaoh Amenhotep IV, who took the name Akhenaten and instituted a monotheistic cult, Freud especially followed the interpretation put forward by the American Egyptologist J. H. Breasted in two books, *A History of Egypt* (1906) and *The Dawn of Conscience* (1934). He might be criticized for relying so heavily on such a popular account as the latter book; but in the 1930s he scarcely had leisure or energy to keep up with the learned journals of Egyptology. Hence it is unfair to blame him, as Emanuel Rice has recently done, for ignoring certain archaeological discoveries that suggested a more negative picture of Akhenaten. Rice tells us that the remains of Akhenaten's mummy, discovered in 1907, suggested that he was in his late twenties when he died; since he ruled for seventeen years, he must have come to the throne at the age of eleven or earlier; therefore he was probably manipulated by political intriguers, rather than taking the initiative, let alone founding a new religion.[13] The alleged discovery of Akhenaten's mummy is not mentioned by Breasted; and rightly so, for (as Rice does not mention) the mummy in question, on careful re-examination, proved to be that of a young man who died in his twentieth year and therefore was not Akhenaten.[14] One should not, therefore, be too hasty in attacking Freud's use of data.

However, Freud's interpretation of his data reveals some obvious biases. Some result from the commitment to psychoanalytic theory which makes him seize the flimsiest evidence for primeval acts of totemism or parricide. Others, notably his idealization of Akhenaten, indicate the view of history that Freud took for granted in approaching the ancient world, and that seemed confirmed by his major source, the books by Breasted.

The overall conception of intellectual history that governs Freud's excursions into anthropology is set out in *Totem and Taboo*: "The human race, if we are to follow the authorities, have in the course of ages developed three such systems of thought—three great pictures of the universe: animistic (or mythological), religious and scientific" (SE 13:77). This scheme, reminiscent of Comte, goes back to Freud's early immersion in positivist thought.[15] The notion of an ascent from religion to science, however, can be traced to his teens, when he acquired a conception of history as a narrative of individuation and secularization. In a letter of 30 October 1927 to Julie Braun-Vogelstein, widow of the Socialist politician Heinrich Braun, Freud recalls how, during their schoolboy friendship, Braun encouraged him to read Buckle's *History of Civilization* and "a similar work by Lecky."[16] Buckle's *Introduction to the History of Civilization in England* is an essay in comparative intellectual sociology, whose pioneering ambition does much to compensate for its occasional crudity. Buckle sees history as the ascent of "that bold, inquisitive, and scientific spirit, which is constantly advancing, and on which all future progress must depend."[17] He intends to contribute to this process by extending positivistic science to discover regular laws in history. In opposition to the pieties of Victorian England, he insists that civilization depends not on moral progress but on intellectual progress; it is the latter, not the former, which has swept away one of the two greatest evils, religious persecution, and promises to abolish the other, namely war.

The book by Lecky that Freud read was most probably *History of the Rise and Influence of the Spirit of Rationalism in Europe*, in which rationalism is defined as the antithesis of dogmatic theology. Lecky recounts three associated narratives: the intellectual development away from belief in miracles and anthropomorphic conceptions of God and towards reliance on empirical evidence; the moral development away from rule by fear and towards the authority of the individual conscience; and the political development of secularization and democracy. These developments, however, do not themselves result from rational persuasion but from changes in outlook—as we might now say, in worldviews or *mentalités*. To take the example discussed in Lecky's first chapter: the existence of witches was taken for granted in the early modern period, yet by the mid-eighteenth century most people thought it absurd. Although Lecky is vague about how such changes in outlook occur, he ascribes the main responsibility to the example of enlightened individuals who are prepared to challenge authority. In this case, the belief in witchcraft was decisively challenged by Montaigne, "the first great representative of the modern secular and rationalistic spirit." "By extricating his mind from the trammels of the past, he had learned to judge the narratives of diabolical intervention by a standard and with a spirit that had been long unknown."[18] This of course does not explain why worldviews change—where did Montaigne acquire his rationalism, and why did people listen to him?—but it establishes a model of intellectual history in which enlightened individuals repeatedly enter into conflict with traditional and dogmatic authority and ultimately succeed because their views correspond to empirical reality.

Freud found a similar model underlying Breasted's two books. From *A History of Egypt* Freud quoted Breasted's description of Akhenaten as "the first individual in human history" (SE 23:21n.).[19] Breasted's metanarrative becomes more explicit in *The Dawn of Conscience*, in which he undertakes to recount the early stages in the development of conscience (that is, a moral sense emphasizing the responsibility of the individual), and to oppose orthodox Christian assumptions by displacing the ancient Hebrews from their central role in this narrative and substituting the ancient Egyptians. The greatest advance in the development of conscience was due to Akhenaten (or, as Breasted transliterates his name, Ikhnaton):

Ikhnaton was the first individual in history. Consciously and deliberately, by intellectual process he gained his position, and then placed himself squarely in the face of tradition and swept it aside. He appeals to no myths, to no ancient and widely accepted versions of the dominion of the gods, to no customs sanctified by centuries—he appeals only to the present and visible evidences of the god's dominion, evidences open to all.[20]

Thus Akhenaten fits the model of Lecky's intellectual heroes. He relies on empirical evidence; he opposes tradition; and his opponents, to whom Breasted attributes all kinds of malice, are the priesthood of the dethroned god Amon. At a later stage, indeed, Breasted practically equates the Egyptian priesthood with the Roman Catholic Church. When in the fifteenth century B.C. the High Priest of Amon was made primate of all the priesthoods of Egypt, he established an "Amonite papacy," a "sacerdotal state," ruled by a "crafty priesthood"; they erected magnificent buildings but ignored the moral content of religion, which "survived only in the breasts of poor and lowly believers."[21] This makes Egypt sound like the Rome of Pope Julius II. Freud does not go so far, but he does rely heavily on Breasted's account of Akhenaten's unique personality, his opposition to tradition, and the "fanatical vindictiveness" (SE 23:23) which he provoked among the suppressed priesthood.

Breasted also argues at great length that the ancient Hebrews owed much to Egypt. He finds strong Egyptian influence in the wisdom literature of the Old Testament and in the social teaching of the prophets. Psalm 104 shows the direct influence of Akhenaten's Hymn to the Sun. There seems to be nothing eccentric about these suggestions: after all, once the history recounted in the Bible is placed in perspective, it seems impossible that the Hebrews should not have been influenced by the more developed civilizations of the ancient Near East. In arguing that the actual doctrine of monotheism came from Egypt, Freud is merely going further along this road. And it is possible that some at least of the opprobrium *Moses and Monotheism* has received is inspired not only by Freud's defective scholarship but also by his daring to question the singularity of Biblical monotheism.

2

Thanks to the Standard Edition, Freud's works are familiar to the majority of readers only in an English version. In order to render Freud academically respectable, this version, as we now know, was deliberately given a more scientific color than the original.[22] Readers unfamiliar with German culture are doubtless surprised by the many quotations which need to be explained in footnotes, and simply unaware how many half-concealed quotations and allusions enhance the texture of Freud's prose, as a natural product of the humanistic education (*Bildung*) that he had undergone and appreciated. In the best study of this aspect of Freud's writing, Walter Schönau sums up Freud's indebtedness to literature:

The extent of his reading can to some extent be inferred from the wealth of quotations in his correspondence and in his writings. The writers he admires, however, are those universally acknowledged: Shakespeare, Lessing, Goethe, Schiller, Fontane, Heine, and also, in particular, C. F. Meyer. Among contemporary authors he knew personally Arnold and Stefan Zweig, Rilke, Schnitzler, and Thomas Mann, among others. But he had a special fondness for the great literary classics.[23]

Freud's reading in literature, however, did not only affect his style. In a work like *Moses and Monotheism*, which is so much an imaginative construction, parts of the argument can be traced back to literary origins. Indeed, his original intention was to write something like a historical novel. He told Arnold Zweig in a letter of 30 September 1934 that he was at work on *The Man Moses, a Historical Novel*.[24] In the 1934 draft of *Moses and Monotheism* from which Yerushalmi quotes, Freud makes it clear that he did not intend to write a work of fiction but to use imagination in filling in the many gaps left by the Biblical tradition:

One undertakes to treat each possibility in the text as a clue, and to fill the gap between one fragment and another according to the law, so to speak, of least resistance, that is—to give preference to the assumption that has the greatest probability. That which one can obtain by means of this technique can also be called a kind of "historical novel," since it has no proven reality, or only an unconfirmable one, for even the greatest probability does not necessarily correspond to the truth.[25]

Yerushalmi plausibly interprets this to mean that Freud initially considered writing a character study of Moses, but afterwards became more interested in other aspects. Soon afterwards Freud wrote to Max Eitingon: "I am no good at historical novels; let us leave them to Thomas Mann."[26] This strongly suggests that his original conception was inspired by Thomas Mann's *Joseph* novels, the first two of which were published in 1933 and 1934.[27]

Contemporary literature, however, was generally less important to Freud than the classics, particularly Goethe, Schiller, Lessing and Heine. All these authors may have contributed something to Freud's text, particularly Goethe, whose works Freud knew so well that he could often quote from quite obscure passages.[28]

After adducing Sellin's claim that Moses was murdered by his followers, Freud says that this hypothesis was "also, strange to say, accepted by the young Goethe without any evidence" (SE 23:89). There might seem to be an error here, since Freud is alluding to the essay "Israel in the Wilderness" ["Israel in der Wüste"] which is among those appended to the *West-Eastern Divan* [*Der West-östliche Divan*], the collection of

Orientalizing poems that Goethe published in 1819, at the age of seventy. However, Goethe tells us in introducing the essay that it is a much earlier work, reflecting the youthful interest in the Old Testament that he has already described in his autobiography, *Poetry and Truth* [*Dichtung und Wahrheit*]. The essay was in fact written in 1797, but in his autobiography (with which Freud was undoubtedly familiar) Goethe describes how, while still at school in Frankfurt, he learnt Hebrew and made a close study of the last four books of the Pentateuch.[29]

"Israel in the Wilderness" is of special interest as an exercise in the historical study of the Bible. Goethe sympathized with this approach, pioneered in eighteenth-century Germany by Michaelis, Herder, and Eichhorn, and in a later passage from *Poetry and Truth* he formulates his own principle of historical criticism. "Nobody will now deny that there are contradictions in the Bible. People sought to reconcile them by taking the clearest passage as a basis and trying to adjust the contradictory, less clear one to fit it. I, however, wanted to establish by investigation which passage best conveyed the sense of the matter; I adhered to this one and rejected the others as inauthentic additions."[30] In "Israel in the Wilderness" Goethe applies this method to Exodus, Leviticus, Numbers and Deuteronomy. Having separated the laws from the narrative, he examines the latter on two assumptions: that events were crucially determined by Moses' personality; and that the Israelites can barely have spent two years in the wilderness, let alone twenty. His account of Moses' personality is unflattering and often ironic. He depicts Moses as a rough, unreflective man of action, ill-equipped to act as leader or general, who caused much unnecessary loss of life through sheer incompetence. Finally, Goethe suggests, Moses' exasperated followers decided to dispose of him: "Moses himself disappeared, as Aaron had disappeared, and unless we are much mistaken, Joshua and Caleb thought it best to terminate the rule of a mediocrity [*eines beschränkten Mannes*] which they had endured for several years, and to send him after the many unfortunate people whom he had dispatched in advance."[31]

The method Goethe describes is very close to Freud's and carries a similar danger of circularity. One must have already decided what "the sense of the matter" is before one can judge which passage best conveys it. Goethe's adoption of this method, however, must have strengthened Freud's confidence in his approach and reinforced his hostility to the professional Biblical scholars of his day. On the other hand, Goethe's ironic criticism of Moses finds no echo in Freud's work; nor could it, given the lifelong identification with Moses that is apparent especially in *The Moses of Michelangelo* as well as in *Moses and Monotheism*.[32] The reason Goethe gives for Moses' murder, namely his insufferable ineptitude, has understandably been suppressed.

It is tempting to associate *Moses and Monotheism* also with an essay by Schiller, "Moses' Mission" ["Die Sendung Moses," 1790]. Yerushalmi thinks that, since Schiller was "one of Freud's favourite poets," it is "highly probable" that Freud had read this essay.[33] Perhaps; but while Freud's quotations from Schiller's poems and plays were part of his educational repertoire, "Moses' Mission" has no such standard status, and is indeed one of Schiller's least-known works. Its argument, however, does partially anticipate Freud's. Schiller surmises that the idea of a single Supreme Being arose among the Egyptian priests but was confined to a small circle of initiates; that Moses, as part of his Egyptian upbringing, became such an initiate; that, having rediscovered his Hebrew identity, he sought to inspire the degenerate Hebrews with courage by persuading them that theirs was the one true God. Thus Moses was teaching them a true doctrine, but rendering it acceptable by means of invented ceremonies, like that of removing one's shoes in God's presence. Schiller emphasizes the absolute power which Moses derived from this combination of truth and charlatanry: "If he can legitimate himself for his brethren as this God's organ and emissary, then they are a ball in his hands; he can lead them just as he pleases."[34] If Freud had at some time read this essay, it would no doubt have encouraged him to conceive of Moses as virtually creating the Jewish people.

In a footnote to *Moses and Monotheism* Freud finds in Heine an anticipation of his theory that Jewish monotheism originated in Egypt. He quotes from the poem "On the New Jewish Hospital in Hamburg" Heine's description of Judaism as "the plague dragged along from the Nile Valley, the unhealthy beliefs of Ancient Egypt" (SE 23:30n.).[35] Since Freud had a remarkable knowledge of Heine's works, it is likely that he knew at least two other passages in which the late Heine speaks of Moses. One is in the poem "Vitzliputzli," part of the collection *Romanzero* (1851). Describing how Columbus presented mankind with a whole new world, Heine digresses to Moses:

Only one, a single hero,
Gave us more, and something better,
Than Columbus did, and that is
He who gave to us a God.

Amram was his noble father,
Jochebed his mother, and he
Bore himself the name of Moses,
And he is my greatest hero.[36]

The other is in the *Confessions* (*Geständnisse*, 1854), which contain a passage about Moses so interesting that it is worth quoting at length:

How small Sinai appears when Moses is standing on it! The mountain is only the pedestal for the feet of the man whose head rises into the sky, where he speaks with God—God pardon me the sin, but sometimes I fancy that this Mosaic God is only the reflected radiance of Moses himself, whom he so much resembles, both in wrath and in love—It would be a great sin, it would be anthropomorphism, to assume such an identity between God and his prophet—but the resemblance is striking.

I used to have no particular liking for Moses, probably because I was under the sway of the Hellenistic spirit and could not forgive the legislator of the Jews for his hatred of all visual representation, all sculpture. I did not see that, despite his enmity to art, Moses was himself a great artist and possessed the true artistic spirit. Only in him, as with his Egyptian compatriots, this artistic spirit was focused only on the colossal and imperishable. Unlike the Egyptians, however, he did not shape his artistic works from brick and granite; rather, he built human pyramids, he chiselled human obelisks, he took a poor pastoral tribe and made it into a nation that would likewise bid defiance to the centuries—a great, everlasting, holy nation, a nation of God, that could serve as a model to all other nations, and indeed as a prototype to the whole of mankind: he created Israel! This artist, the son of Amram and the midwife Jochebeth, may boast with more justification than the Roman poet that he erected a monument that will outlast anything made of bronze![37]

Heine strikingly anticipates Freud's fascination with Moses; his identification of Moses with Yahweh; and his view of Moses as shaping the Jewish people. Moreover, an important theme common to Heine's *Confessions* and *Moses and Monotheism* is the conflict between Hellenism and Hebraism.[38] Heine tells us how a crippling illness has weakened his attachment to Hellenic ideals of sensuous beauty and increased his respect for the Jews' rigorous morality. "I see now [Heine continues] that the

Greeks were only beautiful youths, while the Jews were always men, mighty and unyielding men, not only in those days but down to the present, despite eighteen centuries of persecution and misery." Freud notes with evident regret: "Harmony in the cultivation of intellectual and physical activity, such as was achieved by the Greek people, was denied to the Jews" (SE 23:115); but he commends them for choosing intellectuality over the development of muscular strength and the tendency to violence that that usually produces. In both these passages from Heine and Freud there is, of course, not merely an antithesis but a triangle: Christianity is implicitly present and antagonistic to both Hellenism and Hebraism. For Heine, Christianity is opposed both to Hellenic sensuousness and to Hebraic moral rigor, while for Freud it is inferior to Hellenic harmony and to Jewish intellectuality.

Another writer of great importance for Freud (as for Heine) was Lessing. Freud deliberately took Lessing's flexible and witty style as a model for his own.[39] He must also have admired the intellectual courage which Lessing showed especially in attacking dogmatic theologians, upholding religious tolerance, and championing the reputation of the Jews. The best-known testimony to Lessing's philo-Semitism is the play *Nathan der Weise* (1779). Renate Böschenstein has recently commented on the importance for Freud of its central character, the idealized Jew Nathan.[40] Freud's identification with Moses is well known; Böschenstein suggests that in Freud's imagination Moses fused with Lessing's Nathan. In *The Moses of Michelangelo* Freud interprets Michelangelo's statue as an image of self-restraint. Shocked by the sight of the Israelites worshiping the Golden Calf, Moses is about to drop the tablets on which he has inscribed the Ten Commandments, but hastily clutches them to avoid profanation. Lessing's Nathan similarly represents self-control. We learn towards the end of the play that his wife and seven sons were killed in a fire by Christians, but that Nathan forgave his enemies. Thus in both texts spiritual power is demonstrated, not by vengeance, but by restraint.

Is Lessing's Nathan present also in the Moses of the *Monotheism* book? As Böschenstein points out, Freud contrasts the primitive god Yahweh, "a coarse, narrow-minded, local god, violent and bloodthirsty" (SE 23:50), with the "more highly spiritualized notion of god, the idea of a single deity embracing the whole world, who was not less all-loving than all-powerful, who was averse to all ceremonial and magic and set before men as their highest aim a life in truth and justice" (ibid.). This reads as if Freud has transposed onto the origins of religion the conflict that the Enlightenment saw between a superstitious Christianity and a universalist humanism owing much to Judaism. Such a humanism was represented in literature by Lessing's Nathan, in reality by Lessing himself and by his friend Moses Mendelssohn.

One could, however, go a little further than Böschenstein. *Moses and Monotheism* is crucially concerned with the transmission of a doctrine. On one level, the imposition of monotheism upon the Hebrews, and its re-emergence after a latency period, presumably expresses Freud's hopes and fears about the survival of psychoanalytic doctrines. But on another level it would seem that, in making Moses an Egyptian who takes his monotheism from Egypt, Freud was writing an allegory of the relation between German Jews and the German Enlightenment. The allegory conveys that the humanism of the Enlightenment found a safer home among the Jews than among the Germans: the Jews remained loyal to it while the Germans declined into the barbarism whose most horrifying manifestation was Nazism.

3

Moses and Monotheism is also a covert response to another theory of monotheism, put forward by Father Wilhelm Schmidt, whom Freud describes as follows in a letter to Arnold Zweig:

We live here in an atmosphere of Catholic orthodoxy. They say that the politics of our country are determined by one Pater Schmidt, who lives in St Gabriel near Mödling. He is a confidant of the Pope, and unfortunately he is himself an ethnologist and student of comparative religion, whose books make no secret of his abhorrence of analysis and especially of my totem theory.[41]

Freud added that the journal of psychoanalysis recently founded in Rome had suddenly been banned, and that the ban was thought to have come direct from the Vatican and to have been instigated by Father Schmidt. If Freud were to irritate this person further, his influence in Austria might be used to outlaw psychoanalysis on its home ground. Later, in the prefatory note to part III of *Der Mann Moses,* Freud explained that he had withheld the work from publication because the Catholicism of the Austrian corporate state was the last bulwark against the various barbarisms of Germany, Italy and Russia, and since Catholicism already viewed psychoanalysis with distrust he could not risk strengthening its suspicion (SE 23:57). In a later letter to Zweig he again referred to Schmidt: "And I count it to my credit that our arch enemy P. Schmidt has just been awarded the Austrian decoration of honour for his pious lies in the field of ethnology. Clearly this is meant to console him for the fact that providence has allowed me to achieve the age of 80."[42]

Wilhelm Schmidt (1868–1954) was in his time an anthropologist with an international reputation.[43] While still in his teens he joined the missionary society called the Societas Verbi Divini, and much of his life was spent studying and later teaching at its seminary in St. Gabriel on the edge of Mödling, near Vienna. From 1925 to 1938 he was also Professor of Anthropology at Vienna University. He founded the Anthropos Institute for anthropology, and was also involved in establishing the Museum für Völkerkunde in Vienna. In 1925 he helped to organize an exhibition of missionary work in Rome, and was appointed by the Pope as Director of the Museo missionario etnologico. In 1928 he was honored by a huge Festschrift composed by an international array of authors, including the eminent American anthropologists A. L. Kroeber and Robert Lowie, and also the Austrian reactionary social theorist Othmar Spann.

Schmidt seems not to have done any missionary work or anthropological fieldwork. Although he organized many expeditions, he himself never left Europe until 1935, when he went on a lecture tour of the United States, China, Japan, Korea, and the Philippines. His researches into Australian languages, on which he was an authority, were based on published accounts and on information sent him by missionaries. His productivity was awe-inspiring. Besides his linguistic publications, his main work was *The Origin of the Idea of God [Der Ursprung der Gottesidee]*, in twelve massive volumes which cannot contain less than five million words. A bibliography of his works (not quite complete) lists 647 items, besides over sixty pieces of sacred music.

The political influence which Freud attributes to Schmidt is naturally hard to reconstruct. We know from the diaries of Ignaz Seipel, Chancellor of the First Austrian Republic in the 1920s, that Schmidt was a loyal monarchist who found the Emperor's resignation in 1918 difficult to accept.[44] His public utterances were anti-Socialist and anti-Semitic. He was an enthusiastic supporter of the corporate state (*Ständestaat*) established in 1933 after the dissolution of Parliament. He was the chairman of a commission set up in 1936 by the Austrian episcopate to establish a Catholic university at Salzburg, a project to which he was intensely committed.

All this gives ample reason for Freud to dislike Schmidt. Moreover, Schmidt had already criticized him in print for his venture into anthropology in *Totem and Taboo*. Schmidt's manual of anthropology for students, *The Origin and Growth of Religion*, contains sharp attacks on Freud and Durkheim—both amateurs in anthropology and, not coincidentally, both Jews. Schmidt opposes the argument by Freud that totemism is the basis of religion. He maintains that among the most primitive peoples such practices as parricide and cannibalism are unknown, and defends primitive men against Freud's slanders: "To bring such men into connexion with modern sex-ridden neurotics, as he [Freud] would have us do, and from this connexion to deduce the alleged fact that all thought and feeling, especially subliminal, is founded on and saturated with sex, must remain lost labour. Thus Freud's hypothesis loses its last shadow of hope ever to corroborate or establish any single part of itself, for every part collapses in ruin."[45] That anti-Semitism was among Schmidt's motives is clear from his attack elsewhere on the Jewish anthropologist Salomon Reinach, whom he accuses of adopting the theory of totemism from Robertson Smith's *Religion of the Semites* solely in order to undermine the pre-eminence of Christianity in the history of religions.[46]

Schmidt himself belonged to the diffusionist school, which attempted to explain cultural similarities (in institutions and material products) as resulting not from independent invention but from diffusion from an original center. The German school of diffusionists tried to identify a number of "Kulturkreise" ("cultural circles"), areas within which such diffusion had taken place. Schmidt was particularly interested in the most primitive peoples, such as the Congolese Pygmies, the Andaman Islanders, the Australian Aborigines, and the inhabitants of Tierra del Fuego. Using data collected by explorers, mainly missionaries, Schmidt began by studying these peoples' languages and then passed to their religions. He established to his own satisfaction that all these peoples shared a primeval monotheism. All believed in a Supreme Being who was the author of good. In addition, they led peaceful lives, were monogamous, cared altruistically for children, old people and fertile mothers, and had a clear concept of private property. So perfect was their social order, in fact, that Schmidt found himself driven to conclude that these peoples must have received a direct revelation from God. To have made such an impression on them, God must have appeared in person, in physical form. This conclusion forms the climax of the first six volumes of *The Origin of the Idea of God*, and Schmidt leaves the reader in no doubt that his supernaturalism is absolutely literal:

It was the really existing Supreme Being, the actual Creator of heaven and earth and, in particular, of mankind, who appeared before His most excellent creatures, mankind, and revealed Himself, His own being and workings, disclosed Himself to their minds, wills and emotions immediately after Creation, when He dwelt familiarly together with mankind.[47]

Hence myths about the primeval paradise must be true, and so must the creation myths of the most ancient peoples. After all, as Schmidt observes, they derived their information from God, the most reliable witness to an event which was still recent. Subsequently, however, this happy state was disrupted by sin. Schmidt considers it most probable that the Fall resulted from the excessive pride of the tribal leader who communicated with God on behalf of his followers. Thereafter the male-dominated society of primeval mankind gave way to a matrilocal and matrilineal society, and all the troubles of history followed. Only in remote spots like the Andamans and Tierra del Fuego did remnants survive of man's original paradisal state.

Schmidt's anthropology has not worn well. His supernaturalism makes it clear that despite his pretense of objective research he was guided by his own fantasies. In particular, his account of primitive society sounds much too good to be true. Schmidt's primitives (whom he had never seen in the flesh) seem already to have attained the social harmony which the Austrian corporate state was striving to restore. And by blaming women for the loss of this primeval harmony, Schmidt has translated the myth of the Fall into terms that are anthropological, yet no less mythical.

The enmity between Freud and Schmidt was no mere academic disagreement. Each man held to his convictions the more strongly for their lack of scholarly foundation. Their beliefs were founded, rather, on incompatible ideologies—progressive liberalism versus Catholic conservatism—and on opposed historical myths. Freud sees human history as a slow and painful struggle from primitive animism through theology and philosophy up to the highest stage of consciousness, science, which can at last begin to confer some real instead of illusory benefits upon mankind. For Schmidt, on the other hand, history is a process of loss and decline. A primeval revelation by God himself showed the earliest men the essence of religion and the ideal social life. There could be no compromise between Freud's belief in progress and Schmidt's belief in decline.

Very obviously, *Moses and Monotheism* opposes all that Schmidt stood for by describing Christianity as a neurosis and contrasting it with both Judaism and the modern scientific spirit. But in another way it resembles Schmidt's work. Both Schmidt and Freud are concerned with the transmission of a doctrine. In both cases the doctrine is monotheism. It is transmitted, in Schmidt's account, by diffusion; in Freud's, by repression. Schmidt asserts that God appeared in person to primitive man and taught him a monotheism which was diffused over the globe and, in the process, corrupted and forgotten, except in the refuges of primitive humanity. Freud maintains that the monotheism of the Pharaoh Akhenaten was transmitted by Moses to his followers the Jews, and, though repeatedly forgotten, it survived securely in the unconscious. Thus both Schmidt and Freud were concerned with how doctrines survive—a very understandable concern at a time when Judeo-Christian civilization seemed threatened by both Nazism and Communism. And Schmidt's work should be seen as an important part of the context in and against which Freud's last major book was written.

Notes

1. See Théo Pfrimmer, *Freud lecteur de la Bible* (Paris: Presses Universitaires de France, 1982), for a detailed study of the Philippson Bible.
2. See Yosef Hayim Yerushalmi, *Freud's Moses* (New Haven: Yale University Press, 1991), p. 5.
3. Karl Abraham, "Amenhotep IV. (Echnaton). Psychoanalytische Beiträge zum Verständnis seiner Persönlichkeit und des monotheistischen Aton-Kultes," *Imago*, 1 (1912), 334–60. Abraham and Freud discussed this article in their correspondence: see *A Psycho-Analytic Dialogue: The Letters of Sigmund Freud and Karl Abraham, 1907–1926*, ed. Hilda C. Abraham and Ernst L. Freud, tr. Bernard Marsh and Hilda C. Abraham (London: The

Hogarth Press, 1965), pp. 111–12, 118. On the personal motives that may have led Freud to ignore it later, see Leonard Shengold, "A parapraxis of Freud's in relation to Karl Abraham," *American Imago*, 29 (1972), 123–59.

4. Marthe Robert, *From Oedipus to Moses: Freud's Jewish Identity* (Oxford: Oxford University Press, 1976).

5. Robert Doria-Medina, "On Freud and monotheism," *International Review of Psycho-Analysis*, 18 (1991), 489–500.

6. Marianne Krüll, *Freud and his Father*, tr. Arnold J. Pomerans (London: Hutchinson, 1986).

7. Jerry Victor Diller, *Freud's Jewish Identity* (London and Toronto: Associated University Presses, 1991), p. 140.

8. Ritchie Robertson, "Freud's testament: *Moses and Monotheism*," in Edward Timms and Naomi Segal (eds.), *Freud in Exile* (New Haven and London: Yale University Press, 1988), pp. 80–89.

9. Hugo Gressmann, *Mose und seine Zeit* (Göttingen: Vandenhoeck & Ruprecht, 1913), p. 119.

10. Yerushalmi, pp. 24–25.

11. Ernst Sellin, *Mose und seine Bedeutung für die israelitisch-jüdische Religionsgeschichte* (Leipzig: Deichert, 1922), esp. p. 43. The crucial passages are Hosea 5:1, which Sellin (unlike most translators) interprets as referring to Shittim, the scene of idolatry and violence in Numbers 25, and Hosea 9:7–14.

12. W. Robertson Smith, *Lectures on the Religion of the Semites* (Edinburgh: Adam & Charles Black, 1889), p. 263.

13. Emanuel Rice, *Freud and Moses* (Albany: State University of New York Press, 1990), p. 139.

14. Cyril Aldred, *Akhenaten* (London: Thames & Hudson, 1968), pp. 146–47.

15. See Peter Gay, *Freud: A Life for our Time* (London: Dent, 1988), p. 34.

16. *Letters of Sigmund Freud*, ed. Ernst L. Freud, tr. Tania and James Stern (London: Hogarth Press, 1961), p. 379.

17. Henry Thomas Buckle, *Introduction to the History of Civilization in England*, ed. John M. Robertson (London: Routledge, 1904), p. 75. Originally published in two volumes under the title *History of Civilization in England* (1857–61).

18. W. E. H. Lecky, *History of the Rise and Influence of the Spirit of Rationalism in Europe*, 2 vols. (London: Longman, 1865), 1:103.

19. J. H. Breasted, *A History of Egypt from the Earliest Times to the Persian Conquest* (London: Hodder & Stoughton, 1906), p. 356.

20. Breasted, *The Dawn of Conscience* (New York and London: Scribner's, 1934), pp. 301–2.

21. Ibid., pp. 330, 331.

22. See Sander L. Gilman, "Reading Freud in English: problems, paradoxes, and a solution," in his *Inscribing the Other* (Lincoln and London: University of Nebraska Press, 1991), pp. 191–210; Riccardo Steiner, " 'Die Weltmacht-

stellung des Britischen Reichs": notes on the term 'standard' in the first translations of Freud," in Timms and Segal (eds.), *Freud in Exile*, pp. 181–95, and other papers in the same volume.

23. Walter Schönau, *Sigmund Freuds Prosa* (Stuttgart: Metzler, 1968), p. 16. My translation. Ernst A. Ticho, "The influence of the German-language culture on Freud's thought," *International Journal of Psycho-Analysis*, 67 (1986), 227–34, inadvertently reveals how much of Freud's cultural context, obvious to anyone who knows his works in German, needs to be explained to anglophone readers.

24. *The Letters of Sigmund Freud and Arnold Zweig*, ed. Ernst L. Freud, tr. Elaine and William Robson-Scott (London: The Hogarth Press, 1970), p. 91.

25. Quoted in Yerushalmi, p. 17.

26. Letter of 13 November 1934, quoted in Ernest Jones, *The Life and Work of Sigmund Freud*, 3 vols. (London: The Hogarth Press, 1953–7), 3:194.

27. See Jacques Le Rider, *Modernité viennoise et crises de l'identité* (Paris: Presses Universitaires Françaises, 1990), pp. 292–94.

28. See Schönau passim; Uwe Henrik Peters, "Goethe und Freud," *Goethe-Jahrbuch*, 103 (1986), 86–105.

29. Johann Wolfgang Goethe, *Werke*, ed. Erich Trunz, 14 vols. (Hamburg: Wegner, 1949–60), 9:129ff.

30. Goethe, *Werke*, 9:509. My translation.

31. Goethe, *Werke*, 2:216–17. My translation.

32. See Martin S. Bergmann, "Moses and the evolution of Freud's Jewish identity," *Israel Annals of Psychiatry and Related Disciplines*, 14 (Mar. 1976), 3–26.

33. Yerushalmi, pp. 5, 114 n. 17. This was first suggested by Ernst Blum, "Über Sigmund Freuds *Der Mann Moses und die monotheistische Religion*," *Psyche*, 10 (1956), 367–90 (p. 375).

34. "Die Sendung Moses," in Friedrich Schiller, *Sämtliche Werke*, ed. Gerhard Fricke and Herbert G. Göpfert, 5 vols. (Munich: Hanser, 1958), 4:783–804 (p. 798). My translation.

35. Heine's metaphor of disease derives from the scurrilous ancient tradition, recorded by Josephus and repeated by Tacitus, that the Jews were originally leprous Egyptians banished from their country; see J. N. Sevenster, *The Roots of Pagan Anti-Semitism in the Ancient World* (Leiden: E. J. Brill, 1975), pp. 142–43.

36. *The Complete Poems of Heinrich Heine*, tr. Hal Draper (Oxford: Oxford University Press, 1982), p. 602.

37. Heine, *Geständnisse*, in *Sämtliche Schriften*, ed. Klaus Briegleb, 6 vols. (Munich: Hanser, 1968–76), 6:480–81. My translation.

38. See Ulla Haselstein, "Poets and prophets: the Hebrew and the Hellene in Freud's cultural theory," *German Life and Letters*, 45 (1992), 50–65, especially p. 64 (where Heine and Freud are compared).

39. See Schönau, p. 42.

40. Renate Böschenstein, "Mythos als Wasserscheide. Die jüdische Komponente der Psychoanalyse: Beobachtungen zu ihrem Zusammenhang mit der Literatur des Jahrhundertbeginns," in Hans Otto Horch and Horst Denkler (eds.), *Conditio Judaica: Judentum, Antisemitismus und deutschsprachige Literatur vom 18. Jahrhundert bis zum Ersten Weltkrieg,* 2 vols. (Tübingen: Niemeyer, 1988–89), 2:287–310.

41. *The Letters of Freud and Zweig,* p. 92.

42. Ibid., pp. 130–31.

43. Biographical data on Schmidt are taken from Joseph Henninger, *P. Wilhelm Schmidt S.V.D., 1868–1954: Eine biographische Skizze* (Fribourg: Paulus-druckerei, 1956), and the obituary by Wilhelm Koppers in *Mitteilungen der Anthropologischen Gesellschaft in Wien,* 83 (1954), 87–96. Koppers also edited *Festschrift P. W. Schmidt: 76 sprachwissenschaftliche, ethnologische, religions-wissenschaftliche, prähistorische und andere Studien* (Vienna: Mechitharisten-Congregations-Buchdruckerei, 1928). For Schmidt's bibliography see Fritz Bornemann, "Verzeichnis der Schriften von P. W. Schmidt S.V.D. (1868–1954)," *Anthropos,* 49 (1954), 385–432. For his place in the history of anthropology, see Marvin Harris, *The Rise of Anthropological Theory* (London: Routledge & Kegan Paul, 1969), pp. 382–92.

44. See Friedrich Rennhofer, *Ignaz Seipel, Mensch und Staatsmann* (Vienna, Cologne, Graz: Böhlau, 1978), pp. 115, 155, 727.

45. Wilhelm Schmidt, *The Origin and Growth of Religion,* tr. H. J. Rose (London: Methuen, 1931), p. 115.

46. Schmidt, *Der Ursprung der Gottesidee,* 12 vols. (Münster: Aschendorffsche Verlagsbuchhandlung, 1926–55), 1:39–40. My translation.

47. Schmidt, *Der Ursprung der Gottesidee,* 6:493. My translation. This passage is also quoted, but misattributed, by Harris, p. 391.

Index

Fairbairn, W. R. D., 222
Fall (the), 281
Family romance, 119, 121, 123
Fantasies of crime and punishment
(Freud), 113, 116
Fantasy, 223; reality and, 218–19, 220,
221
Father(s): as castrator, 98, 99, 100, 102–3,
104; in/and Schreber's paranoia, 183,
186–89; split, 103, 104
Father-complex: Schreber case, 188, 189,
190, 191, 193–94
Father image: Moses as, 111
Father-son conflict, 123
Fear of death (Freud), 105
Fechner, Gustav Theodor, 232, 235
Female sexuality, 66–68
Feminine identification, 119
Feminist critique, 224
Feminization: of the Jew, 59–61; in
Schreber case, 186, 187, 196
Ferenczi, Sandor, 115, 116, 160, 199,
204 n. 11, 226
Fetishism, 202
Fiction: Freud's interest in, 130; Freud's
use of, 144
Fictional writing: and clinical writing,
213–15, 217, 219
First International Psycho-Analytical
Congress, 132
Five Lectures on Psycho-Analysis (Freud),
132
Flechsig, Dr., 187, 188, 190, 191, 193, 194
Fleischl, Ernst (von Marxow), 25, 240,
242
Fliess, Wilhelm, 7, 170, 240; Freud's
break with, 111, 226; Freud's
homosexual affect for, 198–99; Freud's
letters to, 30, 32, 34, 37, 79, 82, 85,
119, 258; Freud's relationship with, 25,
34, 35, 131; Freud's transference to,
111, 113; and theory of bisexuality and
infantile sexuality, 117
Fluβ, Emil, 13, 15
Fluβ, Gisela, 12–14, 15
Fontane, Theodor, 272
"Fragment of an Analysis of a Case of
Hysteria" (Freud), 212
Fratricidal wishes (Freud), 113

Freiberg (Pribor), 110–11, 119, 124, 126
Freud, Anna, 32, 257; library of, 253,
260–61
Freud, Jacob (father of Freud), 110, 114,
119, 123; and anti-Semitism, 118
Freud, Julius (brother of Freud), 117;
death of, 113, 224, 226
Freud and Oedipus (Rudnytsky), 224
"Freud and the Man from Stratford"
(Gay), 171
Freud Museum, 215, 253
Freund der Schreber-Vereine, Der, 194
Friedländer, Paul, 39
Frustration. See Versagung (frustration,
refusal, denial)
Fuld, Ludwig, 52
"Further studies on the structure of the
olfactory mucous membrane in
vertebrates" (Exner), 236–37
Future of an Illusion, The (Freud), 110,
213, 246, 255

Gay, Peter, 6, 131, 171
Gaze: Signorelli-Orvieto frescoes, 84, 86,
87–88
Gelassenheit, 155
Geller, Jay, 180–210
Gender: race and, 64
Gender roles, 226
Genetic method (writing), 20 n. 18, 140
Genitalia, 51; female, 66–67, 95, 96; of
Jews, 49
Genius, 2; cult of, 133–34
German culture: cult of the genius in,
133–34
Gilman, Charlotte Perkins, 64
Gilman, Sander L., 47–76
Gladius dei (Mann), 133
Glaube der Hellenen, Der (Wilamowitz-
Möllendorf), 39–40
Gobineau, Count, 53
God, 184, 233–34; primeval revelation by,
281, 282; Schreber's identification with,
188–89, 190, 194
God(s), 277–78
Goethe, Johann von, 38, 130, 131, 134,
174, 258, 262, 272, 273–75
Gomperz, Elise, 27
Gomperz, Heinrich, 27